DONORS, DEVOTEES, AND DAUGHTERS OF GOD

SOUTH ASIA RESEARCH
Series Editor
Richard Lariviere

A Publication Series of
The University of Texas Center for Asian Studies
and Oxford University Press

THE EARLY UPANISADS
Scholar's Edition
Texts, Translations, and Notes by
Patrick Olivelle

INDIAN EPIGRAPHY
A Guide to the Study of Inscriptions in Sanskrit,
Prakrit, and the Other Indo-Aryan Languages
Richard Salomon

A DICTIONARY OF OLD MARATHI
Anne Feldhaus

DONORS, DEVOTEES, AND DAUGHTERS OF GOD
Temple Women in Medieval Tamilnadu
Leslie C. Orr

DONORS, DEVOTEES, AND DAUGHTERS OF GOD

Temple Women in Medieval Tamilnadu

Leslie C. Orr

New York Oxford

Oxford University Press

2000

Oxford University Press

Oxford New York
Athens Auckland Bangkok Bogotá Buenos Aires Calcutta
Cape Town Chennai Dar es Salaam Delhi Florence Hong Kong Istanbul
Karachi Kuala Lumpur Madrid Melbourne Mexico City Mumbai
Nairobi Paris São Paulo Singapore Taipei Tokyo Toronto Warsaw

and associated companies in
Berlin Ibadan

Published by Oxford University Press, Inc.
198 Madison Avenue, New York, New York 10016

Library of Congress Cataloging-in-Publication Data
Orr, Leslie C., 1948–
Donors, devotees, and daughters of God : temple women in medieval
Tamilnadu / Leslie C. Orr.
p. cm.
Includes bibliographical references and index.
ISBN 0-19-509962-1
1. Devadāsīs—India—Tamil Nadu. 2. Tamil Nadu (India)—Religious
life and customs. I. Title.
BL1237.58.D48077 2000
305.43'2945'095482—dc21 98-7533

1 3 5 7 9 8 6 4 2

Printed in the United States of America
on acid-free paper

[redacted]

Preface

As a preface to her book, *Women on the Margins*, Natalie Zemon Davis engages in an imagined conversation with her subjects, three seventeenth-century European women. Davis, displaying considerable courage, confronts the fact that the women she is writing about would not have appreciated or even recognized her description and analysis of their lives. I am in a similar, and perhaps even more dire, predicament with the women who are the subject of this book—the temple women of medieval South India. Being so far removed from them in time and space and hampered by the fact that they have left no personal accounts of their experiences, I can hardly conceive of what my conversation with them might be like. Yet I do feel that I have come to have at least a nodding acquaintance with these women. This acquaintance has been for me an immensely rewarding relationship—if at times a demanding and discomfiting one—which has gradually transformed my way of thinking about the women of India and has challenged my ideas about the location and significance of "women on the margins."

My knowledge of the temple women of medieval Tamilnadu rests on the fact that their activities have been recorded in inscriptions. Thus it is possible to glimpse the actuality of their lives—the details of their relationships with the temple and the down-to-earth realities of where they lived and what they owned and even, if they shared in the food prepared in the temple, what they ate. The information yielded by inscriptional sources is extremely valuable for our understanding of India's social and religious history; it is particularly precious for what it can tell us about women's lives. These sources afford us the opportunity to examine the arrangements and activities with which real human women were involved, opening up a perspective that is quite different from that provided by the mythic and idealized imaging of "the feminine" in Indian literature and religious texts. The inscriptions also allow us to leap-frog backward over postcolonial, colonial, and late pre-colonial delineations and interpretations of the events and structures of the past and find the traces of a particular historical moment represented in its own terms. This book is an exploration of one part of the historical space to which the inscriptions admit us; as so much more remains to be discovered, I hope that my study may encourage other researchers to make further use of inscriptions in the study of Indian history. I also hope that this book will contribute to the ongoing reexamination and reevaluation of "women's place" in religion and society by showing the complexity, multiplicity, and dynamic character of women's identities and activities.

Although it is difficult for me to imagine talking with the temple women who are the subject of this book, I have engaged in much talk about them, and it is a pleasure to acknowledge a few of the many people who have shared in these conversations. To K. Koppedrayer goes the credit for starting the whole thing over fifteen years ago, with her casual suggestion that it might be interesting for me to find out more about the history of the *devadāsīs*. To S. S. Janaki I am grateful for persuading me that it was much better to try to do so by using Tamil inscriptions rather than Sanskrit texts. To M. L. Varadpande I owe thanks for opening many doors, including the one that led me for the first time into an office of the Archaeological Survey of India. To Katherine Young I am deeply indebted for her guidance as my thesis supervisor throughout the long years of my work on this topic, but even more for her extraordinary support as an exemplar, colleague, and friend. She has read many earlier versions of this book—and a great deal more, as well—and her criticism and encouragement have been and continue to be indispensable. To James Heitzman, George Spencer, and Cynthia Talbot go heartfelt thanks for their great generosity—for sharing materials and ideas that have made my labors much easier and more enjoyable and for providing inspiration and detailed suggestions that made possible the transformation of a gigantic dissertation into a book.

My colleagues and students in the Department of Religion at Concordia University have, with patience and interest, borne witness to this process and have particularly contributed to the development of my thinking about women and religion; conversations with and comments on my work by Rosemary Drage Hale, Norma Joseph, Sheila McDonough, and Michael Oppenheim have been especially useful. The length of my bibliography and the number of my notes give an indication of the extent to which this work relies on the foundation of scholarship laid down by others. It is with grateful appreciation that I also acknowledge the help of those who have extended themselves personally to me and have shared with me ideas and information that have been important in the gradual coming into being of this book: John Cort, Richard Davis, Ginni Ishimatsu, Padma Kaimal, Noboru Karashima, Saskia Kersenboom, Mohan Khokar, Anne Monius, Usha Narayanan, Vasudha Narayanan, Indira Peterson, Pamela Price,

Nandini Ramani, Paula Richman, T. Sankaran, S. P. Tewari, Tom Trautmann, K. K. A. Venkatachari, P. Venkatesan, Lakshmi Viswanathan, Joanne Waghorne, Philip Wagoner, and Paul Younger. Many thanks are due also to Steven Collins, for his *parrainage* of this book, and to the editors Richard Lariviere and Patrick Olivelle at the University of Texas and Cynthia Read at Oxford for their remarkable and sympathetic forbearance.

My work would not have been possible without the cooperation of the Office of the Chief Epigraphist of the Archaeological Survey of India, in Mysore, where I have been graciously granted permission to read the transcripts of unpublished inscriptions. I am greatly indebted to Dr. K. V. Ramesh, who was the Director at the time I first undertook my research, and to his successors, Dr. Madhav N. Katti and Dr. M. D. Sampath, for the access they have allowed me to the precious resources in their keeping. In my work I have also relied heavily on the help and knowledge of librarians; I wish especially to acknowledge the assistance of the librarians of the Office of the Chief Epigraphist in Mysore, the Sangeet Natak Akademi in New Delhi, the Institut français d'Indologie in Pondicherry, the Adyar Library in Madras, the library of the Faculty of Religious Studies at McGill University, and the Concordia University Library. I am grateful for the financial support I have enjoyed during the long period of research and writing leading up to the appearance of this book, in the form of fellowships and research grants received from McGill University, Concordia University, the Shastri Indo-Canadian Institute, the Fonds pour la Formation de Chercheurs et l'Aide à la Recherche du Québec, and the Social Sciences and Humanities Research Council of Canada. Thanks are due to Linda Cardella Cournoyer for her excellent work on the index. I would also like to thank the graduate students who have acted as my research assistants—Steven Engler, Michelle Folk, Paul Hammett, Daphne Lazar, Grant Martin, Philip Moscovitch and Tanisha Ramachaudran—for all their help.

My friends and family have long had to endure my preoccupation with this project; I deeply appreciate their patience and encouragement. I especially thank my husband, Jon Kalina, and my daughter, Nathalie, for accommodating me and sustaining me throughout my work. Their confidence in me, their interest and support, have not only gladdened me but have been essential to the very existence of this book.

Contents

Methods of Transliteration, Abbreviation, and Citation

Tamil words are transliterated according to the system of the MTL (*Tamil Lexicon* of the University of Madras), except that, in keeping with medieval inscriptional usage, I do not distinguish between the long and short vowels *e* and *o* when discussing terms and names that appear in inscriptions of the Chola period.

It should be noted that Tamil inscriptions make frequent use of Grantha characters to represent Sanskrit letters, for example, in the words *māheśvara* or *śrīvaiṣṇava*. In these cases and in the case of Sanskrit words, I use the conventional system of transliterating Sanskrit. When the Sanskrit equivalent of a Tamil word is generally well known, I use the Sanskrit form—for example, Sanskrit *maṭha* instead of Tamil *maṭam*, and Sanskrit Śiva instead of Tamil Civaṉ.

I use standard English spellings, without diacritical marks, for place-names and for the names of kings and dynasties.

All translations are my own, except as otherwise noted. The Tamil inscriptions that I have translated for this volume are listed in Appendix III. In the translations of inscriptions, a series of four dots indicates a break in the original text of the inscription, two dots indicate a very small break (of one or two characters), and three dots indicate an ellipsis made by me as the translator of the inscription.

Ta.	Tamil
Ka.	Kannada
Skt.	Sanskrit

MTL	*Tamil Lexicon*, 6 vols. [1927–35] 1982. Madras: University of Madras.
MW	Monier-Williams, Monier. [1899] 1979. *A Sanskrit-English Dictionary*, new ed. Oxford: Oxford University Press.

Apart from MTL and MW, all other abbreviations of this form (ARE, SII, EI, etc.) refer to collections of inscriptions, which are listed in the first part of the bibliography.

Citations of inscriptions are in one of the following forms:

SII 4.223	*South Indian Inscriptions*, Vol. 4, no. 223.
IPS 319	*Inscriptions of the Pudukkottai State* (no vol.) no. 319.
ARE 16 of 1918	*Annual Report on Indian Epigraphy* for 1918, no. 16.
TAS 8,43	*Travancore Archaeological Series*, Vol. 8, p. 43.

Only when a number is preceded by a comma—as in the last example—does it indicate a page number. This method of citing inscriptions is similar to the one I use to refer to primary textual sources. For example, *Maṇimēkalai* 13.95 refers to verse 95 in Chapter 13 of the Tamil work *Maṇimēkalai* (information about the edition consulted can be found in the bibliography).

Secondary sources are cited by page number, preceded by a comma or, in the case of multivolume works, by a colon following the volume number.

DONORS, DEVOTEES, AND DAUGHTERS OF GOD

ONE

Introduction

Devadāsīs and Dancing-girls

Defining the Temple Woman

Every well-appointed Hindu temple aims at being an earthly reproduction of the paradise of the god in whose honour it was built. . . . The Gandharvas are represented by the Temple-band, the Apsarases by the courtesans who sing and dance in the service. These are dedicated to the service of the god; but they give their favours to his worshippers. They are usually called *Devadāsīs*, handmaidens of the god. . . . They dance and sing in the temple-services and also when the images are carried out through the town in procession. Hence the common name for them everywhere is Nautch-girls, Dancing-girls. . . . How foul the atmosphere is in which this custom thrives may be realized from the hideous sculpture visible on the gates and walls of many Hindu temples in Central and Southern India. . . .

—J. N. Farquhar, *Modern Religious Movements in India*, [1914] 1967, 408–9.

Dāsis or Dēva-dāsis (handmaidens of the gods) are dancing-girls attached to the Tamil temples, who subsist by dancing and music, and the practice of 'the oldest profession in the world.' . . . The rise of the caste, and its euphemistic name, seem both of them to date from about the ninth and tenth centuries A.D., during which much activity prevailed in Southern India in the matter of building temples, and elaborating the services held in them. The dancing-girls' duties, then as now, were to fan the idol with chamaras (Tibetan ox tails), to carry the sacred light called kumbarti, and to sing and dance before the god when he was carried in processsion.

—E. Thurston and K. Rangachari, *Castes and Tribes of Southern India*, 1909, 125–26 (quoting the Madras Census Report of 1901).

There can be no doubt that dancing in the East was once exclusively connected with religious devotion. . . . Further, it is well-known that in ancient times women were dedicated to the service of the temples, like the Vestal virgins of Europe. They were held to be married to the god, and had no other duty but to dance before his shrine. Hence they were called the god's slaves (deva-dāsī), and were generally patterns of piety and propriety. In the present day they are still called by the same name, but are rather slaves to the licentious passions of the profligate Brāhmans of the temples to which they belong. What surprised me most was the number and weight of their ornaments, especially in the case of those attached to the temples in Southern India. . . . They drive a profitable trade under the sanction of religion.

—M. Monier-Williams, *Religious Thought and Life in India*, [1883] 1974, 451.

When temples of Hindu gods came to be built and endowed on a magnificent scale, some people began to feel in course of time that there should be singing girls attached to shrines to play music on the occasions of the different services and worships of the day. . . . The introduction of dancing girls in temples tended to lower their moral and spiritual atmosphere. Some people began to visit shrines not so much to pay their respects to deities, as to carry on their love intrigues with the singing girls employed there.

—A. S. Altekar, *The Position of Women in Hindu Civilization*, 1959, 182–83.

For over a thousand years, until they were legislated out of existence in the early twentieth century, women have been associated with temples in various parts of India. These are the temple women, who are the object of the present study. Unique among temple servants because they were women and unusual among Hindu women because they remained unmarried, they have long been an object of fascination and the focus of controversy.

Much of our understanding of the temple women of India is derived from the representations of these women, in the late nineteenth and early twentieth centuries, in ethnographic accounts[1] and in the decisions and debates about their character and status that took place in Indian courts and legislatures and in the press.[2] The conception that most clearly emerges from these sources—a conception that is in many ways superficial and one-sided—is of the temple woman as dancing-girl and prostitute. This is the image of the temple woman presented in the preceding quotations.

This conception of the character and function of temple women, shaped as it was by the political agendas and cultural presuppositions of a particular historical moment and developed in large part with reference to the particular context of South India, was assumed by those who used it to be salient in other places and times throughout India's history, from the early medieval period onward. It is a conception that has continued to exert a strong influence on our ideas about the identity and significance of temple women and has filtered as well into our understanding of the character of medieval Hinduism and of the role of women in Indian religion. In consequence, the *devadāsī* "phenomenon" is judged to be manifest in all kinds of diverse contexts—in sculpture, in myth, and in literature—wherever dance or female sexuality seems to occur within some kind of religious framework.

In an effort to avoid some of the biases and presuppositions that this recently constructed conception of the temple woman brings with it, I have chosen to investigate the activities and roles of temple women within very particular historical and regional parameters and to define as carefully as possible the category of "temple woman." As we see in the preceding passage of Thurston and Rangachari, South India in the early medieval period has long been regarded as a context of great significance in the historical development of the *devadāsī* phenomenon, as well as other features of Hindu religious life. In this study, therefore, the particular historical period I have chosen to examine in detail is the Chola period (A.D. 850–1300), in the Tamil country of South India, in order to discern the features of the lives of temple women within a specific historical framework. In my definition of this group of women, I consider a temple woman to be a woman—who may or may not be a prostitute or a dancer—who is associated with a temple, either by having some kind of regular service function in a temple or because her primary social identity is defined with reference to a temple.

I do not assume that women referred to as *devadāsīs* in various periods of history are necessarily temple women, although *devadāsī* has become in this century the term most commonly applied to temple women. As Marglin explains: "The word *devadāsī* has attained widespread usage since the revival of Indian classical dance, first begun in Tamilnadu in the 1920s. It has become a pan-Indian word, whereas traditionally each region had its own term to designate temple dancers" (1985b, 313). The term *devadāsī*, as it has recently gained currency, appears to be a Sanskritized form of the Tamil term *tevaraṭiyāḷ*, which was one of the most common designations for temple women in Tamilnadu. The term *devadāsī* itself is very rarely encountered in Indian literature or inscriptional records before the present century.

Three very early appearances of the term *devadāsī*, including one inscriptional reference, have provoked a great deal of speculation about the antiquity of the *devadāsī* "institution," but in my reading of the sources where this term occurs I do not find any evidence to suggest that these ancient *devadāsīs* were temple women.[3] The earliest application of the term *devadāsī* to temple women seems to occur in several of the Āgamas, some of which date from before the tenth century. In these texts, the term is occasionally applied to women said to be performing various ritual functions in the temple.[4] The only inscription I have found in which the term *devadāsī* is used to refer to temple women is a twelfth-century Kannada record that uses the term *dēvadāsigaḷ* to refer to women receiving support in a Jain temple (EC 7.Sh97).

Even with my rather cautious definition of temple women, there is evidence that such women were present in various regions and periods in India's history. What kinds of information do we have about the situation, the roles, and the activities of temple women?

Historical Resources: Temple Women in Indian Literature and Travelers' Accounts

Although some scholars maintain that having women serve in temples was an innovation of Puranic religion (Parasher and Naik 1986, 77), there are in fact only four or five passages that actually refer to temple women in the Purāṇas.[5] None of these passages seems to date from before the eighth or ninth century (Hazra 1975; Inden 1985, 53–54; Rocher 1986), and all but one deal with temple women exclusively in the context of exhortations to make gifts of women to the temple. It cannot be assumed that the various references in Puranic literature to dance as a form of worship, to prostitutes, or to *apsarās* ("celestial courtesans") refer to temple women.

In Prakrit and Sanskrit erotic poetry, story literature, and chronicles composed before the late medieval period, there is only a single work, the twelfth-century *Rājataraṅgiṇī*, that seems to refer to temple women. Here we find descriptions both of the gift made by a king of women to a temple and of *nartakīs* (female dancers) as "guardians of the temple" (*Rājataraṅgiṇī* 1.151 and 8.708). In six other works, we find passages that describe prostitutes (*veśyās*, *vilāsinīs*, or *gaṇikās*) who are worshiping or engaged in other activities in or near a temple; there is no indication that these women are temple women, in the sense of being regularly employed in the temple or associated with the temple. With the exception of Kālidāsa's description in *Meghadūta* of prostitutes dancing and waving flywhisks at a Śiva temple, which dates from the fourth or fifth century, all of the other references of this type are from works of the eighth to twelfth centuries, composed either in western India or Kashmir.[6] The temple as a context for the artistic or erotic activities of prostitutes seems to have been an appealing and suggestive image in poetic literature of this period and region.

In ancient Tamil literature of the Cankam period, dancing women and prostitutes are frequently met with (Kersenboom 1981), but temple women are not in evidence. The devotional poems of the Āḻvārs and Nāyaṉmārs—composed in Tamil in the sixth to ninth centuries—refer to women, celestial and human, offering worship in temples, and to singing and dancing, but they do not refer to temple women (Orr and Young 1986—cf. Pope [1900] 1970, 85; Hardy 1983, 477, n. 189, n. 199; Kersenboom 1987, 23–24; A. Singh 1990, 52; Sadasivan 1993, 31–35). I have found only one work of ancient or medieval Tamil literature that seems to refer to such women—the twelfth-century hagiography *Periya Purāṇam*. In describing the birth of Paravai, the first wife of the saint Cuntaramūrtti, the text says: "As if a radiant jewel had been born, she appeared in the family of temple women (*patiyilār*), of Rudra's courtesans (*uruttira kaṇikais*)" (*Periya Purāṇam* Tatuttāṭkonta Purāṇam 132). Although there are no other indications in this text (nor in the poems of Cuntaramūrtti, composed three centuries earlier) of Paravai's identity as a temple woman, we find here the use of a term (*patiyilār*) that means "temple woman" in Tamil inscriptions of the same period as this text.

In the analysis of poetic and religious literature it is necessary to take particular care to distinguish between temple women and *apsarās*, the celestial women associated in myth with skill in dance and with the power to seduce mortals, frequently connected with the heavenly court of the god Indra and described as the beautiful attendants who await the courageous and the virtuous after death (Vatsyayan 1968). These divine beings are often encountered in Sanskrit literature, where they may be referred to by terms that, to some, suggest a link to temple women, for example, *devagaṇikā*, or *devaveśyā* (Sternbach 1942–50). In South India, various female spirits (*cūrara makaḷir*, *varaiyara makaḷir*, and *vāṉara makaḷir*) and the celestial women who awaited fallen warriors in heaven came to be identified with *apsarās* (*Index des Mots*; *Puṟanāṉūṟu* 287.10–12; Clothey 1978, 29–30, 160f).[7] For example, in Tamil literature (of perhaps the fifth or sixth century) we find in *Maṇimēkalai* (13.95) a reference to a "divine courtesan" (*kaṭavuṭ kaṇikai*) and in *Cilappatikāram* (3.4) a description of the courtesan Mātavi's descent from "heavenly women" (*vāṉavar makaḷir*). The possibilities for confusion of these divine figures with human temple women are compounded by the fact that some twentieth-century temple women connect themselves with *apsarās* in legends about the origins of their communities; some of the South Indian temple women whom Srinivasan studied, for instance, claimed a connection with the *apsarās* by virtue of belonging to the lineage of Mātavi, whose story is told in *Cilappatikāram* (A. Srinivasan 1984, 140–41; see also Marglin 1985b, 91, 145; Gorringe 1998, 10, 31).

Another category of literature provides more direct information about the possible activities of human women in the temple context. These are the Āgamas, the ritual handbooks and compendia of sectarian lore compiled in Sanskrit by the Śaivas and Vaiṣṇavas in the period A.D. 500–1500 (Schrader [1916] 1973; H. Smith 1975; Gonda 1977; R. Davis 1986.) Although these texts are primarily focused on knowledge and procedures relevant to priests, they do refer in passing to the participation of others, including women, in temple rituals. I have collected fifty-three passages that refer to women's ritual roles in twenty-two different Agamic texts—seven Śaivāgamas, three Vaikhānasa texts, and twelve Pāñcarātra texts.[8] Not all of these passages necessarily refer to temple women but may in some cases describe the ritual participation of women of the community, including prostitutes, who were not associated in any formal way with the temple. Nor can we assume that women necessarily did perform the tasks in the temple that the Āgamas indicate as possibilities in their formulations of ideal patterns of worship.

Nonetheless these texts are a rich resource in terms of indicating the types of ritual roles sanctioned for women in the medieval temple milieu. In the references I have collected, the roles most frequently mentioned are singing and dancing, and the context for women's participation most frequently mentioned is festival celebration. These texts are also interesting because they seem very often to describe women's participation in temple rituals as occasional or optional.

There are a few references to women who may have been temple women in the accounts of Chinese, Arab, and European travelers to western and southern India between the seventh and sixteenth centuries. In some cases, particularly in the earlier Chinese and Arab reports from western India, it is not clear whether travelers encountered actual temple women—that is, women with an established and regular connection to the temple—or professional performers or prostitutes who sang, danced, and made music in the area around the temple or during festivals.[9] The later accounts of European visitors to South India give us a few more shreds of evidence concerning the existence and activities of temple women, including, for example, their participation in the court life of Vijayanagara in the sixteenth century.[10]

The scattered and fragmentary character of the evidence relating to temple women in religious and secular literature and in foreign travelers' accounts—as well as its idealized, mythic, prescriptive, or polemical character—makes it quite difficult to use these sources as a basis for understanding or reconstructing the history of temple women in India. Authors basing their studies of temple women on such sources (e.g., Penzer 1924; S. Chatterjee 1945; Bonoff 1973) have been forced by the nature of the evidence to produce accounts that are quite general and that lack any historical specificity.

Temple Women in the Modern Period: Characterizations and Conceptualizations

Fortunately, full descriptive accounts of the lives and ritual activities of temple women in recent history are available to us through the efforts of several anthropologists—in particular, Frédérique Marglin, Amrit Srinivasan, and Saskia Kersenboom. The new ethnographies produced by these scholars have illuminated and altered previous understandings of the character of temple women; they are especially valuable in demonstrating how temple women, rather than being anomalous figures, have a place within the framework of Indian society and religion. These scholars have questioned the notion that the identities of temple women are primarily bound up with prostitution; instead they have given us an image of the temple woman, as she has survived into the early twentieth century, defined by three characteristics: her hereditary status, that is, her birth or adoption into a particular community; her status as dependent on ritual dedication to temple service through a ceremony of "marriage" to the temple deity; and her professional expertise—her mastery of a dance tradition.

This recent ethnography and analysis challenges some of the prevailing ideas about temple women and corroborates others. Ideas about temple women that have gained currency in the last hundred years seem to be linked to four interrelated themes. These themes are associated with a series of general interpretations and ideas about history, religion, and women in India that pervade academic study but that seem particularly persistent and troublesome in the vicinity of the figure of the temple woman: (1) the assumption that there is a pan-Indian and transhistorical *devadāsī* phenomenon; (2) the idea of the degeneration of the *devadāsī* institution; (3) the notion of the *devadāsī* as the passive victim of social forces or elite interests; and (4) the focus on the *devadāsī*'s role as being defined primarily with respect to her identity as a woman, in terms either of her sexuality or of her representation of some peculiarly feminine power. I would like to briefly review these ideas about temple women to show how the present study may cast new light on these conceptions and may contribute to a more complete picture of Indian religion and of the history of women in India.

The first of the four themes is linked to the fact that the study of Indian society and religion and the study of Indian women have been in large part dominated by a tradition of scholarship that has focused on abstract images and values, treating them as though they stand outside of history. The foundations of Indian culture, or of the role and status of Indian women, have been sought in such timeless and basic "Hindu" categories and concepts as *dharma* or purity, hierarchy or spirituality, *māyā* or *śakti*.[11] The idea that these essential principles have shaped Indian civilization is linked, by rather circular reasoning, to the notion that Indian society and tradition have remained changeless. In part, this notion was promoted by the bearers of that tradition themselves, but the idea of India as a place without history was further developed by Orientalist scholars and colonial administrators and continues to exert considerable influence.[12]

Contemporary studies of India's religious and social history tend to be marked by this legacy, and studies of India's women are especially likely to be conducted primarily or exclusively with reference to transhistorical and transcendental images and ideals. In this case, one must struggle not only with the Indological orientation toward abstract religious concepts but also with the particular problems associated with the study of women that Rita Gross has identified as belonging to androcentric scholarship. Androcentrism, like Orientalism, objectifies and essentializes the object of study—women are considered with reference to cultural stereotypes, goddesses and female symbolism, and men's views about women. Androcentric scholarship treats women as if their lives have been shaped by structures and a history that are not their own (Johansson 1976, 402–5, 416–17; Gross 1977, 9–10; 1987, 38–39; Mohanty 1988, 78–80; O'Hanlon 1991, 73–74). There is still a very strong tendency to see Indian women's lives as having been defined and circumscribed, from ancient times to the present, by the prescriptions of religious and legal treatises and to view the codes of behavior prescribed for women as being not only consistently "applied" throughout the course of Indian history but also as uniform and monolithic in character (Leslie 1989, 1–4, 19–22, 325–29; cf. Jamison 1996, 9–10, 15–17).

Because of the scholarly traditions we have inherited, much of our understanding of Indian history and society, and of women's part in that history and society, comes from the study of religious texts and of myths, symbols, and rituals. This kind of study is essential insofar as it allows us to recognize patterns, models, ideals, and values that have salience in Indian culture and history and in the lives of Indian women.[13] But equally important is attention to the behavior and experience of individuals—to particularity, difference, and change.

This type of study seems to be especially needed in the case of temple women. In recent scholarship, the *devadāsīs*' role has been interpreted almost entirely with reference to abstract, overarching conceptions such as *śakti* or auspiciousness.[14] Frédérique Marglin's (1985b) analysis of the temple women of Puri develops the concept of auspiciousness as a key to understanding the ritual and symbolic significance of these women. In Saskia Kersenboom's study of the *devadāsī* tradition of South India, we find the idea that auspiciousness and identity with the goddess (Śakti) are understandings of the "meaning" of temple women and other female ritual specialists that are universally applicable in "all historical layers of South Indian culture" (1987, 192). This approach obscures historical and regional variations in the activities and circumstances of temple women, effaces the individuality of temple women, and conceals change. The aim of the present study is to move from abstract, transhistorical meanings toward specificity and historicity.

The second theme prevalent in thinking about temple women—the idea that the *devadāsī* institution has degenerated—contains a number of different component strands: notions of the general decline of Indian civilization and of the decadence of the medieval period, ideas about the history of the status of women in India, and concerns about the "real" character of the temple woman in the context of Hindu reform and revival.

Both Indologists and Indian nationalist historians have shared the view that India's political, social, and religious integrity degenerated over time; disagreements among members of the two camps on this issue are focused mainly on the time and the cause of this decline. European scholars were inclined to date the onset of degeneration relatively early, imputing it to some inherent cultural, religious, or racial failing, whereas Indian nationalists have tended to attribute deterioration to more recent experiences of conquest and influence by foreigners.[15] Despite differences about the precise sequence of events and the reasons for decline, Indian and Western scholars have, even in recent times, frequently agreed that "medieval" Indian society and religion ought to be characterized as decadent. A whole constellation of features—none of them particularly positive—is attributed to the India of post-Gupta times, beginning in the seventh century or a few centuries later: political fragmentation, feudalism, rigidity of social hierarchy and Brahmanical domination, regionalism, sectarianism, conservatism, cultural ossification, Tantrism, and emotionalism and eroticism. "Early medieval is seen as a breakdown of the civilizational matrix of early historical India" (Chattopadhyaya 1994, 13).[16]

The persistence of this characterization of the medieval era in historical writings, together with the glorification of India's ancient religion by Orientalists and Hindu reformers, has had an impact on our understanding of religious life in medieval India. Kosambi, for example, recounts the "dismal tale of rapid growth and long degeneration," which resulted, in the medieval period, in the decline of cities, of the economy, and of learning, as well as an "incredible proliferation of senseless ritual" (1969, 166–76, 196). In Devangana Desai's view, the "atmosphere of the Medieval temple was a breeding ground for luxurious living and degenerate sexual practices" (1975, 160). We often encounter the notion that the development in the medieval period of the devotional ethos of *bhakti*, together with the patronage of Brahmans and temples, entrenched "feudal" hierarchies and made the general population vulnerable to political subjugation and to the control of priestly or Brahmanical authority (Nagarkar 1893, 767–76; Nandi 1973, 10–13; Narayanan and Veluthat 1978; Chattopadhyaya 1990, 10–11, 127–28; 1994, 10–12, 28–31; Veluthat 1993, 198–211, 240–41).

There is another aspect of the notion of degeneration in India's history that touches our assessment of the situation of temple women. This is the idea of the decline in the status of women generally, from a "golden age" when women were honored and participated fully in religious life to a later age when women were denied access to religious ritual and education and suffered such abuses as child marriage and *sati*.[17] This view of the experience of Hindu women over the course of India's history does not directly link women's degraded status with the social and religious developments that are supposed to have occurred in the medieval period that I have outlined. The suppression of women's rights and freedoms is usually depicted as occurring considerably earlier, beginning, according to some accounts, in the late Vedic period, in tandem with the rise of elaborate ritualism, priestly specialization, and increasingly rigid social hierarchy.

If, as is often assumed, normative roles for Hindu women had become by the medieval period restrictive and repressive and exclusively defined with reference to the role of the chaste wife, the presence of temple women in medieval Hindu temples is rather problematic. Again, the theme of decline has been pressed into service in a number of different scenarios: either the temple woman of the early medieval period is seen as another type of chaste wife, pure and nunlike in her dedication to God, who was transformed in the course of time into a temple prostitute; or temple women are considered to have engaged in sexual activity from their earliest appearance, but changes in the context for this activity are seen as having brought about the decadence of the *devadāsī* institution by medieval times—"sacred prostitution" in the context of ancient fertility rites having been replaced by hedonistic sex in the "degenerate" milieu of the medieval temple.[18]

These historical reconstructions, particularly those in which the temple woman's original nunlike character was stressed, were important in the early twentieth century as a means through which Hindus, and temple women themselves, could express pride in their religious traditions (Jordan 1989, 260, 271–74; 1993, 264; see also Marglin 1985b, 9–11, 93–94; Meduri 1996, 178–81). But these histories were also weapons that were used to drive the *devadāsīs* out of existence and to divest them of their special claim to traditional expertise in classical Indian dance. The hypothesis of decline could be turned to a number of political uses, depending on whether the focus was on the pure origins of the *devadāsī* institution or on its present degenerate manifestation: "The reformers presented the extant temple-dancer as a 'prostitute' in order to do away with her; the revivalists presented the ancient Hindu temple-dancer as a 'nun' in order to incarnate her afresh" in the form of the high-caste professional classical dancer who performed "pure" traditional dance on the concert stage rather than in the temple (A. Srinivasan 1983, 96). Closely linked to the idea of the ancient temple woman as nun is the idea of dance as a form of worship or yoga, a notion that was promoted by those who wanted to make Indian classical dance respectable (Rukmini Devi 1957; Gaur 1963; Ramanujan, Narayana Rao, and Shulman 1994, 28–29; Meduri 1996, 219–72, 326–36).

The notions of the degeneration over time of the roles and character of temple women, of the declining status of women generally, and of the decadence of the medieval period seem to have been built up more on political grounds than on a firm foundation of historical evidence. In this study, the examination of the activities of temple women within a specific medieval context will allow us to assess the validity of these ideas and to create a fuller, less stereotyped image of medieval social and religious life in a particular time and place.

The third theme that is prominent in much of what has been written about temple women—their portrayal as passive, as lacking agency, and as victims—is linked, like the theme of decline just discussed, to ideas about India's history and about the role of women in that history. The denial of agency to the people of India is characteristic of the Orientalist studies of the colonial period (Said 1979, 207–9; Inden 1990, 22–23, 73; Haynes and Prakash 1991, 5). Ronald Inden points out that we need in our study of India to overcome the legacy of colonialism and to recognize the agency of Indian people: "Colonialism consisted quite precisely of the attempt to make previously autonomous (or more autonomous) agents into instruments . . . through which the colonizers could fulfil their desires and into patients, those who had to be variously pacified or punished, saved, reformed, or developed" (Inden 1990, 23). Indian women in particular seem to have been regarded as instruments and patients, not only by colonizers, missionaries, and Indologists, but also by Indian nationalists and social reformers. Even today, there is a tendency among scholars, including Western feminists, to see the history of the women of India and of "third-world" women generally as a history of submission and victimization; such scholarship does not consider the possibility that these women may have possessed autonomy or agency in shaping their circumstances.[19]

In the nineteenth and early twentieth centuries, "women's issues" loomed large in debates among colonial authorities, Western and Hindu reformers, and Indian nationalists.

> For all their overt concern with women, however, these debates [about such issues as *sati*, child marriage, and the condition of widows] neither offered women any voice as subjects themselves, nor admitted that they possessed any power of agency. Rather, they stressed the weakness and ignorance which made women easy victims, either for domineering male relatives or for a manipulative priesthood. . . . The real concern and point of contest in these debates was not women at all. Rather they were arguments about the status of Hindu tradition and the legitimacy of colonial power. (O'Hanlon 1991, 74–75)

The Indian woman came to be regarded as the very embodiment of tradition, in a vision that was shared both by those who wished to protect and promote tradition and by those who aimed for its reform. Indian women, representative of Indian society as a whole, were variously considered to be ennobled by tradition, to be oppressed by tradition, or to be oppressed by customs that were only degenerate remnants of India's true tradition—but in all cases, women were seen as being acted upon rather than as actors.[20]

Temple women, of course, were an object of concern in these debates. The late nineteenth- and early twentieth-century conception of temple women as prostitutes and dancing-girls made it difficult to find a place for them in the emerging image of Hindu womanhood characterized by purity, chastity, domesticity, spirituality, and self-sacrifice. Perhaps because of this lack of fit, temple women attracted the special attention of reformers.[21] Hindu reformers also had difficulty in finding a place for temple women in the context of a Hinduism that sought to deemphasize "idolatry," mythology, ritual, and those aspects of customary practice viewed by Christian and colonial critics as superstitious and backward [Farquhar (1914) 1967, 435, 437–39, 442; Nair 1994, 3159; Price 1996, 153–58].

Among British reformers, in contrast, the major focus in the *devadāsī* reform movement was the issue of women's "age of consent" and the prostitution of minors. A great deal of concern was expressed about the sexual victimization of would-be *devadāsīs*; the recruitment (possibly through kidnapping or purchase) and the dedication of minor girls as temple women were problematic from the point of view of both the girl's inability to make a decision for herself in the matter of dedication and the possibility of her being compelled to engage in sexual activity at a very young age.[22] The idea that girls were forced against their will or against the wishes of their families to be dedicated to the temple seems to have very little basis in fact.[23] If girls had no choice in this matter and if girls dedicated to the temple were likely to be involved in sexual activity soon after attaining puberty, their situation was identical to that of virtually every girl, who in the normal course of events would be given in marriage. It was, of course, much easier for reformers and legislators to tackle these "abuses" among *devadāsīs* than to take on these issues among the Indian population at large. There were a few faint protests—notably by *devadāsīs* themselves—that the characterization of their lives in terms of violence and victimization was a complete misrepresentation; for the most part, however, the Indian reaction was embarrassment about rather than refutation of such portrayals (Jordan 1989, 220–21, 238–40, 254, 259–60, 272; Anandhi 1991, 740–41; Nair 1994, 3162–63; Kannabiran 1995, WS66–67; Meduri 1996, 176–83, 209, 225–27).

The depiction of the *devadāsī*—or the potential *devadāsī*—as victim was extremely influential and crucial to the success of the movement to legislate against the continuing existence of the *devadāsī* community. The concept of the *devadāsī* as victim, or as being in other ways the passive object of manipulation by others, is also characteristic of much of the historical speculation centered on temple women, which was formulated in the same period as the reform movement against *devadāsī* dedication. Whether the scenario of decline was that of the transformation of nun into prostitute or of the perversion of sacred prostitution, the reasons adduced for the degeneration were, most frequently, manipulation and coercion by priests or by members of royal or noble elites. One of my main aims in this study is to reexamine the notion that temple women were so entirely without agency by considering the character of their activities and roles in a particular historical context.

The fourth theme—the femininity and sexuality of the *devadāsī*—is linked to the concept of the *devadāsī* as victim in several ways. First, she was perceived as a sexual victim. In addition, perversely, the notion that she had not chosen to be dedicated—her passivity in the matter of becoming a temple woman—focused even more attention on her sexuality and enhanced the conception of her as a quintessentially feminine, erotic being. Kabbani's (1986, 26) description of European feelings about "Oriental women" as harem women, sexually enslaved and erotically expert—fluctuating "between desire, pity, contempt and outrage"—perfectly expresses Western reactions to the *devadāsī*.[24] But from another perspective, the sexuality of the *devadāsī* was viewed as being predatory. Not only was she represented as responsible for the victimization of the girls whose dedication she arranged, who were supposed in some cases to have been bought or kidnapped by her, but also, as a prostitute, she was regarded as a calculating and mercenary being, cynically manipulating the desires and weaknesses of men.

Prostitution in colonial India was a complex issue, evoking mixed attitudes and policies within official British, missionary, and Hindu reformist circles. In the late nineteenth century, British colonial administrators and military authorities were primarily concerned with prostitution as a health problem for British soldiers in India but attempted at the same time to respond to British public and missionary opinion, which decried the sanctioning of prostitution through the institution of controls over Indian prostitutes (Oddie 1979, 105; Ballhatchet 1980; Burton 1992; cf. Walkowitz 1980). In the same period, the focus of concern for Hindu reformers with respect to prostitution seemed to be the threat posed to family life—for example, the possibility that a (high-caste) woman, particularly a young widow, might become a prostitute (Kishwar 1986, 155–58; Rule 1987, 67–72; I. Chatterjee 1990, 27–28; J. Whitehead 1995, 203–4). In addition, Hindu reformers of the late nineteenth century were disturbed by the idea that the *devadāsī* institution provided religious sanction for prostitution. For them, the anti-nautch campaign was a way to reform Hinduism and to express condemnation of public immorality (Oddie 1979, 102–3). The overlap between British and Hindu concerns about prostitution was remarkably slight: on one hand, Indian legislators were extremely reluctant to address the problem of Indian women being prostituted for the benefit of British soldiers (Ballhatchett 1980, 156–57); on the other, British courts and legislatures in India did not accede for decades to Hindu reformers' requests to have *devadāsīs* legally declared prostitutes, even though these requests were supported by British missionaries (Oddie 1979, 102, 105–9; Jordan 1989, 230–33; 1993).

Where British and Indian attitudes and responses to prostitution seemed to be in accord was in their utter lack of sympathy for the prostitute, or the *devadāsī*. The sexual nature seen as the core of her identity was perceived as a threat—a threat to the health of British and Indian men, a threat to the social distance that ought to prevail between the British and the natives of India and between members of different castes and classes, a threat to the idealized Hindu family and to chaste Hindu wives and innocent girls, and a threat to the reputation of the Hindu religion. This perception led to various efforts to define, confine, and control the women who embodied this social threat.[25]

In colonial India, the British definition of the prostitute was linked to their understanding of the nature of Indian society. Although military authorities, who were in essence procuring women for British troops (Ballhatchet 1980, 62–63, 162–64), certainly had a vested interest in maintaining the belief that there were in India "hereditary prostitutes," this belief was consistent with the official colonial vision of Indian society as an assemblage of discrete "castes and tribes," each with a prescribed position in the social hierarchy and with a traditional occupation (see, e.g., Crooke [1896] 1974; Thurston and Rangachari 1909). In some cases, the British authorities had come to believe that members of some of these communities were professional prostitutes or criminals, who came by their calling hereditarily, that is, by virtue of their birth into the group (Gordon 1969; Nigam 1990). The concept of a prostitute caste was easily applied to the *devadāsīs*, as well as to other groups.[26]

When prostitution was seen as an activity that belonged to particular identifiable communities, it was tempting for reformers to imagine that an attack on such a community was a blow against prostitution. This seems to be precisely what happened in the case of the *devadāsīs* (A. Srinivasan 1983, 76, 95). As the reform movement progressed—the campaign against the employment of *devadāsīs* as entertainers and against *devadāsī* dedication—and as the men of their community actually joined forces with the reformers, *devadāsīs* became increasingly vulnerable (A. Srinivasan 1985,

1873–74; Anandhi 1991, 741; Meduri 1996, 364–66). And in time, of course, the *devadāsī* disappeared, irrevocably branded as a prostitute, as legislation banning dedication was passed in various parts of India in the 1930s and 1940s.[27]

This history of attention to the temple woman's primary identity as a prostitute has inspired a whole series of ideas about her character, history, and significance that continue to have wide currency. The irony is that many of the temple women in recent history may not have been prostitutes, in the sense of having numerous sexual partners or exchanging sex for money.[28] Nonetheless, the concerns of the reformers about the *devadāsī*'s sexuality have influenced popular and scholarly understandings of Hindu temple women up to the present day—although today the *devadāsī*'s sexuality may be construed in more positive terms.

One of the ways in which the sexuality of temple women has been interpreted is through the concept of sacred prostitution. The notion of sacred prostitution was originally presented as an explanation of the presumed sexual activities of priestesses and other dedicated women in the temples of the ancient Near East. The central idea of sacred prostitution is that sexual acts performed in a sacred setting, often between a priestess who embodies some form of female divinity and a king, would ensure fertility and prosperity (Frazer 1957, 184–95; see also Harman 1989a, 254–58). Many scholars consider that the temple women of India were sacred prostitutes in this sense (e.g., Farquhar [1914] 1967, 409; Sinha and Basu 1933, 13–21; Gonda 1961, 82–85, 94; D. Desai 1975, 88–92, 103–7; Marglin 1987; Kopf 1993, 146–152). It is, however, important to bear in mind that the whole concept of sacred prostitution may not be a valid one even in the context of the ancient Near East; although this was where the notion at first seemed useful, a number of authors have recently challenged the idea that sacred prostitution is an accurate description of the cultic practices of this region and period (Fisher 1976; Oden 1987; P. Bird 1989; Hackett 1989).

An idea that seems to be related to the notion of sacred prostitution has been suggested by Hardy (1978, 140) and Kersenboom (1987, 166, n. 34)—the *devadāsī* as *prasāda*. In the context of Hindu worship, offerings made to the image of the deity, which the god has presumably enjoyed or touched in some way, are frequently distributed as *prasāda* among worshipers as a mark of the god's grace and as a means through which the worshiper can have contact with the divine presence. The idea that a temple woman is a form of *prasāda* rests, evidently, on the notion that a woman belonging to the deity might be also enjoyed sexually by the worshipers of that deity and that such a woman would thereby act as a kind of conduit of divine favor from the god to his (male) devotees.

Another way of understanding the sexuality and femininity of the temple woman in ritual and symbolic terms is with reference to the Indian system of Tantra. The evidence for a connection between temple women and

Tantric sexual ritual is, however, very slim, consisting only of a possible reference to temple women in a late eighteenth-century Tantric text and the existence of Tantric interpretations of temple rituals performed by *devadāsīs* at Puri.[29]

All of these formulations—sacred prostitution, the *devadāsī* as *prasāda*, and Tantric interpretations—consider sexual activity as ritual activity. Temple women have, however, been most visible in ritual contexts in which overt sexuality is condemned. The Indian temple, as a precinct where rules of purity are closely observed, has no place for ritual sex. Even if, as contemporary anthropological study has indicated, sexual symbolism is important in the devotional ethos and in the ritual performed by the *devadāsīs*, sexual activity had no place in the temple cult in which these women participated. Nor does it seem, according to the careful study of temple women in recent times, that their sexual activity was in any way ritualized (A. Srinivasan 1984, 183–84, 279; Marglin 1985b; Kersenboom 1987).

Although recent studies by Marglin, Kersenboom, and others have for the most part rejected the idea that prostitution and ritualized sex were features in the lives of temple women, such studies have, in another way, focused on the femininity and sexuality of these women. Marglin, for example, suggests that it is the temple woman's sexuality—which connects her with prostitutes and *apsarās*, as well as married women—that makes her a preeminent representative of the auspicious (Marglin 1985b, 70, 96, 101, 144–45, 286). Marglin (1985b, 95, 217) also interprets the temple woman's dance as a symbol of sexual union. On another level, the temple woman's femininity is critical insofar as she represents the goddess Lakṣmī (Marglin 1985b, 174–75). In Kersenboom's interpretation, too, the *devadāsī* is regarded as the representative of the supreme goddess, Śakti. Kersenboom considers the *devadāsī*'s femaleness as essential to her ritual function, inasmuch as she acts as the female counterbalance to the male deity enshrined in the temple and as a female ritual specialist capable of controlling or channeling dangerous but divine feminine energies (1987, 185–86, 192–98).[30]

Although we find in these interpretations a celebration, rather than a condemnation, of temple women's femininity and sexuality, there is still the risk that too narrow a focus on feminine identity and sexuality will limit our capacity to fully understand these women's significance and their activities. This focus—the last of the four themes that for the last century have dominated the description and interpretation of temple women's roles—allows for only a partial and narrow view of what temple women do and what they represent. This orientation toward understanding temple women—like the other three themes of transhistoricity, degeneration, and passivity—has deeply colored our perception of the history of temple women and of their place in history. It would seem both possible and profitable to escape from the limitations that these themes impose on our investigations.

In a Different Landscape: The Temple Women of Medieval Tamilnadu

Historical Resources: Temple Women in Inscriptions of the Chola Period

In the eighteenth year of the reign of Nirupatoṅkavarmaṉ, Nakkaṉ Kāḷi, a temple woman (*tevaṉār makaḷ*) of Śrīkaṇṭapuram, gave 12 *kaḻañcu* of pure gold for a perpetual lamp for [the god] Tirukkaṭaimuṭi Perumāṉaṭikaḷ.

This gold, the wealth of the Lord (*perumāṉaṭikaḷ*), received from this person of the *peruñceri* of Śrīkaṇṭapuram, is to yield a daily interest of 1 *uḻakku* [of ghee].

May the *paṉmāheśvarar* protect this [endowment].

—SII 7.526: this inscription was engraved in A.D. 872 at the Śaḍaiyar temple in Tiruccennampundi, Tanjavur district.

In the forty-ninth year of the reign of Śrī Kulottuṅkacoḻadevar, this deed of land sale was declared and recorded in Maṉāvaṇakkaḷamānāṭu, in Nakaṟañcoḻakeraḷapuṟam, in Veṇkuṉṟanāṭu, in Veṇkuṉṟakoṭṭam, in Cayaṅkoṇṭacoḻamaṇṭalam, with the agreement, on behalf of the town (*nakaram*), of us, the *nakarattār* of this town, including Neṟkuṉṟaṅ Kiḻāṉ Kuṭameṟatiruvaṭikaḷ, Kaṉṉuva Pākkiḻāṉ Vaṭavāyi. . . . Cātinta Āccinataraṭippaṉ, Neṟkuṉṟaṅ Kiḻāṉ Kaliyaṉ Makiyāṉ, Maṇappākkīḻaṉ Karaikkiyemaṟṟayilaiyāṉ, Nalluḻāṉ Svāmi Amutu, and Neṟkuṉṟa Kiḻāṉ Oṟi Vaṭavāyil.

Cuntari Utayaiñceytāḷ alias Pūventiyacoḻa-māṇikkam, a temple woman (*devaraṭiyār*) of Lord Matukulamātevīśvaram of this village (*ūr*), purchased from the town (*nakaram*) and donated 2 *veli* of land (whose boundaries are described in detail), to provide offerings (*tirupaṭimāṟṟu*) and festival lamps for this god and for the goddess ("Queen of the Bedchamber"—*tirupaḷḷiyaṟai nampirāṭṭiyaṭiyār*) whom she had set up. The whole of this 2 *veli* of land which we the *nakarattār* of Coḻakeraḷapuṟam agreed to sell, Pūventiyacoḻa-māṇikkam bought and donated as *devadāṉam* for the goddess.

I, the accountant Māmpākkamuṭaiyāṉ Māṟkaṇṭaiyaṉ Civakkoḻuntāṉ Catturukālamakalātittaṉ, sign this deed of sale that has been declared by these people.

He who destroys or seizes this charity will be as one who has sinned on the banks of the Ganges and the shores of Kanyakumari.

—SITI 118: this inscription was engraved in A.D. 1119 at the Manukulamahādeva temple in Salukki, North Arcot district.

In the thirty-fifth year of the reign of Śrī Tirupuvaṉavīratevar, we, the temple servants (*tevarkaṉmikaḷ*) of Āticaṇṭeśvaratevar of the temple. . . .

Uṭaiyavaḷ alias Nāṟpatteṇṇāyira-māṇikkam, one of the temple women (*tevaraṭiyār*) of this temple. . . . [having set up the deities] Tiruvācuranāyanār, Periyatevar, and Nācciyār and made a taxfree land endowment for the temple of this Lord, [was assigned] a position (*muṟai*) when worship is offered at the early morning service (*tiruveḻucci*), and a senior (?) place at the hunting festival (*tiruveṭṭai*), and [the singing of] the seventh verse of Tiruvempāvai at the Tiruvātirai festival in the month of Mārkaḻi. . . . in the order [of worship] in this temple. . . . and [her] descendents (*vaṟkattār*). . . .

We the temple servants of. . . . of this temple sign [this agreement]: the temple accountant Muṉṉūṟruvappiriyaṉ, the temple manager (śrīkāriyam) Teṉṉavaṉ mūventaveḷāṉ, the *śrīmāheśvara* supervisor Koṇṭāṉ, the temple servant (*tevakaṉmam*) Muṉṉūṟruvapaṭṭaṉ, Pālaṟāvāyaṉ, and Amutaṉ Campaṉtaṉ.

—NK 134: this inscription was engraved in A.D. 1213 at the Kālahastīśvara temple in Tirupampuram, Tanjavur district.

These three medieval Tamil inscriptions, engraved in stone on the walls of South Indian temples, are among the hundreds of epigraphical records that provide specific and detailed information about the activities and identities of temple women of the past. I have located close to seven hundred inscriptions that refer to temple women. These inscriptions range in date from the seventh or eighth century up to the eighteenth and early nineteenth centuries and are found throughout India; two-thirds come from the early medieval period—A.D. 850–1300—and the vast majority come from South India, from the present-day states of Tamilnadu, Kerala, Andhra Pradesh, and Karnataka (see appendix I). In this early medieval period, the Tamil country—defined for my purposes as the region in which the Tamil language was current and used for inscriptions—extended far beyond the current limits of the state of Tamilnadu; stone inscriptions written in Tamil were produced in large numbers and are particularly rich in references to temple women. I have found over 300 such references (see appendixes II and III). The abundance of inscriptional resources available for the study of temple women and of other aspects of social and religious life—combined with the significance of this period and region for the evolution of the *devadāsī* "institution," among other religious developments—has induced me to base my study on these sources and within this historical context.

The region under study roughly corresponds to present-day Tamilnadu but overlaps into what are today Andhra Pradesh, Karnataka, Kerala, and even Sri Lanka (see appendixes I and II). The geographic limits of this study are broadly defined because inscriptions in Tamil are found so extensively throughout South India, Tamil language and culture being widely disseminated in the medieval period—at least in part because of the political hegemony of the Pallava, Pandya, and Chola rulers based in various parts of the Tamil country. To aid in the analysis of regional variation, I have considered this broad area to be divided into five smaller regions: (1) a northern region (traditionally referred to as Tondai-mandalam) made up of North Arcot, Chingleput, and Chittoor districts and other Tamil-influenced parts of Andhra; (2) a core Chola region (Chola-mandalam) consisting of Tanjavur and Tiruchirappalli districts; (3) a "middle" region (Nadu-nadu) between the Chola region and the north, consisting of South Arcot district; (4) a southern region (Pandi-mandalam, the "Pandya territory") made up of Madurai, Ramnad, Tirunelveli, and Kanyakumari districts, as well as Travancore and

Malabar; and (5) a western region made up of Coimbatore and Salem districts, and overlapping into the southern and eastern parts of present day Karnataka (see figure 1.1).

The chronological framework of this study is linked to the dynastic politics of the imperial Cholas. I refer to the period under study—A.D. 850–1300—as the Chola period, but I must stress at the outset that the Chola kings did not exercise control or even influence over the whole of the Tamil country or through the whole of the period. Before, during, and after the reign of the Chola kings, whose dynasty came to an end in A.D. 1279, other powers held sway in various parts of the region—either rulers who identified themselves with one of the other great South Indian dynasties, like the Pallavas or the Pandyas, or local rulers, chiefs, and lords.

Figure 1.1 The Tamil country and its regions (see Appendix 1 for an explanation of the definition of district boundaries).

The first of the imperial Cholas, Vijayalaya, and his immediate successors had to struggle to establish and maintain Chola power against such rivals. In the first subperiod (A.D. 850–985), from the establishment of the Chola capital in Tanjavur to the end of Uttama's rule, Chola control over territory to the north and south waxed and waned, in the face of formidable challenges.[31]

The second subperiod (A.D. 985–1070) began with the accession to the Chola throne of the great king Rajaraja I and ended with the beginning of Kulottunga I's reign. During this period, Chola armies conquered vast areas of South India, fighting against the Pandyas and Eastern and Western Chalukyas, and made forays into Southeast Asia; this was the zenith of Chola power.

The third subperiod (A.D. 1070–1178) began with Chola power fairly secure; as the period continued, however, Chola forces were driven out of Sri Lanka, Chola territory in the west reverted to the Western Chalukyas, and Chola control in the northern and southern regions was weakened by the rising power of local chiefs and claimants to the Pandya throne.

The fourth and last subperiod (A.D. 1178–1300), which began with the accession of Kulottunga III, saw the final collapse of Chola power, as forces to the north and south—latter-day "Pallavas," Telugu Chodas, and imperial Pandyas—consolidated power and the Hoysalas in Karnataka and Kakatiyas in Andhra established new dynasties.

This division of the whole of the Chola period into these subperiods produces four spans of time, each of about one hundred years and corresponding approximately to the tenth, eleventh, twelfth, or thirteenth century A.D. I consider the first two subperiods as the early Chola period and the last two as the later Chola period.

What Chola Period Inscriptions Can Tell Us

Approximately 15,000 Chola period inscriptions have been found so far, and about a third of these have been published.[32] Most of the unpublished inscriptions have been reported and their contents summarized in the *Annual Report on Indian Epigraphy*, published by the Archaeological Survey of India since 1887. Scholars have been allowed access—particularly since the early 1980s—to the transcripts of unpublished inscriptions that have been copied by the Archaeological Survey of India, at the Office of the Director of Epigraphy in Mysore.[33] The corpus of Chola period inscriptions thus constitutes an extremely rich resource for historical investigation.

Basing their work largely on inscriptional sources, the eminent Indian historians A. Appadorai, T. V. Mahalingam, and K. A. Nilakanta Sastri began in the late 1920s to produce a detailed and textured picture of political, administrative, economic, and social life in the Chola period. Building on this foundation, scholars like R. Champakalakshmi, Kenneth Hall, Noboru Karashima, George Spencer, Burton Stein, Y. Subbarayalu, and R. Tirumalai have explored in more detail such issues as the character of kingship, the constitution of the state, economic dynamics, the character of religious institutions, and the organization of society in medieval Tamilnadu. These issues have been further illuminated by the work of the most recent generation of historians, including Arjun Appadurai, Carol Breckenridge, Nicholas Dirks, and James Heitzman. The potential of inscriptional sources for the investigation of the history of religions and of women in medieval Tamilnadu has, however, barely begun to be exploited.

Almost all of the Chola period inscriptions are engraved in stone, originally on temple walls, and record in Tamil a multitude of transactions and arrangements relating to temple affairs, most of which center around donations made to temples. The inscription makes explicit and public the identity of the donor, the nature of the gift, and details about how the endowment is to be put to use in order to maintain worship in the temple. By commissioning the engraving of an inscription, a donor could ensure that her or his generosity would be recognized, both immediately and in the long term, and that the arrangements for worship made in the donor's name would continue "for as long as the moon and the sun," as inscriptions themselves commonly declare.

The corpus of Chola period inscriptions is distinctive, in comparison with the inscriptional record of other regions and periods, not only because of the large quantity of inscriptions that have been written and preserved but also because of their relative ubiquity throughout the Tamil country and the fact that they are almost exclusively records of gifts to temples—and not records of the foundation of temples or of the establishment of Brahman settlements (*brahmadeyas*). It is not entirely clear why Chola period inscriptions are so much more numerous than those of other regions or of the Tamil country itself after the thirteenth century.[34] But part of the explanation for the distinctive features of the Chola period inscriptions—in terms of their distribution and their recording of gifts to already existing temples—lies in the fact that by the beginning of the period, an extensive network of Hindu sacred places had been established throughout Tamilnadu (Spencer 1970; Young 1978; Peterson 1982; Hardy 1983, 256–61). These shrines, celebrated by the Śaiva and Vaiṣṇava poet-saints of the sixth to ninth centuries, came to be the primary focus for worship and patronage during the Chola period.

In the centuries preceding the Chola period, the Ā̱lvārs, devoted to Viṣṇu, and the Nāyan̲mārs, devoted to Śiva, composed poems in Tamil that invited worshipers to join with those who, in shrines throughout the Tamil country, fervently and exclusively worshiped a Supreme Lord in a spirit of devotion, service, and surrender (*bhakti*). This proselytizing message was explicitly inclusive: people of low status and women were not only incorporated into the community of devotees but also in some cases were held up as paradigmatic worshipers of the Lord. The *bhakti* poet-saints even included women among their number—the Vaiṣṇava Āṇṭāḷ and the Śaiva Kāraikkāl Ammaiyār. During the Chola period, the concept of *bhakti* was intellectually elaborated by the great South Indian sectarian teachers (*ācāryas*) who developed the sophisticated theological systems of Śaiva Siddhānta and Śrīvaiṣṇavism. The *ācāryas* produced texts which continue to be studied by scholars and devotees, from both within and without the sectarian traditions.[35] Meanwhile, the concept of *bhakti* was socially and ritually elaborated within the communities of people—devotees, pilgrims, patrons, priests, teachers, students, ascetics, and temple servants—who congregated in the sacred places praised in the poems of the Āḻvārs and Nāyaṉmārs. These people produced inscriptions.

In the course of the Chola period, the temples became increasingly wealthier, larger, and more complex. They grew into grand and beautiful stone structures, whose walls came to be covered with inscriptions, and which to this day ornament the landscape of Tamilnadu.[36] Śaiva temples were particularly numerous and well supported during the Chola period, but Vaiṣṇava institutions also grew and strengthened. The Chola period inherited not only a network of sacred places but also a way of conceptualizing the divine in terms of an idiom of locality. In the poems of the Āḻvārs and Nāyaṉmārs, Viṣṇu and Śiva are praised as the lords of specific villages and towns in Tamilnadu, where they are present in iconic form (Hardy 1978, 122–23; Peterson 1989, 143–79). In the inscriptions, these deities are named in precisely the same way, as the sovereigns of particular places. Indeed, the fact that this idiom was so widely shared in Chola period inscriptions means that there is a blurring of sectarian distinctions; it is frequently difficult to determine, if we look only at the text of an inscription, whether the deity to whom donations are being made is Śiva, Viṣṇu—or a Jain Tīrthaṅkara.

The religious landscape of the Chola period contained not only places where the great Hindu gods were honored but also shrines where Jains and Buddhists worshiped. Well before this period, Jainism and Buddhism had become widespread in Tamilnadu, and these religious traditions persisted through the period and beyond—in the case of Jainism, until the present day. The number of Buddhist sites and inscriptions that have so far been discovered is small, but numerous Buddhist images reflect the existence of Buddhist worshipers in the Chola period. There is ample inscriptional evidence that Jainism was a continuing presence in some of the areas where it had long been established—in the northern and middle regions of Tamilnadu; in the far south; and in the southeastern part of the core Chola territory, bordering on the southern districts.[37] There are many parallels among the Jainism, Buddhism, and Hinduism of medieval Tamilnadu. Jain and Buddhist devotional poetry in Tamil was very similar to the works of the Śaiva and Vaiṣṇava poet-saints (Nagaswamy 1975, 129; Vijayavenugopal 1979; Kandaswamy 1981). The ways in which worship was conducted and the ways in which the object of worship was conceptualized—as the "lord" of a particular place, present in iconic form, and as the recipient of gifts, offerings, and services—were virtually identical for Jains and Hindus, according to the inscriptions they have left us (Orr forthcoming a).

The earliest of these inscriptions, recording endowments to support the worship of Hindu and Jain deities and Tīrthaṅkaras in Tamilnadu, date to the sixth and seventh centuries.[38] In subsequent centuries, such inscriptions rapidly came to displace the records of gifts made in support of ascetics and

Brahmans characteristic of the period of early Pandya and Pallava rule in Tamilnadu. Perhaps the earliest inscription that provides details of the character of Hindu worship in medieval Tamilnadu is the Kuram copper-plate inscription (SII 1.151), the record of a late seventh-century Pallava royal grant for a temple and a *brahmadeya* near Kanchipuram in Chingleput district. This grant established support for worship with water and fire; for the recitation of the *Bhārata*; and for providing the temple deity with "worship, bathing, flowers, perfumes, incense, lamps, food offerings, conches, drums, etc." (*pūjya-snāpana-kusuma-gandha-dhūpa-dīpa-havirupahārabali-śaṃkha-paṭaha-ādi*). These services are very similar to those referred to in the Jain inscriptions of this period, in the Tamil poems of the Āḻvārs and the Nāyaṉmārs of the sixth to ninth century, and in earlier Tamil literature.[39] Literary and inscriptional sources from outside South India indicate that many of these elements were part of a pan-Indian pattern of worship that was widespread even before the efflorescence of *bhakti* in the Tamil country and that was common in Buddhist and Jain practice, as well as in early Hindu ritual.[40]

Hardy (1983, 29–33) has characterized this pattern of worship—using flowers, perfumes, incense, flags, banners, cloth, lamps, and music—as "folk religion" and has emphasized its lack of connection with Vedic, Vedāntin, yogic, and elite Buddhist ritual practice.[41] He suggests that in Tamilnadu the temple milieu, which began to be prominent from about the sixth century—and which was marked "with a pronounced 'brahmanism,'" bearing "totally new features, derived from Sanskritic culture and religion"—only gradually came to incorporate elements from the folk culture, and that this fusion between elite and folk cultures never took place in the case of South Indian Buddhism and Jainism (1983, 225–33). The early material evidence of Jain, Buddhist, and Hindu worship in Tamilnadu, which we have just reviewed, would seem to challenge the notion that Brahmanical and folk religious traditions—or "heterodox" and Hindu ones—ought to be treated in such dualistic terms.

The picture that Burton Stein has given us of religious life in Tamilnadu is similarly polarized: according to Stein, temples in Tamilnadu dedicated to Śiva and Viṣṇu continued, even in the Chola period, to have a Brahmanical, "Vedic," "canonical," or "sastric" character—in contrast to localized, non-Brahmanical, popular cults based in smaller shrines dedicated to tutelary deities, particularly goddesses (1980, 232–33, 237–39, 324–31). In fact, the inscriptional evidence does not support this view, inasmuch as religious practice in Chola period temples can be shown to have continuity, in ritual terms, with the folk idiom of worship just described and presents itself, in sociological terms, as both popular and local, with many non-Brahmans involved as patrons, worshipers, and temple servants.[42] And although the inscriptions are incapable of providing details about the type of worship that was conducted in this period at small and impermanent shrines—in cities and towns, in villages, or in homes—there is no reason to believe that this worship was primarily goddess-oriented. The dichotomy between a Brahman-dominated, orthodox religion of the great Śaiva and Vaiṣṇava temples and a highly localized goddess cult of the villages may be meaningful for much later times, when social and political structures had undergone considerable change, but it seems to have little to do with the religious environment of the Chola period.[43]

The inscriptional and iconographical evidence suggests that many of the goddesses worshiped in the early Chola period were pan-Indian "high" deities—associated with Jain and Buddhist, as well as Hindu, pantheons—rather than local agricultural or clan deities (Orr forthcoming a). In the later Chola period, we find more and more goddesses who are depicted as the consorts of the great Hindu gods and who are housed in shrines built within the compounds of Śaiva and Vaiṣṇava temples; images of these *nācciyār* (consort goddesses), shrines built for them, and inscriptions referring to them are especially in evidence at the end of the period, in the thirteenth century (K. Srinivasan 1960, 21–33; Stein 1973, 77–79; Champakalakshmi 1981b, 222; Orr forthcoming a). These developments were accompanied by a movement within South Indian Hindu theology of the twelfth and thirteenth centuries, in which increasing emphasis was placed on the association of Śiva and Viṣṇu with powers or principles—*śakti* and Śrī—personified as the "wives" of these male deities (Sivaraman 1973, 177–89, 520–21, n. 44; Nayar 1992, 367–415). Suggestions that these religious developments of the later Chola period are linked to an effort to assimilate local goddesses into an orthodox Hindu pantheon or to "ground" the great Hindu gods in the Tamil country through myths of marriage with local goddesses differentiate too sharply between Brahmanical and local traditions—and ignore the fact that by the late Chola period, "Sanskritic" deities, both male and female, had been rooted in the Tamil religious landscape for many centuries.[44]

If Chola period inscriptions suggest that elite and folk religious practices were not entirely distinct, the evidence further suggests that the boundaries between Hindu and non-Hindu were not definitely demarcated and that the people whom we retrospectively classify as Hindus, Jains, and Buddhists shared a common religious culture.[45] There was a sharing not only of patterns of worship and conceptions of the character of the object of worship—as a divine or holy being present in and sovereign over a particular place in the Tamil country—but also donative activity was conceptualized and carried out in the same ways regardless of the sectarian identity of the institution that was receiving the donation. In medieval Tamil inscriptions, gifts to temples were described as gifts to the deity (or Buddha or Tīrthaṅkara) enshrined in the temple, who was regarded as receiving them in the same way a human being would.[46]

The many thousands of inscriptions that record such gifts attest to the prevalence and importance of donation as a religious activity in the Chola period. Yet there are remarkably few precedents in the pre-Chola era—at least within the Hindu context—for this donative behavior. The Dharmaśāstras declare that *dāna*, making gifts, is the chief form of religious practice in the Kali age in which we live (*Manusmṛti* 1.86), but these texts and inscriptional records of Hindu religious gifts in the pre-Chola period are almost exclusively concerned with gift giving to Brahmans.[47] The Tamil devotional literature of the pre-Chola period, written by the Āḻvārs and Nāyaṉmārs, does not mention giving gifts to shrines or deities as a part of the practice of the ideal devotee but focuses instead on worship and pilgrimage. It seems that the earliest examples, in South India and elsewhere, of gifts being given to an institution or to a divine or superhuman figure are found in the Buddhist and Jain contexts. It is interesting as well that so many of those engaged in the patronage of Buddhism and Jainism were women.[48]

Although Chola period inscriptions carefully describe the substance of gifts to temples (e.g., gold, livestock, or land) and very frequently indicate the object of the gift (e.g., the support of a perpetual lamp or a festival service), the motive for making the gift is seldom mentioned. Gifts were presumably made, at least in part, with the intention of generating religious merit or possibly to fulfill a vow or expiate a sin.[49] The idea that religious donations produced merit is indicated by the fact that inscriptions occasionally mention that the donor has made a gift "for" or "on behalf of" (*āka*, or *cārtti*) another person. The transfer of merit is, however, atypical of Chola period inscriptions; only rarely do we find that a gift has been made "for the sake of" another person. And in contrast to later Tamil inscriptions and to inscriptions from outside of Tamilnadu that more frequently refer to such transfers of merit, we do not even find in the Chola period inscriptions a word (e.g., *puṇya*) that refers directly to the merit obtained by making a gift.[50]

Patronage of religious institutions, and recording it in an inscription, was also motivated by goals other than purely religious ones. Apart from merit, one could acquire social recognition and political and economic advantages through donations to temples.[51] In some cases, inscriptions describe in considerable detail the consequences that followed from making a gift—which might involve the acquisition of a position or privilege, obtaining the right to take charge of some portion of the wealth possessed by the temple, or the opportunity to become implicated in some other way in the network of economic and political transactions that centered on the temple.

The inscriptions' attention to the results of religious donation opens a window onto the situations and intentions of donors. Although there are those who disparage the usefulness of inscriptional evidence as "distorted and highly fragmentary" because "the inner reality, the linkages, the motivations" are not revealed (Shulman 1985, 8, 24; also Narayana Rao, Shulman, and Subrahmanyam 1992, 31–32), others are more optimistic: "We may be able to study even the mentality of the people associated with inscriptions" (Karashima 1996). The argument is about the value of evidence derived from inscriptions in comparison to what one may learn from literary sources.

On the one hand, there are several great advantages in using inscriptions rather than the texts that more usually serve as the basis for our reconstruction of the social and religious history of India. Perhaps the most striking virtue of inscriptional sources, in contrast to religious and legal texts, is that they allow us to determine with great precision the date and place of their production. Chola period inscriptions almost invariably begin by giving the date, in terms of the regnal year of a king, identifiable by his name or epithets. Despite the fact that some of the records are fragmentary, it is possible to chronologically situate 90 percent of the Chola period inscriptions (Heitzman 1985, 40). In terms of locating these inscriptions geographically, very often the place where the inscription is found is the temple or village to which the record refers. Furthermore, the inscriptions tend to be very precise in specifying the location of the temple that is receiving the donation, of any lands that may be the substance of the gift or whose revenues are to be transferred to the temple, and of the hometowns of donors and other people named in the inscription.

There are other important ways in which inscriptions differ from texts that prove advantageous. These records are not normative and prescriptive. They are formulaic in style and may serve as exemplary models, but they record particular and individual events rather than an idealized and abstract pattern; that is, they present precedents rather than paradigms (Waghorne 1984, 46–47). Although forged inscriptions are not unheard of and the terms of the endowments, even if they are literally written in stone, can be and eventually are superceded by subsequent arrangements and the "interpretation" of temple practice, these records are far less prone than many texts to alteration, interpolation, mythic elaboration, or being read through the lens of later commentary and tradition.[52]

On the other hand, there are limitations to the usefulness of epigraphical sources. "The inscriptions by their very nature tend to cause the historian to lay disproportionate stress on the institutions which house them—namely the temples" (Narayana Rao, Shulman, and Subrahmanyam 1992, 31–32; see also Dirks 1987, 288). In fact, 98 percent of Chola period inscriptions are concerned with temple affairs (Heitzman 1985, 39). Furthermore, because their purpose was usually to record some change or addition to temple acquisitions, services, or organization, inscriptions refer only in passing to routine procedures and standing arrangements; these records do not show the system "at rest" (Granda 1984, 183). Also, certain types of changes are more likely than others to be recorded: donors and temple officials would be particularly motivated to record endowments in inscriptions when the gift was of a durable nature—land that would yield agricultural produce, a sum of money that would produce interest, or a herd of livestock that would produce ghee for ritual lamps (Talbot 1988b, 33–34).

The value of inscriptional evidence may also be compromised and its accuracy skewed as a consequence of the way in which it has been gathered and presented during the last century. The fact that inscriptions are most likely to have been copied from the walls of large, famous, and still living temples means that sites that were important in the Chola period, but later fell into disuse, are underrepresented in the inscriptional corpus. Another problem arises in consequence of the fact that epigraphists have copied inscriptions with scant concern for the context in which they were found; the extraction of the text of an inscription from its material matrix, and the neglect of the art historical and archaeological information that is yielded by the inscription's context, in many cases detracts from our efforts to interpret inscriptional data (Folkert 1989; Orr forthcoming a).

Despite these limitations, inscriptions are precious to the historian inasmuch as they document economic, religious, political, and social realities, occurring in a particular place and time. Inscriptions describe actual events—but it is important to acknowledge that they are not simply objective reports of these events. Inscriptions record donations in particular ways, using specific kinds of terms and certain styles of composition and language (Inden 1990, 232). It was Burton Stein who first highlighted the importance of what he called the "ritual" aspect of Chola period inscriptions, the intention of inscriptional records "to present a particular understanding of relations among persons and institutions" (Stein 1980, 352). Stein and others who have studied the shape and style of Chola period inscriptions (Stein 1980, 352–61; Spencer 1984; Shulman 1985, 25–27) have focused particularly on the way in which they express something about the Chola king's relations with his domain and his subjects; these scholars have provided analyses of *meykkīrttis* (Skt. *praśastis*), the eulogistic prefaces of grants that recount the genealogy and exploits of the king and "express socio-political realities through a mytho-poetic medium" (Talbot 1988a, 189).

But there are many other ritual elements in inscriptions apart from *meykkīrttis* that give us clues about the motives, perceptions, and values held by a donor and those people around him or her who were in some way involved in the donative activity (see Alayev 1985, 34–35). The order in which the elements of an inscription are arranged and the amount of space allotted to each element provide information about the significance of the transaction recorded. Chola period inscriptions usually emphasize the importance of the deity, who is typically mentioned at the very beginning of the record, following the *meykkīrtti* (if it is present) and the date, and is described as the lord of a particular locality, which is itself identified at length. The donor's connection with the temple or with other local social structures may be further underlined by the mention of corporate groups who sanction the transaction or of individuals acting as witnesses or signatories; such individuals—often local notables or temple functionaries—are mentioned with increasing frequency in the course of the Chola period. Inscriptions are thus capable of articulating a whole range of religious, social, and political relations—including many that have nothing to do with the king.

Almost all Chola period inscriptions mention the name of a king or chief at the beginning of the record as a means of dating the record, but only about a third of the inscriptions have *meykkīrttis* (cf. Stein 1980, 358). Even when a *meykkīrtti* is present as the preface to an inscription, this does not indicate that there was any association between the king and the transaction recorded (Granda 1984, 51–52). Kings are very rarely the central actors in the arrangements described by the inscriptions—although queens, especially in the early Chola period, are frequently represented as taking active roles as donors. The king is visible in Chola period inscriptions, but he is not as dominant a figure as recent analyses of the South Indian temple have suggested (Appadurai and Breckenridge 1976; Dirks 1976 and 1987; Breckenridge 1978; Stein 1980; Appadurai 1981; Reiniche 1985; Shulman 1985; Younger 1995). The features emphasized in these analyses—the role of the king as the premier temple patron, the king's utilization of the temple in legitimating his sovereignty and integrating his polity, and the parallels between court and temple ritual—seem to belong much more to the late precolonial era than to the Chola period.[53] In fact, in the few cases in which we find a Chola king showing interest in the affairs of a temple, he does not seem to have acted as a model for others who imitated his patronage nor did his participation encourage the growth of the network of relationships centering on the temple; on the contrary, the king's presence seems to have had a dampening effect on nonroyal patronage and to have undermined local political and economic structures (Hall 1980, 200–1; 1981, 404–9; Heitzman 1987a, 41–44; 1995, 86). For the most part, rulers in the Chola period remained aloof from involvement in local affairs.

In reaction to the earlier view of the "Chola Empire" as a vast bureaucratic state, Burton Stein (1980) has conceptualized the Chola polity as a "segmentary state," in which the ruler's sovereignty was more "ritual" than it was politically or administratively effectual at the local level. Others regard South Indian society in this period as "feudal" (Jha 1974; R. Sharma 1974; Narayanan and Veluthat 1978). Although I will avoid the debate about whether any of these models adequately describes the political system of medieval Tamilnadu (see Kulke 1982; Heitzman 1987a; Karashima 1992; Chattopadhyaya 1994), I must emphasize that a particular model of the medieval feudal economy—in which the control of resources by temples, Brahmans, vassals, and officials is seen as bringing about economic stagnation and the impoverishment of local people[54]—is clearly inapplicable to the Chola period. In this period there was a rapidly expanding agrarian economy, extensive trade and use of money, and a complex system of rights to and uses of property that allowed local individuals and institutions to acquire increasing economic power (Hall 1980; Heitzman 1985; 1987b; 1995). Although many economic and political arrangements were strongly local in character, the people involved in them were not isolated. Local communities were nodes in broad networks, as were local temples. The village in the Chola period was not insular and self-sufficient but was involved in a wide range of economic and cultural links to other parts of Tamilnadu (Hall 1981, 394–96; Kulke 1982, 262; Chattopadhyaya 1990, 9–11; cf. Mahalingam 1967, 342–44; Jha 1974, 207). There was not a sharp distinction between urban and rural economies or societies; even large towns contained fields and gardens, interspersed among residential, market, and temple areas (Heitzman 1987b and forthcoming). A good deal of wealth was channeled into the temples in this period, but a very large proportion of this wealth was redistributed and recirculated, encouraging trade, craft production, and the growth of agriculture.[55] The inscriptions engraved on the walls of the temples provide evidence of the dynamic and complex character of relationships among people in Chola period society.

These inscriptions give us information about a wide range of types of people and a picture of the workings of society that goes much deeper than the level of the activities of kings, nobles, or "feudatories"—the level of court culture, military manouvers, political alliances, and the deliberations and pronouncements of the learned and the powerful. The inscriptions thus offer us a view "from below"—but it is not a view from the bottom. The people who are most frequently represented as actors in the transactions and relationships recorded in the inscriptions are those with access to enough wealth to make gifts to the temple and to commission the engraving of the inscription and those connected in one way or another with the life of the temple. The inscriptions provide a good deal of information about local lords and Brahmans, village administrators, and temple servants but very little about those people with few economic and political resources.

It is interesting, therefore, that these records can tell us as much as they do about women. Were we to rely solely on normative and mythological texts for an understanding of women's roles and activities in India's past, as so often has been done, we would never even suspect the existence of this evidence of women's involvement in economic and religious life. The fact that the inscriptions are descriptive, recording specific and concrete events, makes them extremely valuable for the study of women's history. These records allow us to catch a glimpse of the actuality of women's participation in society, which is frequently obscured in literary and religious texts.[56]

Chola period inscriptions provide evidence that challenges our ideas not only about the situation and activity of women but also about the structuring of society in general. In contrast to what Brahmanical legal texts may lead us to expect, we do not find that caste is the organizing principle of society or that boundaries between different social groups are sharply demarcated.[57] In the inscriptions, it is extremely rare to find individuals who identify themselves or others with reference to caste affiliation.

Even for those belonging to the group with the most clearly defined caste identity—the Brahmans—the term *brāhmaṇa* is scarcely used, their identity as Brahmans is not well marked, and it is only as a result of a certain amount of sleuthing that one can establish that they actually are Brahmans.[58] Those individuals mentioned in the inscriptions whom we can identify as Brahmans are not, typically, temple Brahmans. For the most part, they were not directly involved in the administration of the temple or with temple ritual. Individual Brahmans are frequently mentioned in Chola period inscriptions as landowners and temple patrons. Groups of Brahmans, organized into the corporate bodies referred to in the inscriptions as *sabhais* (Skt. *sabhā*), or Brahman "assemblies," are commonly referred to, especially in the inscriptions of the early Chola period, as managers of local affairs, overseeing property transfers and tax matters.

Sabhais are not the only type of local administrative body mentioned in the inscriptions. We also find assemblies of villagers (*ūrār*); townsmen (*nakarattār*); and *nāṭṭār*, or representatives of the agricultural locality (*nāṭu*)

(Nilakanta Sastri 1955, 486–519; Hall 1980, 19–70; 1981; Stein 1980, 105–31, 163–70). In the course of the Chola period, the relations among these groups, the *sabhais*, and bodies of temple authorities, and their relative importance and power underwent various changes (Champakalakshmi 1981a; Hall 1981).

It has been assumed by some authors that in the Chola period and even earlier, the non-Brahman administrators of villages and *nāṭus* were *veḷḷāḷas*, members of a group that is today the dominant agricultural caste in Tamilnadu (Subbarayalu 1973, 36; Stein 1980; Gough 1981, 106–7; Karashima 1984, 58; Veluthat 1993, 233–38; Younger 1995, 131–32, 190–91, 201–2). Indeed, *veḷḷāḷas* are mentioned in Chola period inscriptions and, apart from Brahmans, are the only group of people resembling a caste for which we have evidence in this period. We do not, however, have evidence that they were primarily identified as agriculturalists, or had the dominant economic position or the high ritual status that they have today. Nor is it clear that their identity as a caste was at all well defined; the social boundary between *veḷḷāḷa* and non*veḷḷāḷa*, as between Brahman and non-Brahman, may have been considerably more porous than it is today.[59]

If the inscriptions do not tell us that *veḷḷāḷas* were the major landholders and cultivators of Chola period society, they do provide information about another group of people with considerable local and regional influence. These people, whom Heitzman (1995) terms "lords," are those described by the inscriptions as "possessors" (*uṭaiyār*) of villages or regions. These men typically had property rights and administrative or honorific positions in several localities and were active as donors to temples. Another group whom we encounter in Chola period inscriptions, and who also figure prominently as donors, are merchants (*viyāpāri*). Merchants took part in local administrative affairs as members of the corporate groups known as *nakarattār*.[60]

The inscriptions do not tell us a great deal about the people who were at the base of the economic and political ladder, but they do show us that such people did not hold fixed positions at the bottom of a well-articulated social and ritual hierarchy, as is the case in the caste system of today. For example, people referred to as *paṟaiyar* (the name of a low caste in contemporary South India, from which the English word "pariah" is derived) are described in some Chola period inscriptions as living in separate areas within villages, and they are mentioned in contexts that clearly indicate that they were considered to have a degraded status. But there are also several inscriptions recording gifts made by *paṟaiyar* to temples, suggesting that they cannot in all cases have been without economic resources or have been regarded as "outcastes." Social stratification and the bondage of people to the land or to fixed service relations seem to have been on the increase through the Chola period, but even at the end of the period, systems of caste, slavery, or serfdom do not appear to be widely or firmly entrenched features of society in Tamilnadu.[61]

Chola period inscriptions, because they are primarily records of gifts to the temple, provide a considerable amount of information about the various types of people involved in the administration of temple affairs and in temple ritual and service. Temple administrators are often referred to as corporate groups rather than as individuals, particularly in the early Chola period. The inscriptions use a variety of terms for these groups, including *tāṉattār* (from Skt. *sthāna*, "place, abode"), *śivabrāhmaṇas* or *māheśvaras* (in the case of Śaiva temples), *śrīvaiṣṇavas* (in Vaiṣṇava temples), supervisors (*kaṇkāṇi ceyvār*), managers (*śrīkāriyam ceyvār*), and accountants (*kaṇakkar*).[62] In inscriptions of the later Chola period, people performing the same functions as these groups—such as accepting gifts on behalf of the temple, managing or overseeing the use of temple resources, and acting as witnesses to agreements into which the temple entered—are increasingly mentioned by name, as individuals. Among those serving in the temple, the inscriptions refer to an array of groups and individuals, including priests (*arccippār, nampimār, ācāriyar, śivabrāhmaṇas*), who were assisted by *māṇis* (Skt. *brahmacārins*), as well as drummers and musicians, potters and other artisans, cooks, cleaners, gardeners, and garland makers.

The great majority of the people associated in these various ways with the temple were men. Some, however, were women—which gives me a reason for writing this book. But there is another category of people referred to in the inscriptions that appears to be almost exclusively male, particularly in the Hindu context. These are the ascetics (*tapasyar, sannyāsis, aṭikaḷmār, vairāgyar, śivayogis*) and those associated with *maṭhas* ("mutts," Ta. *maṭam*). Although not mentioned very frequently in Chola period inscriptions, these figures are of interest because of their importance in the later religious landscape of Tamilnadu. One must, however, guard against an anachronistic understanding of medieval religious institutions. *Maṭhas* were not, as they later came to be, the exclusive preserve of ascetics and members of sectarian elites. These institutions, which came increasingly to be associated with Hindu temples in the course of the Chola period, closely resembled the Jain *paḷḷis* of early medieval Tamilnadu (Orr 1998). They appear to have served primarily as feeding houses for pilgrims, ascetics, and Brahmans, in addition to being places of worship. By the end of the Chola period, some of them may have begun to take on the character of schools and monasteries.[63]

Chola period inscriptions mention a wide range of different types of people, whether referring to them in passing as anonymous members of corporate groups or highlighting for posterity their names and affiliations. The identities of donors are generally given preeminence. But apart from the donor, people with various other functions may appear, mentioned either collectively or by name: relatives of the donor, temple functionaries who received the gift on behalf of the deity, local administrators who carried out the terms of the grant, temple servants who received support from the gift, landowners mentioned in the boundary specifications of a piece of land, or people with whom the gift might be invested. Inscriptions may yield information about people's profession (merchant, priest, potter, drummer); about their place of residence, property holdings, or kinship relations; or about their affiliation with a particular group or institution (a caste, a military body, a royal court, a temple). The inscriptions provide an image of society, as well as a representation of change in that society, that is based on the identities and activities of individuals.

In attempting to understand the way in which one group of those individuals, temple women, may have been effective in shaping their own history, I have found useful the analysis of the relationship between individual and system, between actor and structure, formulated in practice theory (Bourdieu 1977). My thinking has been furthered by the discussions by Ortner, Inden, and others about the nature of human agency, subjectivity, intentionality, ideology, and consciousness—discussions that have been inspired, at least in part, by practice theory.[64] In this book I explore the question of how the temple women whose history I describe were able to act and were acted upon; my aim is to provide an analysis of temple women's agency in the context of the evolution of the institutions and ideologies of medieval Tamil society.

Using Inscriptions to Reconstruct Temple Women's History

Earlier studies of the history of temple women in India have in a number of cases utilized inscriptional sources. Although some of these studies are quite valuable, they are unable to accomplish the task I undertake here, either because they are focused on a different region (e.g., for Karnataka: Sathyanarayana 1969, Parasher and Naik 1986, and Parasher-Sen 1993; for Kerala: M. Narayanan 1973 and Gurukkal 1979), or because their wide scope does not allow for description and analysis of temple women's roles and activities within a specific historical context (Mankodi 1966; Gaston 1980; Prasad 1983; Varadpande 1983; Kersenboom 1987; Sadasivan 1993). Furthermore, there has been a tendency in the way that inscriptional evidence relating to temple women has been used toward "impressionistic interpretations" (Heitzman 1985, 41–42) based on a few interesting and unusual inscriptions. My approach here is rather to undertake a systematic and aggregate analysis of the entire corpus of inscriptions that provide information about temple women in order to effectively utilize the mass of details available and to create a more complete and dynamic portrait of temple women in the Chola period.

Just as virtually every treatment of the topic of women in India provides a quotation from Manu, so does virtually every account of the history of South Indian temple women refer to a single inscription. This inscription (SII 2.66), dated A.D. 1014, records King Rajaraja I's establishment of 400 women in the streets around the great Rājarājeśvara temple, which he had founded in Tanjavur, and is cited again and again as a characteristic portrait of the circumstances of temple women in the Chola period.

> In the twenty-ninth year of the reign of Śrī Rājarājadevar, shares [were assigned] as allowances (*nivantam*) to the temple servants (*nivantakkāṟar*)

given by Lord Śrī Rājarājadevar as temple servants for [the deity] Lord Śrī Rājarājīśvaram Uṭaiyār, and to the women of the temple quarter (*taḷicceri peṇṭukaḷ*) who [formerly] dwelled in the temple quarters of the Chola region and had been brought and established [here] as women of the temple quarter of Lord Śrī Rājarājīśvaram Uṭaiyār.

Each share consists of [the produce of] one *veli* of land, equal to 100 *kalam* of paddy measured by the *marakkāl* named Āṭavallā<u>n</u>, constituting a *rājakesari*.

To the substitutes for those who have been thus allotted shares but have died or [gone] abroad [to seek] wealth, the position (*mu<u>r</u>ai*) is assigned: these people are to receive this support (*kāṇi*) and to perform the service (*paṇi*). If those to whom the position is assigned are not suitable, some other person among those who are suitable should be appointed to perform the service and receive compensation. If those to whom the position is assigned are not members of the appropriate group (*niyāyaṅkaḷ*), a suitable member of the group should be appointed, and he is to receive the support.

This is the royal order issued by Lord Śrī Rājarājadevar, to be engraved in stone.

The women of the temple quarter (*taḷicceri peṇṭukaḷ*) [are assigned]:

One share to Nakka<u>n</u> Ceramaṅkai of Olokamahādevi-īśvaram [temple] at Tiruvaiyā<u>r</u>u, [who resides in] the first house on the south side of the temple quarter to the south;

One share to Nakka<u>n</u> Iraṇamukarāmi of this [same] temple, [who resides in] the second house . . .

The inscription goes on to name a total of 400 women, identifying them according to their hometowns or home temples and their place of residence in the streets around the Rājarājeśvara temple. Each of these women is assigned one share in support from the temple, although no particular duties are specified. Following this list are the names of 108 men—identified as dance masters, singers, musicians, drummers, artisans, bearers, and accountants—who are assigned various numbers of shares.

Neither this uncommonly lengthy inscription nor the situation at the Tanjavur temple can be regarded as typical. The very fact that this temple is a royal foundation makes it unusual in the Tamil country, and the scale of the building and numbers of temple personnel are unmatched elsewhere—the product of a spectacular royal gesture (Spencer 1969; Heitzman 1991). To understand what was actually characteristic of temple life and of temple women's lives in the Chola period, we must capitalize on the fact that there are an extremely large number of inscriptions from this period, including many that mention temple women. An analysis that takes into account the whole body of available inscriptional evidence is likely to give us a more complete picture—and one that points up regional differences and historical changes—than that afforded by this one important but unusual inscription.

This is precisely what I have undertaken in the present study. I located and collected the texts of inscriptions that refer to temple women by surveying a wide variety of secondary sources, by reading all the *Annual Reports on Indian Epigraphy*, by examining all the published Chola period inscriptions, and by going over the relevant unpublished inscriptions at the Office of the Director of Epigraphy in Mysore. I translated those inscriptions that I thought would be useful from Tamil into English and entered information from them into a computer database to facilitate aggregate analysis. The total number of inscriptions in the database is 1,457; a subset of these, the 820 inscriptions that fall inside the geographic and chronological parameters of my study, constitute my dataset, and 304 of these inscriptions refer directly to temple women (see appendix II). Most of my analysis is based on these 304 inscriptions. I sorted through them in a number of different ways, aggregating the separate bits of information contained in each, to see what kinds of patterns emerged with respect to the character and roles of the temple women. These patterns were analyzed with special reference to regional and chronological variation—mapping them onto a time and space grid constructed by using the four subperiods of the Chola period and the various districts and regions of Tamilnadu.

In addition to my various analyses of the Chola period inscriptions that refer directly to temple women, I have used several other analytic approaches that allow me to compare temple women with other groups of people. I have been especially interested in comparing temple women with other kinds of women and with "temple men"—those men associated with the temple whose situation parallels that of temple women. In this comparative project I am utilizing a method of study very similar to the "gender relations" approach (Kelly-Gadol 1976; J. Scott 1986 and 1987; Bock 1989, 15). That is, instead of constructing a history focused exclusively on a particular group of women, adding on a supplementary chapter to the history of the Chola period that we already have, I have attempted to analyze the actions and situation of the women I am studying in terms of a broader context of relationships. My aim is to discover how temple women were related to one another, to other kinds of women, to men, and to various social systems—and how these relationships were different from those in which other types of women and temple men were implicated.

Because there has been very little study of women or of temple men in the Chola period, I have used the inscriptional evidence to create comparison groups for my purposes. In some cases, these groups are quite large and complete; for example, I have collected information about palace women and Jain religious women—groups who will be described in the next chapter—as systematically as I have done for temple women. In other cases, when the comparison groups were potentially extremely large (e.g., "temple men," "all women," or "people in general"), I have used a fraction of the available inscriptional data and constructed sample groups that I hoped would be representative of the total populations in each case. In constructing some of these sample comparison groups, I have utilized the method of area study worked out by James Heitzman, involving the examination of all available inscriptions from a number of taluk-sized study areas, chosen to represent the variety of economic, political, and religious situations present in medieval Tamilnadu (Heitzman 1985, 44, 57–58). The area studies I have done to construct the sample comparison groups of "people in general" and "temple men" are based on the examination of the Tamil texts of published inscriptions from four study areas: Tirukkoyilur taluk in South Arcot district, Kumbakonam taluk in Tanjavur district, Kulattur taluk in Tiruchirappalli district, and Kanchipuram taluk in Chingleput district.[65] To obtain information about "all women," I took as a representative population all the women named in *A Concordance of the Names in the Cōḻa Inscriptions* (Karashima, Subbarayalu, and Matsui 1978).[66] By constructing these frameworks of comparison, I am able both to situate temple women in the context of medieval Tamil society and to discern the particularities of their roles and activities.

Having discussed the ways in which Chola period inscriptions open up a new perspective on the history of women in general and temple women in particular, I show in the next chapter how the inscriptions represent temple women as a social category distinct from other types of women, as individuals present and active in various times and places in medieval Tamilnadu, and as people primarily identified as "devotees" and "daughters of God."

TWO

Discerning and Delineating the Figure of the Temple Woman

Definitions and Locations

The Temple Woman as a Social Category

Women are frequently mentioned in Chola period inscriptions, most often as donors. The inscriptions provide clues that allow us to distinguish different types of women, although titles or professional identifications are applied less often to women than to men, and there are a number of inscriptional references to women in which no information beyond a name is given. Nonetheless, it is possible to discern several categories of women, including temple women, Jain religious women, queens, palace women, Brahman women, and a rather heterogeneous group of family women.

My first task in this chapter is to provide a definition for the category of temple women. Following this, I will define or characterize each of the other types of women, in order to determine to what extent each of these categories might overlap with the category of temple women.

I define a temple woman as a woman who has at least one of the following characteristics:

a. She is referred to in the inscriptions by one of several terms—*tevaraṭiyāḷ* (or a related term that similarly has the meaning of "devotee," e.g., *emperumāṉaṭiyāḷ*); *tevaṉār makaḷ* ("daughter of God"); and *patiy(il)ār* or *taḷiy(il)ār* ("temple woman").
b. She is said to have some function in a temple or *maṭha* and/or to receive on a regular basis food, rice, cloth, or gold, or rights over land from the temple.
c. She is identified in the inscription as being a woman "of this temple" or a servant or devotee "of the Lord of such-and-such a place."

The set of 304 Chola period inscriptions that I consider to refer to temple women has been constructed with reference to this definition. When I use the term "temple woman" to refer to women outside of the area and period of study, I have the same definition in mind as this one, although the "temple woman" terms found elsewhere are, naturally, different from those that are part of the definition for medieval Tamilnadu.

The category circumscribed by my definition is internally coherent and is sufficiently homogeneous a grouping to be considered to correspond to a recognized social identity. This can be demonstrated by examining the extent to which the three definitional features overlap. I took, as a subset of the 304 Chola period inscriptions that refer to temple women according to the definition, those which are clearly datable, for which I have complete texts, and which definitely refer to women. This subset consists of 177 references to temple women, which I analyzed according to the three features of the definition (see figure 2.1). Of these 177 references, 134 (76 percent) show feature a ("temple woman" terms), 55 (31 percent) show feature b (function in or support by temple or *maṭha*), and 110 (62 percent) show feature c (being of the temple). The references that mention more than one feature (which fall in the shaded areas at the center of figure 2.1) make up 64 percent of the total. This conjunction of definitional features provides strong evidence for the notion that the three characteristics are in fact correlated with one another and that they are indicative of a coherent social category.

Most of the overlapping among the definitional features occurs between feature a (the "temple woman" terms) and one of the other two features. Only in seven cases (4 percent of the total) is there overlap between features b and c and only five (3 percent) of the references give all three of the definitional characteristics, probably because of the differences in how the inscriptions identify people in different roles. Donors, for instance, are named, whereas people performing ritual functions and receiving support from the temple are frequently referred to as an anonymous group. Women termed *tevaraṭiyār* (feature a) who were donors would be more likely to have their home temple (feature c) mentioned than would a collective group of female *tevaraṭiyār* (feature a) who performed tasks in or received support from the temple (feature b). Although they do not overlap with each other, both features b and c consistently overlap with the set of characteristic "temple woman" terms (feature a). Of the total of 177 references analyzed here, 134 (76 percent) use one of the four "temple woman" terms.[1] The terms have a central definitional role.

The extent of the correlation of definitional features varies in different times and regions. It occurs with the greatest frequency in inscriptions from the southern districts of Tirunelveli, Madurai, and Ramnad and is least in evidence in the core Chola area (Tiruchirappalli and Tanjavur districts), although even here well over 50 percent of the references to temple women mention more than one of the definitional features.[2]

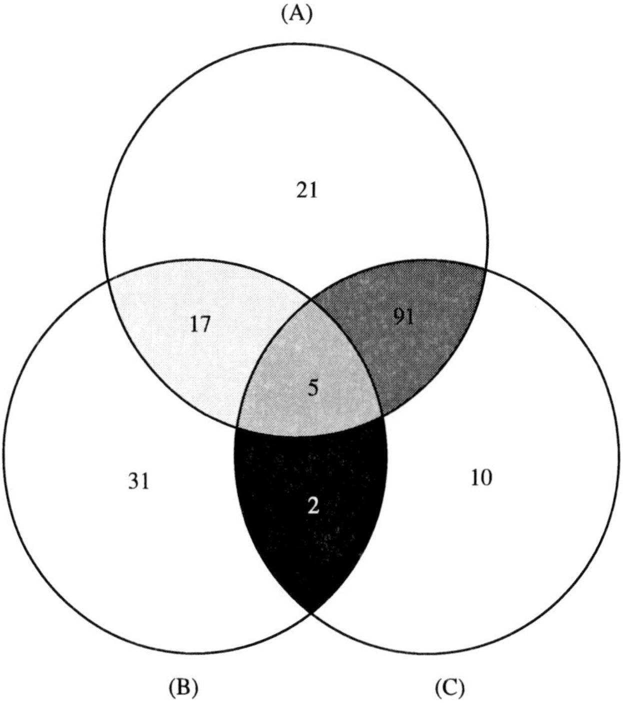

Figure 2.1 Correlation of the definitional features of the category "temple woman." (A) Referred to by specific terms tevaraṭiyār and related terms; tevaṉār makaḷ; patiy(il)ār; or taḷiy(il)ār); (B) function in or support from the temple; (C) being "of the temple."

In terms of chronological variation, we find that the conjunction of features is much more characteristic of the later Chola period than the earlier. Table 2.1 shows the percentage of overlap between the definitional features in each of the four subperiods. In the second subperiod, fewer than half of the references to temple women mention more than one of the definitional features, and this subperiod also marks the low point in the number of inscriptions that refer to temple women—both in the subset of inscriptions being considered here and, as we will see in the next section, in the whole

Table 2.1 Overlapping of definitional features of the category "temple woman"

	Number of references	Percentage with two or more features
Chola 1 (A.D. 850-985)	32	53
Chola 2 (A.D. 985-1070)	21	43
Chola 3 (A.D. 1070-1178)	42	79
Chola 4 (A.D. 1178-1300)	82	72

collection of inscriptions referring to temple women. In the second subperiod there is little correlation between "temple woman" terms and either feature b or c. In the third subperiod there is a sharp rise (to 79 percent) in the proportion of references to temple women with conjoined definitional features. The correlation between "temple woman" terms and feature b—employment in or support by the temple—is much higher in the third subperiod than in the other subperiods; there is *no* overlap between these two features in the first subperiod and quite a low correlation in the second.[3] Overall, this pattern seems to indicate a transition—a shift in the understanding of the character and role of temple women that took place during the second subperiod and resulted in the emergence of a more well-defined conception of temple women in the third subperiod.

By analyzing the correlations among the three features in the definition of temple women, I have demonstrated that the definition frames a coherent social category. Another result of this analysis is the finding that the definition is most salient in the later Chola period and that there may have been important changes in the significance of the category "temple woman" during the eleventh century.

To show the distinctiveness of the category of temple women, the next task is to examine its relationship with other groupings of women who are represented in Chola period inscriptions. First, I briefly describe each of these other groupings.

Jain religious women, defined in a way that parallels the definition for temple women, are those women (a) who are referred to by the term *kuratti* ("teacher," from Skt. *guru*) or *māṇākkiyār* ("student," related to Ta. *māṇi*, found in the Hindu inscriptional context referring to *brahmacārins*, or male celibate students), (b) who functioned in or received support from a Jain institution, or (c) who are described as belonging, in some sense, to a Jain institution. The Tamil inscriptions do not refer to these women as nuns or ascetics or as members of specific Jain monastic communities (*gaṇas* or *saṅghas*), but the fact that they are generally identified with reference to a disciplic succession rather than a kinship group seems to indicate their status as renunciates. These women are particularly in evidence in inscriptions of the eighth century, before the beginning of the Chola period, when they are prominent as donors of the Jain images found in caves and on rock faces in Tirunelveli district, in the far south of Tamilnadu (Orr 1998).

I categorize as queens those women who are given in the inscriptions the titles *teviyār* (from Skt. *devī*) or *pirāṭṭiyār* (the feminine equivalent of Ta. *pirāṉ*, "lord") or who are identified as the wives, mothers, daughters, or sisters of kings—including local rulers, as well as rulers of the major South Indian dynasties. The majority of queens in Chola period inscriptions do in fact belong to the Chola dynasty, and they are especially active as donors in the core Chola region in the first half of the period, in the tenth and eleventh centuries.[4]

A palace woman has at least one of the following two characteristics: (a) she is referred to in the inscription as belonging to a *veḷam* ("palace") or *parivāram* ("retinue") or as an *aṇukki* ("intimate") or *poki* ("concubine") of a king or chief; (b) she is identified in the inscription, with or without the use of such terms, as being associated with a particular queen, king, chief, or palace establishment. Although in some cases the term used for these women indicates or suggests a sexual relationship with a chief or king, most of these palace women seem to have been ladies-in-waiting, or attendants, rather than concubines or royal courtesans. In any case, the palace women mentioned in Chola period inscriptions appear to have enjoyed a high status in society and to have had considerable wealth.[5] Palace women, like queens, were especially visible in inscriptions of the early Chola period. In the course of this study, when I use the expression "royal women," I am referring to both queens and palace women.

Brahman women are those women who are termed *brāhmaṇī* (or Tamil variants such as *pirāmaṇi*). The equivalent male term is scarcely ever found in Chola period inscriptions, although there are a number of other indicators of Brahman status for men, including the mention of *gotras* (Orr 1995a and 1995c). The term *brāhmaṇī*, which is very frequently used in Chola period inscriptions as a synonym for "wife," is virtually the only marker of a woman's status as a Brahman. Inscriptions throughout the whole of the Chola period refer to Brahman women; they are often described as the owners or sellers of land, as well as donors (Orr forthcoming b).

The category of family women includes women other than queens and Brahmans who are identified as the wives, mothers, sisters, or daughters of various sorts of men—including shepherds, merchants, and landowners. Although this is a very large group, it does not include all the women mentioned in inscriptions who are not classed into one of the other categories because over half of all the women mentioned in Chola period inscriptions are not identified with reference to family relationships (Orr forthcoming b), including many who cannot be placed in the category of temple women, Jain religious women, queens, palace women, or Brahman women.

The inscriptional evidence does not provide the foundation for a complete system of social classification; the categories of women I have described are not exhaustive. But this is of less concern for the present study than the question of whether the categories are distinct from one another. It is particularly important to determine whether women defined as temple women might also belong to one of the other categories. Although I have shown how the category of temple women is internally coherent, we must now ascertain the extent to which it is a discrete social category.

There is some overlap between the category of temple women and that of Jain religious women. There are three inscriptions whose location and language indicate that they refer to women associated with the Jain milieu, but the more capacious definition of the category temple women also includes them, because they are identified in the inscriptions as being "of the temple" or another religious institution; they also seem to receive some type of support from or be provided with a place of residence by the institutions to which they belong. In two of the inscriptions (SII 3.92 and SII

14.40), both of the ninth century, the women are referred to as *koyiṟpiḷḷaikaḷ*, "children of the temple." There is nothing distinctively Jain about this language, and indeed these inscriptions provide a good example of the blurring of sectarian boundaries and of the shared religious culture of medieval Tamilnadu, which is described in chapter 1.[6] The third inscription (SII 7.56), dating from the tenth century, uses more characteristically Jain terminology in referring to a "women's *paḷḷi*" (*peṇpaḷḷi*), which is provided with a well and a house site.[7] The women of this *paḷḷi*—which may be regarded as a shrine, a rest house, or a monastery—are evidently Jain religious women, but they also fall into the category of temple women because they received support from and were identified with a religious institution.

We encounter two women who seem to be both queens and temple women in the inscriptions of the Śiva temple of Melapaluvur in Tiruchirappalli district. One of them, Nakkaṉ Akkāranaṅkaiyār, is referred to in two tenth-century inscriptions (SII 13.153 and 154) both as the queen of Piḷḷai Ceramāṉār (the Chera prince) and as a *tevaṉār makaḷ*—a daughter of the god of "this temple," the temple of Lord Avanikantaṟpa Īśvara. She is thus, according to my definition, a temple woman, as well as a queen. The second woman is another *tevaṉār makaḷ* of the same temple, named Nakkaṉ Pañcavaṉ-mātevi, who is identified as one of the queens of Rajaraja I in an inscription of the early eleventh century (ARE 385 of 1924).[8]

In two cases the categories of temple women and of palace women seem to overlap. In the first, in an inscription (SII 22.87) that dates from the late eleventh century, a woman named Puṇṇiyañceytāḷ is mentioned as the mother of a female donor and is described both as the *aṉukki* of a chief and as one of the *tevaraṭiyār* in the temple of Lord Tiruvekampam in Kanchipuram. The second case is less clear. A late thirteenth-century inscription from Tanjavur district refers to a woman named Āyutaiṉācci, who is the mother of a male donor (ARE 560 of 1921). She is identified both as a *tevaraṭiyāḷ* (and is thus a temple woman) and as a member of a *parivāram* (and is thus a palace woman). However, the inscription does not specify whose *parivāram* she belongs to, beyond identifying him as a *kāṇiyuṭaiyār*—the possessor of a *kāṇi*, rights in land or privileges. *Kāṇi*-holders were in some cases members of local elites, in other cases temple servants (Heitzman 1985, 128–47). I believe that we are dealing here with a temple woman who was part of the retinue of a temple functionary rather than a palace woman.

It is striking that in the Chola period inscriptions we can point definitely to only a single case in which the identities of temple women and palace women were blurred. The notion, frequently encountered in descriptions and interpretations of the *devadāsī*, that temple women and palace women had similar roles or overlapping identities is not borne out by this evidence. The idea of an intimate connection between the temple and the court—including the sharing of ritual forms, of dance and music traditions, and of personnel—and of the *devadāsī* as a key figure in these transactions and associations springs from a situation that apparently did not exist before the seventeenth century, when a particular type of royal culture began to develop in the courts of the Nayaka rulers and of other princes in South India and elsewhere.[9] In the Chola period, this melding of the royal and religious had not yet occurred, and there was a definite and distinct boundary between temple women and palace women with respect to their identities and activities.

We do not encounter in the inscriptions any Brahman women who would also be classified as temple women. There are, however, six inscriptions in which women fall into the categories both of temple women and family women, according to my definitions. In three of these inscriptions, temple women—a *tevaraṭiyāḷ*, a *tevaṉār makaḷ*, and a *maṭha* slave—are identified as wives (*akamuṭaiyāḷ*) (ARE 147 of 1912; SITI 28; ARE 409 of 1925). In three other inscriptions (SII 22.141; NK 157; KK 255), temple women are described as the mother, daughter, or sister of a man; in two cases they are slaves (*aṭiyāḷ*, *aṭimai*) of a temple or *maṭha*, and in the third, a woman is classified as a temple woman because she is said to be a *tevaraṭiyāḷ*.

Of the 304 Chola period inscriptions that refer to temple women, there are only a dozen cases in which they can also be classified as belonging to another group—Jain religious women, queens, palace women, or family women. This demonstrates that the category "temple women" as I have defined it is not only internally coherent but also distinctive and salient in terms of the social classifications represented in the inscriptions of this time and place.

Temple Women's Visibility in Chola Period Inscriptions

Having established that there were such beings as temple women, distinguishable from other types of women, we would like to know more about when and where they appear in the inscriptional record. Table 2.2 shows the geographical and chronological distribution of the 304 inscriptions that are the foundation of this study.

Forty-eight inscriptions, or 16 percent of the total, date from the first subperiod; the number, and proportion, goes down to 40 (13 percent) in the second subperiod; in the third subperiod the number doubles; and in the fourth subperiod, the steep rise continues, so that this single subperiod contributes 135 inscriptions, 44 percent of the total.

Tanjavur district contributes by far the most inscriptions—75 out of the total of 304. Chingleput district, in the far north of Tamilnadu, also makes a respectable contribution, providing 57 inscriptions out of the total. Figure 2.2 shows that the bulk of the inscriptions come from the core Chola region (Tanjavur and Tiruchirappalli districts) and from districts to the north. In the southern region, only Tirunelveli district has a substantial number of inscriptions referring to temple women, and there are only a few inscriptions from the western region.

In addition to the geographical mapping, the sectarian distribution of inscriptional references to temple women among Śaiva and Vaiṣṇava temples

Table 2.2 Chronological and geographical distribution of references to temple women

District	Subperiod 1 (850–985)	Subperiod 2 (985–1070)	Subperiod 3 (1070–1178)	Subperiod 4 (1178–1300)	Total
Northern region					
Chingleput	5 (9%)	13 (23%)	19 (33%)	20 (35%)	57
North Arcot	4 (15%)	6 (22%)	5 (19%)	12 (44%)	27
Chittoor	4 (50%)	1 (12%)	2 (25%)	1 (12%)	8
Middle region					
South Arcot	3 (9%)	4 (12%)	13 (39%)	13 (39%)	33
Chola region					
Tanjavur	18 (24%)	8 (11%)	22 (29%)	27 (36%)	75
Tiruchirappalli	6 (19%)	2 (6%)	6 (19%)	18 (56%)	32
Southern region					
Tirunelveli	3 (12%)	2 (8%)	—	21 (81%)	26
Madurai	—	2 (22%)	2 (22%)	5 (56%)	9
Kanyakumari	1 (11%)	1 (11%)	1 (11%)	6 (67%)	9
Malabar/Travancore	3 (50%)	—	2 (33%)	1 (17%)	6
Ramnad	1 (17%)	—	—	5 (83%)	6
Western region					
Coimbatore	—	1 (20%)	3 (60%)	1 (20%)	5
Salem	—	—	—	1 (100%)	1
Kolar	—	—	3 (60%)	2 (40%)	5
Mysore	—	—	—	1 (100%)	1
Bangalore	—	—	1 (100%)	—	1
Godavari	—	—	1 (100%)	—	1
Sri Lanka	—	—	1 (50%)	1 (50%)	2
TOTAL	48 (16%)	40 (13%)	81 (27%)	135 (44%)	304

The percentages represent the contribution of each subperiod to the total number of references to temple women, for each district.

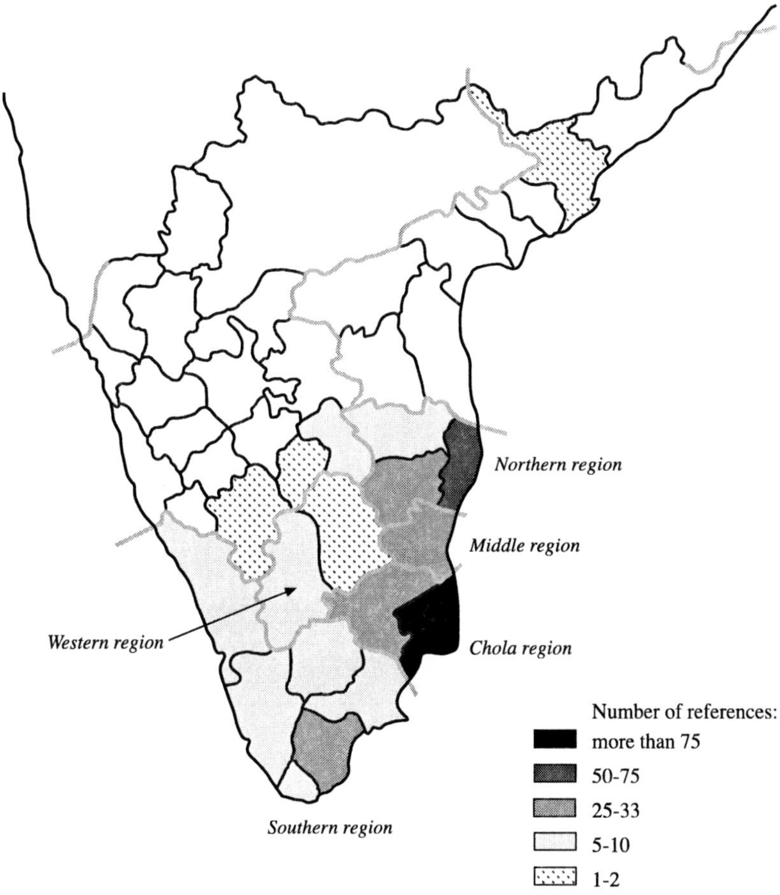

Figure 2.2 Distribution of inscriptional references to temple women in the Tamil country.

may be of interest. Of the 304 inscriptions, only 26 (9 percent) come from Vaiṣṇava temples. Half of these are from various temples in Chingleput district, and only 1 is found in the core Chola region. The 26 inscriptions are fairly evenly distributed chronologically, with a rise in the last subperiod: there are 7 inscriptions in the first subperiod, 5 each in the second and third subperiods, and 9 in the last subperiod. The relatively small number of references to temple women in Vaiṣṇava temples can be explained by the fact that in the Chola period, as today, Śaiva temples were more numerous in Tamilnadu than Vaiṣṇava temples. There are no major differences between the inscriptions' presentation of the activities and identities of Vaiṣṇava temple women and those of Śaiva temple women. It would appear that the temple women of Śaiva and Vaiṣṇava temples were very similar.[10]

The pattern of change over time I have described—a dip in the number of references to temple women in the second subperiod, followed by a rapid rise through the third and fourth subperiods—is not found in all regions (see table 2.2). This pattern is characteristic of the two core Chola districts, Tanjavur and Tiruchirappalli, although in Tanjavur district, the increase in references to temple women in the fourth subperiod is not very marked. In the southern region, this increase in the last subperiod is extremely pronounced and follows a dip in the third subperiod (rather than the second). In the northern region, there is a steady rise, without any dips. In the middle region between the north and the core Chola area, apart from an increase between the second and third subperiods, there are no other ups and downs in the number of inscriptions that refer to temple women. What we see, then, is an overall increase from the beginning to the end of the Chola period in all regions of Tamilnadu but differences among regions in how the greater number of references to temple women in the last subperiod is arrived at: in general, the northern and middle regions show a steady and gradual increase, the core Chola area has a more pronounced increase in the third and fourth subperiods, and the southern region shows an abrupt and rapid increase only in the last century of the Chola period.

The significance of the increasing numbers of references to temple women will become clearer if we view these numbers against the chronological and geographical distribution patterns of the corpus of Chola period inscriptions as a whole. Rather than utilizing this larger corpus of inscriptions, which is the basis for my study, most analyses of distribution patterns have focused only on "Chola inscriptions"—i.e., those inscriptions dated in the regnal year of a Chola king (Sitaraman, Karashima, and Subbarayalu 1976; Karashima, Subbarayalu, and Matsui 1978; Subbarayalu 1982). To compare my data on temple women with the patterns that have been discerned in these analyses, I took as a subset of my collection of 304 inscriptions only those that would be considered "Chola inscriptions." This involved eliminating nearly 100 inscriptions dated in the reigns of kings other than Cholas—about a third of my total. More than three-quarters of these non-Chola inscriptions come from the last subperiod, and most are from either the southern region or the north. They are dated in the reigns of various non-Chola kings—in many cases Pandya rulers but also later "Pallavas" and Telugu Chodas. The mention of a king's name to date an inscription does not in any way imply his involvement in the transaction recorded, but references to non-Chola rulers—especially the references in the northern districts of Chingleput and North Arcot to a variety of different rulers—do indicate political change and competition for sovereignty in the regions where these inscriptions are found. In the course of the present study, I will be exploring the question of why we find such a large number of inscriptions that refer to the activities of temple women in areas where Chola rule was insecurely established.

This mass of non-Chola inscriptions that refer to temple women would seem to account for some of the increases we see in the last subperiod, particularly the rapid rise in references to temple women in inscriptions from the far south of Tamilnadu, the heart of the Pandya territory. But even when we remove these non-Chola inscriptions, we still find that there are considerably more inscriptions that refer to temple women in the later Chola period than in the earlier. My subset of 205 Chola inscriptions are proportionately distributed as follows: 18 percent in the first subperiod, 19 percent in the second, 35 percent in the third, and 28 percent in the fourth. When we consider that there are approximately the same number of Chola inscriptions in each of the four subperiods (Subbarayalu 1982, 305), we must conclude that the increasing number of references to temple women in the later Chola period is not attributable to an increasing number of inscriptions in general; rather, this pattern seems to indicate a real increase in temple women's activity and involvement in temple affairs.

Temple women are not the only people who gain increasing visibility in Chola period records. During the Chola period, more and more individuals—many of whom, as local notables or temple functionaries, acted as witnesses or signatories to land transactions and grants—are mentioned in each inscription. Table 2.3, which provides figures for the number of names per inscription in the four study areas (see note 65 in chapter 1), shows this increase as a rise from 1.87 names per inscription in the first subperiod to 5.7 names per inscription in the last.

Of the 304 inscriptions that refer to temple women, 222, or close to three-quarters, provide their names. The proportion of inscriptions that mention temple women by name, rather than referring to them as an anonymous group, increases steadily through the Chola period, from 59 percent in the first subperiod to 83 percent in the fourth. Because there are increasingly more inscriptions that refer to temple women in the later Chola period, we find a sharp rise in the numbers of temple women named toward the end of the Chola period. One hundred thirty-three temple women are mentioned by name in the last subperiod, more than the number named in the three other subperiods combined—excluding the 383 *taḷicceri peṇṭukaḷ* named in the Tanjavur inscription, which dates from the early part of the second subperiod (see table 2.3).

Although temple women may be seen as participating in a general epigraphical pattern of increasing specification of individual identity and increasing recognition of participation in affairs centering on the temple, the rise in their visibility in the course of the Chola period, and especially the steep rise in the thirteenth century, appear to be more marked than for many other types of people. And their increasing visibility contrasts dramatically with the declining representation of other kinds of women in the inscriptional record (see Orr 1998 and forthcoming b). Table 2.3 shows that in the four study areas there is not only a decline in the absolute number of women named but also a steep decline in the average number of women named per inscription, which falls from .29 (a woman named in every three or four inscriptions) to .05 (a woman named only once in every twenty inscriptions). For royal women—queens and palace women—there is an especially precipitous drop in visibility between the early and later Chola periods.

Although temple women represent only a tiny fraction of the people mentioned in Chola period inscriptions, I have demonstrated that they can

Table 2.3 The visibility of men and women in Chola period inscriptions: area study

	Subperiod 1 (850–985)	Subperiod 2 (985–1070)	Subperiod 3 (1070–1178)	Subperiod 4 (1178–1300)	Total
Number of inscriptions	260	99	149	92	600
Total names	486	431	586	524	2027
Names per inscription	1.87	4.35	3.93	5.70	3.38
Men's names	410	405	560	518	1893
Men's names per inscription	1.58	4.09	3.76	5.63	3.16
Women's names	76	26	26	6	134
Women's names per inscription	0.29	0.26	0.17	0.05	0.22
Royal women	26	21	1	0	48
Brahman women	5	1	6	2	14
Temple women	23	0	5	1	29
Other women	22	4	14	3	43
Temple women named in entire corpus	44	26	35	133	238

The figures in this table are numbers of names. They are based on the examination of inscriptions in four study areas (see note 65 in chapter 1), except for the last row of figures for temple women, which is drawn from the whole corpus of Chola period inscriptions (except SII 2.66, the Tanjavur inscription, which names 383 temple women).

be located in the inscriptions as a distinct and coherent category. Our survey of the chronological distribution of inscriptional references to temple women shows that in the course of the Chola period, an increasing number of inscriptions mention temple women, and that, particularly in the last century of the period, an increasing number of individual temple women are named in these inscriptions. This increasing visibility contrasts with the declining presence of other types of women in the inscriptional record and appears to be linked to the destabilization of Chola dynastic rule. The rising visibility of temple women and the highlighting of their individual identities also correlate with the more consistent conjunction of the definitional features of the temple woman that is evident in the later Chola period. This increasing conjunction, which seems to indicate an increasing recognition and definition of the temple woman's status, centers around the characteristic terms that were applied to temple women in Chola period inscriptions, which we now examine.

Devotees and Daughters of God

"Temple Woman" Terminology in India: Prostitutes and Ladies

Almost all of the 304 Chola period inscriptions referring to temple women apply some sort of term to them: 195 inscriptions use one of the "temple woman" terms of the definition outlined in the previous section—*tevaraṭiyār* or a related term meaning "devotee," *tevaṉār makaḷ* ("daughter of God"), and *patiy(il)ār* or *taḷiy(il)ār* ("temple woman")—and another 98 inscriptions use some other term. Only 11 inscriptions do not apply any term to temple women. A study of the meanings and applications of the various terms should illuminate the functions and character of temple women, and the changes that occurred over the course of the Chola period. Before undertaking this detailed study, however, I would like to show how, in general, the types of terms used to refer to temple women in Chola period inscriptions in Tamilnadu may have differed from those used in the inscriptions of other parts of India.

Among the earliest inscriptions that refer to temple women are those in Tamil, of the ninth century, which mention *tevaṉār makaḷs* and *tevaraṭiyār*. But early medieval inscriptions from other parts of India provide a different kind of vocabulary. In Andhra Pradesh and Karnataka, eighth- and ninth-century inscriptions refer to *vilāsinīs* ("charming" or "coquettish" women), who were evidently temple women. Other early inscriptional references to temple women include a seventh-century reference from Rajasthan to a *gaṇikā* ("courtesan") associated with a temple, an eighth-century reference from Orissa to *dārikās* ("female servants"), and ninth- and tenth-century references to *sūḷeyar* ("prostitutes") from Karnataka. There are tenth-century inscriptions from Kerala that refer to temple women as *naṅkaimār* ("ladies") and eleventh-century references in Andhra to temple women who are also termed "ladies"—*sānis*.

It is striking that in inscriptions outside of the Tamil country, there are *no* terms equivalent in meaning to the definitional terms applied to most temple women in Chola period inscriptions—terms meaning "devotee," "daughter of God," or "temple woman."[11] There is some overlap in terminology between Tamil and non-Tamil inscriptions when terms meaning "servant," "dancer," or "singer" are applied to temple women. But such terms are not particularly common either in Tamil or in non-Tamil inscriptions.

Table 2.4 shows the kinds of terms for temple women that are most frequently found in non-Tamil inscriptions dating from before 1300 in the three regions of North India, Karnataka, and Andhra Pradesh, as well as in Tamil inscriptions of the same period.[12] The table demonstrates that there were significant differences not only between these areas and Tamilnadu but also among these areas.

Only a small number of inscriptions that refer to temple women are from the vast region of "North India," and these show considerable variety in the types of terms used. But a quarter of these inscriptions (four of sixteen) use terms that mean "prostitute." An even larger proportion (29 percent) of the inscriptions from Karnataka use terms with the same meaning; in almost all cases the Kannada term used in this context is *sūḷe*.[13]

Such terminology in North India and Karnataka contrasts sharply with the usage in Andhra Pradesh and Tamilnadu. In inscriptions from Andhra Pradesh, I have come across only four references that refer to temple women as prostitutes (constituting 3 percent of the total number of references to temple women); these four appear in Sanskrit rather than Telugu inscriptions. In *none* of the Chola period inscriptions nor in later Tamil inscriptions are temple women referred to as prostitutes.

Temple women begin to be mentioned in the inscriptions of these four regions—North India, Karnataka, Andhra Pradesh, and Tamilnadu—at approximately the same time, in about the ninth century. It does not appear, therefore, that the practice of attaching temple women to temples spread from one region to another, one of these regions providing the model for the others. I think it is likely that the temple woman "phenomenon" in Tamilnadu arose independently of developments in other regions and that the use of a distinctive set of terms for temple women is one of the indications of this independent evolution. It is beyond the scope of this study to interpret the significance of the use of "prostitute" terms for temple women in the inscriptions of Karnataka and northern India or to relate this use to what appear to be parallel references in the Āgamas. But it should be emphasized that only between about a quarter and a third of the inscriptional references to temple women in Karnataka and North India in fact use "prostitute" terminology, and that this terminology is of a different character than that utilized in the Agamic texts.[14] If, nonetheless, we consider that temple women in Karnataka and North India *were* in fact prostitutes, this does not mean that their counterparts in Tamilnadu necessarily were also.

Even in Karnataka, other aspects of temple women's character and their functions in the temple and in society may have been of much greater importance than their identities as prostitutes (cf. Parasher and Naik 1986, 75–78; Parasher-Sen 1993, 254–55). In fact, in the inscriptions of Karnataka, temple women are more frequently referred to as *pātrās* than as prostitutes; the term *pātrā* is found in 35 percent of the inscriptions referring to temple women. This is the feminine form of a Sanskrit word that includes among its meanings "a capable or competent person" and "an actor or an actor's part or character in a play" (MW, 613). It may be that the temple women termed *pātrā* in the Kannada inscriptions were responsible for providing some kind of performance, such as song or dance, in the temple.[15]

In the inscriptions of Andhra Pradesh, the terms for temple women are quite different from those of Karnataka and of Tamilnadu. Over half of the inscriptions from Andhra use the term *sāni*, the Telugu form of the Sanskrit *svāminī*, "lady," a term also commonly used as a title for women other than temple women (MW, 1284; C. P. Brown 1985, 1330; Talbot 1988b, 107–8). It is interesting to compare this term with that most widely applied to temple women in Chola period inscriptions, *tevaraṭiyāḷ*. Although the Telugu term connotes mastery and the Tamil term servitude, they are both honorific terms, conferring social or ritual status. In neither case do they indicate anything about the ritual function or profession of temple women, as the most frequently found terms in Kannada inscriptions seem to.

It is now time to examine what meanings are conveyed—how, where, and when—by this Tamil term, *tevaraṭiyāḷ*, and by the other terms applied to temple women in Chola period inscriptions. Although, in the course of

Table 2.4 Terms used in pre-1300 inscriptions that refer to temple women

	"Servant"	"Dancer," "Singer"	*Pātrā*	"Prostitute"	*Sāni*	Other	All temple woman inscriptions
North India							
	3 19%	1 6%	0	4 25%	0	8	16
Karnataka							
	2 2%	2 2%	31 35%	25 29%	0	38	85
Andhra Pradesh							
	4 3%	12 9%	7 5%	4 3%	76 55%	41	138
Tamilnadu							
	10 4%	6 2%	0	0	0	288	304

Percentages express the proportion of terms in each category out of the total numbers of inscriptions that refer to temple women in each region.

For districts and areas included in each region and chronological distribution, see appendix I.

the Chola period, "temple woman" terms seem to have become technically specific, being increasingly applied exclusively to temple women, their literal meanings may reveal something of temple women's character and activities. Furthermore, an investigation of the changing usages of these terms will illuminate the processes by which temple women's identities became consolidated in the later Chola period.

Tamil Terminology: Slaves and Devotees

In the twelfth year of Ko Rājakecaripa<u>n</u>mar alias Cakkaravattikaḷ Śrī Kulottuṅkaco<u>l</u>adevar,

Irājacuntari, a temple woman (*mahā-devaraṭiyāḷ*) [lit. "devotee of the Great God"] of Tiruttānto<u>nr</u>i in Virarājentrapuram, gave land at Nallaraicūr for *po<u>n</u>akam* food offerings for the early morning service (*ci<u>r</u>ukālai santi*) for [the deity] Parameśvara, Lord of the *ūr* (village)—for 4 *nāḷi* of rice, fried curry (*po<u>r</u>ikka<u>r</u>i*) offerings, ghee offerings, yoghurt offerings, and betel offerings.

[The land is briefly described.]

She also gave 15 *kalam* of paddy. We, the *civabrāhmaṇar* (*śivabrāhmaṇas*) of this temple (*stānam*), who are responsible for these expenses, take in hand this land and this paddy. May the *pa<u>n</u>māheśvarar* protect this endowment.

—SII 22.153: this inscription was engraved in A.D. 1145 at the Grāmārdhanātha temple in Elvanasur, South Arcot district.

In the Chola period inscriptions, *tevaraṭiyāḷ* (or its plural form *tevaraṭiyār*) is the term most frequently used to denote temple women (see table 2.5). This is a compound term made up of the words *tēvar* ("god, lord") and *aṭiyāḷ* ("female slave, servant, devotee"). (In inscriptional orthography, there is no long *e,* so *tēvar* is spelled *tevar.*) The plural form *tevaraṭiyār* is the form most frequently found in inscriptional usage, either as an honorific plural that refers to a single individual or as a collective plural. This plural form obscures gender, which means that it is sometimes difficult to determine whether the *tevaraṭiyār* mentioned in inscriptions are women or men. Over half of the references to temple women use this term or synonymous terms such as *emperumāṉaṭiyāḷ* or *āḻvāṉaṭiyāḷ*, in which *emperumāṉ* and *āḻvāṉ*, like *tevar*, mean "god" or "lord." *Tevaraṭiyāḷ* and these related terms are found in inscriptions from all regions of Tamilnadu.

The term *tevaraṭiyār* is a compound whose two components are inherited from an earlier literature and religious ethos associated with the Tamil *bhakti* movement of the sixth to ninth centuries. But the *combination* of the two words *tevar* and *aṭiyār* is something that appears for the first time in inscriptions of the early Chola period.

The first part of the compound, *tēvar*, means "god" or "king" and is the honorific plural of *tēvaṉ*, derived from the Sanskrit *deva* (MTL, 2068). Often, in fact, the term *tevaraṭiyār* is spelled *devaraṭiyār* in the Chola period inscriptions, with the Grantha letter *d* instead of Tamil *t*. Although other Tamil forms of the word *deva*, such as *teyvam* ("divinity") and *tēvu* ("deity") were current in the early Cankam literature, it was only after the seventh century that the terms *tēvaṉ* and *tēvi*, referring to specific gods and goddesses, came into widespread use in Tamil (Zvelebil 1977, 227).

The word *tēvar* has no sectarian connotations; it does not refer specifically to Śiva or Viṣṇu. The nonsectarian quality of *tevaraṭiyār* is in keeping with the type of language used in general in Chola period inscriptions.[16] Temple deities—and *tevaraṭiyār*—are not identified with reference to a pantheon that includes the great gods Śiva and Viṣṇu, but rather with reference to a particular place. The deity is described as the lord (frequently, the *uṭaiyār*, "possessor") of a specific village, and the *tevaraṭiyāḷ* is the devotee of a particular deity. This localization and specificity of connection is expressed by the frequent identification of temple women through such phrases as *ittevaraṭiyāḷ* ("the devotee of *this* god") or *ikkoyiṟ-tevaraṭiyāḷ* ("the devotee of the god of *this* temple").

The second part of the term *tevaraṭiyār* is derived from *aṭi*, the Tamil word for "foot." The (male) *aṭiyāṉ* or the (female) *aṭiyāḷ* is one who is at the feet of another, as a slave, servant, or devotee (MTL, 51). The term underscores the lowliness and humility of the *aṭiyāṉ*, relative to his master. The concept of the devotee as being at God's feet has deep roots in Tamil religious history,[17] and came to be particularly emphasized by the Vaiṣṇava Āḻvārs and the Śaiva Nāyaṉmārs, the Tamil poet-saints whose poems deeply influenced Hindu liturgy and theology as these took shape

Table 2.5 Chronological distribution of terms used for Tamil temple women

Term	Subperiod 1 (850–985)	Subperiod 2 (985–1070)	Subperiod 3 (1070–1178)	Subperiod 4 (1178–1300)	Total
aṭiyār	1 (2%)	3 (8%)	1 (1%)	5 (4%)	10
tevaraṭiyār	12 (25%)	12 (30%)	55 (68%)	75 (56%)	154
tevaṉār makaḷ	17 (35%)	5 (12%)	1 (1%)	1 (1%)	24
patiyār/taḷiyār	2 (4%)	4 (10%)	2 (2%)	10 (8%)	18
Total	48	40	81	135	304

This table gives the number of inscriptions in each subperiod that use a particular term to refer to temple women, as well as the percentage of such usages out of the total number of inscriptions that refer to temple women in each subperiod (indicated in the last row).

during the Chola period. In the ninth-century *Tiruvācakam* by the Śaiva saint Māṇikkavācakar, for instance, there are hundreds of references to the feet of God—which the devotee is to touch, serve, adorn, worship, and take refuge in—and the most frequently used term for devotee is *aṭiyāṉ* (Yocum 1982, 173–74, 206, n. 61).

The idea of the *aṭiyār*, as it is expressed in the poems of the Āḻvārs and Nāyaṉmārs, is tied less to the notion of slavery in a literal sense than to the unworthiness and lowliness of the devotee relative to God or to other devotees. That the identity of the *aṭiyār* is linked to a relative rather than an absolute status is demonstrated by the way in which the poet-saints compete with one another—each trying to prove that he, among all the devotees, is the *most* humble, servile, and selfless.[18] In fact, in a very significant sense, *aṭiyār* is an honorific term, which in the Tamil *bhakti* context is a great privilege to bear.

These honorific connotations are also present in the inscriptions of the early Chola period, where *aṭiyār* is more often applied to "devotees" than to "slaves"—and where temple women are counted among both *aṭiyār*-devotees and *aṭiyār*-slaves. In surveying the Chola period inscriptions, I have located a total of nineteen that employ the term *aṭiyār*, of which ten are from the first two subperiods. Three of the ten early Chola period inscriptions use *aṭiyār* to refer to people whose high ritual status as honored devotees is indicated by the fact that they were offered food in the temple. In two of these three inscriptions (NK 69 and SII 8.66), arrangements were made to feed *aṭiyār* on the occasion of temple festivals; it is not clear whether these groups of *aṭiyār* included women. The third inscription, from Tanjavur district, does not indicate any particular occasion for feeding the devotees but does specify that two parts of the endowment were earmarked for feeding female devotees (*peṇṇaṭiyārkaḷmār*), and one part was for the male devotees (*āṉaṭiyār*) (SII 13.218). We get a very clear impression of the esteem in which these *aṭiyār* were held from the string of honorific plural suffixes attached to the term *aṭiyār* in this inscription, in the case of the female devotees, and from the language of one of the other inscriptions (SII 8.66) which describes the devotees as "graciously condescending to take food" (*co<u>r</u>u prasādañ ceytaruḷa*), just as a deity would receive food offerings.[19]

The most common meaning of *aṭiyār* in early Chola period inscriptions is neither "devotee" nor "slave" but something like "royal attendant" or "retainer." Half of the ten inscriptions from the early period describe the *aṭiyār* as donors or people on whose behalf a donation was made; these four men (*aṭiyā<u>n</u>*) and one woman (*aṭiyāḷ*) are said to be the "servants" of royal figures. Here we see the use of the term *aṭiyār* to denote people who have the means to make donations and who have privileged standing in a royal court, people whose status is not low in absolute terms—who may, in fact, command considerable respect—but who are simply subordinate to another figure.

Only two of the ten inscriptions from the early Chola period apply the term *aṭiyār* to slaves rather than to retainers or devotees; in both cases these *aṭiyār* are temple women (ARE 149 of 1936–37; SII 22.141). In the later Chola period, however, we see a changing pattern of the use of *aṭiyār*, accompanied by an increase in the number of references to temple women who had the status of slaves. Of the nine inscriptions of the later period that use the term *aṭiyār*, six apply it to people who were owned, given, or sold. Most of these inscriptions are found in Tanjavur district, date from the thirteenth century, and apply the term to women. One of them, for example, describes the sale by two brothers, who were temple accountants, of five women to the temple at Sulamangalam—Mātāṇṭi, her two daughters, Nācci and Aḷuṭainācci, and two granddaughters, Celvi and Cokki (ARE 296 of 1911).

Although there is a continuing use in the later Chola period inscriptions of the term *aṭiyār* to denote persons of relatively high social standing—one inscription uses the term for a retainer of a local chief or notable and two refer to the feeding of *aṭiyār*-devotees, using the same kind of honorific language as in the earlier period—a semantic shift seems to have taken place. References to slavery, even in the thirteenth century, are still relatively rare, but the term *aṭiyār* is increasingly applied to people, primarily temple women, who had the status of slaves.[20]

In the early Chola period, and in the preceding centuries, the *aṭiyār* was a person for whom the fact of subordination, of "serving," was itself a source of status; to be connected with a divine or royal figure was an honor. It is possible that the earlier honorific connotations of *aṭiyār* may, in the later period, as slavery in a real sense became more prevalent, have served to legitimize the use of and obscure the actual status of people, especially women, who worked in the temple as slaves. Table 2.5 shows that ten Chola period inscriptions use the term *aṭiyār* to refer to temple women; in five cases these temple women are *aṭiyār*-devotees and in the other five they are *aṭiyār*-slaves. All but one of the latter five inscriptions comes from the later part of the Chola period.

This examination allows us to evaluate the claim made by some scholars that the word *tevaraṭiyāḷ* is simply a translation into Tamil of the Sanskrit word *devadāsī*, the term today used most frequently to refer to temple women (Kersenboom 1987, 28; Parasher and Naik 1986, 65). Apart from the fact that the Sanskrit term has not been in widespread use until the present century, whereas *tevaraṭiyāḷ* is commonly found in inscriptions from the early Chola period onward, the word *aṭiyāḷ* has a very different range of meanings and connotations from those associated with *dāsī*.

While early medieval literature and inscriptions in Tamil reveal that the primary meaning of *aṭiyāḷ* is "devotee," the *dāsī* as she is described in Sanskrit literature and in North Indian inscriptions is primarily a slave or a menial servant—and secondarily a prostitute.[21] The conception of the *aṭiyāḷ* is predicated on relationship; in contrast, the idea of the *dāsī* is centered more on status and function. Although the male term *dāsa* increasingly takes on devotional connotations in North Indian and Sanskrit usage, it is extremely rare to find the term *dāsī* carrying any religious significance. For example, inscriptions and literature of the fourth to sixth centuries indicate that Brahmans, kings, and other men of high social standing bore such names as Varāhadāsa, Viṣṇudāsa, Kālidāsa, and Buddhadāsa, indicative of their religious identities (Kane 1930, 2:251; Jaiswal 1967, 113; T. Sharma 1978, 41, 51, 48, 60, 66, 71–72, 107–112; EZ 4.13). But the women in Sanskrit literature that bear *dāsī* names—Puṣpadāsī, Caraṇadāsī, Rāmadāsī, and Pradyumnadāsī—are prostitutes, not devotees.[22]

This semantic split along gender lines, evident in the case of *dāsī* and *dāsa*, is absent for *aṭiyāḷ* and *aṭiyāṉ*, where the shared range of meanings is demonstrated by their use in medieval Tamil inscriptions, as we have seen. Even the particular ethos associated with the Sanskrit term *dāsī* seems absent from the Tamil context. In the early Tamil *puṟam* literature, concerned with the affairs of kings and chiefs, we do not find royal courts filled with *dāsīs* or the king's generosity praised because of his gifts of women as we do in the Buddhist, Epic, and Puranic literature of the North. Later, in the Chola period, the literature and inscriptions that describe the activities and charities of the Chola kings do not depict these rulers as being surrounded by large groups of slave women, prostitutes, or serving women nor as making gifts of such women—in contrast to their contemporaries in North India.[23] The differences between the Tamil and North Indian cultural milieux reinforced the distinctiveness of the conceptualization and usage of the two terms *aṭiyāḷ* and *dāsī*.

The devotional connotations that *aṭiyāḷ* inherited from the earlier *bhakti* era were enhanced even further in the Chola period when this word was compounded with *tevar*. *Tevaraṭiyār* (or a synonym) is the term most frequently used to designate temple women, and in the course of the Chola period, the frequency with which temple women are referred to by this term increases (see table 2.5).[24] In the first subperiod, only 25 percent of the inscriptions that refer to temple women use the term *tevaraṭiyār*, and in the second subperiod, 30 percent use this term for temple women. In the third subperiod, however, the proportion rises to over two-thirds (68 percent), and in the last subperiod, the figure is 56 percent.

Not only are temple women increasingly referred to as *tevaraṭiyār* in the course of the Chola period, with a particularly marked leap between the second and third subperiods, but also the term is increasingly applied specifically to individual women rather than to groups of devotees, which may or may not have included women. In the early Chola period, groups of *tevaraṭiyār* are mentioned in the inscriptions as recipients of food offered in the temple (just as in the case of *aṭiyār*), as receiving support from the temple, or as performers of ritual or administrative tasks for the temple. For example, a tenth-century inscription from Uttaramerur in Chingleput district makes the *tevaraṭiyār* responsible for collecting a fine if the sheep donated to the temple by a Chola queen are not properly tended (SII 3.195). I suspect that at least some of these groups did include women because when the term *tevaraṭiyār* is used to refer to individuals, it is applied far more frequently to women than it is to men, even at the beginning of the Chola period, and because in a few cases the female character of groups of *tevaraṭiyār* who received support from or performed services in the temple is specifically mentioned.[25] But the individual and female character of *tevaraṭiyār* is increasingly emphasized in the course of the Chola period. The pattern is very striking: of the twelve inscriptions that refer to *tevaraṭiyār* in the first subperiod (see table 2.5), only four (a third) apply the term to individual women; in the second subperiod, the proportion is six out of twelve (a half); in the third subperiod, 43 out of 55 (over three-quarters); and in the last subperiod, 68 out of 75 (91 percent). Although *tevaraṭiyār* was used in the earlier inscriptions to signify "devotees" in a rather general and eclectic way, this term had, by the end of the Chola period, come to have a much more narrow—and exclusively feminine—field of application.

The frequency with which the term *tevaraṭiyār* was used to refer to anonymous groups of devotees, of unspecified gender, who were fed or supported by the temple or who took charge of temple affairs in various ways declined dramatically in the course of the Chola period. Concommitant with the increasing definition of the *tevaraṭiyār* as an individual and as a temple woman were shifts in the ways in which such devotees and their activities and authority were defined and acknowledged. The inscriptions reflect two types of developments: a new nomenclature for devotees in groups engaged in temple management or receiving food offerings, which laid more stress on sectarian identity, and an expanding recognition of individuals in administrative roles, which emphasized a more exclusively male identity.[26]

Groups of "honored devotees" were referred to less and less frequently as *tevaraṭiyār*, and instead were referred to by such terms as *māheśvara*, *śivabrāhmaṇa*, and *śrīvaiṣṇava*. And individual men, who were not called *tevaraṭiyār*, were increasingly affiliated with temple affairs in ways that individual women, who were referred to as *tevaraṭiyār*, were not. But the term *tevaraṭiyār* nonetheless continued to carry honorific connotations and to be used in contexts that demonstrated the high status of those women to whom it was applied.

In large part these were donors or the relatives of donors. That the records of *tevaraṭiyār*'s gifts were inscribed on temple walls indicates that they had access to wealth and that their patronage received public and official recognition from the temple authorities. The use of the term *tevaraṭiyār* for these women may be itself regarded as a marker of their social standing and this ritual recognition. The fact that other donors identified themselves for posterity as the daughters, the sons or grandsons, the sisters, or the brothers of female *tevaraṭiyār* also indicates that the term was linked to high ritual or social status, which the *tevaraṭiyār*'s relatives were anxious to highlight rather than to hide. The roles of donor and relative of donor were much more prominent among *tevaraṭiyār* of the later Chola period than they were in the earlier period. Of the 24 early Chola period references to *tevaraṭiyār*, in only 7, or less than a third, did the *tevaraṭiyār* act in the role of donor or relative of a donor. In the 130 inscriptions dating from the later Chola period, 95, or nearly three-quarters, of *tevaraṭiyār* had one of these two roles.

Tevaraṭiyār in the later Chola period are involved in one type of donation that is of particular interest, which I term making "deals" with the temple—acquiring the right to perform some task in the temple or to receive support from the temple as a direct consequence of providing a gift to the temple. Twelve inscriptions from the later Chola period mention that *tevaraṭiyār* were engaged in this kind of transaction. For example, there are five inscriptions from Nallur in South Arcot district that record how the temple received gold from a number of different female *tevaraṭiyār* and, in exchange, assigned to them the various tasks of performing song and dance at a festival and of singing portions of the sacred hymn *Tiruvempāvai* as part of the temple ritual, as well as granting them the privilege of having precedence in festival processions (ARE 143, 144, 149, 160, and 161 of 1940–41; cf. NK 134, translated in chapter 1). Such deals are not recorded until the later Chola period and they almost invariably involve women, many of whom are referred to as *tevaraṭiyār*. Was becoming a *tevaraṭiyār*, gaining the right to use the honorific term "devotee" to identify oneself, a part of the deal? As men with special status or privilege in the temple were referred to less and less as *tevaraṭiyār*, and their identities were increasingly defined as masculine or in terms of groups (*māheśvaras*, *śivabrāhmaṇas*, and *śrīvaiṣṇavas*) from which women were excluded,[27] were women carving out another type of identity as "devotee" through their activities as temple patrons?

Tamil Terminology: Daughters of God

In the eleventh year of Ko Parakesaripaṉmar, Nakkaṉ Piratamātevi alias Mumuṭicoḻat-talaikkoli, a temple woman (*tevaṉār makaḷ*) (literally, "daughter of God") of Śrī Ārūr, gave gold to [the deity] Tiruvaṉantīśvarattu Paramasvāmi of Śrīviranārāyaṇac-caturvvetimaṅkalam, a *brahmadeyam* on the northern bank, for one perpetual lamp.

The temple managers (*śrīkāriyañ ceyvār*) will be responsible for burning [the lamp] by supplying to the temple 1 *uḻakku* of oil daily, for as long as the moon and the sun shall shine. She [also] donated a standing lamp.

—SII 19.283: this inscription was engraved in the tenth century at the Anantīśvara temple in Udaiyargudi, South Arcot district.

Tevaraṭiyār is by far the most common term for temple women, particularly in the later Chola period, but in the earliest inscriptions the term *tevaṉār makaḷ*, "daughter of God," is more frequently encountered. Although this term appears in only 8 percent of all references to temple women in Chola period inscriptions, it is used in over a third of the inscriptions of the first subperiod (see table 2.5). It is in especially common use in the core Chola region (Tanjavur and Tiruchirappalli districts) and in North Arcot district.

We also find in early Chola period inscriptions the parallel masculine term *tevaṉār makaṉ*, "son of God," although it is less frequently used than its feminine counterpart.[28] Given the gender-specificity of *makaḷ* ("daughter") and *makaṉ* ("son"), even in their plural forms, there are many fewer problems in determining the sex of those to whom these terms are applied than in the case of the term *tevaraṭiyār*. But we run into another kind of difficulty: the problem of ascertaining whether the *tevaṉār* was human or divine. In Chola period inscriptions, terms that mean "lord"—such as *tevar*, *tevaṉār*, *uṭaiyār*, and *āḻvār*—may be applied both to kings and human lords and to deities. Other words, like the prefix *tiru*, meaning "eminent" or "holy," may similarly be used in connection with the speech, meals, baths, and buildings of both kings and gods. Potentially, therefore, a *tevaṉār makaḷ* might be either a "daughter of God" or the daughter of a king or local chief. For the most part, however, clues from within the inscription or from other inscriptions of the same place allow us to determine whether the *tevaṉār* was a man or a god[29]—and in virtually every case, *tevaṉār makaḷ* refers to a woman who was a "daughter of God."

The twenty-four inscriptions that refer to temple women as *tevaṉār makaḷs* are records of the gifts of these women or their relatives in all but two cases. In one of these, the inscription is too fragmentary to make out more than a few names, and the other, which is also fragmentary, seems to be a record of the assignment of shares (*paṅku*) in temple property to a *tevaṉār makaḷ*, among others, at Tiruvidaimarudur in Tanjavur district (SII 19.92A). The fact that *tevaṉār makaḷ* (and its male equivalent, *tevaṉār makaṉ*) was most frequently applied to donors or the relatives of donors points to its association with people of high social and economic standing and its honorific character, just as we have seen for the term *tevaraṭiyār* in the later Chola period. In fact, the way in which *tevaṉār makaḷ* was used in the early Chola period, particularly the first subperiod—for individual, named temple women who acted in donative roles—seems to anticipate the use of the term *tevaraṭiyār* in the later period. A comparison of the early use of *tevaṉār makaḷ* with the later use of *tevaraṭiyār* also highlights the shift that took place between the earlier and later Chola periods, from the shared use by men and women of honorific terms with religious connotations in the earlier period toward more gender-specificity in the later period.

In the case of *tevaṉār makaḷ*, it hardly seems necessary to examine the context of its application to demonstrate its honorific character. The meaning of the term clearly points to the notion of divine favor and intimate relationship with God. We occasionally find elsewhere in Chola period inscriptions other ways in which this special recognition of being regarded as the child of God is expressed; for example, a palace man, one of the companions (*aṇukkar*) of the Chola king, is referred to by the god Vītiviṭaṅkaṉ of Tiruvarur as "our son" (*nammakkaḷ*) in a twelfth-century record purportedly issued by the deity (SII 17.593).[30] Here and with the term *tevaṉār makaḷ*, as we have also seen in the case of *tevaraṭiyār*, the devotee's privileged connection is not with the transcendent god Śiva or Viṣṇu but with a particular deity dwelling in a specific location. And, it is interesting that references to *tevaṉār makaḷs* (and *makaṉs*) are especially concentrated at a few sites—at Tiruvidaimarudur and Tiruchatturai in Tanjavur district, and at Takkolam in North Arcot district.[31] It would seem that not every temple deity condescended to designate his special devotees as his daughters and sons.

It has been suggested that temple women in the Chola period were considered to be daughters of the deity because they could not trace their paternal line. Subbarayalu, for example, says of the temple women of the Tanjavur temple: "They had all one and the same 'father' . . . the god Śiva himself. For, the poor girls could not point to their 'genitor', though they had all rights to claim the supreme god as their 'pater'" (1976, Chap. 7). This interpretation seems to be based on nineteenth- and twentieth-century images of the *devadāsī*, which stress her character as a prostitute and the custom of her "marriage" to the temple deity. The logic is, then, that the offspring of the *devadāsī*, uncertain of their true paternity, would consider the deity to be their father. This logic, however, does not seem to have been relevant to temple women even in recent history.[32] In the Chola period, there is even less justification for considering the use of a term that means "daughter of God" to be a confession of problematic parentage. It is evident, from its use in the inscriptions, that it has an honorific character. Furthermore, because there is nothing in the inscriptions to indicate that the idea or the practice of marriage to God was part of the definition of a temple woman, it seems that the significance of the term ought to be considered more in the light of its literal meaning, "daughter of God," than as being linked to the later conception of temple women as the "wives of God" (Marglin 1985b; Kersenboom 1987).

The identification of temple women in the early Chola period as *tevaṉār makaḷs*, "daughters of God," is evocative of the *bhakti* ethos of the preceding centuries. The Āḻvārs and Nāyaṉmārs describe the relationship between devotee and God by referring to a variety of human relationships (Young 1978, 23, 26–27). Although recent scholarship on the Tamil *bhakti* hymns has focused on the relationship of lover and beloved,[33] other kinds of relationships, including that between parent and child, may be equally important in the theological imagination and expression of the *bhakti* poets.[34] The romantic or erotic devotional ethos is not nearly as prominent in the Śaiva literature as it is for the Vaiṣṇavas; the Śaiva poet-saints are more likely to address God as "father" than as "beloved" (see, e.g., Yocum 1982, 90). It is, perhaps, no coincidence that all the *tevaṉār makaḷs* and *makaṉs* mentioned in Chola period inscriptions appear to be associated with temples dedicated to Śiva. Given the dominance and popularity of Śaivism and the widespread liturgical use of Śaiva *bhakti* literature in the Chola period, we might expect that the Śaiva poet-saints' notion of the devotees as God's sons and daughters had some impact on religious ideas and was significant in shaping the meaning of the term *tevaṉār makaḷ*.

Tamil Terminology: Temple Women

> In the sixth year of the reign of Vikkiramcoḻatevar, Nakkaṉ Cāṇi, the daughter of Kām. . . . ḷi, a temple woman (*taḷiyilāḷ*) of Tiruvekampam Uṭaiyār of Kāñcipuram in Toṇṭaināṭu alias Jayaṅkoṇṭacoḻamaṇṭalam, remitted 5 *kācu* to the [temple] treasury, the interest from which was to be used for burning a perpetual lamp, as long as the moon and sun shall shine, for Lord Tiruviṭaimaruṭaiyār.
>
> May the *paṉmāheśvarar* protect this gift.
>
> A lamp was also given.
>
> —SII 5.701: this inscription was engraved in A.D. 1124 at the Mahāliṅgasvāmi temple in Tiruvidaimarudur, Tanjavur district.

Eighteen Chola period inscriptions use terms that mean "temple woman" or "those of the temple" (see table 2.5). These terms—*taḷiyār*, *taḷiyilār*, *patiyār*, and *patiyilār*—like *tevaraṭiyār* and *tevaṉār makaḷ*, are linked to the definition of temple women outlined at the beginning of this chapter. Like *tevaraṭiyār*, these terms are most frequently found in the plural form, which obscures gender; the singular feminine *taḷiyilāḷ* and *patiyilāḷ* are occasionally encountered but not the singular masculine forms. These terms are formed by the addition to a word for "temple" (*taḷi* or *pati*) of the personal ending (plural *-ār*), with or without the locative infix *il*.[35] The terms *patiyār* and *patiyilār* are more commonly used (in thirteen inscriptions) than *taḷiyār* and *taḷiyilār* and are found particularly in inscriptions of the thirteenth century. The *pati/taḷi* ("temple") terms are not distributed evenly throughout Tamilnadu; their use is especially concentrated in three rather disparate localities—Tirunelveli district in the far south, Tanjavur district in the Chola country, and Chingleput district in the far north.

The pattern of use of these "temple" terms closely resembles the case of *tevaraṭiyār*: in the early Chola period, the terms are applied to groups of devotees, and in the later Chola period, to individual women. Six of the eighteen inscriptions using these terms are from the early Chola period, and in five of these six, "those of the temple" are members of anonymous corporate groups. There are, for example, references to the support of *patiyār* as temple servants or to the offering of food to *patiyār*, a reference to *taḷiyār* acting as parties to an agreement concerning a property transaction, and another inscription that mentions that the *taḷiyilār* are to provide song and dance in the temple. The only case in which an individual identity emerges in the early Chola period is in an inscription in which a particular woman, a *patiyilāḷ*, is named as one of the four *patiyār* who are among the overseers (*kaṇkāṇi*) of a royal endowment (SII 5.520).

Of the twelve inscriptions of the later Chola period in which "temple" terms are used, only two refer to groups rather than individuals. One of these details the arrangements made for the dance performance of the *patiyilār* (SII 8.333) and the other mentions that a group of *taḷiyār tevaraṭiyār* were to sing in the temple (SII 5.705). The ten inscriptions that mention individuals by name include two that similarly suggest temple service: one mentions the provision of support by the temple to two female *taḷiyilār* (EC 10.Kl121), and the other records that King Rajaraja III issued an order after having seen *akamāṟkam* (a form of song or dance) performed by one of the *patiyilār* at the temple on a festival day (SITI 520).

Eight, or all the rest of the later Chola period inscriptions that refer to *patiyār*, *patiyilār*, *taḷiyār*, or *taḷiyilār*, use these terms to designate individual women who themselves, or whose relatives, made gifts to the temple or acted as land sellers. One of these inscriptions (SII 5.707) indicates that the term *patiyilār* might have been conferred as an honorary title. This inscription records a donation made by Ariyapirāṭṭi Utaiyap-perumāḷ, a woman who is identified both as one of the *patiyilār* of Rājarājīśvaram (probably the great temple of Tanjavur) and as one of the *paṇimūppimār* of the western row of houses (*tirumāḷikai*) outside the first enclosing wall (*prākāra*) of the temple of the Lord of Tiruvidaimarudur, to whom her donation was made.[36] That a woman described in terms of her residence in the immediate proximity of the temple at Tiruvidaimarudur should also be identified as one of the *patiyilār* of another temple suggests that the term *patiyilār* did not carry the sense of an exclusive relationship of devotion or service to a particular deity but that it was possible to gain recognition as one of "those of the temple" from several different temples.

Another of the late Chola period inscriptions that records the gifts of *patiyilār* similarly points to the honorary character of this term (ARE 468 of 1916). This is a record from the Arikeśanātha temple at Giriyambapuram in Tirunelveli district, which describes a deal made by Nakkaṉ Ceṇṭāḻvi alias Vīrābharaṇa-talaikkoli, "one of the *patiyilār* of this temple," who, having constructed and endowed a goddess shrine, received shares in the temple property from the *śivabrāhmaṇas*. In this case, it seems quite possible that Nakkaṉ Ceṇṭāḻvi was, in exchange for her patronage of the temple, granted not only the right of support from the temple but also the right to be acknowledged as "one of the *patiyilār* of this temple." She may also have been, in consequence of her charitable acts, given sanction to use the title *talaikkoli* as part of her name.

In Chola period inscriptions, the title *talaikkoli* is found only in the names of temple women, and it is borne by virtually every woman who is said to be a *patiyilār*; of the thirteen *patiyilār* who are named in the inscriptions, twelve have *talaikkoli* as part of their names.[37] The title is formed by the addition of the feminine suffix *-i* to *talai*, meaning "head; that which is first, best, highest; or person of highest quality and rank," and *kōl*, meaning "rod, stick; branch; staff; or sceptre" (MTL, 1774, 1194; Agesthialingom and Shanmugam 1970, 106), producing a word that means something like "she of the illustrious staff." The Tamil epic *Cilappatikāram*, written some centuries before the Chola period, uses the word *talaikkōl* to signify both a scepter that represents Chola sovereignty and a title, evidently bestowed by the Chola king, that was granted to women skilled in dance.[38] In the usage of Chola period inscriptions, we see a continuation of the honorific significance of the term *talaikkoli*, but the links with royalty and skill in dance seem somewhat attentuated. As we have seen, several of the inscriptions with the terms *patiyār*, *patiyilār*, *taḷiyār*, or *taḷiyilār* apply them to people said to perform song or dance; in one of these (SITI 520), the *patiyilār* is named and bears the title *talaikkoli*. In two other inscriptions (SII 17.593 and SII 17.606), in which the "temple" terms are not used, *talaikkoli* is part of the names of dancers.

But far more frequently these terms and this title are used for people with other functions and other kinds of connections to the temple—for the most part, for women who acted as temple patrons. And if the connection with Chola royal authority is the key to the importance of the title *talaikkōl* in *Cilappatikāram*, it is the connection with the temple that is most significant in the case of the *talaikkoli* titles borne by Chola period temple women. That these women were granted the right to bear these titles by the temple and not by the Chola ruler is indicated by the fact that their *talaikkoli* titles were more often suffixed to the name of a deity (e.g., Tillaināyakat-talaikkoli, "she of the illustrious staff of the Lord of Tillai") than to the name of a king, that most *talaikkoli* titles were held by temple women from outside the core Chola region, and that *talaikkoli* titles were borne exclusively by temple women. If the title *talaikkōl* in *Cilappatikāram* was a mark of royal recognition for a woman's skill in dance, the *talaikkoli* titles borne by Chola period temple women seem rather to acknowledge a woman's special status as a devotee of a temple and to indicate her eligibility to participate in temple affairs or temple ritual. The context of most of the inscriptional references to the name *talaikkoli* and the terms *patiyilār* and *taḷiyilār* suggests that the acquisition of these titles, with their concommitant rank and privileges in the temple, was linked to the temple woman's activity as a temple patron.

This chapter began with a consideration of the coherence and distinctiveness of the category of the temple woman in medieval Tamilnadu. We saw that the coherence of this category, which increased in the course of the Chola period, rested on the overlapping of two definitional features, being "of the temple," and working in or being supported by the temple, with a third definitional feature, being referred to by one of a set of "temple woman" terms. These terms—*tevaraṭiyār*, *tevaṉār makaḷ*, *patiyilār*, and *taḷiyilār*—are at the core of the definition, and the salience, of the category. It is appropriate, therefore, having completed our survey of these terms, to compare their significance and application to determine whether the category of temple women is homogeneous or whether, as has been suggested,[39] these terms apply to separate and distinguishable groups within the broader category of temple woman.

The "temple woman" terms used in medieval Tamil inscriptions closely resemble one another—and are distinct from the terms in inscriptional use outside of Tamilnadu—with respect to their honorific and devotional meanings. All of these terms convey the idea of a privileged relationship with a temple deity. *Tevaraṭiyār* and *tevaṉār makaḷ* carry religious connotations derived from the *bhakti* idiom of the Āḻvārs and Nāyaṉmārs of the pre-Chola period, in their identification of temple women as "devotees" and "daughters of God." All of the terms underscore the fact of relationship with a particular temple deity rather than with a sectarian community.

There is also consistency among all the "temple woman" terms in their application. The activities of *tevaraṭiyār* are not substantially different from those of *tevaṉār makaḷs*, *patiyilār*, or *taḷiyilār*. All of these terms were most commonly used to refer to women who made temple donations or who were the relatives of donors. In the early Chola period, this was especially the case for *tevaṉār makaḷs*; as this term fell out of use in the later Chola period, we find the increasing application of the terms *tevaraṭiyār*, *patiyilār*, and *taḷiyilār* to individual women named in the inscriptions as temple patrons. None of these terms is linked, in application or in meaning, with any particular function or role; they are, instead, markers of status. Increasing numbers of women were referred to by these terms; they were identified as donors and their "temple woman" status was acknowledged by the temple. Temple women were also involved in deals, in which donations were exchanged for position and privilege—and perhaps for the title of "temple woman" itself. In many ways the acquisition of the status associated with these terms seems to be tied to temple women's donative activities, and it is to an examination of these activities that we turn in the next chapter.

THREE

Temple Women as Temple Patrons

Property and Piety: Women and the Temple

Temple Women and Other Donors

In the fourth year of the reign of Ko Virājakecaripaṉmar, Centaṉ Ceyyavāymaṇi, a temple woman (*tevaraṭiyāḷ*) of Tiruvaraṅkam, gave 10 *kaḻañcu* of gold to the Mahādevar (Great God) of Teṉkailāyam in Śrīkaṇṭa-caturvvetimaṅkalam, for one twilight lamp and one pot of river water for offerings daily.

This 10 *kaḻañcu* of gold was received by the Lord of the holy temple. Thus we, the worshipers (*upāsakar*) at this holy temple, will be responsible for this grant as long as the moon and stars shall shine. May the *paṉmāheśvarar* protect this endowment.

—SII 13.88: this inscription was probably engraved in A.D. 875 at the Pipīlikeśvara temple in Tiruverumbur, Tiruchirappalli district.

In the ninth year of the reign of Tiripuvaṉaccakuravarttikaḷ Śrī Rājādhirājadevar—since in previous years there had not been engraved records of the various gifts of perpetual lamps made to Lord Tiru Oṟṟiyūr Uṭaiyār of Puḻaṟkoṭṭam in Jayaṅkoṇṭacoḻamaṇṭalam—a record was inscribed that was seen in the registry of the temple accountant Tiru Oṟṟiyūr Uṭaiyāṉ Uṟavākkiṉāṉ [which said that] Cāṇi Oṟṟiāḻvi, a temple woman (*tevaraṭiyāḷ*) of this temple, gave to Lord Tiru Oṟṟiyūr Uṭaiyār 32 cows to maintain one perpetual lamp [and that] Paṭampakūṉ Vallamuṭaiyāṉ, one of the shepherds (*maṉṟāṭikaḷ*) of Tiripuvaṉacuntara street of the "lamp group" (*tiruviḷakku kuṭi*) of this god, was to [tend the cows and] supply 114 *nāḻi* of ghee.

We undertake thus to measure out 114 *nāḻi* with the *perāyiram oṟṟi* measure [named after the deity] and bring the ghee.

—SII 5.1360: this inscription was engraved in A.D. 1172 at the Ādhipurīśvara temple in Tiruvorriyur, Chingleput district.

The role of temple women most frequently seen in Chola period inscriptions is that of donor to the temple. Of the 304 inscriptions that mention temple women, 112 (37 percent) describe them as having this role; when we add the 21 inscriptions that describe temple women as making deals—exchanging gifts for privileges and functions in the temple—we have a total of 133 inscriptions (44 percent of the total) that record the gifts of temple women to the temple (see table 3.1). This role is the most prominent one by far for temple women in all four subperiods. It is especially important in the third subperiod, when 56 percent of all inscriptions that mention temple women describe them as making gifts to the temple. In the fourth subperiod, the figure is 41 percent, but another 21 percent refer to temple women as the relatives of donors. Apart from the role of temple patron, the next most commonly mentioned role for temple women is that of temple servant, but this role is mentioned on the average only half as frequently as that of donor.

Temple women's gifts, in substance and value, were very similar to those of other kinds of donors. Most of the gifts recorded in inscriptions of the early Chola period were in support of perpetual lamps to be burned in the temple. In the later Chola period, endowments for support of lamps contin-

Table 3.1 Chronological distribution of the roles of temple women

Role	Subperiod 1 (850–985)	Subperiod 2 (985–1070)	Subperiod 3 (1070–1178)	Subperiod 4 (1178–1300)	Total
Donor	19 40%	13 32%	38 47%	42 31%	112 37%
Deal	—	—	7 9%	14 10%	21 7%
Relative of donor	3 6%	5 12%	2 2%	28 21%	38 12%
Temple service	11 23%	9 22%	16 20%	22 16%	58 19%
Responsibility function	9 19%	3 8%	2 2%	10 7%	24 8%
Slave	1 2%	1 2%	6 7%	13 10%	21 7%
Offered food	5 10%	7 18%	10 12%	1 1%	23 8%
Other	2 4%	2 5%	2 2%	6 4%	12 4%
Total	50	40	83	136	309
Total number of inscriptions	48	40	81	135	304

The percentages represent the proportion of inscriptions that specify a given role in each subperiod out of the total number of inscriptions that refer to temple women in that subperiod.

ued, but gifts were also made to support daily or festival services or temple personnel or to help build temples or install images. We do not see any differences among the various types of donors—queens, palace women, temple women, Brahman women, Brahman men, local lords, merchants, and so forth—in the object of donation nor in the apparent value of their gifts. It is difficult to determine the relative value of the various gifts of land, livestock, gold, jewelry, and gold or currency in different times and places, but the range does not appear to be very great, nor are there many donors whose generosity is especially conspicuous.[1]

It is perhaps not very surprising that the role of donor for temple women should be so often mentioned in Chola period inscriptions, which, after all, are primarily the records of gifts to the temple. The fact that temple women frequently acted as temple patrons and that their gifts resembled those of other donors would not be in the least remarkable, except that these facts distinguish temple women from those groups with whom we would expect them to be most similar—other women and temple men.

I define temple men in a way that parallels my definition of temple women: they are men described by the inscriptions as being "of the temple" or as receiving support from or performing some function in the temple. A wide range of terms is applied to temple men; the inscriptions mention *śivabrāhmaṇas*, *śrīmāheśvaras*, *vaikhānasas*, *tevarkaṉmikaḷ* (temple servants), *kaṇakkar* (accountants), *maṉṟāṭis* (shepherds), *uvaccar* (drummers), *taccar* (carpenters), and *arccippār* (priests), among others. Thus the definition of a temple man does not center around a set of particular terms, as is the case for the temple woman, and the range of terms used for temple men is indicative of the heterogeneous character of this group. Temple men are much more frequently mentioned than temple women in Chola period inscriptions. Of the 2,027 people named in inscriptions of the four study areas, 219, or over 10 percent, are temple men.[2]

But temple men's visibility in the inscriptions has very little to do with their activity as donors. Table 3.2 shows the involvement of different sorts of donors in temple patronage, indicating the extent to which temple men, women in general, and men in general were named as donors in inscriptions of the four study areas (the figures for temple women are drawn from the corpus of Chola period inscriptions as a whole). Only 3 of the 219 temple men named, a mere 1 percent, were identified as temple patrons.[3] In contrast, 99 of the 238 temple women named, 42 percent, were so identified.

If very few temple men appear in the inscriptions as donors, other types of men are represented as temple patrons. Close to half of Chola period donations were made by men who were represented as landowners or who, given the kinds of titles they bear, may be considered local notables or lords. Thirteen percent of male donors in the four study areas were Brahmans and 8 percent were merchants. Kings or other royal figures constitute less than 1 percent of male donors.

Most donors were male, but there are many records of women's gifts to Hindu temples. In the four study areas taken together, 17 percent of the do-

Table 3.2 Donative activities of different kinds of donors in each of the four subperiods

	Subperiod 1 (850–985)	Subperiod 2 (985–1070)	Subperiod 3 (1070–1178)	Subperiod 4 (1178–1300)	Total Donors	Total Names
Temple women	25 25%	9 9%	27 27%	38 38%	99 100%	238
Temple men	—	—	2 67%	1 33%	3 100%	219
Women	47 53%	19 21%	16 18%	7 8%	89 100%	134
Men	176 41%	58 13%	99 23%	98 23%	431 100%	1893

These figures represent the numbers of individuals named in the four study areas, except for the top row of figures, for temple women, which comes from the corpus of Chola period inscriptions as a whole (excluding SII 2.66). The percentages represent the proportion of donors of each group whose gifts were made in a particular subperiod out of donors of that group in the whole of the Chola period.

nors were women; this proportion was as high as 25 percent in the second subperiod and declined to 7 percent in the last subperiod. About a quarter of the female donors in the four study areas were queens, and another 13 percent were palace women; these two types of women were especially active as donors in the the second subperiod and in Kumbakonam taluk in Tanjavur district. Brahman women account for 11 percent of the female donors, and various other kinds of women make up the rest of the group.[4]

Temple women appear as donors in increasing numbers in the course of the Chola period, but women in general are less and less in evidence. This contrast is shown in table 3.2: three-quarters of all gifts made by women in general were made in the early Chola period, whereas three-quarters of all gifts made by temple women were made in the later Chola period.[5] The first subperiod was the period in which women in general were most active as donors; this activity declined drastically in the second subperiod and continued to decrease through the later Chola period. The activity of men generally follows a similar pattern, except that after a steep decline in the second subperiod, men's donations picked up again, to some extent, in the later Chola period. Temple women, in contrast, were not particularly active as donors in the first subperiod, but this activity was increasingly in evidence through the later Chola period, rising steadily and steeply after the second subperiod.

That there was in the second subperiod a decline in the number of donations made by all groups of people—men, women, and temple women—suggests a development that had a dampening effect on temple patronage for a wide range of potential donors. Perhaps opportunities for donors to participate in the affairs and the rituals of temples were reduced because of changes in the temples' institutional structure. As hierarchies of temple authorities—priests, teachers, sectarian leaders, and functionaries—came to be established in Hindu temples throughout Tamilnadu, and as interest in certain temples on the part of Chola kings may have introduced new political complexities, temples might not have welcomed gifts made with the expectation that the donor would become involved in temple affairs as a consequence. This may have been particularly true in the case of potential donors who were female.[6] If such changes in temple organization and temple politics may, for a time, have discouraged patronage, a readjustment seems to have been made, so that various individuals were again motivated to make gifts to temples and temples were eager to acknowledge them. But the previous level of donations by women—except for temple women—was never restored. Relations between donors and temples seem to have been resumed on a somewhat different footing, in which women's participation in the public affairs of temple life was evidently more restricted. Temple women, however, demonstrate an increasing engagement with the temple in the course of the Chola period. Whatever the character of the new types of connections that were established between the temple and the community, temple women seem to have been able to participate in this network of linkages in a way that other women were not.

The differences between the chronological pattern of temple women's donations and the patterns for other kinds of women are particularly marked when we compare temple women to royal women, including both queens and palace women. Of the thirty-nine royal women who made gifts to temples in the four study areas, only one did so in the later Chola period. The steep decline in the number of royal women's donations, from the middle of the eleventh century, is evident throughout the Tamil country (Orr 1992; 1999).

This comparison reveals differences not only in chronological patterns but in geographical ones as well. Royal women's patronage was concentrated in the core Chola region; most of their gifts were made to temples in Tanjavur and Tiruchirappalli districts.[7] In contrast, temple women's gifts were distributed throughout the whole of the Tamil country. If there is any focus of concentration for their donations, it is Chingleput district, where over a quarter of their gifts were made.[8] Queens and palace women followed one another's examples in their choices of temples to endow: queens modeled themselves after other queens and sometimes palace women, and palace women followed the example of queens (Orr 1992). Particular temples received numerous gifts from queens; temple women's donations were dispersed more diffusely.[9]

In contrast to the pattern for royal women, in which specific temples came to be the recipients of gifts in a kind of bandwagon effect, there seems to have been no group strategy on the part of temple women that rested on consistent or cumulative patronage of a single temple. Chola royal women, on the one hand, as a result of the mutually reinforcing donative style they adopted, may have acquired considerable local influence through their gifts to specific temples—although, as we have seen, their donations and their influence did not continue into the later Chola period. Temple women, on the other hand, did not act in concert with one another in their patronage of temples, but as individuals—and, as time passed, were increasingly implicated in the life of numerous temples throughout Tamilnadu as a consequence of their donations.

Women's Property Rights: The Special Case of the Temple Woman

In the seventh year of the reign of Sakalabhuvaṉaccakkaravattikaḷ Śrī Avaṉiyāḷappiṟantār alias Ko Peruñciṅkatevar, the order of Coḻa Koṉ was seen and sent forth by Teṉṉavaṉ Brahmamārāyar, Jayatuṅkapallavaraiyar, Tillaiampalapallavaraiyar, the *śrīmāheśvara* supervisors of the temple of Lord Tirucciṟṟampalamuṭaiyār, the temple managers (*śrīkāriyañ ceyvārkaḷ*), the *sāmutāyañ ceyvārkaḷ*, the *koyilnāyakañ ceyvārkaḷ*, the *tirumāḷikaikkūṟu ceyvārkaḷ*, and the accountants:

Piḷḷaiyār Ciṟṟiṭai Arivai, one of the temple women (*tevaraṭiyār*), bought 1 *mā* of *ūrppaṭi* land, in the name [through the agency] of Kavuṇiyaṉ Tirucciṟṟampalamuṭaiyāṉ Viṉāyakaṉ, from Uḻaiccāṇaṉ Tirunaṭṭapperumāḷ Civaṉ of Kaṭavācceri, a hamlet of Perumpaṟṟappuliyūr [= Chidambaram], as a gift to the temple, to make a garden for the adornment [of the deity].

She also bought land from the Brahman woman, the wife of Kulottuṅkacoḻa Piramārāyaṉ of Caṇṭeśuranallūr, a hamlet of this village (*ūr*), as a "garden grant" (*tirunantavaṉappuṟam*) to support one man (*āḷ*) to tend the garden. She bought 4 *mā* of *ūrppaṭi* land, which she named Civakāmacuntari viḷākam, from Teṉṉavaṉ Brahmamārāyar of Iḷanāṅkūr, a hamlet of this village.

One *mā* of the *ūrppaṭi* land, of the land called Cirāviḷākam, is to provide for food (*koṟṟu*). She has had made a garden in order to adorn [with flowers] [the goddess] Periyanācciyār, mistress of Tirukkāmakkoṭṭam. She has bought 100 *kuḻi* of land from Tirukkaḷiṟṟupaṭittoṇṭaṉ of Naṭuvilkarai, a hamlet of this village.

She arranged for a "garden grant" (*tirunantavaṉappuṟam*) to support one man (*āḷ*) to tend the garden. She bought 7 *mā* of *ūrppaṭi* land, which she named Cirāviḷākam, from Teṉṉavaṉ Brahmamārāyar of Iḷanāṅkūr, a hamlet of this village, to provide for food (*koṟṟu*) for two men, at the rate of 1 *kuṟuṇi* and 4 *nāḻi* [of paddy] per man per day, who are to supply garlands to the "flower *maṇṭapam*."

This is the deed of sale for the land bought for the garden and as "garden grant" to provide for food. The *mulaparuṣaiyār* (Brahman assembly) of Perumpaṟṟappuliyūr have given the order that the taxes to be remitted on these lands be deposited in the temple treasury. Thus is this inscription made on the temple wall. This is signed and caused to be inscribed here by Coḻa Koṉ.

—SII 12.151: this inscription was engraved in about A.D. 1250 on the north wall of the third *prākāra* of the Nāṭarāja temple in Chidambaram, South Arcot district.

Although the visibility and donative activity of most kinds of women declined in the course of the Chola period, the inscriptions show that women had a much greater public presence and considerably more economic autonomy than would be possible if women in this period had acted in conformity with the norms outlined in the Dharmaśāstras. This literature defines women primarily within the framework of the patrilineal family, as wives whose access to wealth and property were severely restricted; because of her lack of personal resources, a woman's religious activity was assumed to be dependent on the support and permission of her husband.[10] The inscriptions, however, tell a different story.[11] In the record translated above, for example, there is evidence of the engagement of two different types of women—a temple woman and a Brahman woman—in property transactions, with the full acknowledgement of local political and temple authorities and the Brahman assembly and with little interference from male figures. Although the Brahman woman is nameless, identified only as a wife, she is represented as selling her own land as an independent agent, without the mediation or authorization of her husband, father, or son. Piḷḷaiyār Ciṟṟiṭai Arivai, the temple woman, is able, in consequence of her purchase of five plots of land from four different individuals, to sponsor religious activities in the great temple of Chidambaram—the offering of flowers and the adornment of the goddess's image with flowers. In only one of the five property transactions is there the mention of an intermediary, and her donation to the temple is made directly and in her own name.[12]

Women in the Chola period evidently had more access to property and more autonomy in disposing of their property than the normative texts would lead us to expect, but this access and autonomy for most types of women was less than that of men. Table 3.3 indicates the extent of the involvement of women in the ownership and transfer of property relative to that of men in the four study areas. The percentages represent the proportion of people who were women out of all the individuals named in the inscriptions as possessors, sellers, purchasers, or donors of property—currency, livestock, gold, ornaments and furnishings, buildings and images, or land—in each of the four subperiods.

This table shows that only a fraction of these property transactions were undertaken by women. The fact that women are mentioned less frequently than men in this regard suggests that their property rights were not equivalent to those of men. This table also indicates that women's ability to acquire and dispose of wealth was diminished in the course of the Chola period. Women were not, even in the early Chola period, as prominent as men in the arena of property transactions, although they were nearly so in the second subperiod in Kumbakonam taluk of Tanjavur district, because of the activities of palace women and queens; but women's involvement in the possession and transfer of property, relative to men's, declined markedly in the later Chola period, particularly in the last subperiod.

There is, however, actually an increase in the later Chola period in the proportion of women who are described as the owners, donors, buyers, or sellers of land.[13] Many of the women mentioned in inscriptions of the twelfth and thirteenth centuries who possessed or acquired land are either Brahman

Table 3.3 Extent of women's involvement with property in the four study areas

	Chola 1	Chola 2	Chola 3	Chola 4	All subperiods
Kumbakonam taluk (Tanjavur district)	19%	48%	18%	9%	21%
Kulattur taluk (Tiruchirappalli district)	29%	0%	3%	6%	13%
Tirukkoyilur taluk (South Arcot district)	17%	12%	8%	6%	11%
Kanchipuram taluk (Chingleput district)	10%	6%	24%	3%	11%

women or temple women—as is illustrated in the preceding inscription from Chidambaram.[14] This inscription also illustrates another feature of women's involvement in land transactions in the twelfth and thirteenth centuries: the mediation of a male agent. In the Chidambaram inscription, it is a temple woman whose purchase of land is transacted by an intermediary, but more typically it was Brahman women whose land transactions were mediated by agents—often termed *mutukaṉs* ("guardians")—who were frequently their sons or other male relatives.

Even though most of their land transactions were carried out by women themselves, independently of any outside agent or male relative,[15] the appearance of the *mutukaṉ* in this context suggests that there were certain limitations and qualifications of women's property rights, specifically their rights to own land, which may have become increasingly salient in the course of the Chola period. The mixed message we get from the epigraphical evidence—that women had the opportunity to acquire wealth, including land, but that they did not have complete autonomy in the disposition of their property—comes through particularly in the references in the medieval Tamil inscriptions to *strīdhana* (Ta. *citanam*). For example, there are inscriptions in which a woman's son, acting as *mutukaṉ*, is involved in the sale of land that she had acquired as *strīdhana*, property presumably given to her by her natal family at the time of marriage (SII 8.708; SII 19.404). In another case, a woman who was making a gift, for the merit of her son, of the land she had acquired from her father as *strīdhana* had another man acting as *mutukaṉ* (SII 17.604).

These examples suggest that *strīdhana*, "women's wealth," was not entirely under a woman's control and that the male members of her marital family had some interest in the property she acquired from her natal family. In fact, when *strīdhana* is mentioned in Chola period inscriptions, it most often refers to property that belongs to a man. A number of inscriptions indicate clearly that a woman's *strīdhana*—in the form of land or of rights to property (*kāṇi*)—might not be considered hers at all but was under the control of her husband.[16] The transfer of *strīdhana* in the Chola period was more often than not the transfer from one man to another, from a man to his son-in-law, rather than the transfer of property from a mother or a family to a daughter, as described in the Dharmaśāstras.[17] Nor do the Chola period inscriptions give us evidence of women's inheritance of property from their natal families, although I have found two references to inheritance by sons—both of which also mention inheritance by sons-in-law or nephews (*marumakaṉ*) (SII 22.27 and IPS 198).[18]

If on the one hand women in medieval Tamilnadu did not acquire property as daughters, in the form of *strīdhana* or inheritance from their natal families, or had to share control of this property with their husbands and sons, there is, on the other hand evidence that they acquired property rights as wives at the time of their marriage or as a result of their marriage. For example, the junior wife of a Brahman was given land (probably by her husband) on the occasion of her marriage (SII 13.251); another Brahman woman donated articles of her "lesser dowry" (*iḷakku aṅkamaṇi*) to the temple (SII 6.314). A married woman had rights in (and responsibilities toward) the joint property of her husband's household, although this property may in principle have been in the charge of her husband, and she inherited wealth from her husband.[19] Thus the inscriptions indicate that the sources of a woman's property—as well as the restrictions on her control of it—was linked to a woman's status as a wife.

Although women in general, in the course of the Chola period, are less and less visible in the inscriptional record, become less active as donors, and are represented as having decreasing access to and control of property, the reverse is true for temple women. Not only were temple women unique among women in medieval Tamilnadu, in that they constituted a group whose economic activity and autonomy was not reduced in the course of the Chola period, but they were also different from other women in the means by which they acquired property. Access to wealth for most women seems to have been linked to marriage. But Chola period temple women did not marry and, in some cases, traced kinship through the maternal line, rather than being part of a patrilineal family structure. They thus may have acquired property through inheritance from their mothers.[20] Certainly any wealth that temple women received from their natal families would not have passed out of their control, as in the case of the *strīdhana* of married women.

In addition to the possibility of receiving property from their natal families, in the context of a nonpatrilineal kinship system, the arrangements that temple women had with the temple could result in their acquisition of land, houses, clothing, gold, or daily or yearly allowances of food or grain. Even when temple women were not directly supported by the temple, simply having the status of a temple woman may have given them the opportunity to acquire wealth. Connections with a temple—particularly as the temple became increasingly important as a political and economic center of the community—were frequently financially rewarding. We see this in the case of men who became involved with the temple as donors or temple functionaries, and temple women may have reaped similar economic advantages.

We can glean some idea of how the status of temple woman may have served as a magnet for wealth in the Chola period by looking at the economic arrangements in present-day Hindu temples and at the life-style and means of livelihood of temple women in recent times, as described by anthropologists such as Srinivasan and Marglin. Here we see that gifts were made to temple women as exemplary devotees or as individuals having a special connection with the temple. Temple women in recent times received payments for particular services they performed, in the temple or in the course of a temple festival, on behalf of worshipers. They were also paid for professional or ritual tasks performed outside the temple (e.g., celebration of marriages or singing for pilgrims).[21]

In the Chola period, temple women were different from other women both in their relationship to property and in their social identities. These differences are tied to each other: over the course of the Chola period, most women—*because* they were economically, as well as socially, defined by marriage—found themselves in an increasingly weaker position, whereas for temple women the *absence* of a connection to marriage, and the alternative linkage to the temple provided a context in which their economic power was strengthened.[22]

Our understanding of temple women's association with the temple as a type of social and economic definition that parallels the defining structure of marriage for most other women perhaps provides a clue to the origin of the idea that a temple woman is married to God rather than to a mortal husband. This notion and the associated ritual seem to be unknown before the seventeenth century, although in more recent history it is seen, both by *devadāsīs* and by those who have studied them, as perhaps the most important defining feature of their identity and status. But even though Chola period temple women were not in fact married to the temple deity, as later temple women were, there may have been a growing recognition that their relationship with the temple was equivalent to marriage for other women.

It is clear, in any case, that the *distinction* between temple women and women defined by marriage became greater. We have seen, in the previous chapter, that the status of temple woman came to be increasingly well defined in the later Chola period and that there was a rising visibility and highlighting of the individual identity of temple women—whereas other kinds of women were less and less in evidence as actors in the public arena described by the records on temple walls. In the present chapter, I have suggested that the decline in the later Chola period of non-temple women's donative activity was linked to changes in temple organization and temple politics, whereas temple women were able to come to terms with these changes. Their continuing access to property was tied to the fact that their social identities were predicated on relationships with temples rather than with husbands, and they increasingly established and reinforced these relationships through their patronage of the temple.

Patterns of Patronage of Temple Women

Give and Take

On Sunday, in the Aśvati *nakṣatra*, the eighth day in the month of Mīṉa, in the Kollam year 428, Ceṅkoṭaṉ Pūvāṇṭi, a temple woman (*tevaraṭiyāḷ*) of this temple—who had set up the Goddess (Nācciyār) for [the deity] Kuṉṟameṟinta Piḷḷaiyār in the holy temple of Rājendracoḻīśvaramuṭaiyār Mahādeva, Lord of Tirukkoṭṭār alias Mummuticoḻanallūr—gave a total of 20 *accu* (gold coins) for thrice-daily food offerings for this Goddess.

Having received [this money] from her hand, we, the temple servants (*tevarkaṉmikaḷ*) and the *śrīmāheśvara* supervisors of this temple, deposited it in the treasury to provide for offerings, the daily interest being 5 *nāḻi* of paddy, or 2 *nāḻi* of husked rice, for food offerings for the Goddess.

From this paddy, [Ceṅkoṭaṉ Pūvāṇṭi] will measure out on the top of the plank 2 *nāḻi* of rice, and after the food has been offered, we will give her 1 *nāḻi* of the cooked rice daily. On the festival day of the *tīrttam* (bath of the deity), we will give her the *parivaṭṭam* (cloth used in worship). And we will give this 1 *nāḻi* of cooked rice, the *parivaṭṭam*, and the paddy to the descendents (*santāṉapraveśam*) of Ceṅkoṭaṉ Pūvāṇṭi.

Thus we, the temple servants (*tevarkaṉmikaḷ*) and the *śrīmāheśvara* supervisors, having received and deposited in the treasury these 20 *accu*, issue this agreement in stone and copper to Ceṅkoṭaṉ Pūvāṇṭi that the 2 *nāḻi* of rice will be provided [to the Goddess] for as long as the moon and sun shall shine.

—TAS 6.15 (= KK 256): this inscription was engraved in A.D. 1252 at the Coḻīśvaram temple in Cholapuram, Kanyakumari district.

A unique feature of temple women's giving was their involvement in deals with the temple. In these transactions, temple women received, in exchange for a gift, certain rights, privileges, or support from the temple. Twenty-one inscriptions record such interchanges; thus over 15 percent of the records of temple women's donations explicitly mention some type of "return" on their gifts, apart from purely spiritual benefits.

In South Indian inscriptions of the post-Chola period, such deals were often made—by various donors—particularly deals resembling that described in the inscription above, in which donors were granted temple honors in the form of food or other materials sanctified by contact with the temple deity.[23] But in Chola period inscriptions, deals are not at all common. Apart from the twenty-one records of temple women's deals, I have found only six descriptions of deals that men made with the temple and just a single case in which a woman who was not a temple woman was involved in a deal.

Of the twenty-one Chola period inscriptions recording deals made by temple women, all are from the later Chola period: seven are from the third subperiod, and fourteen are from the last subperiod. Thirteen come from the northern, western, or middle regions of Tamilnadu (Chingleput, North

Arcot, South Arcot, and Salem districts), five are from the southern districts, and only three are from the core Chola region. Three of the twenty-one deals resulted in arrangements for the support by the temple of the donating temple woman. But in the other eighteen deals, the consequence of the gift was the receipt of temple honors. In a few cases these honors involved the right to receive some object with which the deity had come into contact or cooked food that had been prepared in the temple (*amutu*, *coṟu*, *coṟṟu*).[24] More frequently, however, the privilege granted was precedence or proximity to the deity in the performance of a ritual task—for example, being assigned a place near the deity in a festival procession or the right to sing portions of the hymn *Tiruvempāvai* before the deity. Ten of the eighteen inscriptions, including the inscription translated above, indicate that the honors granted to temple women were hereditary. Given that in the Chola period there were very few links to the temple that seem to have been hereditary—whether these were associated with a particular status or function in or support from the temple—this characteristic of the privileges acquired by temple women through their deals is of some significance. Another quality of the arrangements that resulted from temple women's deals distinguishes them: whereas temple women's service functions or ritual tasks are ordinarily rather ill defined in Chola period inscriptions, they are exceptionally clearly specified in the case of deals.

Temple women's deals not only outnumber those of other kinds of people—a striking fact because temple women represent only a tiny fraction of the donors mentioned in Chola period inscriptions—but also their deals are of a different character. Men's deals, although they are chronologically situated, like temple women's deals, in the later Chola period, are located differently in terms of geography. Of the six inscriptions recording men's deals, four are from the core Chola region; two are from the south; and none are from the northern, western, and middle regions, where the majority of temple women's deals were made. The single inscription recording the deal of a nontemple woman is, like most of the records of men's deals, from the core Chola region.[25] Whereas the majority of temple women's deals resulted in the receipt of temple honors and only a few in arrangements for the support of temple women, the pattern is reversed in the case of men's deals.[26] Four of the six records of deals made by men describe the establishment by the temple of a means of support for them as a consequence of their donations, and only two inscriptions describe the receipt by male donors of temple honors—in both cases, they were granted the privilege of participation in ritual and proximity to the deity. Another point of difference is that the temple services to be performed by the men in these two cases are quite vaguely defined, in contrast to the detailed specification of ritual tasks in the records of temple women's deals. Furthermore, whereas nearly half of all the deals made by temple women resulted in arrangements with the temple that could be passed on hereditarily, this is true of only one of the six deals made by men.

The deals made by temple women in the Chola period closely resemble in their consequences the transactions that were to become increasingly common in the post-Chola period. Temple women appear to be in the vanguard of a development from which Chola period men were largely excluded in both the extent and the nature of their involvement with deals. To understand why temple women became engaged in this kind of activity so early, it may be useful to consider where it was taking place. Most of their deals were transacted in regions peripheral to the core Chola territory. As Chola power waned in these areas, during the twelfth and thirteenth centuries, temple and local officials may have seized the opportunity to establish themselves as brokers of power and status, using the temple as a base for their authority and using temple honors as a means of creating a network of local linkages—and simultaneously increasing the wealth of the temple by exchanging temple privileges for gifts. In fact, of the eighteen deals negotiated by temple women in exchange for honors, in sixteen the honors were granted by temple or local authorities (*tā<u>n</u>attār*, *tevarka<u>n</u>mikaḷ*, *mahāsabhaiyār*).[27] Political circumstances made such transactions possible, but why were women and not men, temple women and not other women, attracted to this possibility?

The Chola period inscriptions recording deals describe women and men differently. None of the six men who made deals with the temple is identified as a temple man, although in half of these cases (all involving Brahman men), the transaction seems to have resulted in the creation of a position for the man—that is, his transformation into a temple man. In contrast, of the twenty-two women who made deals, only one is not identified as a temple woman; all of the other twenty-one are described as women of the temple. The implication is that these women already had some association with the temple but that by making donations they could enhance their ritual status and increase their opportunity for participation in temple ritual. The main object of these women in making deals, then, seems not to have been to acquire a title or a position but rather to establish themselves in particular ritual roles or to receive honors to which they might not otherwise be entitled. That entitlement to such roles was not primarily conceived of in terms of obtaining support or a sinecure is borne out by what temple women received in exchange for their gifts.

Perhaps more women than men made deals with the temple because women had fewer other means through which links to the temple could be secured and service rights in the temple acquired. There are two routes by which men became associated with the temple to which women evidently did not have access. The first is, rather ironically, the acquisition of position or privileges in the temple through *strīdhana*. As we have seen, *strīdhana* was essentially, in the Chola period, the transmission to a son-in-law of what had been possessed by his father-in-law. That this could include property and position in the temple is made clear in a twelfth-century inscription from North Arcot district (SII 22.235), recording the grant of property rights to a *śivabrāhmaṇa* and his descendents, which notes that such rights were obtainable by gift, by purchase, or by *strīdhana*. It is not difficult to find in the inscriptions examples of the acquisition through *strīdhana*, by both Brahman and non-Brahman men, of the right to serve in such positions as priest, dance master, or drummer.[28] Women, obviously, would not have obtained rights in this manner; nor do we find, in the case of temple women, any indication of parallel types of transfer of rights and privileges, for example, from aunt to niece.

Another way in which temple service rights might be acquired by men, which is mentioned in the inscription just cited, was by purchase. It appears that women were in most cases barred from engaging in this kind of trade. Rights were bought not from the temple, as in the case of a deal, but from someone who owned them. A number of Chola period inscriptions describe men, especially Brahmans who obtained temple rights in this manner, but none record the purchase of rights to temple property or position by temple women. Two inscriptions, both from the last subperiod and from the far northern or western regions of Tamilnadu, refer to temple women's sale of such rights, but these transactions are hedged about with restrictions and sanctions imposed by temple or village authorities: in one case, a temple woman was ordered to sell her rights, and in the other case was fined for having done so.[29] It is clear that temple women did not have the same freedom as men to trade in temple service rights.

By making deals with the temple, temple women were able to acquire position, property, and—above all—privileges in Chola period temples. Although temple women could not avail themselves of all of the means through which men secured relationships with the temple, they were able to enhance their ritual status through their activity as temple patrons. Unique among donors in the Chola period in what they sought in exchange for their gifts, temple women took advantage of local political circumstances—particularly at the periphery of the Chola realm—to implicate themselves in the network of relationships that radiated outward from the temple. In the next section, we turn to a consideration of the character of the temples that temple women patronized and the manner in which their gifts provided links with the temple community and underwrote their identities as temple women.

A Question of Place

In the sixth year of Ko Māṟapaṉmar alias Tripuvaṉacakkaravattikaḷ Coṇāṭukoṇṭaruḷiṉa Śrī Cuntarapāṇṭiyatevar, we the *civappirāmaṇar* (*śivabrāhmaṇas*) of the temple of Lord Nālāyira Īccura Uṭaiyār in Kallaṭaikuṟicci, a southern hamlet of Śrīrājarājac-caturppetimaṅkalam, a *brahmadeyam* in Muḷḷināṭu, received 6½ *accu*, which was deposited in the temple treasury, from Ūyakkoṇṭāṉ Civallapatevi, one of the temple women (*tevaraṭiyār*) of this deity, for one perpetual lamp for this deity to last as long as the moon and sun shall shine.

We, the *civappirāmaṇar*, make this stone record of our undertaking to provide daily the expenses [for this lamp]. Signed: Cattaṉ Māṉaticcuraṉ alias Viranārāyaṇapaṭṭaṉ, Poṉṉampi Veḷḷantāṅkiṉāṉ Tirucciṟṟampalapaṭṭaṉ, Eccavarākaṉ Āṇṭamāl alias Kotukulapaṭṭaṉ, Umaiyāḻvāṉāviṉ Kaṉṟu alias

Niyāyaparipālapaṭṭaṉ, Ciṟiyāṉ Cevakattevaṉ alias Nāṟpatteṇṇāyirapaṭṭaṉ, Perumāḷ alias Kirāmarācapaṭṭaṉ, Eccavarākaṉ Mātevapaṭṭaṉ, and Poṉṉampi Umaiāḻvāṉ alias Āyirattaḷipaṭṭaṉ.

—SII 23.102: this inscription was engraved in A.D. 1220 at the Nāgeśvaram temple in Kallidaikkuricci, Tirunelveli district.

In the twentieth year of the reign of Śrī Kulottuṅkacoḻatevar, we, the *tāṉattār* of the temple of Tirumaṇañceri Uṭaiya Nāyaṉār, the Lord of Puṉṟiṟkūṟṟam in Irācarācavaḷanāṭu, and we the *śrī uruttira śrīmāyecurarār* (*śrīmāheśvarar*) of this temple, and we among the *nālukuṭi* who guard (*kāppu*) this deity, received 500 *kācu* from Tillaivaṉamuṭaiyāḷ Matatilli, a temple woman (*tevaraṭiyāḷ*) of this temple, as an endowment for offerings to [the deity] Kṣettirapāla Piḷḷaiyār whom she had set up in the temple of this Lord.

This 500 *kācu* being deposited in the temple treasury as an endowment is to provide each day 2 *nāḻi* of rice and to provide without fail for a lamp, for as long as the moon and sun shall shine, by the agreement of us, the *tāṉattār* of the temple, the *śrī uruttira śrīmāyecurarār*, and we among the *nālukuṭi* who guard this deity.

—IPS 152: this inscription was engraved in A.D. 1198 at the Śiva temple in Tirumananjeri, Tiruchirappalli district.

One of the most striking features of temple women's donations is that a very high proportion of their gifts were made to their home temples. Temple women, like other people mentioned in Chola period inscriptions, are often identified with reference to a "hometown." Temple women might, for example, be identified as the "devotee" or "daughter" of a particular temple deity or as belonging to a particular temple or village.[30] The hometown identifications associated with temples or deities serve to mark an individual as a temple woman (or a temple man), whereas those that link individuals to villages or other localities are more widely shared—although they are much less frequently found as part of the identification of women in general than they are of temple women.[31] It is difficult to determine whether hometown identifiers are places of birth or mark other kinds of links to a specific locale, but they seem in many cases to indicate a place of residence and individual (rather than family or group) association with a particular town or temple.

Table 3.4 provides a breakdown of the kinds of hometown identifications of temple women and other donors—no hometown identifier ("None"), a hometown different from the place of donation ("Elsewhere"), or a hometown that was the place where the gift was made ("Here"). A very high proportion of temple women are identified by their hometowns, and they typically endowed their home temples. Of the 108 temple woman donors mentioned in inscriptions (where enough of the text is available to permit this analysis), 101, or 94 percent, are identified with reference to their hometowns. In twenty-one cases, these hometowns are not local, but eighty, or nearly three-quarters, record gifts made by temple women to their home temples or to temples in their hometowns. In contrast, in the four study areas, only 54 percent of donors in general bore hometown identifiers, and only one-fifth made gifts to temples in their hometowns (table 3.4). These figures suggest that the motives of temple women in making donations were different from those of other donors: a temple woman's patronage was concentrated on the temple where she had temple woman status and was intended to secure this status, whereas other donors might be impelled to make gifts to temples outside of their home base to create a more "ramified personal network of lands and public duties" (Heitzman 1995).

Table 3.4 also provides information about the extent of hometown temple patronage in each of the four study areas. Here we see that donors in Kumbakonam taluk, in Tanjavur district, and in Tirukkoyilur taluk, in South Arcot district, bore the least resemblance to temple women: only an eighth of the individuals who made gifts in these study areas were identified as being from the locality. The pattern is quite different in the case of Kulattur taluk, in Tiruchirappalli district, where the proportion of donors making gifts to temples in their hometowns is considerably higher (37 percent), although it is still only half the rate for temple women. The pattern here may be attributed to differences between this study area and the other three.

Kulattur taluk is in an arid, agriculturally poor area; it was relatively remote from Chola authority and seems to have developed strong local authority structures (Tirumalai 1981, 336–38; Heitzman 1985, 79–81, 418–19; 1987a, 59; cf. Chattopadhyaya 1994, 215–22). Although the temple at Kudumiyamalai, in Kulattur taluk, was an important one, it does not seem to have attracted as many donations or donations from as far afield as did the major temple centers in the other three study areas, which in some cases (e.g., Tiruvidaimarudur

Table 3.4 Gifts to home temples and elsewhere: temple woman and study-area donors

	None	Elsewhere	Home	Total
Temple women	7 6%	21 19%	80 74%	108
Kumbakonam taluk, Tanjavur district	67 49%	53 39%	16 12%	136
Tirukkoyilur taluk, South Arcot district	76 56%	42 31%	17 13%	135
Kanchipuram taluk, Chingleput district	36 41%	30 34%	21 24%	87
Kulattur taluk, Tiruchirappalli district	30 31%	32 33%	36 37%	98
Total study areas	209 46%	157 34%	90 20%	456

in Kumbakonam taluk and Kanchipuram in Kanchipuram taluk) were commercial centers, as well as famous sacred sites (Hall 1981, 397–99; Tirumalai 1981, 63–111, 342–44; Heitzman 1985, 213, 215; 1995). Perhaps there is a resemblance between temple woman donors and donors in Kulattur taluk because temple women were frequently active as donors in circumstances that were similar to those found in Kulattur taluk—in areas somewhat removed from central Chola control, where temples were not too large, and where local politics were dynamic. The two inscriptions translated at the beginning of this section, for instance, show temple women as donors in this context. Such circumstances seem, on one hand, to have encouraged hometown temple patronage and, on the other, to have provided opportunities for temple women to make gifts as a means of enhancing relations with their home temples.

We have already seen that most of the deals made by temple women were transacted in regions peripheral to the core Chola territory. An examination of the political circumstances under which temple women and their relatives acted as temple patrons reinforces the idea that possibilities for their participation in temple life were particularly available in times when and places where Chola power was relatively weak. Of the 133 records of donations by temple women, 36, or more than a quarter, are dated in the reigns of kings or lords who were not Cholas; and of the 38 records of the gifts of temple women's relatives, 21—over half—are dated in non-Chola reigns. These political conditions seem to have been conducive to the development of local economic and political networks centered on the temple with which temple women and their relatives could become engaged through their patronage.

Although the great majority of temple women's gifts were made to temples in their hometowns, we may be able to discern something about their patronage if we consider the exceptions to this pattern, the crossover donations which temple women made in places other than their hometowns. In table 3.4, we see that there were twenty-one such gifts—19 percent of all the donations made by temple women. We might, of course, expect temple women, like other donors, to be drawn to give gifts to temples of particular fame and religious importance, even though they were not local. But the crossover donations of temple women were not, for the most part, gifts to large and famous temples.[32] Instead, the temple women who made crossover gifts were more often than not *from* famous temples—for example, the temples of Kanchipuram and Tirumukkudal in Chingleput district, Tanjavur and Tiruvarur in Tanjavur district, and Jambai in South Arcot district. We see here that even when temple women patronized temples outside their hometowns, they seem to have been less attracted by the prospect of becoming donors to large and famous temples than by the opportunities associated with patronage of smaller-scale institutions.

To further investigate the kinds of temples that received gifts from temple women and to compare temple women with other donors, I have constructed a typology of temple towns in five study areas, based on the numbers of donations they received.[33] Table 3.5 shows the fourfold system of classification: type I temples—very large temples—are those that received more than 40 percent of all donations made by individuals in the study area in the course of the Chola period; type II—large—temples received between 11 percent and 40 percent of donations; type III—medium-sized—temples received 5 percent to 10 percent; and type IV—small—temples received less than 5 percent of the donations made in the study area. This classification indicates the importance of a particular temple town relative to others in the immediate vicinity.[34] In each study area, one or two temple towns are classified as type I or type II; these were more prominent than others in the region in the number of endowments they received. Altogether, this tabulation takes into account 1,567 donations distributed among 133 temple towns.

Twenty-four temple women made gifts in eighteen of these temple towns.[35] If temple women were "average" donors—conforming to the pattern of patronage of donors generally—we would expect to find them as donors of type I and type II temples. As we see in table 3.5, temple women were indeed among the patrons of both of the two very large type I temples in the study areas—Vedaranyam (Tirutturaippundi taluk, Tanjavur district) and Kudumiyamalai (Kulattur taluk, Tiruchirappalli district). But only one of the five type II temples, Tiruvidaimarudur (Kumbakonam taluk, Tanjavur district), was endowed by a temple woman; the other type II temples—Tiruvisalur (Kumbakonam taluk, Tanjavur district), Kilur and Tirunamanallur (both in Tirukkoyilur taluk, South Arcot district), and Srirangam (Tiruchirappalli taluk, Tiruchirappalli district)—received no gifts from temple women.

Instead, it appears that the sort of temple that most frequently attracted temple women's gifts was the medium-sized type III temple. Table 3.5 indicates that half of all the temples patronized by temple women in the five study areas were of this type. Furthermore, of the twenty-seven temples that are so classified a third received gifts from temple women; this is quite a high proportion, given the relatively small number of temple woman donors in the area study.

Not only does the pattern of temple women's patronage diverge from that of the average donor, but also temple women differ from the typical female donor in the kinds of temples they chose to endow. In the five study areas, I found records of gifts from 117 royal women (queens, princesses, or palace women) at 32 different temples and gifts from 127 women who were neither royal women nor temple women at 39 different temples. Although the number of different temples patronized by temple women (18) was nearly as great as the number of temple woman donors (24), the figures here reinforce the idea, already introduced in considering royal women's donations, that the gift giving of women in general was much more concentrated on specific temples, in contrast to temple women's more diffuse and individualistic patronage. Table 3.5 shows that all the very large and large (type I and type II) temples were included among the temples on which both royal and nonroyal women's patronage was especially focused.[36] And whereas the groups of royal and nonroyal woman donors in the study areas are each about five times as large as the group of temple woman donors, the nontemple women patronized only twice as many medium and small (type III and type IV) temples as the temple women.

The medium-sized temples that particularly attracted temple women's patronage—well established but with neither a huge supply of incoming wealth nor a superabundance of donors—would appear to have provided a context in which temple women's gifts were welcomed and in which these gifts may have had the capacity to secure certain privileges for their donors. In temples of this size, such privileges may have been less jealously guarded and competition with other donors for recognition by the temple may have been less intense than at larger temples. At the same time, in contrast to smaller temples, the medium-sized temple would have had enough economic and political importance in the community to encourage the establishment and strengthening of relationships with the temple.

Temple women's patronage is distinctive with respect to the situation and character of the temples these women chose to endow. Temple women departed from the norm in the extent to which they made gifts to their hometown temples, to medium-sized temples, and to temples outside the sphere of Chola dominance. If we turn from the question of where they were active as donors to a consideration of how they recorded their donations, we may gain some insight into the nature of the relationships they forged through their gifts. Donative inscriptions invariably highlight the identity of the donor, but they may also refer to a variety of other people with whom the donor becomes linked through the act of donation.

One category of such people are those on whose behalf the donor makes his or her gift. Chola period inscriptions do not often record such transfers of merit, and there are only three inscriptions that describe temple women as making donations for the benefit of someone else—their daughters in two cases and a mother in another (ARE 159 of 1920; ARE 47 of 1922; ARE 505 of 1962–63).[37] When nontemple women transfer the merit of their gifts, it is almost always to family members and most often their male relatives, particularly their sons or husbands (Orr 1999). That these references to the transfer of merit by temple women, although few, are unanimous in indicating matrilineal connections would appear to be of some significance for our understanding of the family structure of temple women.

Another aspect of donation that we might explore is the involvement of temple women in group donations, or the recording of their gifts together with those of other people. Such patterns, should they exist, would be likely to indicate the kinds of social or political links that temple women sought to establish or reinforce through their gifts.[38] In fact, a large majority of their gifts were made, and recorded, as individual donations. This is in keeping with the general character of temple patronage and of property transactions in medieval Tamilnadu, which were typically described in the inscriptions as matters of individual responsibility and initiative (Granda 1984, 345; Heitzman 1995, 75). Deals negotiated by temple women were never made corporately or cooperatively, except insofar as privileges were secured for

Table 3.5 Proportion of temples of various types patronized by temple women and by other women

	Kumbakonam taluk	Kulattur and Alangudi taluks	Tirukkoyilur taluk	Tiruchirappalli taluk	Tirutturaippundi taluk	Total
			Temple women n = 24			
Temple Type						
Type 1 (41%–59%)	0/0	1/1	0/0	0/0	1/1	2/2
Type II (11%–40%)	1/2	0/0	0/2	0/1	0/0	1/5
Type III (5%–10%)	3/6	1/3	2/6	3/7	0/5	9/27
Type IV (below 5%)	1/28	4/21	1/36	0/8	0/6	6/99
Total	5/36	6/25	3/44	3/16	1/12	18/133
			Royal women n = 117			
Temple Type						
Type I (41%–59%)	0/0	1/1	0/0	0/0	1/1	2/2
Type II (11%–40%)	2/2	0/0	2/2	1/1	0/0	5/5
Type III (5%–10%)	5/6	0/3	3/6	6/7	0/5	14/27
Type IV (below 5%)	8/28	0/21	1/36	2/8	0/6	11/99
Total	15/36	1/25	6/44	9/16	1/12	32/133
			Nonroyal women n = 127			
Temple Type						
Type I (41%–59%)	0/0	1/1	0/0	0/0	1/1	2/2
Type II (11%–40%)	2/2	0/0	2/2	1/1	0/0	5/5
Type III (5%–10%)	5/6	0/3	6/6	4/7	2/5	17/27
Type IV (below 5%)	5/28	2/21	5/36	2/8	1/6	15/99
Total	12/36	3/25	13/44	7/16	4/12	39/133

a temple woman's descendents. Of the 112 other inscriptions that record temple women's gifts, 17 describe gifts made with other individuals. In 11 of these 17 inscriptions, the others mentioned as codonors are themselves temple women or the female relatives (especially sisters) of temple women.[39] Whatever linkages were established by temple women by making or recording donations with others, these connections seem to be primarily with women of their own family or community.

Apart from codonors and the recipients of merit, other kinds of people appear in Chola period inscriptions recording donations. The figure who has attracted the most scholarly attention is the king. Most inscriptions mention the king in passing, simply as a means of fixing the date of the record in a regnal year. In about a third of the inscriptions, the royal presence looms larger because the record is prefaced by a *meykkīrtti*, a eulogy of the king's attainments and conquests. Very few of the records of temple women's gifts include a *meykkīrtti*. If, as Burton Stein (1980, 352–53) has suggested, the appearance of the *meykkīrtti* indicates acknowledgement of the king's authority or signals interest by the sponsor of the inscription in participating in the ritual polity centered on the king, the virtual absence of this feature in temple women's records would suggest a lack of connection between their donations and the politics and symbols associated with the sovereignty of the Cholas or other early medieval South Indian dynasties. In the records of temple women's gifts, there are only three instances in which the king is involved in the donation or its recording: a tenth-century inscription, mentioning that the king was present on the occasion of a temple woman's donation (SII 3.102); a case in which a temple woman is said to have received royal sanction for her gift (ARE 179 of 1916); and the record of a temple woman's request to a king to turn over tax revenues to a temple (ARE 385 of 1924).

In contrast to the very few references to the king are the large numbers of people from the locality—village or temple authorities, individually named or in groups—who, according to the testimony of the inscriptions, are implicated in the system of relationships brought into being through

---

Temple towns of each study area are classified by type according to the percentage of donations recorded in a specfic place as a proportion of all donations made in the study area (see note 33). The number of temples of each type is represented by the denominators of the fractions. The numerator represents the number of temple towns of a given type in each study area that received gifts from temple women, royal women, or nonroyal (nontemple) women.

In Kumbakonam taluk (Tanjavur district), 468 donations were made. Tiruvidaimarudur received 19 percent (type II) and Tiruvisalur received 14 percent (type II).

In Kulattur and Alangudi taluks (Tiruchirappalli district/former Pudukkottai State), 134 donations were made. Kudumiyamalai received 41 percent (type I).

In Tirukkoyilur taluk (South Arcot district), 449 donations were made. Kilur received 13 percent (type II) and Tirunamanallur received 11 percent (type II).

In Tiruchirappalli taluk (Tiruchirappalli district), 363 donations were made. Srirangam received 31 percent (type II).

In Tirutturaippundi taluk (Tanjavur district), 153 donations were made. Vedaranyam received 59 percent (type I).

temple women's donations. Over half of the donative inscriptions of temple women refer to the participation of village or temple authorities; the two inscriptions that introduce this section show how temple authorities, in particular, played a part in the donations of temple women. Indeed, it appears that a larger proportion of temple women than of other kinds of donors established links with temple authorities through their donations: whereas 40 percent of temple women's donative inscriptions refer to temple authorities, for other donors the proportion is less than a quarter.[40]

In the course of the Chola period there is a marked increase in the mention of temple authorities by all donors—in part, at the expense of references to village authorities (Champakalakshmi 1981a, 418; Hall 1981, 408; Orr 1995c)—but the increase is especially dramatic for temple women. By the last subperiod, two-thirds of the records of their gifts refer to temple authorities.[41] As the internal structure of the temple underwent change and the prominence and autonomy of the temple in local politics increased, temple women, as temple patrons, seem to have been especially interested in forging links with those at the center of the temple-based web of relationships.

The system with which temple women sought to become engaged through their gifts was not the royal ritual polity, the extensive network of "lordly" influence, or a local network of landholding, mercantile, and political interests; it was instead the ritual, economic, and social structure based in their home temples. Their interest in participating or being recognized in this system, although not unique to them, was especially marked among them. And temple women's engagement with this system became increasingly important to them in the course of the Chola period, as is demonstrated by the increasing proportion of temple woman donors who gave to temples in their hometowns and who mentioned temple authorities in their records. When we consider that these increasing proportions—rising especially in the middle of the Chola period—coincided with an increase in the absolute numbers of temple women acting as donors, we may conclude that temple women, through their patronage, were actively taking advantage of the opportunities that the changing structure and standing of the temple afforded them.

Temple women, as one of the many groups of people who acted as temple patrons, maneuvered through these changing circumstances in their own unique way. In using temple patronage as a way to secure status or identity, they engaged in a type of negotiation for relationship with the temple that marked them as being entirely different from temple men, who virtually never acted as temple patrons. The male counterparts of temple women had other means of making connections with and enhancing their position within the temple, which evidently were unavailable to temple women because of their sex. But the donative activity of temple women also sets them apart from other women: while temple patronage was, in the course of the Chola period, increasingly important for temple women, other women were less and less active as donors. That temple women were able to maintain and even expand their involvement with the temple while other women were not is attributable both to changes in the internal structuring of the temple—toward increasing complexity, hierarchy, and formality—and to the differences in the social and economic definition of the positions of temple women and other women. The temple woman, whose access to wealth was not tied to her status as a wife, had greater autonomy and was better able to maneuver in and around the changing contours of the institutional landscape of the temple.

Temple women's gift giving was not only distinctive in terms of its very existence—in contrast to the virtual absence of such activity by temple men and its radical decline for women in general—but also exhibits a number of other particular characteristics that sets it apart from the temple patronage of other donors. The inscriptions that record temple women's donations make explicit mention of privileges and honors that they received in exchange for their gifts; there is no evidence that other donors made such deals with the temple. Deals and other donations made by temple women and their relatives are more commonly found in areas peripheral to Chola political dominance than are the gifts of other donors. The pattern of temple women's patronage is more diffuse than that of other donors: it is less concentrated on the larger, more famous temples of Tamilnadu and more focused on medium-sized temples, particularly on temple women's own home temples. The greater number of, and increasing, references to temple authorities in the records of temple women's gifts, as well as the mention of their mothers, sisters, and daughters as codonors or recipients of the merit of their gifts, show that the relationships that they established and strengthened through their donations were different from those of other temple patrons.

In the last chapter, we saw that in the course of the Chola period, the status of temple woman became increasingly well defined. The characteristic features of temple women's patronage that have been described in this chapter point to the importance of their gifts in acquiring and maintaining this status, in reinforcing the identity of the temple woman in relationship to a particular temple, and in securing the privileges and recognition that were concommitants of this identity. In some cases, as we have seen, the temple confirmed this identity and acknowledged and rewarded temple women's patronage by granting rights to perform ritual roles and service functions. In the next chapter, we turn to a more detailed examination of the ways in which temple women participated in such activities in the temple.

FOUR

Temple Women as Temple Servants

The Design of Temple Life in Medieval Tamilnadu

. . . . Under the new arrangement, (a certain amount of) land is assigned for [maintaining] perpetual lamps and another plot of land, bordering it, is set aside as a garden for areca nuts, coconuts, and flowers.

As for the temple servants (*devarkaṉmikaḷ*) who are in the [deity's] presence, those among the temple servants (*tirukoyiluṭaiyarkaḷ*) who were formerly doing the three [services] of the *māṇi* (assistant, *brahmacārin*) will continue to have custody of their land so long as they do the three [services] of the *māṇi*. The temple servants (*tirukoyiluṭaiyarkaḷ*), the drummers (*ukaccarkaḷ*), he who is temple manager (*śrīkāriyañ ceyvāṉ*) by the king's authority, the devotees (*aṭikaḷmār*), and the flywhisk women (*kavarip-piṇākkaḷ*) are assigned residences in the temple precincts.

[The following section of the inscription describes the provision of land and house sites for the temple servants responsible for burning lamps and for other groups (*kuṭikaḷ*) of temple servants; gives details of the food to be prepared for offerings to the deity (*āḻvār*); and lists the amount of paddy (and quantity of land) required to produce these offerings, to provide oil for lamps and other requisites of worship, and to support the temple personnel.]

. . . . For one Brahman to perform worship (*tiruvārātiṉai*) of the deity, including his cloth allowance, 1 *patakku* and 4 *nāḻi* [of paddy] daily, amounting to 70 *kalam* yearly [requiring a certain amount of land].

1 *kuṟuṇi* and 4 *nāḻi* of paddy are required twice daily to provide for those among the temple servants (*tirukoyiluṭaiyarkaḷ*) who are in charge of the land,

together with those doing the three [services] of the *māṇi*, to provide for rice offerings and water for the sacred bath and for poured water offerings, and to provide for those who give assistance (*paricārakam*) to the *nampi* doing the worship, who perform the anointing of the deity, and who carry the canopy. Altogether, 40 *kalam* of paddy is required four times a year [which is the yield of a certain amount of land].

For three garland makers, 1 *kuṟuṇi* and 4 *nāḻi* of paddy, amounting to 40 *kalam* yearly [requiring a certain amount of land].

For three people to sweep and smear the courtyard (*tirumuṟṟam*), 1 *kuṟuṇi* and 4 *nāḻi* of paddy, amounting to 40 *kalam* yearly [requiring a certain amount of land].

For twelve drummers (*ukaccu*)—one to beat the *talaippaṟai* (chief drum), one the *mattaḷam* (drum), one the *kaṟaṭikai* (rattle?), two to play the *caṅku* (conch), two the *kāḷam* (trumpet), one the *cekaṇṭikai* (gong), two the *tāḷam* (cymbals), and two the *kaimaṇi* (hand-bells)—at the time of the sacred bath, and at the times of the food offerings, *bhūtabali*, *śrībali*, *arddhayāmam* (midnight service), and *paḷḷiyeḻucci* (early morning service)—2 *tūṇi*, 1 *kuṟuṇi*, and 2 *nāḻi* of paddy daily, amounting to 277 *kalam*, 1 *tūṇi*, and 1 *patakku* yearly [requiring a certain amount of land].

For two temple watchmen (*tirumeykāppār*), including their cloth allowance, 3 *kuṟuṇi* of paddy daily, amounting to 90 *kalam* yearly [requiring a certain amount of land].

For one accountant (*karaṇattāṉ*), 60 *kalam* daily [should be yearly] [requiring a certain amount of land].

For him who is the temple manager (*śrīkāryañ ceyvāṉ*) by order of the king, 1 *patakku* of paddy daily, amounting to 60 *kalam* yearly [requiring a certain amount of land].

. . . . for hymn singers (*tiruppatiyam pāṭuvār*). . . . for potters (*kalamiṭu kucavar*). . . .

[The inscription continues with an accounting of the amount of paddy (and land) required for various services, including the monthly bathing of the deity with 108 pots. Then follows a damaged section that seems to refer to a royal grant and an agreement about land.]

This agreement is confirmed, recording the building of this stone temple and the gift. . . . to this deity by Queen Cempiyaṉ Mahādeviyār, the mother of Śrī Uttamacoḻa, in the seventh year of Ko Rājarājakesaripaṉmar.

. . . . Cāramuṭaiyāṉ Araṭṭaṉ Ikāṭutevaṉ of the royal retinue. . . . and Appūruṭaiyāṉ Āccaṉ Paṭṭālakaṉ of the junior division of the keepers of the royal ornaments, and Āccaṉ Kampaṉ alias Tirumaṇañceri Tirukaṟṟaḷippiccaṉ convey the command of this queen who orders these temple arrangements, that these lands are to provide for the temple expenses.

[In the following lines are details of the yearly expenses to be met by the yield from the land—for sandal paste for the daily adornment of the deity; for the renovations of temple buildings and other repairs; and for setting up a garden to produce, among other things, sandal, flowers, and coconut. Land is also to be set aside to support temple servants . . .]

. . . . for three people (*kuṭikaḷ*) to tend [the garden]. . . . for two drummers (*uvaccarkaḷ*) to play the conch as formerly, and for the expenses of renovations . . . .

[The inscription then describes the amount of land to be provided for the players of drum and conch, for those who make garlands, for those who carry the hand-lamps for *śrībali*, for those who sweep and smear the temple courtyard, for three ascetics (*tapasyar*) who dwell in the temple precincts of this god in Pallavapurāṇapuram, for two hymn singers, and for rice offerings for the god Amarapucaṅkadevar. Details of the boundaries of the land are then given, including mention of arecanut gardens named after Queen Cempiyaṉ Mātevi and A̲lakiya Co̲laṉ, and of land given to twenty-five Brahmans for recitation for the deity of the Talavakara Sāmaveda, the Taittirīya Veda, and the Chāndogya Sāmaveda.]

Thus we undertake to provide for these expenses. Signed: Māṭalaṉ Maticūtar Cāttanāṉ Impānāyarpaṭṭaṉ, Māṭilaṉ Coti Co̲lapāṇṭiyaṉ, Māṭilaṉ Nātittañcāttaṉ alias Pañcavaṉ Mātevipaṭṭaṉ, and Māṭalaṉ Ānū̲r̲r̲eṇmaṉ Piccaṉ.

—SII 13.170: This inscription was engraved in A.D. 992 on the east and north walls of the central shrine of the Uktavedīśvara temple in Kuttalam, Tanjavur district.

This inscription records the extensive rebuilding and rearrangement of temple affairs at a temple in the core Chola region by Queen Cempiyaṉ Mahādevi, the wife of King Gandaraditya and the mother of Uttama Chola. Although the beginning of this inscription is missing and it is fragmentary, it provides an outline of the services and personnel considered appropriate for a medium-sized temple with substantial resources in the late tenth century. Among those receiving support from this temple are a Brahman priest and his assistants (*māṇis*), drummers and musicians, gardeners and garland makers, hymn singers and Brahmans chanting sacred texts, flywhisk women, watchmen, people to clean the temple courtyard, potters, devotees, ascetics, accountants, and a temple manager. Most Chola period inscriptions do not provide such a full picture of temple life because they are records of additions to or alterations of existing arrangements—the gift of yet another perpetual lamp, provisions for offerings of flowers or food in daily worship, or the institution of a special service at the celebration of a festival. But there are a number of "set-up grants" that carried out more massive modifications of the temple arrangements formerly in place and were sponsored by major donors, some of whom were, like Queen Cempiyaṉ Mahādevi, royal patrons.[1] These set-up grants provide us with the opportunity not only to appreciate the variety of roles played by temple servants but also to see which among them were considered most important in the conduct of temple rituals and temple affairs.

Our first discovery is that female temple servants were not regarded as essential personnel. In the course of surveying the corpus of Chola period inscriptions, I have collected fifty-nine examples of set-up grants, each of which record the assignment of tasks and the provision of support to at least three different categories of temple servants. This group of fifty-nine inscriptions is doubtless only a fraction of the total number of such inscriptions, but I believe that it includes all the set-up grants that mention temple women—and these number only sixteen. Another five inscriptions mention groups of temple servants, such as garland makers or those involved in food preparation—groups which might have been female or have included women—but the vast majority of the people whose services were required in the running of the temple are clearly male.

Table 4.1 shows which of these services were most in demand. It would appear that the people deemed most essential to temple life were priests and their assistants, gardeners and garland makers, and drummers. There is a reference to each of these types of temple servants in approximately half of the fifty-nine set-up grants. It is not surprising to find priests among those whose services were most needed by the temple, but it is interesting, first, that priests are not mentioned more frequently as key figures in the set-up grants and, second, that there are other kinds of temple servants whose services are represented as being nearly as significant as those of priests.

There is a very clear indication of the importance in medieval temple ritual of flowers, as offerings to and adornments for the deities, in the fact that there are so many references in the set-up grants to the need for people to weave flowers into garlands and for gardeners to tend the plots where coconuts, arecanuts, sandalwood—and, above all, flowers—were grown.[2] The role of the drummer (*uvaccaṉ*) also looms large in Chola period temple life. The preceding translation is not unusual in its specification of the membership of the group of drummers, the instruments to be played (including conch and trumpet, as well as percussion instruments), and the ritual occasions on which the drummers were required to perform. Many Chola period inscriptions record provisions made for bands of drummers—most often groups

Table 4.1 Temple personnel referred to in set-up grants

Service	Inscriptions
Priests: priests, *śivabrāhmaṇas, māṇis, ācāryas*	30
Gardeners and garland makers	27
Drummers	26
Singers and reciters	24
Artisans: mostly potters (also carpenters and metal workers)	23
Cleaners of floors	20
Menial tasks in the preparation of food and other offerings	14
Responsibility functions (managers, accountants, supervisors)	12
Attendance on the deity (bearers, participants in processions, etc.)	12
Cooks	11
Musicians (excluding drummers)	11
Washermen	9
Watchmen	9
Dancers	4
Total number of set-up grants	59

of five or seven men but sometimes groups as large as twenty or more. Drumming seems to have been an essential element of temple worship and is particularly mentioned in the context of the *śrībali* offerings that were a part of the services carried out three times daily for the temple's main deity. Although other musicians, players of wind and string instruments, are mentioned in a number of the set-up grants, they are considerably less prominent than drummers.

Close behind the priests, gardeners and garland makers, and drummers in importance are singers and reciters, artisans, and those whose duty it was to clean the temple precincts. There are many references, in both the set-up grants and in the corpus of Chola period inscriptions as a whole, to the singing of hymns—the Tamil poems composed by the Āḻvārs and Nāyaṉmārs, which had, by the tenth century, been set to music.[3] Less frequently, there are references to the recitation, typically by Brahmans, of Sanskrit scriptures. The Tamil sacred texts are much more in evidence than the Sanskrit ones and clearly had an important place in temple ritual. It is also significant that singing as an element in temple ritual is much more prominent than dancing: whereas twenty-four of the fifty-nine set-up grants refer to the support of singers, only four mention dancers as members of the corps of temple personnel.

References in the set-up grants to artisans and to the cleaning staff of the temple, like the references to gardeners and garland makers, take us behind the scenes and help us to understand what kinds of work needed to be done to support the ritual performances conducted for the benefit of the deities enshrined in the temple. Twenty-three of the set-up grants arrange for artisans to serve the temple, and in all but two cases the artisans mentioned include potters. That potters were so much in evidence suggests that the cooking of food—for feeding devotees, pilgrims, ascetics, and Brahmans, as well as for offerings to the gods—was a central activity of the temple in medieval Tamilnadu (Orr 1994b). This is borne out as well by the frequent references to the assignment of menial tasks associated with food preparation, such as bringing firewood or husking paddy (in fourteen of the fifty-nine set-up grants) and to the employment of cooks by the temple (in eleven set-up grants). Several of the twenty references in the set-up grants to the need for people to clean the temple also indicate a connection with food: in addition to performing such duties as sweeping floors and purifying them with cow dung, cleaners might also be responsible for the removal of the leavings after people were fed in the temple precincts. Among the other menial tasks mentioned are those performed by washermen and watchmen; the regularity of references to these tasks is indicative of their importance in the functioning of the temple.

Twelve of the set-up grants make provisions for people with "responsibility functions" in the temple, performing such tasks as managing or overseeing the use of temple resources or representing the temple by accepting gifts or signing agreements with individuals who had transactions with the temple. For example, in the preceding translation arrangements are made for the housing of the temple manager (*śrīkāriyañ ceyvāṉ*) and for the provision to him and the temple accountant (*karaṇattāṉ*) of paddy from the temple lands. As we have seen in the previous chapters, inscriptions increasingly refer to such people in the course of the Chola period, identifying them more and more as individuals rather than as anonymous functionaries or groups of temple authorities. As numerous as these people are, most were not the recipients of support from the temple, as are the temple manager and the accountant referred to in the preceding translation, and seem rather to have held their positions or exercised their functions more in an honorary than a professional sense.

Another group of participants in temple life whose work was conceived in various contexts as either a privilege or a job were those who served as attendants on the deity. These were people who adorned the image of the god; accompanied the god, bearing lamps, parasols, or flywhisks; or were members of the entourage of the deity during festival processions. In twelve of the fifty-nine set-up inscriptions, functions of this sort are specifically assigned or their performers are provided with some form of support by the temple. In the preceding inscription, for example, the flywhisk women are given places of residence in the temple precincts, and various other people are charged with the tasks of carrying the canopy during the daily worship and carrying lamps during *śrībali*, and they are compensated for performing these duties. Sometimes, however, as we have seen in the case of the deals made by temple women, such tasks were regarded as privileges. It may well be that these duties, like responsibility functions, came to have an increasingly honorific character in the course of the Chola period.

Having surveyed the variety of functions and activities that took place in the medieval temples of Tamilnadu—and having ordered these functions and activities according to their apparent importance, in pragmatic terms, to the organization of temple life—I wish now to locate temple women within this milieu. There are two aspects of this problem: first, the extent of women's participation in these various forms of temple service and, second, the centrality of temple service in the identity of temple women. The figures in table 4.2 provide us with the opportunity to investigate both these questions.

A comparison of this table with table 4.1 makes it clear that there were entire categories of temple service from which women were excluded, including several of the functions that, judging from their prominence in the set-up grants, were regarded as essential to the conduct of temple ritual—most notably the roles of priest and drummer. At the same time, among the tasks that temple women did perform, the most frequently mentioned function—that of dancer—was evidently not of great ritual importance, given the small number of references to this role among the set-up grants. Nor were any of the roles played by temple women in medieval temple life—whether as dancers, cleaners and menial workers, attendants, singers, or garland makers—exclusively female.

We might expect that temple ritual and temple affairs were dominated by men. But given that popular and scholarly images of the temple woman

Table 4.2 Roles of women in the temple

Service	Subperiod 1 (850–985)	Subperiod 2 (985–1070)	Subperiod 3 (1070–1178)	Subperiod 4 (1178–1300)	Total
Non-specified service	—	2 5%	1 1%	8 6%	11 4%
Garland makers	—	3 8%	1 1%	1 1%	5 2%
Singers	2 4%	2 5%	6 7%	2 1%	12 4%
Menial: cleaners and food preparers	1 2%	3 8%	4 5%	10 7%	18 6%
Attendance	2 4%	2 5%	4 5%	9 7%	17 6%
Dancers	3 6%	3 8%	11 14%	7 5%	24 8%
Total service	8 17%	9 22%	19 24%	31 23%	67 22%
Responsibility functions	9 19%	3 8%	2 2%	10 7%	24 8%
Support only	8 17%	10 25%	21 26%	19 14%	58 19%
Total inscriptions	48	40	81	135	304

Pecentages represent the proportion of inscriptions that refer to a particular role for temple women out of the total number of inscriptions that refer to temple women in each subperiod.

have so often centered on her persona as a ritual specialist or a skilled professional—and particularly on her role as a temple dancer—it is somewhat surprising to discover that fewer than half of the 304 inscriptions that refer to temple women in the Chola period indicate in any way that they were involved in temple activities, apart from being donors to the temple. Sixty-seven, or less than a quarter of the inscriptions, describe their engagement in temple service and many of these inscriptions represent the character of this service only in vague and general terms. Another 24 inscriptions (or 8 percent) mention temple women as the performers of responsibility functions, and 58 (19 percent) refer to the provision by the temple of some type of support for women, without specifying that any particular duties were required of them.[4]

Temple women's identities in the Chola period were evidently not particularly tied to functions they may have performed in the temple. This situation can be contrasted not only with what we know of temple women in the twentieth century but also with the character of temple *men* in the Chola period. Table 4.3 allows us to compare the roles of individual temple women who were named in inscriptions of the Chola period with the roles of temple men named in inscriptions of the four study areas.[5] The figures in this table

Table 4.3 The roles of temple women and temple men mentioned by name in Chola period inscriptions

	Subperiod 1 (850–985)	Subperiod 2 (985–1070)	Subperiod 3 (1070–1178)	Subperiod 4 (1178–1300)	Total
Temple Women					
Service function/ support	16	1	7	52	76 32%
Responsibility function	—	11	—	19	30 13%
Donor	25	9	27	38	99 42%
Relative of donor	3	5	1	24	33 14%
Total temple women	44	26	35	133	238
Temple men					
Service function/ support	3	6	5	6	20 9%
Responsibility function	18	30	94	52	194 89%
Donor	—	—	2	1	3 1%
Relative of donor	—	—	2	—	2 1%
Total temple men	21	36	103	59	219

underscore the overwhelming dominance of men as temple servants and temple administrators: nearly as many temple men are named in the published inscriptions of four very small study areas, a tiny fraction of the total number of Chola period inscriptions, as temple women are named in the entire inscriptional corpus. And the reasons for this visibility of temple men are entirely different from those that bring temple women into view. Table 4.3 shows us that 42 percent of the temple women named in Chola period inscriptions are represented as donors and another 14 percent as the relatives of donors. In contrast, a mere 1 percent of the temple men in the area study are described as having either of these roles. This points up the very different character of temple women's and temple men's relationships with the temple and reinforces the idea, presented in the last chapter, that temple women's links to the temple were particularly and uniquely associated with their roles as temple patrons.

If the role of donor is the one that seems most important for temple women, the next most commonly mentioned role is that of temple servant, broadly defined: 32 percent of named temple women are described as performing some kind of service function or as receiving support from the temple. It is important to remember that both the performance of services and the receipt of support were often regarded as privileges rather than aspects of a "job." We have seen, for example, that in exchange for their gifts to the temple, temple women would be granted the honor of serving the deity as a hymn singer or an attendant in a festival procession or have the right to receive food that had been prepared in the temple. Table 4.3 shows that nearly all of the individual temple women described as having service functions or receiving temple support appear in inscriptions of the last subperiod, when temple women's donations and deals were also very numerous. The last subperiod also produces a relatively large number of references to individual temple women with responsibility functions. This role is one played overall by 13 percent of the temple women named in Chola period inscriptions but is mentioned only in inscriptions of the second and fourth subperiods.

Temple men are different from temple women not only because they so rarely acted as donors but also because of the much greater emphasis on responsibility functions as their primary role. Whereas considerably more temple women are named in connection with temple service or support than as performers of responsibility functions, the opposite pattern prevails for temple men. Only 9 percent of the temple men mentioned by name in the inscriptions of the four study areas perform temple services or receive temple support, and in contrast to temple women, approximately the same number of such men appear in inscriptions of each of the four subperiods.[6]

I do not mean to suggest that relatively few men, or a small proportion of temple men, were involved in temple service. As we see in the set-up grant translated at the beginning of the chapter, large numbers of men were employed in a variety of functions by the temple. What we see here, rather, is that the individual identities of temple men were not so much highlighted in connection with their roles as performers of ritual, professional, or menial services as they were with respect to their performance of responsibility functions. Eighty-nine percent of the temple men named in the area study—a very large majority—performed such roles as taking charge of gifts to the temple, signing agreements on behalf of the temple, or supervising temple affairs. In table 4.3 the sharp increase between the second and third subperiods in the number of temple men is the direct result of there being a very large number of temple men with responsibility functions who were named in inscriptions of the third subperiod. These include a whole range of types—temple managers, treasurers and accountants, Brahmans, and individuals associated with *maṭhas*—but a large number of these men were identified in sectarian terms, as *śivabrāhmaṇas* or *śrīvaiṣṇavas*, for example.

The emergence of these figures in positions of authority in the temple and the various indications of a proliferation of responsibility functions increasingly exercised by individuals specifically named in the inscriptions suggest that in the course of the Chola period the internal politics of the temple were becoming more and more complex and carefully articulated. Privileges and responsibilities were increasingly divided, defined, and assigned to members of groups and individuals who had particular kinds of status. In this connection, we may recollect the discussion in chapter 2 of the shift in the use of the term *tevaraṭiyār* from its application to groups of "honored devotees," who were offered food or entrusted with administrative responsibilities, to its almost exclusive application to individual temple women, who did not have these roles. This shift was accompanied by the emergence in the later Chola period of both a new, more sectarian nomenclature for groups of honored devotees and a greater recognition of individual men who had authority in temple affairs. The increasing elaboration of the ways in which these affairs were conducted and recorded in inscriptions, together with the increasing specification of individual identities and entitlements to participate in these affairs, seems to have created a system in which temple women were progressively excluded from involvement with responsibility functions. In the next section, we explore this issue further.

Reputation, Recognition, and Responsibility

In the thirty-second year of the reign of Śrī Rājādhirājadevar, for the god Lord Olokamātevi-īśvara of Tiruvaiyāṟu in Poykaināṭu, in Rājendraciṅkavaḷanāṭu, on the north bank [of the Kāvēri River], with the following acting as supervisors: Aṇuttarapallavaraiyaṉ, *atikāricci* (female palace superintendant) Comayaṉ Amittiravalli, temple manager Nantanūruṭaiyaṉ Celvaṉ Mayilai, Āttiriyaṉ Nampi Kāṭanampi who performs temple worship on behalf of the *stānamuṭaiyar* ("possessor" of the temple) Kettira Civa-paṇṭitar, *māṉamutali* Pāratāyan Celvaṉ Naraṅkaṉ alias Rājamāttāṇṭa-brahmamārāyaṉ, *vaṇṇakku* (tester of coins) Cāttaṉ Niṉrāṉ alias Viracoḻa-aṇukka Māyilaṭṭi, the *patiyār* (temple women)—including *patiyilāḷ* Nakkaṉ Araṅkam alias Jayaṅkoṇṭacoḻat-talaikkoli, Nakkaṉ Pūmi alias Paramākkaviṭaṅkat-talaikkoli, Nakkaṉ Coḻa-viccāti alias Olokamātevit-talaikkoli, and Nakkaṉ Pavaḻakkuṉru alias Maturāntakat-talaikkoli—the *karaṇattāṉ* (accountant) Kecuvaṉ Maturāntakaṉ, and the *porppaṇṭāri* (treasurer) Maṇimatti Mātavakkiramavittaṉ,

Prince (*piḷḷaiyār*) Śrīviṣṇuvattanadevar graciously bestowed 300 *rājarājaṉ māṭai* (gold coins) to be used to provide 150 golden waterlilies, each golden waterlily weighing 2¼ *kaḻañcu*, for a total of 337½ *kaḻañcu* in gold, measured with the *kuṭiñaikkal* weight. The aforementioned acted as supervisors.

In the thirty-first year of the reign of Lord Śrī Rājādhirājadevar, Prince Śrīviṣṇuvattanadevar worshiped the [deity's] sacred feet and graciously gave an anklet ornament of gold. The anklet, weighing 5 *kaḻañcu* and ¾ *mañcāṭi* in gold, measured with the *kuṭiñaikkal* weight, he graciously presented to the god Caṇṭeśvara. And [he gave] an ornament for the festival procession, to be worn at the [deity's] waist, weighing 6¼ *mā*, or, together with its stone, 6 *kaḻañcu*, 1 *mañcāṭi*, and 6 *mā*. . . . The aforementioned acted as supervisors.

In the twenty-seventh year of the reign of the great king who conquered the Gaṅgā and the eastern lands, Prince Śrīviṣṇuvattanadevar graciously bestowed 99¼ *māṭai*. He graciously presented to Āṭavallār [Śiva as Nāṭarāja] two necklaces and four armlets, weighing 79 *kaḻañcu*, 2 *mañcāṭi*, and 1 *kuṉri* in gold, measured with the *kuṭiñaikkal* weight. And he graciously presented to this deity, at his holy feet, [ornaments] of gold, weighing altogether 32¼ *kaḻañcu*, including 4 metal plates, 23 golden flowers, 2 curved plates (crescent moons?), 1 short plate, 11 pear blossoms, and 2 pleated ornaments.

He graciously presented to this [deity] 4 necklaces containing 851 pearls and weighing 22 *kaḻañcu*, 6 *mañcāṭi*, and 2 *mā*. [He also gave] an ornament for the foot composed of 1,109 pearls and a cloth sewn with 315 pearls, with a weight of 47 *kaḻañcu*, 6 *mañcāṭi*, and 1 *mā*. Altogether [the total is] 2,285 pearls, and a weight of 72 *kaḻañcu*, 1 *mañcāṭi*, and 3 *mā*.

—SII 5.520: this inscription, which begins with a very long *meykkīrtti*, was engraved in A.D. 1050 on the north wall of the Uttara Kailāsa shrine of the Pañcanadīśvara temple in Tiruvaiyaru, Tanjavur district.

In the whole of the corpus of Chola period inscriptions, I have found only nine inscriptions like this one, which name women with responsibility functions. Three of these inscriptions date from the second subperiod, and the other six are from the last subperiod. Another fifteen mention groups of people with responsibility functions, using "temple woman" terms (e.g., *tevaraṭiyār*) which may refer to women (as well as to men). Inscriptions of this type are found especially in the first subperiod. The total of twenty-four inscriptions that refer to temple women with responsibility functions constitute 8 percent of all inscriptions that mention temple women, but there is little evidence to suggest a definite chronological pattern of their increasing or decreasing involvement in temple affairs. Mostly, they simply were not involved.

It is certainly clear that temple women were not part of the development characteristic for men—the very sharp increase between the second and third subperiods in the number of named individuals with responsibility functions. This increase between the early and later Chola periods seems to be the result, at least in part, of the fact that more and more men had the function of "taking in hand" (*kaikkoṇṭa*) an endowment, receiving a gift on behalf of the temple. Women, in contrast, do not seem to have performed this function; the only case I have found is that of a temple woman (*tevaraṭiyār*) who "took in hand" the gift that a queen made to a temple in Kanyakumari district in the thirteenth century (KK 194 = TAS 8, 34). Another important administrative function in the temple that is quite commonly mentioned as belonging to men, either as individuals or in groups, is that of "supervisor" (*kaṇkāṇi*). Here again, I have come across just one inscription in which a named woman has this function—the preceding translation—in which four temple women (*patiyilār*) shared the role of supervisor with other temple functionaries.

If these roles were extremely rare for women, what types of responsibility functions did temple women have? Table 4.4 shows the numbers of inscriptions that mention temple women in connection with each of five types of responsibility functions, considering separately the nine inscriptions in which temple women are named (and definitely female) and the fifteen in-

Table 4.4 Types of responsibility functions performed by temple women

	Named	Group	Total
Administration	3	4	7
Collection of taxes and fines	—	4	4
Tending	4	2	6
Party to agreement	2	2	4
Protection	—	3	3
Total	9	15	24

scriptions that refer to groups of temple women (*tevaraṭiyār*, *emperumāṉaṭiyār*, etc.). I have arranged these types of responsibility functions roughly in order, beginning with those roles that seem to have involved the most decision-making powers and control and ending with those that were more nominal and honorific in character and peripheral to the workings of the temple.

The two functions already discussed, marked by the terms *kaikkoṇṭa* and *kaṇkāṇi*, are classified as functions of the first sort, administrative functions, as are other kinds of active engagement in the conduct of temple affairs. People charged with the second category of responsibility functions, collection of taxes and fines, received property on behalf of the temple but would not have been involved in decision making or management of the temple's wealth. The third category, people who "tended" temple resources, are those with whom livestock, land, or gold was invested by the temple in expectation of a certain regular return in the form of ghee for lamps, paddy, or other supplies used by the temple. In Chola period inscriptions, there are many examples of shepherds involved in such "tending" relationships with the temple. For example, at the great temple of Tanjavur, specific shepherds, together with their relatives, would be assigned ninety-six sheep or forty-eight cows, in exchange for which they would be expected to provide daily enough ghee to fuel a perpetual lamp; the shepherds, their relatives, and their relatives' relatives were supposed to maintain this arrangement in perpetuity (SII 2.63, 2.64, 2.94, 2.95). Temple Brahmans also frequently entered into these tending relationships.[7]

Neither the fourth nor the fifth category of responsibility functions necessarily involved any active hand in or control over temple affairs, although people with these functions were acknowledged to have at least some connection with and authority in the business of the temple. The fourth category includes individuals who acted as signatories to grants and groups that represented interests in the temple in drawing up agreements. People who were engaged in the fifth type of responsibility function, invariably in groups, were said to ensure the protection (*rakṣai*) of the grant recorded in an inscription; typically, *paṉmāheśvarar* or *śrīvaiṣṇavas* were said to exercise this role.

Table 4.4 shows us that temple women as individuals were not closely linked to the inner workings of the temple. Of the responsibility functions that involved some degree of control over temple resources, individual temple women are named as temple administrators in three inscriptions and in the category of those who tended temple property in four inscriptions.

We find a few more references to control over temple resources, as well as to other types of responsibility functions, in inscriptions that refer to groups of people (particularly people termed *tevaraṭiyār*), who may have been temple women. Four inscriptions include such groups among supervisory or managerial personnel, and in four others, groups of *tevaraṭiyār* are given the responsibility for the collection of fines or taxes. There are three inscriptions, all dating from the first subperiod and found in Tirupati in Chittoor district (in the northernmost part of the Tamil country, in what is today Andhra Pradesh), in which we encounter the expression *emperumāṉaṭiyār rakṣai*. Because *emperumāṉaṭiyār* is one of the "temple woman" terms and was applied in other inscriptional contexts to people who were definitely women, it is possible that it indicates the designation of temple women as "protectors" of grants. But even in the case of groups, only a very small number of inscriptions represent temple women—or groups that might include or consist of temple women—as performing responsibility functions.

We may contrast these small numbers not only with the much larger numbers of male temple officials who, as individuals or in groups, engaged in responsibility functions central to the workings of the Chola period temple but also with the numbers of temple women—referred to as *sānis*—who were involved in such functions in medieval Andhra Pradesh. In Telugu inscriptions contemporary with the Chola period inscriptions in Tamil, *sānis*, very often together with male temple officials such as *māṇis* or *sthānapatis*, or as a group termed the "three hundred *sānis*," frequently took charge of or supervised the administration of gifts to the temple (Talbot 1988b, 105–7; Ramaswamy 1989, 96–97). In the Tamil country, in contrast, the responsibility for temple affairs seems to have rested solely with men, and it is extremely rare to find managerial tasks, even of the most nominal sort, shared with temple women.[8]

The almost complete lack of engagement of temple women in responsibility functions means that they were not authorized to exercise power within the institutional structure of the temple nor to have direct access to the economic resources of the temple. But they were also denied the opportunity, which so many men took advantage of in the later Chola period, to use involvement in temple affairs as a means of gaining status and public prominence. The men whose names increasingly multiply in the records engraved on temple walls were—through the inscription of the record itself, as well as through the encounters, transactions, and solemn ceremonies of donation and witnessing that the record represents—accorded recognition by the temple and the local society, in terms both of their reputations and social connections in the short term and of their fame for posterity.[9] Temple women may have realized these aims through their activity as donors—an avenue that temple men did not follow—but they did not acquire or enhance their status and position by participating in temple affairs, as temple men did. Temple women did, however, participate in temple service, and we now examine this aspect of their identity and activity.

Serving in the Temple

Dancing and Singing

In the third year of the reign of Ko Māṟapaṉmar alias Tiripuvaṉacakkaravattikaḷ Śrī Vikkirama Pāṇṭiyatevar, the sacred order [of the deity] concerning the *patiyilār* and the *tevaraṭiyār* of the temple of Lord Tiruviraṭṭanamuṭaiya Nāyaṉār [was given]: that when the [deities] Chief (*mutaliyār*) Nāṭaṟkariyakūttar and Nāyakar are brought into the hundred-pillar *maṇṭapam*, the *patiyilār* are responsible for dancing before the raising of the curtain and the *tevaraṭiyār* are responsible for dancing after the raising of the curtain.

—SII 8.333: this inscription was engraved in the thirteenth century on the southern *gopura* at the Viraṭṭaneśvara temple in Tiruvadi, South Arcot district.

In the ninth year of the reign of Śrī Kulottuṅkacoḻadevar, it is agreed (this) first day of the ninth year that gold and paddy are to be provided as they were formerly provided for the *pāṇar* in this temple, at the rate of 1 *kalam* of paddy, measured by the *ūrkkāl*, per person, for the basic living allowance (*mutal kāṇipeṟṟapaṭi*) for Irumuṭicoḻaṉ Pirāṉ alias Acañcalapperayaṉ—who is to sing for the Lord of Tiruviṭaimarutu in Tiraimūrnāṭu in Uyyakoṇṭārvaḷanāṭu, who is to cause the *taḷiyillār tevaraṭiyār* to sing in the temple, and who is to dwell here as the person of this place responsible for the *pāṇar*—and for his descendents (*vaṅśattār*).

We, together with those servants of the temple (*palapaṇi nivantakkārar*) who are partners in this agreement, assign, as formerly to the *pāṇar*, the land necessary to produce this paddy and additional expense money—land that is part of the *tevatānam* of this god—as land for the support of *pāṇar* (*pāṇakāṇi*), as their "livelihood" (*jīvitam*).

And, as a place of residence, a house is given for dwelling here, and the terms of this allowance (*paṭi*) are inscribed in stone as what is approved this ninth year and first day, according to royal order (*tirumukam*).

This royal proclamation (*tirumantira olai*) is signed by Malaiyappirāyar and Putukkaṭaiyār, the tax accountants Neṭumaṇamuṭaiyāṉ, Ponnuḻāṉ, Paṇṇainallūruṭaiyāṉ, Veḷārkiḻavaṉ, Aracūruṭaiyāṉ, and Ceṟṟūruṭaiyāṉ, [and others].

[The boundaries of the land are given and the yield in paddy.]

Signed: the temple accountant Kuṇṭaiyūrkiḻavaṉ, the temple servant (*tevarkaṉmi*) Tirucciṟṟampalapaṭṭaṉ, the temple manager (*śrīkāriyam*) Mulaṅkuṭaiyāṉ, and the *śrīmāheśvara kaṇkāṇi* Tiruviti Anpaṟkaracu.

[More details of the land boundaries are given, and the names of these signatories are again inscribed].

—SII 5.705: this inscription, which begins with a very long *meykkīrtti*, was engraved in A.D. 1142 at the Mahāliṅgasvāmi temple in Tiruvidaimarudur, Tanjavur district.

The art of the *devadāsīs*, their expertise in dancing and singing, has been at the center of much of the attention paid to these women in the last century. One frequently encounters the idea that the entire *devadāsī* institution is tied to the introduction of song and dance into rituals of worship, that the very raison d'être of the temple woman was to serve as a performer in the temple (e.g., Sadasivan 1993, 31). Several of the scholars who have made substantial contributions to our understanding of temple women in recent times have themselves been dancers, and their work conveys a vivid appreciation of the artistic tradition and professional skill of the surviving members of *devadāsī* communities.[10] But the *devadāsīs*' artistic heritage is not particularly ancient. Their traditions—including the repertoire of particular music and dance forms and the performance of dance at specified moments in temple ritual—seem to have been developed and codified in the eighteenth and nineteenth centuries (Khokar 1979, 64; Kersenboom 1987, 43–48; Meduri 1996, 40–45). It is not really possible to trace back to early times a continuous lineage for the *devadāsī* as we think of her today, as a temple servant whose ritual expertise was dance. Songs and dances do not seem to have been formal liturgical elements or offerings made to the temple deity in the temple ritual of early South India, as it is reflected in the Tamil *bhakti* literature of the sixth to ninth centuries, nor was the singing and dancing that was a part of early devotional life of the same character or performed by the same types of people as the temple songs and dances of later times (Young and Orr 1985; Orr and Young 1986). As we have seen in the analysis of Chola period setup grants at the beginning of this chapter, hymn singing did become a more established feature of temple liturgy in succeeding centuries, but dance seems to have been a minor component in the ritual life of the medieval temple. The Agamic texts similarly give the impression that dance was an optional element in temple ritual.[11] And between medieval and modern times, many factors have been at work which have altered the ritual contexts in which temple women had a part to play, the artistic traditions that shaped the forms of temple dance, and the associations between temple dance and temple women.

Despite the fact that temple women are so frequently referred to as "dancing-girls"—or, more respectfully, "temple dancers"—in scholarly and popular literature, the inscriptions of medieval India only rarely refer to them in this way (see table 2.3). Of the 304 Chola period inscriptions that mention temple women, only 4 use terms that mean "dancer." In 2 of these inscriptions, both of which refer to groups of singers, as well as dancers, it is not even certain that these performers are female. The first, an early Chola period inscription from Chittoor district in the far north, records that *kūttu-āṭiṉār* ("*kūttu* dancers") and *pāṭiṉār* ("singers") were to receive payment for their services, apparently on the occasion of a festival for the god Indra (SII 8.529). The second is an eleventh-century inscription from Kolar district, in the northwest, which mentions the provisions made for the *āṭiṉār* and *pāṭiṉār* who were to perform at a festival (EC 10.Kl 108). These inscriptions, although separated in time, come from the same general geographical area, and the use of the term *aṭiṉār* for "dancers" seems restricted to this region. In 2 other inscriptions that record arrangements for temple dance, and refer to the performers as dancers, there is much more certainty that these are women. Both are mid-twelfth century inscriptions from Tiruvengavasal in Tiruchirappalli district, which name the women who were commissioned to dance at temple festivals. In one of these inscriptions (IPS 139), the woman is referred to as a *cāntikkūtti*. *Kūtti* is the feminine form for "dancer," derived from *kūttu* ("dance, dancing"). A *cāntikkūtti* is a woman who performs the *cānti* dance; *cānti* (from Skt. *śānti*, "peace") is perhaps best translated in this context as "festival" (MTL, 1370).[12] The other inscription (IPS 128) names a woman who is to act as an *āṭuvāḷ* ("female dancer"), and specifies that she is to perform the *cāntikkūttu*.

Very few temple women are referred to as dancers, and it is equally the case that all female dancers were not temple women. Four Chola period inscriptions refer to *kūttis* or *cāntikkūttis* who do not appear to have had any connection with the temple. Two are eleventh-century inscriptions with references to a "dancer-tax" (*kūtti kāl*) (EI 22.34; SII 7.467).[13] And two thirteenth-century inscriptions (IPS 219 and SII 17.463) record the donations of women said to be *cāntikkūttis* "of our town" or "in this place"—not "of the temple." One of these (IPS 219) describes the donor as the daughter of a man named (or titled) Periyanāṭṭācāriyaṉ, "great teacher (*ācāriyaṉ*) of the district (*nāṭu*)," a name that indicates high professional standing. This man is not identified as a *cāntikkūttaṉ*, but there are several inscriptions in which male dancers are referred to by this term. In one (SII 2.67H), the *cāntikkūttaṉ*—who was employed to perform a play or a dance called the "Rājarājeśvaranāṭakam" at the big temple of Tanjavur—also has *ācāriyaṉ* ("teacher") as part of his name. In another (IPS 275), a *cāntikkūttaṉ* "of this district (*nāṭu*)" is said to have received land from the same temple of Tiruvengavasal that employed the two female dancers (the *cāntikkūtti* and the *āṭuvāḷ*) already mentioned.

Although all the inscriptions that refer to men as *cāntikkūttar* do so in connection with support from or performance in a temple, it seems to me that there are a number of indications that *cāntikkūttar* were professional dancers who were independent of the temple, in family-based occupational groups in which both men and women were involved in performances in various contexts. The constellation of features shown by the inscriptions that refer to *cāntikkūttar*—their identification as being of the town or district rather than of the temple; the word *ācāriyaṉ* as part of the names of several of the men; the employment of *cāntikkūttar* in the temple specifically for dance performances; the mention of a father-daughter kinship relation—suggest that the *cāntikkūttar* were an occupational group not primarily identified with temple service but employed by the temple as performers, especially during festivals.[14]

Among those—*cāntikkūttar* and others—who danced in the temple, men were more prominent than women, particularly in the earlier Chola period. Table 4.5 shows the numbers of inscriptions that refer to temple dancers or performers of drama (*nāṭakam*) in each of the four subperiods, indicating whether we can identify them as women, men, or neither. The first thing we notice in this table is how small these numbers are. That my careful scrutiny of the entire corpus of Chola period inscriptions has uncovered only thirty-eight inscriptions that refer to temple dancers underscores the minor and inessential character of dance as an element of medieval temple ritual. In twelve of the inscriptions, it is not possible to ascertain the sex of the performer; I have nonetheless taken these inscriptions to refer to temple women in my overall tabulation (e.g., in table 4.2) because it seems quite possible that some of these anonymous dancers were women. When we turn to a comparison of the two groups of inscriptions in which the dancers are clearly male or female, we see that in the earlier Chola period men were much more frequently given the task of dancing in the temple than were women: nine inscriptions refer to male dancers and only two to female dancers. In the later Chola period, however, the situation is reversed: twice as many temple dancers are identified as women than as men.

We see a similar and even more dramatic reversal in comparing male and female dancers with respect to the contexts of their performances. In the first two subperiods, six inscriptions assign men to the function of dancing at festivals, and only one assigns women to this function; in the last two subperiods, just 1 inscription designates men as festival dancers, whereas seven designate women. In the later Chola period, then, women became increasingly visible as temple dancers, and although they did not entirely monopolize temple dance, women seem to have effectively displaced men from a role that had formerly been largely a male preserve—dancing at festivals.

The seven inscriptions that describe temple women as festival dancers represent a small fraction of the total number of inscriptions that refer to temple women and their activities and an even tinier fraction of all the Chola period inscriptions that refer to temple ritual in general and to arrangements

Table 4.5 Temple dancers in Chola period inscriptions

	Chola 1	Chola 2	Chola 3	Chola 4	Total
Women	1	1	6	4	12
?	2	2	5	3	12
Men	3	6	3	2	14
Total	6	9	14	9	38

for festivals in particular. In other words, dancing at festivals was a relatively unimportant aspect of temple women's lives, and having temple women dance was not at all necessary for the conduct of temple festivals. Nonetheless, the pattern of displacement that these inscriptions reveal, in however minor a way, may be significant for our understanding of changes in both the circumstances of temple women and the organization of temple life. As temple women in the later Chola period were taking over from men the responsibility for performing festival dances, they were moving into a specialization that was to become in later centuries central to their identity and their place in the structure of temple service.[15]

But the way—or one of the ways—in which Chola period temple women accomplished this move sets them apart from their counterparts of a later age and from their male counterparts in their own times. In at least two of the seven inscriptions from the later Chola period that describe women performing festival dances, these women purchased from the temple the right to perform this service, as well as the right to sing the Tamil devotional song *Tiruvempāvai* (ARE 160 and 161 of 1940–41). These temple women were not inheriting the right to perform dance but were, instead, acquiring it by making a deal with the temple.[16] Thus, along with the shift in the identity of festival dancers from male to female, there was also a shift from the employment of members of a professional community, who were not necessarily associated with a particular temple, to the employment of temple women who regarded dancing at festivals more as a privilege and mark of status than a duty for which they would be remunerated. The first of the two inscriptions translated at the beginning of this section, fixing the order in which the *patiyilār* and *tevaraṭiyār* were to perform dance in the course of daily worship, provides another indication of the concern for rank and ritual rights that seems to characterize temple women's involvement with dance in the later Chola period.

Temple women were not, of course, the only people who regarded temple service in this light, and the structuring of temple life around concepts of privilege and honor was to become more and more important for all types of tasks and positions in the post-Chola period. But during the Chola period itself, we find a kind of patchwork in which some of the roles associated with the functioning of the temple seem to have had an honorary character, some were more in the nature of "jobs" of either a menial or professional nature, and others were a mixture of these two types or were transitional from one type to another—tending in most cases toward becoming increasingly honorary. The complexity of this pattern becomes even greater when we take into account not only the different kinds of tasks there were to perform in the context of the temple but also the variety of people who might perform them and the possibility of competition among them. In the case we are considering here, I have suggested that the role of dancer, and particularly festival dancer, was in the early Chola period filled largely by members—mostly but not exclusively male—of a professional, family-based occupational group, the *cāntikkūttar*. In the later Chola period, the *cāntikkūttar* lost ground to women who were temple- rather than family-based and who regarded this role as a privilege rather than a profession. This is not to say that these women lacked skill in dance, but they differed dramatically from the *cāntikkūttar* in that their primary identity was not that of dancer.

Yet another group is associated with temple dance: the *naṭṭuvar*, or "dance masters."[17] They are different from the *cāntikkūttar* because they were not displaced from their role in the temple by temple women, and they are different from the temple women because their role continued throughout the Chola period to be a professional and family-based right rather than a matter of personal privilege. *Naṭṭuvar* are mentioned in thirteen Chola period inscriptions that I have located. In every case, the *naṭṭuvaṉ* is male and is described as receiving support from the temple for his services, and in two of the inscriptions, the *naṭṭuvaṉ*'s service rights are transferred to male relatives. The *naṭṭuvar* are not linked explicitly to temple women in the inscriptions,[18] but in several cases *naṭṭuvar* are associated with drummers (*uvaccar*) or other musicians. An eleventh-century inscription (SII 8.644) records that a *naṭṭuvar* was assigned an *uvacca-kāṇi*, "drummer's service right," and a thirteenth-century inscription (EC 10.Bp38a) describes a *naṭṭuvaṉ* as the head of a group of *uvaccar*. We have seen, earlier in this chapter, how important drummers were in the ritual life of the temple. References to *uvaccar*, as key ritual specialists, are particularly abundant in the early Chola period, but by the early twentieth century, members of this community—who became known as Ōcchar—had suffered a marked decline in social status and had a much more marginal ritual status as drummers and priests who served village goddesses (Thurston and Rangachari 1909, 5: 419–20; Pillay 1953, 248).[19]

The inscriptions of the later Chola period that show *naṭṭuvar* as supervisors of groups of *uvaccar* or as possessors of *uvaccar*'s service rights may provide a clue to how the *uvaccar* lost their ritual status. As the *naṭṭuvar* maintained and strengthened their position within the temple structure, they may, in the later Chola period, have begun to compete with the *uvaccar* and take over some of their functions. Eventually, the *uvaccar* were entirely displaced as ritual specialists within the great temples. Another function with which the *naṭṭuvar* might have increasingly been involved, and which is related to drumming, was that of dance teacher: the Chola period temple women who were not members of *cāntikkūttar* families perhaps received instruction from *naṭṭuvar*—just as, in recent South Indian history, *devadāsīs* have been taught by *naṭṭuvaṉār*.[20]

When we consider the roles of temple women and other temple servants as singers in Chola period temples, we see a pattern of competition and displacement similar to that for dance but with the opposite result: whereas temple women appear to have been increasingly implicated in dance, particularly festival dance, they were progressively excluded from the role of hymn singer.

Just as temple women were rarely referred to as dancers, so, too, were terms that mean "singer" scarcely ever applied to them. Temple women were very different from male temple servants in this regard. In the Chola period inscriptions, two types of terms are used for "singers": general terms, including those based on the Tamil verb *pāṭu*, "to sing," and those derived from the Sanskrit *gandharva* (the term for the celestial musicians who are, in myth, the companions of the *apsarās*); and technical terms, like *viṇṇappañ ceyvār*, those who "sing sacred hymns in the presence of the deity" (MTL, 3664). The general terms may be found in combination with expressions that provide somewhat more ritual specificity, with respect to the kind of song to be performed; for example, *tiruppatiyam pāṭuvar* are "those who sing (Tamil) hymns." In many cases, the plural form of these terms and the anonymity of the singers obscure their sex, but when we can ascertain whether those identified as singers are female or male, they are almost invariably the latter.

The technical terms are never applied to women,[21] and there are only two inscriptions in which women are referred to as singers, using the general terms. One of these, a tenth-century inscription from Travancore, in southern Kerala, records an agreement between the Chera king and the authorities of a Śiva temple about the payments to be made for various temple services and temple servants, including the *naṅkaimār kāntarpikaḷ*, the "lady singers" (TAS 8,43). The term used here for "singer," *kāntarpikaḷ*, has its male equivalent in the terms *gāndharvar* or *kāntarppar*, which are found elsewhere in Tamil inscriptions of the Chola period (e.g., SII 23.264 and SII 4.867). The second inscription comes from Kanchipuram in Chingleput district and records the gift of villages by a Telugu Choda chief to support the "women who sing (*pāṭum peṇṭukaḷ*) before the Lord"—who is in this case a form of Viṣṇu, Śrī Varadarājasvāmi (SITI 393). In contrast to this single inscription that applies terms derived from *pāṭu* to women,[22] I have found eight inscriptions in which they are applied to men. The term *pāṭuvar*, "singer," is used to refer to men in five inscriptions, but there are no cases in which it definitely refers to women.

Not only is there a preponderance of men among those who are identified as singers in Chola period inscriptions, but also the task of singing in the temple is assigned much more frequently to men than to women. The predominance of men as hymn singers has made me decide to handle the inscriptions in which the sex of the singers is unclear in a different way than I have for dancers: I have included in the category of temple women only those singers who are definitely female. Table 4.6 indicates the numbers of inscriptions that refer to singers in the temple, as women, as men, or as people whose sex cannot be ascertained. Men are more numerous as temple singers in all subperiods except the third, when an equal number of inscriptions describe women as filling this function. All six of the inscriptions in this subperiod that describe women as temple singers are from a single temple in Nallur, in South Arcot district, and they are all records of deals made by individual *tevaraṭiyār*: each of these women, having made a gift of gold to the temple, received the right to sing a particular portion of the hymn *Tiruvempāvai* and, in several cases—as we have already seen in the discussion of temple women's involvement in festival dance—to perform cer-

Table 4.6 Temple singers in Chola period inscriptions

	Chola 1	Chola 2	Chola 3	Chola 4	Total
Women	2	2	6	2	12
?	14	15	5	8	42
Men	4	13	6	5	28
Total	20	30	17	15	82

tain dances or to be otherwise involved in the conduct of festivals (ARE 143, 144, 149, 160, 161, and 176 of 1940–41).

Tiruvempāvai, a composition of the Śaiva poet-saint Māṇikkavācakar, is referred to not only in this set of inscriptions but also in an eleventh-century record from Tiruvorriyur in Chingleput district, in which sixteen *tevaraṭiyār* are given the responsibility for its performance (ARE 128 of 1912). It is striking that this is the only specific hymn mentioned by name as part of the temple liturgy to be performed by female singers. It may be that this particular devotional work, which is cast in the feminine voice, was regarded as being particularly appropriate for women to sing—as it continues to be in contemporary Tamilnadu (Orr and Young 1986; Young 1993). But other compositions—for example, *Tiruvāymoḻi*, part of the Vaiṣṇava canon of devotional hymns in Tamil—seem to have been considered as suitable only for male performers.[23]

Chola period inscriptions indicate that until the thirteenth century, many different types of people filled the role of hymn singer: in the early period, this task was assigned, on the one hand, to a woman who was a slave (ARE 149 of 1936–37), and, on the other hand, to high-status men, such as Brahmans (including those bearing the title *paṭṭar*, from Skt. *bhaṭṭar*) and *aṭikaḷmār* (ascetics or "honored devotees"). In the third subperiod, there continue to be hymn singers of various types and status: apart from the temple women who negotiated for the privilege of singing *Tiruvempāvai*, there are references to men who were *uvaccar* or *pāṇar* and who served as singers in this period. One of the inscriptions translated at the beginning of this section (SII 5.705) shows how members of this latter community were associated with hymn singing at a temple in Tiruvidaimarudur, in Tanjavur district, in the twelfth century.

The *pāṇar* are known to us from early Cankam literature as itinerant bards who sang and played the stringed *yāḻ*, but there are very few references to this group in Chola period inscriptions—not enough to shed light on the way in which, in Chola and post-Chola times, their social situation changed dramatically as they shifted in occupation from being musicians to being tailors and came to be considered of low caste (Kailasapathy 1968; Young and Orr 1985 and 1988). In the previous translation, a *pāṇaṉ* (or a man who is taking up the temple service rights of the *pāṇar*) is an active participant in temple life: he is to receive support from the temple, to sing for the temple deity, to oversee the singing of the *tevaraṭiyār* in the temple, and to be responsible for the group of *pāṇar* associated with the temple. But a century later, there are indications that the status of the *pāṇar* had declined[24] and that their eligibility to serve as singers in the temple was being more strictly defined.

In the thirteenth century, hymn singing was increasingly dominated by people of high status—Brahmans and others—and by members of new professional or temple service categories. Already in the eleventh century, in the middle of the Chola period, we begin to encounter the term *viṇṇappañ ceyvār*, which was to become one of the technical terms for hymn singer in the Śrīvaiṣṇava tradition (Jagadeesan 1967), and in the thirteenth century we find the earliest inscriptional references to *otuvār*, the hymn singers in the later South Indian Śaiva tradition (ARE 203 of 1908; SII 23.92; TAS 6.14; Peterson 1989, 56–75). It appears that a relatively open and fluid notion of who might sing hymns in the temple had given way by the end of the Chola period to more restrictive ideas about the ritual qualifications and rights associated with this role. This development may have been tied to the canonization of the two bodies of devotional poems—composed by the Vaiṣṇava and Śaiva poet-saints—and their adaptation and entrenchment in temple liturgy, which took place during the Chola period.[25] Ritual chanting and singing were part of the traditional expertise of Brahmans, and as the Tamil hymns came to be acknowledged as equal in importance to the sacred Vedic texts, the definition of who was eligible to be a hymn singer may have been subject to increasing regulation and definition. In this atmosphere of competition and professionalization, temple women—as well, perhaps, as members of traditional performing communities, like the *pāṇar*—seem to have had little opportunity to further their activities and identities as singers in the temple.

It is clear that the temple women of medieval Tamilnadu were not primarily or originally dancers and singers. They did, nonetheless, occasionally perform songs and dances in the temple—in several cases actually paying for the privilege of doing so—and participated in the processes that were ongoing throughout the Chola period in which different kinds of individuals and groups laid claim to the task or the honor of performing for the deity. The rights to these temple service roles were not, even by the end of the Chola period, exclusively or permanently assigned to particular types of temple personnel, but certain patterns that would persist into later times were beginning to be established. Several groups that had been prominent as singers, musicians, or dancers in the pre-Chola or early Chola period—the *pāṇar*, the *uvaccar*, and the *cāntikkūttar*—had decreasing access to the ritual roles they once played in the life of the temple. The eclipse of these figures is not, however, attributable to a single cause; if, for the *pāṇar*, it was a case of displacement by Brahmans and new categories of professional temple servants, the *cāntikkūttar* may have had temple women to blame for their marginalization.

The increasing involvement of temple women with festival dance may have been possible because this was a service that was not ritually necessary but occasional and optional. We may contrast the role of festival dancing with hymn singing, which was becoming increasingly part of the formal liturgical structure of daily worship; dancing at festivals was an activity in which individual initiative, rather than membership in a particular community or professional group, might have provided the opportunity for participation. If temple women began to take advantage of this opportunity in the late Chola period, they did so only in small numbers. Their dancing at temple festivals was not central either to the definition of what they were or to what constituted a proper temple festival. It is only in retrospect that we can see that temple women's engagement with festival dance in this period was of great significance for their future roles as temple servants.

Temple Women as God's Attendants

In the fifteenth year of the reign of Śrī Uttamacoḻadevar Ko Parakesarivarmaṉ, [an image of] Śrībalidevar, eight trumpets, and flywhisk handles for the twenty-four flywhisk women (*kavarippiṇākaḷ*) were made out of gold and given to Mahādevar (the Great God) of Tiruvoṟṟiyūr, as graciously commanded by Uttamacoḻa and arranged by Ceṉṉiy Eṟipaṭaiccoḻaṉ Uttamacoḻaṉ. . . . [The rest of the inscription is broken off.]

—SII 3.143: this inscription was engraved in A.D. 985 on a slab that is now built into the floor of the verandah around the central shrine of the Ādhipurīśvara temple in Tiruvorriyur, Chingleput district.

On the 116th day in the 30th year of the reign of Tribhuvaṉaviradevar, the emperor of the three worlds who seized Maturai, Īḻam, Caruvūr, and the crowned head of the Pandya king, and who performed the consecration (*abhiṣekam*) of victory and the consecration of the hero, the *tāṉattār* (temple trustees) and the *ūrār* (village assembly) met to determine the order of hymn singing (*tirup-pāṭṭaṭaivu*), carrying the sacred lamps (*tiruvālatti*), and the order of personal attendance (*meykkāṭṭaṭaivu*) [on the deity] of the temple women (*teva aṭiyār*) of the temple of Lord Cuntaracoḻīśvaramuṭaiyār in Kūḻaikuḷattūr; this determination of rank (*muṟai*) before [Śiva's] sacred trident was conveyed to Villavatāy.

[In] the first family (*kuṭi*) . . . . rank are Māṇikkam and Tiruvampalam-pirīyāti alias Catturukāla-māṇikkam.

[In] the second rank (*muṟai*) are Ammaiyāḻvi alias Aṟputakkūtta-māṇikkam and Nācciyāḻvi alias Villavatāy-māṇikkam.

[In] the third rank are Cuntara . . . . ṉuktavaḷate . . . . māṇikkam and her daughter Kaṇavati alias Kulottuṅkacoḻa-māṇikkam and Pollātapiḷḷai alias Tiruñāṉacampanta-māṇikkam and Ciṟuval. . . . yāṟkoyil-māṇikkam.

[In] the fourth rank are Valli alias Irājakempira-māṇikkam and Pollātapiḷḷai alias Coḻakoṉ-māṇikkam.

[In] the fifth rank are Āṭko. . . . ra-māṇikkam and Ciṟupa. . . . alias. . . . Tiruciṟṟampala-māṇikkam.

[In] the sixth rank are Ammaiyāḻvi alias Tiruveṇṇāval-māṇikkam and. . . . Tirukaḷiṟṟupaṭi-māṇikkam.

[In] the seventh rank are Poṟṟu . . . . liviṭṭa . . . . ṟṟucoḻa-māṇikkam and Kūttāṭinācci alias Tirunaṭampuṟinta-māṇikkam.

For the sacred lamps on festival days (*tirunāḷ*), ... and for carrying . . . . on festival days, today. . . . [The rest of the inscription is defaced.]

—IPS 162: this inscription was engraved in A.D. 1207 on the south side of the wall of the ruined Śiva temple in Kulattur, Tiruchirappalli district (Pudukkottai State).

Seventeen Chola period inscriptions refer to temple women as attendants in temple rituals. There are four types of attendance functions that temple women performed: bearing flywhisks (mentioned in eight inscriptions), being present at festivals (in four inscriptions), bearing lamps (in three inscriptions), and acting as a personal attendant on the deity (in two inscriptions). These tasks are similar to singing and dancing in their connotations of special privilege, entailing as they do participation in ritual and proximity to the temple deity, but they are rather different from singing and dancing in that they are entirely unskilled functions.

The most frequently mentioned type of attendance is bearing a flywhisk—the yaktail fan or "chowrie" (Ta. *kavari* or *cāmarai*, from Skt. *cāmarā*). To be fanned with the flywhisk is a mark of distinction particularly associated with kings and deities, who have frequently been depicted in the literature and art of North India, since the early centuries B.C., as flanked by beautiful, female flywhisk bearers (Tewari 1987, 52–70). The association of the flywhisk with both religious and royal contexts is attested to in South India at least since the ninth century A.D.[26] The inscriptional evidence of the Chola period indicates that temple flywhisk bearers were most often women but not exclusively so; at the Srirangam temple, for example, a man was appointed, in the late eleventh century, to do flywhisk service (SII 24.66).[27]

Of the eight inscriptions that refer to temple women as performing this service, three are from the early Chola period, and all three—including the first, the previous translation—use the term *kavarippiṇā*, "flywhisk woman," for the temple women involved.[28] Even though a specific term is applied to these women, it does not appear to entail any particular ritual qualifications or status. In one case, slave women, who have been donated to the temple by a local notable, perform this attendance function: "I have given, with pouring of water, my slave (*aṭiyāḷ*) Uṟaṉ Colai, her daughter Veḷāṉ Pirāṭṭi, and her daughter Aṟamaiyiṇṭaṉ Kaṇṭi to sing hymns (*tiruppatiyam*) and [act as] *kavarippiṇāvarkaḷ* for the Supreme Lord of the temple . . . " (ARE 149 of 1936–37). This tenth-century record clearly spells out their status as chattel but also indicates the privileged character of the role these women are to fulfill by using an honorific double plural for the term "flywhisk women." The honor of attending the deity as a flywhisk bearer is also evident in the five inscriptions of the later Chola period that refer to temple women in this role. They are all thirteenth-century inscriptions from temples in Chingleput district that describe individual temple women as making deals—offering substantial donations to the temple in exchange for the privilege of being a flywhisk bearer (ARE 172, 180, 183, 210, and 211 of 1923).

The fact that these deals were made by temple women suggests that the task itself was not so much a critical ritual function as an incidental adjunct to temple ceremony, whose significance lay primarily in the fact that considerable honor was attached to this role. At the same time, inasmuch as it was a service of attendance borrowed from or shared with the royal context, flywhisk bearing did not need to be performed by a specially qualified or ritually pure person. This activity was an ornamental one, just as in a royal court, where it would be performed by female servants or palace women; the function in the temple was thus perhaps ideally carried out by women, and their identity or status—whether they were slaves or wealthy patrons—was not an issue.[29]

Four Chola period inscriptions refer to temple women's involvement in temple festivals, without specifying any particular function such as singing and dancing. In three of these inscriptions, this involvement means taking part in festival processions, and all three describe the temple woman's right to participate as the consequence of her donation to the temple—once again, a deal. It is clear that what was involved in these deals was the acquisition of a position of honor, of precedence and proximity to the deity in the procession. The fourth inscription mentions in rather vague terms the responsibility of temple women to be present at temple festivals. Chola period temple women seem not to have been extensively involved in festival rituals.[30] When they were involved, their participation had the same character as that of the temple women who bore flywhisks—that is, it was less a matter of performing a ritual function than of (literally) parading the status that had been accorded to them by the temple.

Three of the Chola period inscriptions that refer to temple women as attendants describe them as bearing lamps. In two cases, both from the far south, the task of carrying lamps (*viḷakku*) was assigned to temple women (*tevaraṭiyār* or *tevaṭiccis*) along with menial tasks—weaving garlands or pounding paddy (SII 14.132; TAS 5.24—translations of both follow). In these cases, it is not at all obvious that bearing lamps was actually a ritual duty that involved proximity to the deity; it is possible, for example, that the lamps in question were simply for illumination. But a more formal ritual function for temple women is evident in the third inscription, which is translated at the beginning of this section. In this record, seven *tevaraṭiyār* are each assigned a turn (*muṟai*) to sing, wave the lamp (*ālatti*) before the god, and attend on him (IPS 162). The term *ālatti* that is used for "lamp" in this inscription is derived from the Sanskrit word *ārati*, and we find in this inscription the technical usage *tiruvālattiyeṭu*, "to wave light, etc., before an idol or important personage" (MTL, 246). The careful specification of the order of precedence for the temple women to perform this service indicates the honor associated with this role. But waving and bearing lamps was not a task assigned exclusively to female temple servants, and we find—at least in inscriptions of the early Chola period—men who performed this function, including Brahman men charged with waving the *ālatti* lamp (e.g., SII 3.149). Bearing or waving lamps does not seem to have been a very important role for temple women in the Chola period—in contrast to its apparent significance for South Indian temple women in more recent times[31]—nor does it seem to have been a function that was of particular importance in Chola period temple rituals.

Two thirteenth-century inscriptions refer to temple women who were personal attendants for the image of the deity. One of them has just been discussed, in which the duties assigned in rotation to the temple women of Kulattur included attendance on the god (*meykkāṭṭu*), in addition to waving the *ālatti* lamp before him and singing hymns (IPS 162). The other inscription is another thirteenth-century record, from Tirunelveli district in the far south of Tamilnadu, which assigns a series of roles to various temple women, including cleaning and decorating temple floors, as well as a task that I classify as personal attendance—applying *kāppu* (substances such as sandal paste for ritual protection or adornment) to the images of the deities in the temple (ARE 374 of 1972–73). In both of these inscriptions, in which the names of the temple women are given and their duties and ranks carefully specified, it is clear that personal attendance on the deities was a coveted honor.

This service, like the other attendance functions with which temple women were involved, could be, from the point of view of the person who performed it, a special privilege and, at the same time, from the point of view of the deity or the coordinator or sponsor of temple worship, an optional service, which could be done by a variety of people—or not done at all. Attendance functions do not loom large in the central patterns of ritual life of the medieval South Indian temple or in the range of roles with which temple women were engaged. None of these attendance functions—bearing flywhisks, participating in festivals, bearing or waving lamps, or personally attending the temple deity—was performed exclusively by women. Yet something may be said to be peculiarly feminine about these tasks: close to half of the seventeen inscriptions that refer to temple women's involvement with these duties describe the acquisition of the right to perform these services as the result of a deal. Men may, on occasion, have been involved in the same tasks, but men never arrived at this involvement through these means. The fact that temple women made deals in order to serve in these roles—and that, in other cases, the exact nature of their right to perform these functions was carefully spelled out in the inscription—indicates that what was at stake was not the temple's effort to find someone to fill a job but rather the temple woman's effort to acquire recognition and status in the temple. The indications of the honorary character of these functions are particularly in evidence in the later Chola period; this was also the period of increasing involvement by temple women in these roles—thirteen of the seventeen inscriptions date from the later Chola period.

It is also possible that the temple considered such roles suitable for women. It may be, for example, that the character of these attendance services as marginal or incidental to the basic temple ritual was significant in this regard: women could be allowed to participate in temple ceremony in a capacity that would not aggravate competition for more ritually central roles. Or it may be that women's engagement in these attendance functions was seen as bringing a special quality to the atmosphere of the temple that resonated either with the ornamental character of women's roles in the palace or the auspicious character of women's roles in the home.

Bearing flywhisks—the attendance function of temple women mentioned most frequently—was a "traditionally" feminine occupation that was connected particularly with the royal context. Having women adorn one's court, as part of one's entourage, as personal attendants, or in processions, was a feature of the display and ceremonial associated with the king.[32] Although parallels and mutual borrowings between the temple and the royal palace appear to be more characteristic of the post-Chola period than of the period under study here, it may be that the increasing involvement of temple women with ornamental attendance functions in the later Chola period reflected an early stage in the transfer of aspects of the royal idiom to the temple.[33] It is also possible that some of the attendance functions performed by women in the temple—such as bearing lamps or decorating shrines and images—reflected tasks characteristically performed by women as part of domestic or votive religious observances.[34] Because of these domestic associations, such tasks may have been regarded as auspicious, and because they were performed by women in the home, they may have been considered particularly appropriate activities for temple women.

Preparing Garlands for the Lord

In the fourth year of the reign of Ko Caṭayapaṉmar alias Śrī Cuntaracoḻapāṇṭiyadevar, we the *mahāsabhaiyār* (Brahman assembly) of the *brahmadeyam* Śrī Rājarājac-caturvvetimaṅkalam in Muḷḷināṭu, Muṭikoṇṭacoḻavaḷanāṭu, Irācarācappāṇṭināṭu, met together in the hall (*ampalam*) to make a binding agreement.

We grant land for gardens and houses for the *uvaccakaḷ* (drummers) who are garden laborers (*nandavāṉak-kuṭikaḷ*), for the potters (*kucavakaḷ*), for the temple women (*tevaraṭiyār peṇṭukaḷ*) who carry sacred lamps (*tiruviḷakku*) and weave garlands (*tirupaḷḷittāmam*), for laborer-herdsmen (*veṭṭikkuṭikaḷ iṭaiyar*) who supply ghee for the lamps, and for other expenses of whatever kind for Lord (*āḻvar*) Śrī Rājendracoḻa-viṇṇakar.

[The inscription goes on to describe the boundaries of the land granted; the end of the inscription is missing.]

—SII 14.132: this inscription was engraved in A.D. 1025 on the north wall of the Gopālasvāmi temple in Mannarkoyil, Tirunelveli district.

The tasks associated with providing flowers for the temple—gardening and weaving garlands—present a kind of mirror image to attendance functions. Attendance functions were inessential and optional but brought high honor to their performers, whereas providing flowers was absolutely necessary for the conduct of temple ritual but was considered to be menial labor. Although this task, essential to worship from the earliest *bhakti* times, was viewed as a lowly one, in the "lowlier than thou" ethos of devotion that developed in the *bhakti* period, it was a task that the highest-born devotees felt honored to perform.[35] Something of this same spirit may have been carried forward or revived in the Chola period.

In Chola period inscriptions, most of the work of gardening, picking flowers, and making garlands seems to have been done by men. In only five inscriptions do women perform these functions, and in all of them women are responsible only for picking flowers and making garlands rather than tending the temple gardens. The previous translation illustrates this division of labor: men (in this case, interestingly, *uvaccar*, "drummer") are charged with taking care of the gardens and women (*tevaraṭiyār*) with making the garlands. This inscription is also typical of the handful of records that refer to women in this capacity in that it dates from the second subperiod, when three of the five inscriptions were engraved. In this early Chola period, the other people, apart from temple women, who were assigned to the task of gardening or garland making are, when they are identifiable, invariably men of relatively low status. They are not mentioned by name and are anonymous members of groups; often they are referred to, as in the case of the previous inscription, as *kuṭikaḷ*, "laborers."

In the later Chola period, however, the positions of gardener and garland maker were increasingly assigned to high-status people, including *tavaciyar* ("ascetics") and various categories of "honored devotees," such as *āṇṭār*, *nampis*, and *śrīvaiṣṇavas*.[36] In a number of the later Chola period inscriptions, including a thirteenth-century record that assigns a temple woman the task of weaving garlands (ARE 374 of 1973), those who acquired the responsibility for gardening or garland making are named. The designation of a particular individual usually indicates that some value or prestige was attached to the right to fulfill that role. Although they were essentially unskilled and menial forms of work, gardening and picking and plaiting flowers were forms of service that in the course of the Chola period increasingly involved high-status people interested in securing—in their own names—the right to perform these tasks. It is likely, then, that there was increasing competition for and more and more restricted access to these service roles. This increasing competition and restriction may account for the decline in the engagement of temple women with these tasks, although women had, in any case, never been more than marginally involved with these functions.

Menial Servants and Slaves

According to an earlier royal order, in the nineteenth year of the reign of Tribhuvaṉacakkaravattikaḷ Śrī Rājarājatevar, in the fifth month, on the third *tithi* of the bright fortnight, in the 26th *nakṣatra*, I, Vayalūr-kiḻavaṉ Tiruvekampamuṭaiyaṉ Centāmaraik Kaṇṇaṉ alias Vayirātarāyaṉ of Virukaṉpakkam alias Ceṉṉinallūr in Poṟūrnāṭu in Puliyūrkkoṭṭam alias Kulottuṅkacoḻavaḷanāṭu, in Jayaṅkoṇṭacoḻamaṇṭalam, gave to [the deity] Lord Tiruvoṟṟiyūr-uṭaiya-nāyaṉār five persons—Periyanācci, her daughter Māri, her younger sister Kavuttāḻvi, her younger sister Tiruvāṇṭi, and her younger sister Vaṭukāḻvi—to husk paddy for the feeding hall (*cālai*).

They are to husk paddy for the feeding hall of the god and those who are their descendents (*vaḻi*) are to continue this paddy husking for as long as the sun and moon shall shine.

I, Vayalūr-kiḻavaṉ Tiruvekampamuṭaiyaṉ Centāmaraik Kaṇṇaṉ alias Vayirātarāyaṉ, have had this inscribed in stone.

—SII 4.558: this inscription was engraved in A.D. 1235 on the north wall of the second prakara of the Ādhipurīśvara temple in Tiruvorriyur, Chingleput district.

Paḻuvūr Nakkaṉ, having given the village of Neṭuvāyil and the hamlets surrounding Neṭuvāyil to this deity, and taking responsibility for paying all taxes due from this holy temple and the village, now does obeisance and makes a further undertaking that paddy be measured out in the temple courtyard (*tirumuṟṟam*). . . . to the amount of 1,000 *kalam*, and that 100 *kaḻañcu* of fine quality gold be weighed out. . . . providing for the expenses of cloth, oil, taxes. . . . the expenses [for feeding] 30 *śivayogi* Brahmans and 20 Brahmans—altogether 50 people.

[The inscription goes on to give an account of the amount to be fed to each person per day—of rice, ghee, *kaṟi* (curry), *puḷiṅkaṟi* (tamarind or sour curry), salt, betel, and arecanut—and how much paddy is required for each of these expenses, resulting in a total of 1,605 *kalam*, 2 *tūṇi*, 3 *kuṟuṇi*, and 2 *nāḻi* of paddy annually.]

For one man to bring firewood (*viṟakiṭuvāṉ*), 1 *kuṟuṇi* of paddy daily, and for one cook (*aṭuvāṉ*), 1 *kuṟuṇi* of paddy daily—amounting, for the two men, to 60 *kalam* annually—and for each man an allowance for cloth of 1 *kācu* (money) and 10 *kalam* paddy—totaling 2 *kācu* and 20 *kalam* paddy.

For oil at the time of the solstices and of Saturn for the 30 *śivayogi* Brahmans and the 20 Brahmans—altogether 50 people . . . [a total of 54 *kalam* of paddy is required annually].

[The inscription continues with a detailed account of the amount of paddy required to meet the expenses of providing dal (*payaṟu*), black pepper, and asafoetida on a daily basis—totaling 155 *kalam* and, in money, 15 *kācu*, excluding the money required for "garden duty."]

For one woman to gather and smear and apply powder in the feeding hall (*cālai*), 2 *nāḻi* of paddy daily is required—amounting to 7 *kalam*, 1 *tūṇi*, and 1 *patakku* annually.

For one woman to remove the leavings and [clean] the eating place with earth and put ashes in the pot, 4 *nāḻi* of paddy daily is required, plus an allowance for cloth—amounting to 10 *kalam* annually.

For two hymn singers (*tiruppatiyam viṇṇappañ ceyvār*), 1 *patakku* and 4 *nāḻi* of paddy daily is required—amounting to 75 *kalam* annually.

For a gopuram guard (*kopurattu meykāppāṉ*) responsible for the coming and going, the placement and eviction, of those wishing to eat in the feeding hall, 1 *kuṟuṇi* and 2 *nāḻi* of paddy daily is required, plus an allowance for cloth—amounting to 37 *kalam*, 1 *tūṇi*, and 1 *patakku* annually.

For a potter (*kucavaṉ*) who makes pots for the feeding hall, 2 *nāḻi* of paddy daily is required—amounting to 7 *kalam*, 1 *tūṇi*, and 1 *patakku* annually.

For a proclaimer (*cotivi colluvaṉ*) for 27 days of proclamation from the gopuram, 1 *kuṟuṇi* of paddy daily is required—amounting to 30 *kalam* annually.

For one Brahman man who performs recitation (*adhyayyaṉam*) while the Brahmans are dining (*uttamāgrattil uṇṇum*), 1 *kuṟuṇi* of paddy daily is required—amounting to 30 *kalam* annually, plus 5 *kalam*, or 3½ *kācu* cloth money.

For sandal [paste] for the *śivayogi* Brahmans and the Brahmans who are dining, ½ *kācu* or 5 *kalam* of paddy is required.

[The inscription next provides details of the daily and annual expenses for offerings at the nighttime *śrībali* ritual—including rice, sugar, fruit, and tamarind.]

I, Irājarājapallavaraiyaṉ [= Paḻuvūr Nakkaṉ] made this gift as a tax-free "inner sanctum endowment" (*tiruvuṇṇāḻikaippuṟam*), in the 7th year of the reign of Śrī Irājarājatevar, to this [god] Śrī Vijayamaṅkalatevar, the Great Lord of this *brahmadeyam*, whose temple I constructed in stone, and a record of these arrangements has been here engraved in stone.

[There follows a detailed account of the requirements for thrice daily offerings (to the deity), including rice, ghee, *poṟikkaṟi* (fried curry), areca nut, betel, and curds. Provisions are also made for five perpetual lamps and . . .]

For a cook, 2 *nāḻi* and 1 *aḻakku* of paddy daily, and for the writer of accounts, 4 *nāḻi* of paddy daily; for 2 lamps for the nighttime *śrībali*, [a certain amount of oil required daily—the total annual expense is 365 *kalam*, 7 *kuṟuṇi*, and 4 *nāḻi*].

Between religious acts and evil deeds there is no comparison. May this grant be protected by the *paṉmāheśvarar*.

—SII 19.357 (lines 41–83): this inscription was engraved in A.D. 992 on the north and west walls of the central shrine of Gaṅgājaṭādhara temple in Govindaputtur, Tiruchirappalli district. It is written in continuation of an inscription, dated eight years earlier, that records the gift by the same donor of the village mentioned at the beginning of this record.

Eighteen Chola period inscriptions record the assignment of temple women to menial functions associated with cleaning and food preparation. In half, the women can be identified as slaves, having been sold or—as in the first of the two preceding inscriptions—given to the temple. Such cases are an exception to the rule that the specification of a temple servant's name is a mark of the honor attached to the service: slave women's names are recorded in inscriptions for the same reason that the boundaries of land sold or granted to the temple are indicated in detail—to provide a precise description of the property possessed by the temple.

In only one of the eighteen inscriptions referring to temple women's involvement in menial tasks is there the slightest hint that the task is regarded as a privilege. In the thirteenth-century inscription already discussed (ARE 374 of 1972–73), ten temple women were assigned to various duties, including applying *kāppu* (protective substances or adornments) to the deities—a task that I classified as an attendance function—as well as making decorations (*kolams*) in the great hall (*mahāmaṇḍapa*) of the temple and cleaning and applying *kāppu* in the first and second *prākāras* (surrounding courtyards). This is the only Chola period inscription that specifies that women performed the service of cleaning temple floors, although other people—men or anonymous groups—were often assigned to this task, and as we shall see, women were frequently charged with cleaning the floors of eating halls. Both Tamil and Sanskrit *bhakti* literature exhorts devotees to serve the Lord by cleaning the floors of his shrine,[37] but this is the only inscription that suggests—through its careful assignment of duties to specific women—that cleaning the floors of the temple was considered an honored task in the Chola period. It is also the only inscription that indicates that making auspicious designs (*kōlams*) had a place in the Chola period temple or that this was a distinctively feminine task, as it is in contemporary South India.

For most of the temple women whose duties found them squatting or kneeling on floors, their work was more in the nature of drudgery than auspicious ritual activity. The preceding translation above outlines the specific duties that were required of two women employed by the temple to serve in a feeding hall: one was to smear the floor (probably with cow dung, as a means of purification) to prepare it before a group of Brahmans and *śivayogis* ate, and the other woman was to clear away the leavings and clean up afterward. Altogether eleven Chola period inscriptions refer to temple women acting as servants in feeding houses—*cālais* or *maṭhas*—and although the women's precise tasks are rarely described, it is likely that they were similar to those in the preceding inscription, and that these tasks were normally assigned to women; men who worked in *cālais* or *maṭhas* were typically artisans (especially potters), cooks, or watchmen. In seven of the eleven inscriptions, the women are said to be slaves, which was rarely the case for their male counterparts. It is clear that the type of service performed by temple women in feeding houses was of extremely low status.

In six inscriptions, temple women are involved in the preparation of food that was offered to human or divine recipients. One, an eleventh-century inscription from Chidambaram, specifies that a married woman (*vāḻvacci*) was to bring the water vessel as part of the arrangements made to feed Brahmans (SII 4.223; this inscription is translated at the beginning of the following section). In five inscriptions, all from the later Chola period, temple women had the duty of pounding or husking paddy or dal; two of these, including the first record translated at the beginning of this section, identify the women involved with this work as slaves.

Food preparation tasks of this type were not carried out exclusively by women. But two related types of preparatory functions in the temple were monopolized by men. Both tasks seem to have had more honor attached to them than the work performed by women. The first is the preparation of offerings other than food. For example, while there is one inscription in which a woman fetches water to be used in cooking for Brahmans, numerous inscriptions describe Brahmans with the task of bringing water to bathe the image of the deity. And if temple women pounded paddy to prepare rice for cooking, when the substance pounded was sandalwood or turmeric, used to adorn the image of the deity, the people employed were invariably men—and, again, frequently Brahmans.[38]

The second kind of preparatory function from which women were excluded was the role of cook. The terms used to designate the person who cooked food for the deities or for human recipients in Chola period inscriptions—*aṭuvāṉ*, as in the preceding translation, which describes the arrangements for feeding *śivayogis* and Brahmans, or *maṭaiyaṉ*, as in the following inscription—are clearly masculine forms. It is surprising that the inscriptions contain so little information about the identities of temple cooks; most inscriptions that mention cooks do so in the same breath as potters or the men who were to fetch firewood, without indicating that their ritual status qualified them to prepare food of the requisite purity for gods and Brahmans (Orr 1994b). But the inscriptions do indicate clearly enough that temple cooks were men. Temple cooks and the men involved in the preparation of nonfood offerings may have been engaged in menial tasks, but the ritual location of these tasks was a good deal closer to the divine presence at the center of the temple than were the activities of the temple women. The rice husked by a slave woman in the temple courtyard had a long way to travel before it was transformed into food for the gods.

There are not very many references in Chola period inscriptions to the buying and selling of human beings or to the transfer of people as chattel, and such references are virtually nonexistent in the early Chola period. But almost all references to slavery involve women. I have located twenty-two inscriptions that refer to slavery, and in only one (ARE 280 of 1927–28) are the slaves—"drummer slaves" (*uvacca aṭimai*)—exclusively male. All of the other twenty-one inscriptions refer to slave women attached to the temple. Slave men are almost invariably identified as the children of slave women. Table 3.1 shows how the twenty-one inscriptions are distributed chronologically: there are one in the first and one in the second subperiods, six in the third, and thirteen in the last subperiod.

It is not surprising that virtually all the slaves mentioned in Chola period inscriptions were owned by the temple, given that the inscriptional sources are predominantly focused on temple affairs. Some slaves had a brand or mark (*ilaicciṉai*—from Skt. *lakṣanā*) on their bodies, which indicated their status.[39] As we have seen, the work of slaves that is mentioned most frequently is service in a feeding house attached to a temple; there are also two inscriptions in which female slaves husked paddy for the temple, and one inscription, which we have encountered several times earlier in this chapter, in which the tasks of slave women were to sing hymns and bear flywhisks. It is likely that in the later Chola period, female slaves were owned not only by the temple but also by certain wealthy members of society, and these women performed domestic functions similar to those they carried out in the temple. This may have occured particularly in the core Chola region, where we have the most evidence for temple slaves and where the Chola court may have set a certain royal style for domestic arrangements, and perhaps for temple arrangements as well.[40]

Temple women's involvement with the menial work of cleaning and food preparation is mentioned with increasing frequency in the course of the Chola period: in the first subperiod, just a single inscription refers to these tasks, but by the last subperiod there are ten such inscriptions (see table 4.2). Most of these identify the women as slaves. The rise in this type of female temple service represents the dark underside of the increasing visibility of temple women and their increasingly well-defined status and specialized roles. If, on the one hand, some temple women in the later Chola period were mobilizing their energies and resources to secure special relationships with the temple and to acquire positions of honor, on the other hand, there were those whose connections with the temple were not of their own making and whose work underscored their debased status. Yet in some ways the woman who had the privilege of standing or dancing beside the processional image of the deity and the woman who swept and smeared the floor of the feeding hall may have been regarded in the same light: both might have been referred to as *tevaraṭiyār* and both might have been seen as considered to be carrying out typically feminine functions.

The Overlapping and Obscure Outlines of Female Temple Service

In the twenty-fourth year [of the reign of] Ko Virāca Kecaripaṉmār alias Lord Śrī Rājentiracoḻatevar, through the agreement here drawn up, [to last] as long as the moon and sun shall endure,

Nakkaṉ Paravai, the "intimate" (*aṇukki*) of Lord Rājentiracoḻatevar, [gave] that part [specified herein] of Parākramacoḻanallūr, in Kiṭārankoṇṭacoḻapperiḷamaināṭu, an eastern suburb of the *taṉiyūr* Perumpaṟṟappuliyūr of Rājentiraciṅkavaḷanāṭu, for the expenses on the festival day in [the month of] Āṇi when the Lord—who is the master of Tiruccir̲r̲ampalam—graciously goes forth [in procession], for rice offerings for the Lord, for the distribution of a thousand pots of rice for the *śrīmāheśvaras* at the time when the rice offering is graciously [accepted by the Lord], for the oil necessary for the festival, for the gold which is graciously distributed [by] the Lord, and for the expenses including [provision of] the sacred cloth (*paricaṭṭam*)—totaling 20 *kācu*.

A true copy of the deed of sale [of this land] was taken from the people of the town (*nagaram*) who reside in the place called Kuṇameṅkaipuram [and this deed of sale is recorded here].

[The following lines describe the boundaries of the land bought and donated by Nakkaṉ Paravai and her defrayal of the taxes due (in paddy) through a payment of gold. The inscription goes on to describe a further donation of gold by Paravai . . .]

to provide for what is necessary for the Tiruvātirai festival in Mārkaḻi, including the cloths (*paricaṭṭam*) to be distributed—amounting to an expense of 120 *kācu*;

for the rice offerings at the Tiruvāṉi festival, and for the cloths to be distributed, and for expenses including [provision of] 4 *nāḻi* (of paddy) for lamp oil—180 *kācu*;

for reciters of *Tiruttoṇṭattokai* at the Tirumāci festival—5 *kācu*

—altogether 305 *kācu* were received and this agreement was drawn up.

The communities (*kuṭikaḷ*) who reside in Kuṇameṅkaipuram, including merchants, *veḷḷāḷar*, oil sellers (*caṅkarappāṭiyār*), weavers (*cāliyar*), and *paṭṭiṉavar* (fish sellers?), and the artisan groups (? *kiḻkalaṉaikaḷ*) including carpenters, blacksmiths, goldsmiths, and weavers (*koliyar*) accept the terms of this agreement, and undertake to maintain it for as long as the moon and sun endure.

The inhabitants of this *ūr* (village) gave a part of the land of their *ūr*, called Caṅkoṭiyaṉ Paravainaṅkainallūr [named after the donor Paravai], to cover the expenses of feeding twenty Brahmans in the Ciṅkalāntakaṉ *cālai*.

[The following lines specify the amount of paddy this land will produce, how taxes are to be paid from part of this produce, and how the rest is to be spent to feed the twenty Brahmans: to provide rice, curry, and spices—black pepper, tamarind, salt, turmeric—ghee, curds, betel, arecanut, firewood, plantain, and oil, and to support several servants.]

For one cook for the *cālai* (*cālai-maṭaiyaṉ*) 6 *nāḻi* of paddy, and as clothing allowance for the aforementioned . . [break in the inscription] . . 8 *kalam* of paddy, for one potter (*kucavaṉ*) 4 *nāḻi* of paddy, for one married woman (*vāḻvacci*) who brings the water vessel 4 *nāḻi* of paddy, for five women doing service (*paṇiceyya peṇṭukaḷ*) 1 *kuṟuṇi*, and as clothing allowance for the aforementioned 10 *kalams* of paddy, and as clothing allowance for one honored (overseer of the *cālai*?) 10 *kalams* of paddy—altogether 3 *kalam* and 3 *kuṟuṇi* of paddy per day or 1,226 *kalam*, 7 *kuṟuṇi*, and 4 *nāḻi* of paddy per year, including all the expenses here specified.

[This] agreement shall remain in force, having been engraved in stone, from this twenty-seventh year [of the king's reign] henceforth, as long as the moon and the sun endure.

—SII 4.223: this inscription, which begins with a very long *meykkīrtti*, was inscribed outside the first *prākāra* of the Nāṭarāja temple at Chidambaram, South Arcot district, in A.D. 1039.

[This section of the inscription begins with an account of the quantities of paddy available for the temple, the produce of various lands, amounting to a total of 1,080 *para* of paddy annually.]

Of this total of 1,080 *para* of paddy, 3 *para* are to be taken daily, to produce 48 *nāḻi* of rice, as measured by the god's *iraṭṭamaṭai*, and portions distributed in the following manner:

for the *meṟccānti* (priest) 4 *nāḻi* and 1 *uri*, for one *kiḻccānti* (assistant priest) 3 *nāḻi* and 1 *uri*, for another *kiḻccānti* 3 *nāḻi*, for the sacred parasol [bearer] 2 *nāḻi*, for the feeding of the *vaiśvadeva* ("all gods") at the daily *śrībali* ritual 3 *nāḻi* and 1 *uri*, for the sacred offerings (*tiru amartu*) at dawn 5 *nāḻi*, for the sacred offerings at noon 21 *nāḻi* and 1 *uri*, and for the sacred offerings in the evening 5 *nāḻi*—amounting to a total of 48 *nāḻi* of rice.

This 31 *nāḻi* and 1 *uri* of rice used for sacred offerings [at the daily dawn, noon, and evening services] should be taken and given as follows: 5 *nāḻi* of cooked rice to the supervisor (*vāriyaṉ*), 4 *nāḻi* of cooked rice to feed the garland [supplier], 3 *nāḻi* of cooked rice to the temple watchman who guards the gate, 2 *nāḻi* of cooked rice to the temple woman (*tevaṭicci*) who pounds the paddy for the sacred offerings and carries the hand-lamps, and 2 *nāḻi* and 1 *uri* of cooked rice for each of the seven drummers (*uvaccakaḷ*) who beat the seven instruments for *śrībali*—totaling, for the seven, 17 *nāḻi* and 1 *uri* of cooked rice.

—TAS 5.24 (lines 14–26): this inscription was engraved on copper plates in A.D. 1168; it records a series of endowments to and arrangements made by the Tirupāṟkkaḍal-bhaṭṭāraka temple in Kilimanur, Travancore (Kerala).

Eleven of the Chola period inscriptions that describe temple women as temple servants provide only a vague and general notion of the nature of their roles. Two of these inscriptions date from the second subperiod, one from the third, and eight from the last subperiod (see table 4.2). Several of the inscriptions of this type—one of which (SII 4.223) is translated here—use the phrase "women who do service" (*paṇiceyya peṇṭukaḷ*) without any further specification of the type of service required.[41] Although this kind of expression is found also in references to male temple service, it is usually obvious from the terms used for the men (e.g., "priest" or "drummer") what the nature of the service was.

In general, in fact, whereas the services to be performed by men are often spelled out in some detail—the names of the hymns to be sung or texts to be recited; the exact ritual occasions when the drummers are to perform and what instruments they are to play—this is relatively rare in the case of temple women, as we have seen. The precise description of the forms of temple service to be rendered by women is found most frequently in inscriptions that record their deals. And detailed specifications for women's services most often concern ranking and order of precedence rather than ritual content. It is evident that the particulars of these arrangements are of much greater concern to the individual temple women involved than they are to the temple.

Out of the sixty-seven inscriptions describing temple women's service functions, seven indicate that they performed more than one *type* of task, of the four types of service that I have described—song and dance, attendance, garland making, and menial tasks. Four of the seven involve a combination of song and dance duties along with attendance functions; we have seen, for example, that temple women might serve as hymn singers and at the same time bear lamps and attend on the deity (IPS 162) or that slave women could be assigned both the task of hymn singing and bearing flywhisks (ARE 149 of 1936–37). One of the translations at the beginning of this section (TAS 5.24) shows that bearing lamps, which I have labeled an attendance function, might be combined with the menial task of pounding paddy. In another inscription translated earlier in this chapter (SII 14.132), lamp bearing is combined with garland making. And finally, in the thirteenth-century inscription from Tirunelveli district, we have seen a group of temple women assigned tasks of all four types: dancing, applying pastes to the images of the deities, making garlands, and cleaning the floors of the temple compound (ARE 374 of 1972–73).[42]

The total of seven inscriptions that show temple women with multiple roles is not very many—only a tenth of the inscriptions that indicate that temple women had service functions in the temple—but the fact that we find even a small number of such inscriptions is of interest when we consider that there is nothing that parallels them in the case of temple men: we do not encounter Chola period inscriptions that describe men's activity in the temple with reference to a variety of diverse service functions. Men's employment in the temple seems to have been based on a more clearly established and specific professional foundation than was women's.

The vague and diffuse definition of the roles of temple women presents a contrast not only with the specification of distinct functions for many male temple servants but also with the image of the temple woman as a ritual specialist that has been formulated in recent scholarship. Saskia Kersenboom, for example, maintains that the *devadāsī* of South India has been

> at all times and at all levels of culture and of society a "ritual" person who deals effectively with the divine which is considered dangerously ambivalent. This female ritualist . . . renders her special power effective in three ways:
>
> 1. through her female sexuality that is identified with that of the goddess;
>
> 2. through a number of implements of ritual value like the pot, the lamp, coloured water, certain flowers, fruits and unguents;
>
> 3. through her art.
>
> . . . Her special qualification is her auspiciousness which earns her the epithet *nityasumaṅgalī*. (1987, 67)

Certainly such *nityasumaṅgalīs* have existed in South Indian history—particularly, perhaps, in recent times—but if their defining feature is their role as "ritualists," Chola period temple women should not, it seems to me, be included in their number. The present investigation has shown us, first, that the temple women of the Chola period were not primarily recognized or identified with reference to ritual functions and that, when they did perform services in the temple, their engagement with these tasks—in contrast to men's—frequently seems to have been optional, incidental, and individual. Female temple service in the Chola period was not very organized or well defined, nor was it integrated into the pattern of temple ritual as a whole. Second, there is a lack of fit between the elements of ritual efficacy Kersenboom enumerates and the character of temple women's service in the Chola period temple. We have seen that there is no insistence that the performers of various temple services be female. We have seen very little evidence of temple women's ritual use of pots, lamps, unguents, and so on; the few cases in which such use is in evidence, which we have considered mainly under the category of attendance functions, were less the result of ritual necessity than of the personal efforts of temple women to gain honor and recognition from the temple. And finally, we have seen that the identity of the temple woman was not bound up with the role of singing and dancing; only at the end of the Chola period does she begin to establish a claim to particular rights over or expertise in dance, especially in the context of festivals.

I have suggested that temple women's activities and acquisition of position in the temple occurred in a climate of competition. Temple women's increasing involvement with festival dance seems to have taken place at the expense of men, who had formerly provided this service. Meanwhile, temple women may have been displaced by men in making garlands for the deity and in singing. It appears that in many cases temple service functions were subject to a trend toward greater professionalization and increasingly narrow definitions of eligibility. Temple women's access to various service positions, and the extent of their participation, was from the beginning of the Chola period much more limited than men's, and the changes that occurred in the course of the Chola period in some ways brought about further restrictions on their involvement.

Temple women's roles in the temple were such that their situation was quite different from that of temple men. They were vastly outnumbered by their male counterparts and were entirely or virtually excluded from many of the roles that men fulfilled, including those concerned with the administration of temple affairs. And while there were numerous tasks in the temple and terms for temple functionaries that were exclusively male, the terms and roles assigned to temple women were not exclusively female. We can point to only two sorts of temple service in which women were predominant and in which they became increasingly involved—menial service associated with food preparation and cleaning, and attendance functions. In the former, the tasks were of extremely low status, and in the latter, they were nonessential, occasional, optional, incidental—and perhaps ornamental.

In fact, one or the other of these two characterizations—menial or incidental—can be applied to virtually all of the tasks that were assigned to temple women, most of them of the second type. These activities were not at all central to the ritual life of the temple. With the apparent exception of dance, the services that temple women performed were unskilled and nonprofessional. In many cases, they had more significance in the honor associated with their performance than in the provision of a needed service to the temple. Thus temple women's work had a very different character than that performed by men.

Service, Support, and Status

In the fifth year of the reign of Tribhuvaṉaccakkaravattikaḷ Śrī Irācātirājadevar, I, Araiyaṉ Catiraṉ Irācaṉ alias Kulottuṅkacoḻakkiṭāraiyaṉ of Peruvāyilnāṭu in Jayaciṅkakulakālavaḷanāṭu, bought land [which is briefly described] from the Brahman assembly (*sabhaiyār*) of Tirveṅkaivāyil to be a *kāṇi* (property) to support the dancing of *kūttu* on festival days, including the Tiruvātirai festival in the month Vaikāci, for [the deity] Catiraviṭaṅka Nāyakar whom I established in the temple of Tiruveṅkaivāyilāṇṭār.

[The following lines give a detailed description of the boundaries of the land.]

This land is to be enjoyed by the dancer (*cānti kūtti*) Nācci Umaiyāḻvi Catiraviṭankanaṅkai, who is to perform six dances (*kūttu*).

[The next few lines are damaged but indicate that arrangements about the land were made with the *māheśvarar* and the . . . (?) and that a specified amount of paddy was guaranteed for the person responsible for performing the six dances.]

Thus I, Catiraṉ Irācaṉ alias Kulottuṅkacoḻakkiṭāraiyaṉ, give this [land, as an endowment] to last as long as the moon and sun shall shine. May the *paṉmāheśvarar* protect this [endowment].

—IPS 139: this inscription was engraved in A.D. 1168 at the Vyāghrapurīśvaram temple in Tiruvengavasal, Tiruchirappalli district (Pudukkottai).

Among the advantages of securing a temple position was the possibility that there would be some kind of remuneration. Earlier in this chapter, I have suggested that the performance of responsibility functions might result, indirectly, in obtaining support from the temple, especially in the case of tending arrangements. But many temple servants, including temple women, received support of various kinds directly from the temple. Thirty-two, or about half, of the sixty-seven inscriptions that mention women's temple service functions indicate that they received some kind of support. The following table shows that the proportion of female temple servants who received support from the temple was considerably higher in the early Chola period than in the later period.

Chola 1	Chola 2	Chola 3	Chola 4	Total
5/8 63%	7/9 78%	6/19 32%	14/31 45%	32/67 48%

Between the second and third subperiods there was a major change: although in absolute terms the number of inscriptions that refer to women as temple servants more than doubled, the number that describe them as receiving support from the temple actually declined. In the second subperiod service functions were quite securely linked to support, but in the third subperiod this was no longer the case. This detachment of function from support is in part the result of the fact that temple women in this period began to negotiate deals with the temple that did not involve any remuneration: none of the six deals that temple women made in the third subperiod that resulted in temple service roles included arrangements for their support. In the fourth subperiod, when the absolute number of female temple servants again rose, the proportion who received support from the temple remained below 50 percent. This low percentage is in part due to a continuation of the practice of making deals for service functions without pay, but even more to the increase in the numbers of female slaves assigned service functions—almost none of whom were given any property or regular income.[43]

When temple women were given support, a variety of arrangements were made by the temple, ranging from the most well-defined, official, and permanent arrangements—associated with the granting of *kāṇi*—to more ad hoc and informal forms of support.

Kāṇi usually denoted rights over that part of the produce of a piece of land that was not due to be paid in tax. *Kāṇi* was the form of ownership of agricultural land that was most prevalent in the Chola period and that, to a large extent, continued to prevail in Tamilnadu up until the early nineteenth century under the Persian term *mirās*, the land-grants themselves being termed *māṉiyams* or *ināms* in more recent history (see Fuller 1984, 81 and 91; Karashima 1984, 26–31, 165–80; Heitzman 1985, 123–47, 163–73). *Kāṇi* implied not only rights but also duties and privileges: *kāṇis*, particularly those linked to responsibilities in the temple, were "positions, around which rights and duties remained balanced" and to which "various perquisites were ancillary" (Heitzman 1985, 140; also 135–37).[44] In the present analysis, I am concerned only with *kāṇis* that were bestowed by the temple or connected to temple tasks. Also, I am categorizing as *kāṇi* other sorts of rights to property, which may not have been identical to *kāṇi* but shared its formal, publicly recognized character; these rights are referred to in Chola period inscriptions by the terms *bhogam*, *jīvitam* or *jivanam*, and *vṛtti* (Ta. *virutti*).[45]

Seven inscriptions refer to temple women as the holders of *kāṇi*. Two date from the early Chola period, one from the first and one from the second subperiod, and both are from South Arcot district. The earlier inscription (SII 26.391) is a record of the granting of a *bhogam* to a woman and her *vaṟkattār* to dance at the time of festivals; this is the only reference to *kāṇi* for temple women that indicates that the rights and responsibilities involved were hereditary. In the other early reference, a person, who seems to be a woman, is given as a slave (*aṭiyāḷ*) to the temple and she (or her son) is provided with a *jivanam* for picking flowers in the temple garden (SII 22.141). One inscription of the third subperiod from Tiruvengavasal in Tiruchirappalli district refers to temple women's *kāṇi* and is translated at the beginning of this section; it records the grant of land as *kāṇi* to a woman for performing festival dances (IPS 139). Four of the seven inscriptions that mention temple women as holders of *kāṇi* date from the last subperiod. Two record the purchase of *kāṇi* rights from the temple by *tevaraṭiyār* (IPS 367; SITI 1009), and the other two are grants of *kāṇi* to women (ARE 232 of 1971–72; SII 23.428). In contrast to the three earlier inscriptions, none of these four link the acquisition of *kāṇi* by a temple woman to the performance of any specific function in the temple.

Only a small fraction of temple women had *kāṇi* arrangements, but a somewhat larger number received support from the temple in the form of what I have termed "*kāṇi*-like" arrangements. These are arrangements that are not referred to in the inscriptions by the terms *kāṇi*, *jīvitam*, *bhogam*, or *vṛtti* but that involve, like *kāṇi*, the assignment of land to a particular individual. Twenty-five inscriptions mention *kāṇi*-like arrangements for temple women, and seventeen, or two-thirds, date from the last subperiod. As in the case of *kāṇi* arrangements, most of the references to *kāṇi*-like arrangements appear in inscriptions from the very end of the Chola period.

Kāṇi and *kāṇi*-like arrangements for temple women involved the acquisition and possession of property rights by a particular individual. These arrangements are especially characteristic of the last century of the Chola period, when individual identities were increasingly highlighted and when temple women were more and more engaged in making deals with the temple. Another method by which the temple provided support to temple women was by allocating temple resources according to "shares" or "days."[46] While *kāṇi* and *kāṇi*-like arrangements typically concerned single, named individuals, share arrangements most often involved several different kinds of temple servants, who were frequently referred to as anonymous groups.[47] Twenty-six inscriptions mention temple women as being involved in share arrangements, spread throughout the four subperiods, with somewhat more frequent occurrence in the second and third subperiods. Since the second subperiod is the one in which we find the smallest number of inscriptions that refer to temple women, the eight inscriptions describing share arrangements in this subperiod represent a relatively high proportion—close to half—of all types of support arrangements for temple women.

A comparison of the patterns of support provided to temple women that were typical of the second and of the fourth subperiods indicates that there was a shift in the kinds of relationships that linked temple women to the temple and that connected service, support, and status. In the second subperiod, women were incorporated into temple life as part of a corps of temple servants, who belonged to various groups and were supported by shares in the resources of the temple. But by the last subperiod, the impersonal institutionalized relationship of the share system was much less important for women. Instead, *kāṇi* and *kāṇi*-like arrangements predominated, in which temples and particular temple women entered into well-defined and formal agreements: the temple would provide support for the temple woman, and the temple woman might—or might not—have to perform services in the temple. In the thirteenth century, unlike the eleventh, women were only rarely integrated into the temple establishment as members of groups; instead they negotiated individual relationships with the temple.

In fifty-three Chola period inscriptions it is possible to determine the form of support provided to temple women by the temple. Half of these date from the last subperiod, which suggests that the arrangements made by temple women were being increasingly well defined in terms of the details of their support; at the same time, they were less and less specific about the nature of the services to be performed. The forms of support provided to temple women were similar to those given to other temple servants, and consisted primarily of rice or land. The rice used to pay temple servants was almost always in the form of paddy and was only rarely cooked rice.[48] Agricultural lands were granted to temple servants as a source of regular revenue, usually in the form of paddy, or a temple servant might receive a plot of land as a house site. These two forms of support—grants of rice or of land—are represented approximately equally in the inscriptions that indicate support for temple women throughout the whole of the Chola period.

Some of the inscriptions detail the precise amounts of paddy, rice, or land that temple women received. But because the worth and the units of measure of land and of various commodities varied considerably in different times and places,[49] I have considered the value of grants made to temple women in relative rather than absolute terms, by comparing them to those received by other temple servants mentioned in the same inscription or in other inscriptions of the same period and locale. The types of temple personnel who most frequently received support well above the average level are hymn singers and priests, although other types of personnel are also mentioned. Among the lowest paid are drummers, people charged with the task of cleaning and smearing floors, and those responsible for making garlands. Very generally, menial tasks are least well paid, whereas those of ritual importance and those typically held by Brahmans are most well paid, but this pattern is subject to considerable variation. There are several inscriptions, on the one hand, in which the priest's assistants (*māṇis*) receive support well below the standard; drummers, on the other hand, are in some cases among the best paid temple servants. Temple women, for the most part, are on the lower end of the pay scale.

Twenty-two inscriptions provide enough information about the support of temple women to allow us to arrive at a rough estimate of its relative value.[50] In only three do temple women receive support at an above-average level. These include a tenth-century inscription from Malabar district (TAS 8,43), which describes the provision of paddy for female singers (*naṅkaimār kāntarpikaḷ*); a twelfth-century inscription from Travancore district which records the provision of paddy for four *tevaṭiccis,* whose functions are not specified (TAS 2.3); and a thirteenth-century record from Kolar district, indicating that land was given to several *taḷiyilār* who were "to serve" (*cevikka*) the deity (EC 10.kl 121). Of these three inscriptions, only the first provides any clue to the kinds of duties that might have been required of these temple women, and none records the assignment of specific tasks. All three inscriptions are from regions on the periphery of the Tamil country—two from the Kerala region and one from Kolar district in the west. Thus, what we may consider the highest paying jobs for temple women are not very much like actual "jobs" because they are not associated with particular functions; nor are they either very common or at all typical of the central Tamil country.

This pattern holds even for the middle range of support. Only six of the twenty-two inscriptions can be classified as providing support for temple women at this level. And just one gives the impression that pay was provided in exchange for specific services: this is the thirteenth-century inscription from Tirunelveli district in the far south, which I have referred to several times earlier in this chapter and which records the particular tasks—adorning the images of the deities, cleaning and decorating the temple floors, dancing, and making garlands—and precise amounts of paddy assigned to each of ten temple women. Two inscriptions describing temple women who received an average level of support are from the second subperiod—one (SII 2.66), from the Rājarājeśvara temple in Tanjavur, records the grant of shares to the *taḷicceri peṇṭukaḷ*, and the other (SII 4.223, translated earlier in this chapter), from Chidambaram in South Arcot district, describes the support arranged for a woman who is to bring the water vessel and for five women doing service (*paṇiceyya peṇṭukaḷ*). Three other inscriptions date from the thirteenth century and record deals negotiated by temple women at Uttaramerur in Chingleput district (ALB 8,177; ARE 180 and 183 of 1923). In these three inscriptions, there is an indication that the temple women who had made donations to the temple were entitled to perform certain attendance functions, in addition to receiving support, but these tasks have more the air of privileges than of duties for which the temple women were being paid.

From this discussion, it would appear that the amount of support granted to most temple women was below the level received by the average male temple servant. But it is virtually impossible to demonstrate that temple women received lower pay than men did for equivalent work, for several reasons. First, Chola period inscriptions only infrequently provide information about the tasks performed by temple women—and still less frequently refer also to the amount of support given for the performance of these tasks. Second, temple women did not usually perform the same kinds of tasks that men did.[51] This fact in itself would tend to bring down the level of support that the average temple woman enjoyed, given the exclusion of women from those functions, such as hymn singing or serving as priest, that were most highly remunerated. Even in the realm of menial service, tasks with greater honor—and greater pay—were assigned to men rather than women; this is demonstrated, for example, in the inscription from Chidambaram (SII 4.223), in which the woman assigned to fetch water received two-thirds and each of the five "women who serve" received a quarter of the amount of paddy granted to the male cook.

Temple women, like other temple servants, on occasion received house sites from the temple. I have found twenty-two references that refer, directly or indirectly, to the housing of temple women. These references include inscriptions that mention in passing the "temple women's street" or that identify temple women in terms of their association with the area around the temple. Seventeen, or over three-quarters, of these inscriptions date from the later Chola period. Most of the twenty-two references mention the temple women's residence either in the "temple quarter" (*tirumaṭaiviḷākam*) or in the temple streets (*vīti*, *teru*, etc.). Three inscriptions, all from the early Chola period, associate temple women with the temple *ceri*, or "district."[52]

In the few cases in which the exact locations of temple women's residences are specified, there are various arrangements: for example, the *taḷicceri peṇṭukaḷ* of Rājarājeśvara temple in Tanjavur were housed in the streets to the north and south of the temple (SII 2.66), a temple woman of Tiruvarur lived on the south side of the "holy street" (*tiruvīti*) (SII 17.600), and a temple woman of Tiruvannamalai was a resident of the west street (ARE 232 of 1971–72). In recent times, the assignment of areas around the temple to various groups of temple servants became more fixed, with temple women often housed in the "best" areas, defined by proximity to the deity—directly across the street from the temple walls and close to the main gate of the temple, which was typically on the east side.[53] Such a systematic assignment of residences was evidently not a feature of the Chola period temple community.

Another contrast between Chola period temple women and their modern counterparts is related to the issue of whether temple women—or other types of temple servants—were normally provided with places of residence by the temple. This seems to have become a standard feature of the support of female temple servants by the nineteenth century but is relatively rarely found in the Chola period records. In fact, in the Chola period, the exceptional, negotiable, and honorary character of the assignment of houses is indicated by the fact that the most precise specifications of their locations (the "first house" or "corner house") were made in the case of deals (ARE 29 of 1940–41; ARE 471 of 1962–63). It appears that temple women took advantage of the fact that the assignment of places of residence around the temple was not highly formalized in the Chola period, claiming residence in the vicinity of the temple as a mark of status. That such a privileged association with the temple was increasingly acquired by temple women is indicated by the fact that the greatest proportion of references to the housing of temple women comes from the later Chola period.

A final aspect of the support of temple women to be considered is related to the original source of the property that was granted to them. It has been frequently said that, historically, kings have had a special role in the sponsorship of *devadāsīs* and that, in general, *kāṇis* and other temple "service tenures" were originally rights granted by the king.[54] But the evidence of the Chola period inscriptions supports neither of these views. Some of the links between temple women and the temple were established or sanctioned by royal authority, but most came into being by other means: some were created by temple or village officials, some were the result of gifts made by local notables or residents, and some were established through deals—in consequence of a gift made by the temple woman herself. This diversity of sources is demonstrated by the origins of the *kāṇis* held by temple women. Of the seven *kāṇis* acquired by temple women, three were the consequence of gifts made by local residents, two came into being because of deals made by temple women themselves, one was established by the local Brahman assembly (*sabhai*), and only one was the result of a royal order. There was somewhat more royal interest in the creation of *kāṇis* for male temple servants, but even for men the majority derived from sources other than the king.[55]

There were a variety of different kinds of arrangements through which temple women secured support from the temple, and at no time in the course of the Chola period is there evidence that temple women acquired positions through a particular procedure carried out by the temple or that they were predominantly sponsored by a particular type of patron.[56] Although temple women resembled their male counterparts in receiving support from diverse sources, they were unique among all other types of temple servants in that they, through their deals, became partners with members of the temple establishment in defining the roles they would fulfill in the temple and the remuneration they would receive.

The Chola period temple, dedicated to providing worship for the deities enshrined within, was a focal point for the mobilization of resources, the performance of a wide range of activities, and the participation of many kinds of people. In addition to those who made links to the temple as patrons, many people were employed in the temple in various ways. The patterns of administrative, ritual, and maintenance functions that constituted the life of the temple and defined the temple community were far from fixed; these patterns varied from temple to temple and from region to region and underwent change over time. In this chapter, I have tried to give an idea of the general framework within which these patterns unfolded and of the factors that may have affected the processes of change in order to position temple women within these patterns and processes.

In examining the roles that temple women played in the temple and comparing these with those of their male counterparts, I have attached attributes to the various managerial and service functions that women and men performed and have indicated how the attributes associated with certain functions have shifted over time as different types of people took up these functions. Figure 4.1 gives a schematic view of some of these attributes, representing them as pairs of opposites. Each role in the temple, as fulfilled by a particular type of temple servant at a particular time and place, could in principle be characterized by its location on each of the horizontal lines that join the opposing attributes. The role of temple priest, for example, as it is described in most Chola period inscriptions, would be classified as more "professional" than "honorary," that is, more a job than a privilege, and would also lean

professional ⟷ honorary

essential ⟷ optional

skilled ⟷ unskilled

ritual proximity ⟷ ritual distance

specification of function ⟷ vagueness of function

high pay ⟷ low pay

no pay

negative pay (deal)

Figure 4.1 Attributes of roles and functions in the Chola period temple.

toward the left side of the scales in being relatively skilled, well paid, and associated with specification of function; and would be on the far left end of the scales in terms of the essential character of the role and its association with ritual proximity to the temple deity. The role of the women who purchased the rights to dance and sing *Tiruvempāvai* at festivals from the temple at Nallur (ARE 160 and 161 of 1940–41) would be located differently: toward the left, perhaps, with regard to the skill of the role, ritual proximity, and degree of specification; fairly far to the right in the role's being honorary and optional; and all the way to the right for pay, given that these temple women paid the temple to perform these functions rather than vice versa.

I would like to suggest that although temple men's roles might have a wide range of patterns of attributes—including the clustering of attributes on the left side of the scales, as in the case of the temple priest—the variety of temple women's roles would be much more restricted, would scarcely ever resemble the pattern of the male priest's role, and would instead tend toward the clustering of attributes on the right side of the scales. Men's roles, certainly, might slide to the right as well—many men with responsibility functions were engaged in temple functions that were honorary, optional, not particularly skilled (except, perhaps, in the case of temple accountants), unpaid, and more or less neutral in ritual proximity and specificity of function—but such roles were, typically, not ones that women played.

The attributes on the right side of the chart cannot all be reconciled with one another—it is unlikely, for example, that a role could be regarded as having an honorary character and at the same time involve ritual distance from the divine presence in the temple—but in virtually every type of role that Chola temple women played, it appears that several, if not many, of the right-hand attributes are relevant.[57] The fact that the cluster of characteristics of temple women's roles tend to be located on the right side of this chart does not mean that these roles were, by definition, inferior to the roles played by men. Temple women's roles were, perhaps, more marginal than central to temple life, but we must not assume that those women whose roles were honorary, optional, unpaid, unskilled, and vaguely defined were people who had tried and failed to become highly paid and skilled professional temple servants. Underlying temple women's associations with the temple was a different kind of rationale. Most temple women acquired functions in or support from the temple as a way to enhance a status that was already theirs. A woman's role in the temple was not primarily viewed as a source of livelihood, nor was her role what defined her identity and status—unless, perhaps, she was a slave acquired by the temple specifically to perform menial services. The temple woman's role was, instead, an adjunct or marker of her status.

The identity of the temple woman of the early twentieth century, understood in the context of hereditary, specialized, professional female temple service, seems to be based equally on three carefully defined and interconnected features: ritual tasks and privileges, entitlement to support from the temple, and temple woman status—acquired by birth or adoption into the *devadāsī* community and by a ceremony of dedication to the temple. For Chola period temple woman, we see an entirely different picture. It is the temple woman status that is central to her identity, and temple service roles or support from the temple are accessories to this status. There are only four Chola period inscriptions in which the three aspects—temple service function, support by the temple, and status as denoted by the use of "temple woman" terms—appear in conjunction with one another.[58] If it is the status of being a temple woman that is at the core of her identity—and if, as we begin to suspect rather strongly, this status was acquired and defined very differently for her than it was for the temple woman of the early twentieth century—we must turn now to an examination of its nature.

FIVE

Identity, Geography, Religion, and Kinship

Temple Women and the Medieval Religious Landscape

Ties to God, Temple, and Place

In the twelfth year of the reign of Ko Parakecaripaṉmar alias Tiripuvaṉac-cakkaravattikaḷ Śrī Rājarājatevar [the exact day is also specified], Aṭkoṇṭāṉ Tevuntiruvumuṭaiyāḷ and Kiḻakkaṭaiyaniṉṟāḷ, temple women (*tevaraṭiyār*) who dwell in the temple precincts (*tirumaṭaiviḷākam*) of Lord Tiruvalañcūli Uṭaiyār of Pāmpūrnāṭu in Uyyakoṇṭārvaḷanāṭu, we two. . . . servants receiving support (? . . . . *kāṇi āḷar*) [inscription is broken at several points] . . . . bought land and gave it to provide enjoyment in the temple for [the saints] Tirunāvukkarai-cutevar, Tiruvātavūrāḷikaḷ, and Tirukkaṇṇappatevar.

[the next lines describe the boundaries of the land, which appears to be close to the temple.]

We bought the land from . . . . Tiruveṇkāṭupaṭṭaṉ Tiruvītinampi, in the name (through the agency) of our mother's elder brother Taṇparicuṭaiyār.

[The next two lines are fragmentary but seem to be concerned with taxes on the land.]

We two . . . . present a deed recording this gift of the agreed-upon property for these three [saints] to the holy feet of Tirunāvukkaraicutevar, Tiruvāta-vūrāḷikaḷ, and Tirukkaṇṇappatevar.

> Thus is this deed issued and signed by me, their elder brother [uncle?], Aṭkoṇṭāṉ Taṇparicuṭaiyāṉ, and signed by Aṭkoṇṭaṉ Tevuntiruvumuṭaiyāḷ and by Kiḻakkaṭaiyaniṉṟāḷ.
>
> —SII 8.228: this inscription, which begins with a *meykkīrtti* of several lines, was engraved in A.D. 1158 at the Kapardīśvara temple in Tiruvalanjuli, Tanjavur district.

The temple women of the Chola period, as I have defined them and as they are represented in the inscriptions, are strongly associated with specific places. The characteristic "temple woman" terms link them to deities and temples, and their identities are frequently bound up with particular sacred locations, as in the preceding inscription. In chapter 3, we have seen that a very high proportion of the temple women described as donors were explicitly identified with reference to a "hometown"—connected with a deity, temple, or place—and that the temples they endowed were most often those of their hometowns. The identities of other temple women, not only of temple women who were donors, also seem to have centered around association with a particular place. To gain a deeper understanding of temple woman status and of temple women's identities, I propose to investigate in more detail the character of this association.

There are three distinct ways in which Chola period inscriptions explicitly associate temple women with a particular sacred place. The first is linkage to a particular temple deity (*tevar*, *tevaṉār*, *uṭaiyār*, *īśvara*, or *nāyaṉār*), the second is linkage to a particular temple (*koyil* or *taḷi*), and the third is linkage to a place—to a village or a town (*ūr*, *nagaram*, or *puram*). Table 5.1 gives the proportion of inscriptions in which each of these types is used from all the inscriptions in which temple women are named and the relevant section of the inscription is available for examination (a total of 168 inscriptions). Here we see that 37 percent of the inscriptions use hometown identifiers of the first type (god), 30 percent the second type (temple), and only 4 percent the third type (place).

In each of the four subperiods, approximately the same proportion of inscriptions identify women in terms of their hometowns—ranging between two-thirds and three-quarters—but the nature of this identification changes over time. In the first three subperiods, god identifiers predominate. Almost all of these are associated with the terms *tevaṉār makaḷ* (especially in the early Chola period) or *tevaraṭiyār* (especially in the later Chola period). The demonstrative prefix *i* ("this") may be affixed to produce *ittevaraṭiyāḷ*, "the *aṭiyāḷ* of this god," or *ittevaṉār makaḷ*, "the daughter of this god"; or the word *tevar* or *tevaṉār* that appears at the beginning of the term for temple woman may be construed with preceding names of places or of deities to produce such god identifiers as *tiruviṭaimarutuṭaiyār tevaraṭiyāḷ*, the *aṭiyāḷ* of the Great Lord (literally "Lord Lord," *uṭaiyār tevar*) of Tiruvidaimarudur (SII 23.299).[1]

Temple identifiers are found relatively frequently in the first subperiod, but they are not much in evidence after this—until they reemerge in the last

Table 5.1 Hometown identifications for temple women and temple men

	God	Temple	Place	Hometown Total	Total Inscriptions
Temple women					
Chola 1 (850-985)	12 (41%)	10 (34%)	0	22 (76%)	29
Chola 2 (985-1070)	10 (53%)	1 (5%)	3 (16%)	14 (74%)	19
Chola 3 (1070-1178)	17 (46%)	6 (16%)	0	23 (62%)	37
Chola 4 (1178-1300)	23 (28%)	34 (41%)	3 (4%)	60 (72%)	83
Total	62 (37%)	51 (30%)	6 (4%)	119 (71%)	168
Temple men					
Chola 1 (850-985)	0	2 (10%)	2 (10%)	16 (20%)	20
Chola 2 (985-1070)	2 (9%)	3 (13%)	6 (26%)	9 (39%)	23
Chola 3 (1070-1178)	4 (11%)	22 (58%)	2 (5%)	28 (74%)	38
Chola 4 (1178-1300)	0	14 (58%)	2 (7%)	16 (57%)	28
Total	6 (5%)	41 (36%)	12 (11%)	57 (52%)	109

subperiod in considerable numbers and replace god identifiers as the most important type of hometown identification for temple women. The temple identifiers of the first subperiod are quite different, however, from those of the last. In the early Chola period the term *taḷi* is most often used for "temple." This word seems to have its origin in the Sanskrit word *sthalī* (MTL, 1802), and apart from its use in the hometown identifications of temple women, it is arguably the most widely used term for "temple" in the early Chola period, at least until the beginning of the eleventh century (Suresh Pillai 1968, 440–41). The word *taḷi* predominates in the early Chola period in temple identifiers for temple women, but it is the word *koyil* that is prominent at the end of the period. It is curious that it is not until this late period that we see this usage, despite the native Tamil origins and archaic use of this term in other contexts (MTL, 1190–91; Suresh Pillai 1968, 440–41; Narayana Ayyar 1974, 318–20; Sethu Pillai 1974, 20; Hart 1975, 13). The majority of the inscriptions of the fourth subperiod that identify temple women in terms of their associations with a temple utilize the word *koyil*, particularly in the expression *ikkoyil* ("[of] this temple") or *śrīkoyil* ("[in] the holy temple").

Another kind of temple identification found especially in later Chola period inscriptions is the linkage of women to the parts or precincts of a particular temple.[2] Most often temple women are described in terms of their association with the area around the temple (*tirumaṭaiviḷākam*), as in the preceding translation; there are also references to temple women in connection with the temple street (*tiruvīti* or *teru*), the temple kitchen (*tirumaṭaippaḷḷi*), the row of houses (*tirumāḷikai*) outside the temple wall, or the temple courtyard (*tirumuṟṟam*). These kinds of temple identifiers may, in some cases, indicate the place of residence of the temple women, or they may have a less literal, more honorific sense, suggesting a privileged status of proximity and intimacy with the deity of the temple.

For most of the Chola period, temple women's identities are most strongly articulated in terms of their relationships with the deities of particular places in the Tamil country. But in the fourth subperiod, when more inscriptions mention temple women than in any other subperiod, a higher proportion identify them with reference to their association with a temple rather than with a god or a place. This is significant for our understanding of the changing character of temple women's identity and status, in indicating the formulation of a definition of temple woman that was increasingly tied to the temple as an institutional entity, and in demonstrating that increasing numbers of women identified themselves through this definition.

The temple-linked definition that presents itself in the last part of the Chola period may have roots in the identification of temple women with *taḷis*, which was a feature of the first subperiod. But the scale of the later temple identifications, the increasing number linked to the parts and precincts of the temple, and the enormous increase in *koyil* identifications mark the developments in the last subperiod as something new. Clearly at issue here is the changing character of the institution of the temple itself, as well as the relationship of temple women to it. If we consider that the temple was becoming more firmly established, with increasingly elaborate rituals and entrenched hierarchies, the question arises of whether the temple was an increasingly more salient source of status and identity for society in general or whether the ever-closer relationship between temple women and the temple was in any way unique.

Perhaps the people most interesting to us as a comparison group, in considering this question, are the male counterparts of temple women. Table 5.1 shows the proportions of inscriptions that identify temple men in the four study areas in terms of their connections to deity, temple, or place.[3] The first thing that strikes us is that, unlike temple women, temple men were infrequently identified with reference to a hometown—in any of these three ways—until the later Chola period. Second, whereas temple women were most often identified in terms of their association with a temple deity, this is the type of hometown identification that is least in evidence for temple men. Temple women's identities were, from the very beginning of the Chola period, much more tightly centered around a connection with a sacred place—especially with the god of that place.

When temple men rather suddenly begin, in the third subperiod, to be identified in terms of their hometowns, it is with reference to the temple. As in the case of temple women in the later Chola period, temple identifiers consistently employ the word *koyil*. For temple men, the sharp increase in the proportion of inscriptions with temple identifications takes place in the middle of the Chola period, between the second and the third subperiods. This increase is not accompanied by a massive increase in the number of inscriptions that mention temple men by name, although many more temple men are named in each inscription, particularly as the performers of responsibility functions. For temple women, the increase in temple identifications takes place a century later, and it occurs at the expense of the long-established deity-focused identifications that had earlier been central to temple women's identities. This increase *is* associated with a major jump in the number of inscriptions that refer to temple women by name, and most of these women were donors.

The changing character of the temple—its growing strength and development as an institution—had an impact on both temple men and temple women inasmuch as the temple increasingly became a touchstone for status and identity, as part of the evolving self-definition of both groups. But there are differences between the two groups as well. Temple men seem to have taken up the temple-identified persona earlier than did temple women—who had, in any case, an already-established and related identity focused on a relationship with the temple deity. But most importantly, whereas temple identification for temple men was associated with the performance of administrative duties in the temple—often of a nominal and honorary character—temple identification for temple women was associated with patronage of the temple.

Temple Women in the Temples of Tamilnadu

In the forty-eighth year of the reign of Śrī Kulottuṅkacoḻadevar, we, the *peruṅkuṟi mahāsabhai* [Brahman assembly] of Śrīkulottuṅkacoḻaccaturvvedimaṅkalam in Ūṟṟukkāṭṭunāṭu in Ūṟṟukkāṭṭukkoṭṭam in Jayaṅkoṇṭacoḻamaṇṭalam, wrote this deed of land sale [and gave it to] Cāttaṅkaitoḻi alias Puravarimāṇikkam, a temple woman of that Lord (*avvāḻvāṉaṭiyāḷ*), having received from her 5 *kācu* and sold her the land, which she donated as a perpetually tax-free *maṭappuṟam* (gift to a *maṭha*) to the *maṭha* named [after her] Puravarimāṇikkam, lying to the southwest of the precincts of the temple of Lord (*āḻvāṉ*) Śrīkulottuṅkacoḻaviṇṇakar of the town of Kāñcipuram in Eyiṟkoṭṭam, to provide food offerings (*amutuceykai*) for the temple servants (*tiruvatipaṇiceyvār*) and *śrīvaiṣṇavar* on ten festival days.

[Details of the boundaries and taxes of the gifted land are given.]

We sell this land to be *maṭappuṟam* for this Lord; the temple servants (*devakaṉmikaḷ*) and the *śrīvaiṣṇava* supervisors (*kaṇkāṇiceyvār*) are charged with arranging for its cultivation and providing food offerings for the worthy ones (*svāmivār*). . . . [The last part of the inscription is fragmentary.]

—SII 4.134: this inscription, which begins with a brief *meykkīrtti*, was engraved in A.D. 1118 at the Vaikuṇṭha Perumāḷ temple in Kanchipuram, Chingleput district.

Having established that temple women's identities were, throughout the Chola period, linked to specific sacred shrines, we now consider whether any particular hometowns and home temples were especially significant for temple women.

Of the 158 inscriptions with hometown-identified temple women, 116, or about three-quarters, indicate that the temple woman was from the place where the inscription was engraved—that is, belonging to the god, temple, or town where she was making a donation or, occasionally, receiving support or performing some function. In 32 inscriptions, the temple women were associated with another place. Only one place is prominent in this context, and that is the town of Kanchipuram, in the northern district of Chingleput (see figure 5.1). Kanchipuram is mentioned in 7 of these 32 inscriptions as the hometown of a temple woman; one of these, a twelfth-century inscription from Tiruvidaimarudur in Tanjavur district (SII 5.701) is translated in chapter 2, and another, a thirteenth-century inscription from Jambai in South Arcot district (SII 22.87) follows. When we add to these 7 the 4 inscriptions from Kanchipuram itself, in which temple women are said to be of that place (as in the preceding translation), we have altogether 11 inscriptions in which this town is central to a temple woman's identity.

Figure 5.1 Locations of importance for Chola period temple women.

Eleven inscriptions are not very many, set against the total number of inscriptions that mention temple women. Certainly this small number does not suggest that Kanchipuram was a major location for the "production" of temple women. But it was a famous religious and political center, which, when one did have some connection with it, was clearly worth mentioning. Kanchi was a place of ancient sanctity, important to Buddhists and Jains, as well as to Śaivas and Vaiṣṇavas.[4] It was the capital of the Pallavas from the fourth to the ninth centuries and a provincial capital of the Cholas. In seven of the eleven inscriptions, Lord Tiruvekampan̲, the deity of one of the ancient Śaiva shrines of Kanchi, is specified in the identification. One of the eleven inscriptions—the preceding translation—identifies a temple woman in terms of her connection to the Lord of the Vaiṣṇava shrine of Vaikuṇṭha Perumāḷ, and the other three refer either to other Śaiva temples or simply to the town itself. Most of the eleven inscriptions that link temple women to Kanchipuram date from the later Chola period, although there is one that is very early, from the late ninth century, and two others from the eleventh century, in the second subperiod. Not only is there a range of dates in these eleven inscriptions, but also various terms are used. For example, a temple woman of Lord Tiruvekampan̲ may be referred to as as a *tevan̲ār makaḷ* (ARE 139 of 1912), a *taḷiyilāḷ* (SII 5.701), or a *tevaraṭiyāḷ* (SII 22.87).

Kanchipuram is mentioned in the largest number of Chola period inscriptions as the hometown of temple women. It is also the only place that is mentioned in this context throughout the whole of the Chola period. Two places in Tanjavur district, Tiruvarur and Tiruvidaimarudur are each mentioned in connection with temple women in nine inscriptions, but there is a space of a hundred years, from the early eleventh to the early twelfth century, during which there is no reference that links either of them to temple women.

Tiruvarur is an important and ancient Śaiva center, praised in the hymns of the Nāyan̲mārs. Among the Chola period inscriptions of Tiruvarur, we find altogether seven inscriptions that seem to refer to temple women, and three of these specifically identify these women as being of the place. In addition, a tenth-century inscription from South Arcot district (SII 19.283—translated in chapter 2) identifies a donor as a *tevan̲ār makaḷ* of Tiruvarur. And in the long inscription from Tanjavur (SII 2.66), dated A.D. 1014, which lists 400 *taḷicceri peṇṭukaḷ*, each of whom is identified by her hometown, it is Tiruvarur that is most often mentioned—it is the hometown of 46 of the *taḷicceri peṇṭukaḷ* who were settled in Tanjavur.[5] Thus we have nine inscriptions in total that connect temple women to Tiruvarur: two are from the tenth century, the Tanjavur inscription is from the beginning of the eleventh century, five are from the twelfth century—the earliest dated in A.D. 1119—and one is dated A.D. 1266.

At Tiruvidaimarudur, another place sacred to Lord Śiva, eight inscriptions refer to temple women (including SII 5.705, which is translated in chapter 4), and five of these specifically identify temple women as being of the place. The Tanjavur inscription also mentions Tiruvidaimarudur as the hometown of seventeen *taḷicceri peṇṭukaḷ*. As in the case of Tiruvarur, we have nine inscriptions that link temple women with Tiruvidaimarudur: five are from the tenth century; there is the Tanjavur inscription of A.D. 1014; and then there are three later inscriptions, dated A.D. 1123, A.D. 1142, and A.D. 1218.

It is possible that the hundred-year gap for both Tiruvarur and Tiruvidaimarudur is the result of Rajaraja's imperious commandeering of all available temple women, demanding their presence at his royal temple in Tanjavur (Suresh Pillai 1968, 442–43). There are several other places close to Tanjavur that, having provided *taḷicceri peṇṭukaḷ* in the early eleventh century, seem not to have been associated with temple women in the subsequent period. Vedaranyam, or Tirumaṟaikkāṭu, as it is called in the Tanjavur inscription, sent five women to Tanjavur as *taḷicceri peṇṭukaḷ*. The next evidence we have of a connection between temple women and this place is over 150 years later, in an inscription of A.D. 1177 from Vedaranyam, recording a donation made by a *tevaraṭiyāḷ* of "this village." Another inscription from Vedaranyam, dated in the thirteenth century, records that women were sold as slaves to serve the temple deity.

At Tiruchatturai, a record inscribed fifty years before the Tanjavur inscription refers to a *tevaṉār makaḷ* of "this village" (SII 13.103—the translation follows) and the Tanjavur inscription records that two *taḷicceri peṇṭukaḷ* came from Tiruchatturai. It is not until the thirteenth century, however, that we again hear of an association between the temple at Tiruchatturai and a temple woman. In the case of Melapaluvur (also known as Paluvur), in a nearby area of Tiruchirappalli district, the Tanjavur inscription is the last of a series of four that mention this place as the hometown of temple women. Three earlier inscriptions from Melapaluvur, two dated in A.D. 955 and one in A.D. 1012, describe donations made by temple women (*tevaṉār makaḷs* or *tevaraṭiyār*). The Tanjavur inscription records that nine temple women came from Melapaluvur.

These examples suggest that the transfer of temple women to be *taḷicceri peṇṭukaḷ* at the Rājarājeśvara temple in Tanjavur may have temporarily, or permanently, brought an end to temple women's associations with other temples in the region of the Chola capital. But there are reasons to believe that Rajaraja's royal gesture did not have such a drastic impact. There is the case, for instance, of Tiruvaiyaru, an ancient Śaiva sacred place very close to Tanjavur, which provided nineteen *taḷicceri peṇṭukaḷ* and which, only 35 years later, has a record that mentions four female *patiyār* by name. There is also the fact that apart from the places I have discussed, there is a remarkable lack of correspondance or overlap between the places mentioned in the Tanjavur inscription that provided *taḷicceri peṇṭukaḷ* and the places mentioned in other Chola period inscriptions in connection with temple women. Of the fifty-four towns that are mentioned as the hometowns of *taḷicceri peṇṭukaḷ* in the Tanjavur inscription, only nineteen of them are referred to in any other inscriptions as being the homes of temple women, and only Tiruvarur and Tiruvidaimarudur are prominent in both contexts. Even if the transfer of temple women from various places to Tanjavur depleted the number of temple women in these places, we would still expect to see more inscriptions *predating* the transfer that indicated the existence of temple women associated with these places. It does not seem that the Tanjavur inscription is able to provide an explanation for the geographical and chronological patterns associated with temple women's hometowns; this inscription, indeed, stands out as something of an oddity within the context of these patterns.

Certainly, not all of the places of importance to Chola period temple women were located in the region around Tanjavur. Figure 5.1 shows that in addition to the major "temple woman center" of Kanchipuram, there are several other places in the northern part of Tamilnadu that were prominent as temple women's hometowns. Takkolam is located not far from Kanchipuram; it is a sacred place praised by the Nāyaṉmārs, with temple structures dating from the period of Pallava rule. Four inscriptions at Takkolam, all of the late tenth and early eleventh centuries, identify temple women as being of this place. Another place in the northern part of Tamilnadu, which is, again, praised by the Śaiva poet-saints, is associated with temple women in the later part of the Chola period. This is Tiruvannamalai, in North Arcot district, where we find four inscriptions in which temple women are described as being of this place. A fifth inscription that comes from another part of North Arcot district also refers to a temple woman of Tiruvannamalai. The five inscriptions date from the mid-twelfth to the end of the thirteenth century.

At the other end of the Tamil country, at Tiruvalisvaram in Tirunelveli district, we find another center of activity for temple women in the later Chola period. The temple at Tiruvalisvaram, dedicated to Śiva, seems to have been founded in the period of the early Chola kings, in the late ninth century (K. Swaminathan 1990, 21–22, 27). We find a cluster of four inscriptions from the mid-thirteenth century, in which female donors, or their mothers, are said to belong to the Lord or the temple of that place.

I have now discussed all of the places that are identified in a handful or more of Chola period inscriptions as temple women's hometowns—places that might, in a very loose sense, be regarded as "temple woman centers."[6] There are not very many of these places, and it is striking that some of the largest and most important Chola period temples are missing from the list—notably, the Śaiva temple at Chidambaram and the Vaiṣṇava temple at Srirangam. Consistent with temple women's general tendency to make donations to medium-sized temples and to their home temples, these two major temples did not attract the gifts of temple women. Only one temple woman acted as the patron of either of these temples; her gifts are recorded in two thirteenth-century inscriptions from Chidambaram (SII 12.151—translated in chapter 3; SII 12.172). Only one inscription, again from Chidambaram, refers to the involvement in the life of either of these temples on the part of temple women—a *vāḻvacci* who was to fetch water and women who were to "do service" (SII 4.223—translated in chapter 4). The only suggestion of a temple woman's connection with Srirangam is found in a ninth-century inscription from Tiruverumbur in Tiruchirappalli district, not far from Srirangam, which records the gift made by a temple woman from Tiruvaraṅkam (SII 13.88—translated in chapter 3). Women are conspicuous by their absence from the long lists of temple functionaries, administrators, and committee members whose names fill the inscriptions of Srirangam and Chidambaram (Orr 1995a and 1995c).

Most Chola period temple women are identified in terms of their hometowns, but in most cases these hometowns are neither the most prominent and famous temple towns nor temple woman centers. If one compares the map in figure 5.1, which shows the locations of these centers, with table 2.2 and figure 2.2, it becomes clear that there must have been many places with which temple women were associated that are referred to in only one or two inscriptions. For example, in South Arcot district, thirty-three Chola period inscriptions mention temple women, but there is not even one "temple woman center" in this region. Temple women were not concentrated in a few temple towns; rather their connections were with temples scattered widely across the Tamil country. It is rare to find temple women in groups at a particular temple—the Rājarājeśvara temple in Tanjavur is extremely unusual in this regard—or to find "dynasties" of temple women, that is, a series of references to the association of temple women with a specific place that stretches across time.

Temple women's relationships with temples have a highly individual character. Identification with a particular deity, temple, or place—and identity as a temple woman—were not matters that had to do with membership in a group. That this was a distinctive characteristic of temple women's status has already been suggested by the results of the preceding comparison with temple men. There we saw that whereas for temple men links to the temple were associated with responsibility functions, in which men were involved with other men in the corporate enterprise of representing and acting on behalf of the temple, in the case of temple women these links were associated with individual acts of patronage. That the spatial distribution of the hometown identifications of temple women shows a diffuse rather than nodal pattern confirms the individualistic nature of their connections to the temple and conforms, as well, to the pattern of their donations to the temple.

Names and Places

In the fourth year of the reign of Ko Virācakecaripaṉmar, Nakkaṉ Kavaṭiyakkaṉ, a temple woman (*tevaṉār makaḷ*) of this village, and her younger sister Nakkaṉ Vicciyakkaṉ—these two women, Kavaṭimayakkal and Viccimayakkal, gave . . . .

. . . . for the Goddess (*patāri*), as long as the moon and the sun shall shine, Kavaṭimayakkal . . . . for the Goddess . . . . rice for one . . . .

. . . . for two Brahmans. . . . together with [. . . . *śiva*]*yokiyār*, and for one Brahman woman. . . . 3 *nāḻi* of rice daily. . . . 5 *nāḻi* . . . .

. . . . this year . . . . took . . . . we gave as a gift . . . . for laborers. We two, Nakkaṉ Kavaṭiyakkaṉ and Nakkaṉ Vicciyakkaṉ, thus make this agreement in this village.

—SII 13.103: this inscription was engraved probably in A.D. 953 at the Odanavaneśvara temple in Tiruchchatturai, Tanjavur district.

In addition to the explicit connections mentioned in inscriptions between temple women and particular deities and sacred places, temple women's names also frequently evoke associations with specific gods and temples. The significance of these associations, however, is not as obvious as in the case of hometown identifications, nor are these associations necessarily linked to temple women's identities in the same way as hometown identifications. Temple women's names more often show them as participants in a religious idiom that was shared by society at large than mark them as members of a separate community with its own distinctive forms of relationship with god and temple. I have argued that women indeed were members of such a community; an examination of how temple women's use of god-names and place-names differed from or was similar to those of other people will help us to understand how this community was defined.

That there was no straightforward correspondance between temple women's hometowns and their names is easily demonstrated. We have just seen that the places that have the most claim to be temple woman centers are Kanchipuram (especially the Ekampam temple), Tiruvarur, and Tiruvidaimarudur. These places, however, are not at all prominent in the names of temple women. There are three temple women whose names evoke Kanchipuram's renown and religious importance—two named Ekampam and one, the daughter of a *tevaṉār makaḷ* of the Ekampam temple, named Kāñcipura-naṅkai—but only one of these women appears to have had any actual connection with this place. There is one temple woman who is named Vītiviṭaṅka–māṇikkam, after the Lord at Tiruvarur, but she belongs to a temple in Tirunelveli district, 300 kilometers to the south of Tiruvarur. There are no temple women whose names are associated with Tiruvidaimarudur.

The place-name or name of a specific deity most frequently found as part of the name of a temple woman is that of a temple with which temple women had scarcely any association—the great Śaiva shrine at Chidambaram (Tirucir̲r̲ampalam, Tillai, Poṉṉampalam).[7] This place-name is not only common in temple women's names but also appears as part of the names of hundreds of other people referred to in the Chola period inscriptions, particularly in the third subperiod (Karashima, Subbarayalu, and Matsui 1978, 3:11–12, 231–32, 249–51, 357). As is the case for virtually all of these hundreds of people, the temple women named after this place have no connection with Chidambaram apart from being named for it or for the god enshrined there.[8] None of the records that mention temple women named after this shrine even come from South Arcot district, the district where Chidambaram is located, but are found scattered throughout the entire Tamil region.

Some individuals have names made up of place-names with suffixes, most commonly *uṭaiyār*, that indicate possession. In James Heitzman's analysis of Chola period "lords," he considers such a name to indicate "a point of origin or . . . a site where land is controlled or influence is exercised" (1995, 79).[9] Such names are not borne by temple women, nor do place-names in general have this significance for them. We do find a reference to a temple woman named Tillaivaṉam-uṭaiyāḷ Matatilli, a *tevaraṭiyāḷ* who made a donation to her home temple in Tiruchirappalli district at the end of the twelfth century (IPS 152). The first part of her name means "she who possesses (or is the mistress of) the forest of Tillai (Chidambaram)." But the dense forest of *tillai* shrubs, which in ancient times had surrounded the shrine of Chidambaram, should be understood in terms of its mythic significance (Younger 1995, 84) rather than as a piece of property that someone might have owned. It would seem most sensible to regard this temple woman's name as a feminine form of the name of the deity at Chidambaram, "the Lord of the forest of Tillai."

Temple women's names, when based on place-names, cannot be considered indicative of any special association with the temple or the deity of that place. Such names, for temple women as for many other people in the Chola period, evoke the sanctity and fame of particular temples, without implying any practical connection with them. The widespread use of such names reinforces the idea that the localization of the divine was fundamental to the religious sensibility of the times, and the particular popularity of the name of Chidambaram and its deity suggests its importance in the religious imagination of many people, especially in the later Chola period.[10]

In addition to the names of deities tied to specific sites in the Tamil country, divine names of a more general character were also adopted by temple women. As in the case of the specific local names, these more general names appear to have had patterns of use and significance that were not particularly distinctive for temple women but were for the most part shared by the population at large. These names are, however, different from the specific local names in that they include the names of goddesses.

The idea that temple women acted as representatives of the goddess-consort of the male god enshrined in the temple has been prominent in recent analyses of the meaning of *devadāsīs*' roles and identities (Marglin 1985b; Kersenboom 1987). Thus it may be of interest to see if the use of goddess-names by Chola period temple women suggests such a relationship. Temple women bore the names Tukkai (Skt. Durgā), Kāḷi (Skt. Kālī), Catti (Skt. Śakti), Umai (Skt. Umā), and Tamil goddess-names like Āḷuṭaiya-nācciyār ("Lady of the Sovereign Lord"), Paḷḷiyaṟai-nācciyār ("Lady of the Bed-chamber"), and Ūruṭaiyaperumāḷ-naṅkai ("Lady of the God who is Lord of the Village").[11] The first thing that is clear is that many of these names, especially the Sanskrit-derived names, are those of independent female deities rather than consort-goddesses. And with the exception of the name Umai, none of these names is explicitly Śaiva or Vaiṣṇava. It seems, therefore, that the kinds of goddess-names borne by Chola period temple women generally do not indicate an identification with the divine consorts of the male deities to whose temples these women were connected.[12] Also arguing against the notion that goddess-names had a particular significance for temple women is the fact that these names were borne by many people who were not temple women, including even men and Buddhist women.[13]

Temple women also had the names of male deities, the most prominent of which is Nakkaṉ. Nakkaṉ is related to the Sanskrit *nagna*, meaning "naked" and is a name of Śiva in his ascetic and mendicant aspect.[14] All 383 of the *taḷicceri peṇṭukaḷ* whose names are preserved in the Tanjavur inscription (SII 2.66) bear this name, as do a number of other temple women, including the women mentioned in the inscription translated at the beginning of this section.[15] Apart from its use by temple women, Nakkaṉ is arguably the most common name in Chola period inscriptions; borne by a few women, but mostly by men of various ranks and professions, it is especially popular in Tanjavur and Tiruchirappalli districts in the early Chola period, particularly in the first subperiod (Karashima, Subbarayalu, and Matsui 1978, 1:xxxix, li-lii, 3:265–80).

But temple women seem to have used the name Nakkaṉ somewhat more frequently than did other people, and this leads to the question of whether it had any special significance for them. In many cases, it may be regarded simply as a given name, as in the case of the many other people who bore it. The use of male names as given names for women is not uncommon in Chola period inscriptions. Another possibility is that temple women named Nakkaṉ were taking the name of their fathers. We do find some evidence in the inscriptions of the practice widely followed in present-day Tamilnadu of adopting the father's name as an element of one's own. This naming pattern, however, is far from universal among men named in Chola period inscriptions and seems quite rare for women.[16] In the case of temple women, if Nakkaṉ is taken to designate a father, it might be more appropriate to think of this in religious rather than literal terms.[17]

It is clear from the meaning of the term *tevaṉār makaḷ* that certain temple women were indeed considered, in some sense, daughters of God. It is interesting that a large proportion (eight out of nineteen, or 42 percent) of *tevaṉār makaḷs* whose names we know have Nakkaṉ as a part of their name, and most of the male *tevaṉār makaṉs* also bear the name Nakkaṉ. Here the honor of being considered the daughter or son of God is emphasized through the adoption of God's name. Some temple women may have assumed the name Nakkaṉ when they acquired the status of *tevaṉār makaḷ* or *tevaraṭiyāḷ* or entered into a relationship with a particular temple. Almost certainly this is what happened to the *taḷicceri peṇṭukaḷ* brought to the Rājarājeśvara temple in Tanjavur.[18] We see a similar situation—on a smaller scale—at Tiruvidaimarudur, where, according to a tenth-century inscription (SII 19.92A), all the temple servants who received support from the temple, men as well as a woman (a *tevaṉār makaḷ*), bore the name Nakkaṉ.

It seems best to understand the meaning and importance of the name Nakkaṉ for temple women in several different ways. For most temple women, the significance of the name was the same as for the many other individuals who bore it—and this significance was similar to that of other divine names, whether of goddesses or of deities at specific locales. These names bestowed good fortune on their bearers but did not indicate any special connection between the individual and the deity. However, the name Nakkaṉ as part of the names of the *taḷicceri peṇṭukaḷ* of the Tanjavur temple, and possibly of some of the other temple women who bore it (particularly *tevaṉār makaḷs*), may be considered in a different light—as a name linked to temple woman status and reinforcing temple women's identities as daughters of God.

The higher rate of use of the name Nakkaṉ by temple women than by other kinds of people may be explained by the fact that it was conferred by the temple, particularly on *tevaṉār makaḷs*. In an earlier discussion, in chapter 2, we found that the title *talaikkoli* was used exclusively by temple women, especially by women who were identified as *patiyilār*; in this case, too, I suggested that *talaikkoli* was a title granted by the temple, together with other privileges.[19]

Another title was incorporated into the names of temple women—*māṇikkam*—which, once again, seems to show that their names might be linked to temple woman status. *Māṇikkam* means "ruby" and is derived from Sanskrit *māṇikya* (MTL, 3153).[20] In addition to the seven *taḷicceri peṇṭukaḷ* named in the Tanjavur inscription with *māṇikkam* titles, there are seventy-two other temple women who bear this title—almost a third of the temple women whose names are found in Chola period inscriptions other than the Tanjavur inscription. Of these seventy-two, very few are mentioned in inscriptions of the earlier Chola period, before the end of the eleventh century. In this early period, *māṇikkam* titles are found in only a few inscriptions, and more often with reference to queens and palace women than to temple women. But toward the end of the eleventh century, these titles were increasingly used by temple women. There are four temples, in various parts of South India, that had whole groups of temple women, all bearing *māṇikkam* titles. The earliest example of this kind of phenomenon is from Polannaruwa in Sri Lanka, where a Tamil inscription dated about A.D. 1070 gives the names of seven *tevaraṭiyār*, all with *māṇikkam* titles, who ensured the maintenance of an endowment for a perpetual lamp (SII 4.1388). In the thirteenth century, there are three similar cases—at Vatakatukoyil in Tanjavur district (TK 195), Kulattur in Tiruchirappalli district (IPS 162), and Taruvai in Tirunelveli district (ARE 374 of 1972–73)—in which groups of temple women with responsibility or service functions all had *māṇikkam* titles.

This clustering of *māṇikkam* titles at specific temples parallels what we have seen for the name Nakkaṉ. It seems that certain temples had the practice of granting *māṇikkam* titles to women who had acquired the status of temple woman, and this practice may explain, at least in part, the existence of so many temple women with this title. However, many inscriptions of the later Chola period, particularly in the northern districts, refer to individual temple women with *māṇikkam* titles, most of whom were temple patrons.

There are three types of names borne by temple women—Nakkaṉ, *talaikkoli* names, and *māṇikkam* names—that seem closely associated with temple woman status and which seem in some cases to have been conferred by the temple. It is tempting to consider that these names were acquired by temple women through a ritual of initiation. Sectarian initiation frequently involves taking on a new name—a name associated with the deity worshiped by the sectarian community. And in the practice of South Indian temples in recent history, sectarian initiation is an important element in the process through which certain temple servants become qualified to serve in the temple.[21] But of the three types of names linked to temple woman status, only one—Nakkaṉ—appears a likely candidate as a name bestowed through sectarian initiation. *Talaikkoli* names and *māṇikkam* names often incorporate religious referents, but in sectarian terms these referents are frequently inconsistent and vague. For example, although over half of the *māṇikkam* names borne by temple women can be considered "religious," many lack sectarian specificity. The name Cīkaraṇa-māṇikkam ("ruby of holy action") could refer to any deity. And in at least one case in which there is sectarian specificity, it is evidently inappropriate: a temple woman who was serving in a Śaiva temple, one of the ten women with *māṇikkam* titles at the temple of Taruvai in Tirunelveli district (ARE 374 of 1972–73), had a name—Veṇuvaṉapperumāḷ-māṇikkam ("ruby of the flute-playing Lord")—that refers to Kṛṣṇa, a form of Viṣṇu.

There are no indications in the Chola period inscriptions that the acquisition of names by temple women was ritualized. Given the character of the names, it seems unlikely that they were granted as part of initiation into a sectarian tradition. The idea that Chola period temples conferred Nakkaṉ, *talaikkoli*, or *māṇikkam* names on temple women in some other ceremonial manner rests only on the indirect evidence of the frequency of use and distribution of these names. The inscriptions' silence about the bestowal of names on temple women can be contrasted with the explicit mention of the granting of royal titles to local notables by the king, in Chola period inscriptions, and with the references to the conferring of *māṇikkam* names on temple women in inscriptions of the post-Chola period. These later references, the earliest of which dates from the fifteenth century, describe the granting of a name, together with other honors and the right to serve in the temple, as a formal procedure conducted by the temple authorities.[22]

It is quite possible that such procedures were also carried out for temple women in earlier times, but it does not appear that in the Chola period the official or ritual granting of a name was a necessary prerequisite to or concommitant of the acquisition of temple woman status. It seems clear that some temples did bestow names on temple women and that this was a mark of honor, but for the most part the names of temple women were very similar to those of other individuals in Chola period society. These names are often evocative of deities and sacred places, and only rarely does this religious content appear to have any special significance for temple women's relationships with gods and temples. Where such significance does seem to be present, we find the image of temple women as the daughters—rather than the wives—of God.

Daughters of Women and Daughters of God

Status and Inheritance

In the reign of Vikkiramapāṇṭiyatevar,

Maratakaperumāḷ, the daughter of Vaṭivuṭaiya Maṅkaiyār, one of the temple women (*tevaraṭiyāḷ*) of the first rank (*muṉmuṟai*) in the temple of the god Kaṉṉuṭaiyiccuramuṭaiyār, the Lord of Pullūr, made a gift of the *kaṇṭam* (curtain? bell?) and the *paṭṭikai* (ornamental structure around the wall) in the *maṇṭapam*.

—SII 23.423: this inscription was engraved in the thirteenth century at the Kaṉṉīśvaram temple in Virapandi, Madurai district.

In recent South Indian history, for at least the last two centuries, responsibilities and privileges in the temple have been understood as hereditary, in the case both of "professional" and "devotional" rights—that is, on the one hand, rights to fulfill particular ritual functions and to receive support from the temple and, on the other hand, rights to participate in temple ritual in certain capacities and to receive special marks of the grace of the Lord. During the period of British colonial rule, competition for these hereditary rights was widespread, and many lawsuits were launched to defend or recover them (Appadurai and Breckenridge 1976, 196–204; Breckenridge 1978, 88–104; Appadurai 1981, 165–211; Dirks 1987, 358–83). But the changes wrought by British economic and political control over local and temple affairs in South India may in fact have been in part responsible for producing the perception of such rights (which the British referred to as *mirāsi* rights) as traditional, inviolable, and hereditary.[23] In the Chola period, it is not at all clear that temple duties and honors were closely tied to hereditary claims. In examining the question of how far temple women's rights were hereditary in the Chola period, there are two issues to be addressed: (1) the inheritance of temple woman status and (2) the inheritance of duties and privileges in the temple.

The inscriptional evidence of the Chola period indicates that titles, and the status that went with them, were generally not acquired by inheritance; this fact, among others, indicates that the Chola period was marked by greater social fluidity and less rigid structuring around the principle of heredity than were subsequent eras.[24] Temple women seem to have fit into this general pattern, judging from the infrequency with which such terms as *tevaraṭiyār* and *tevaṉār makaḷ*, as "term- titles" or indicators of a particular status, were inherited. Although daughters of *tevaraṭiyār* and *tevaṉār makaḷs* are mentioned in several inscriptions, including the preceding translation, only in three cases do mothers and daughters share the same term-title. Two of these—one a tenth-century inscription from Ramnad district in the far south of Tamilnadu (SII 14.83) and the other a thirteenth-century inscription from Tiruchirappalli district in the core Chola region (IPS 162)—are simply cases in which both a mother and a daughter are named in a list of *tevaraṭiyār*. The third case is more interesting because, in a series of inscriptions from Takkolam in North Arcot district, we seem to see the process of the acquisition of the term-title *tevaṉār makaḷ* by the daughter of a *tevaṉār makaḷ*. Two inscriptions of the mid-tenth century (SII 3.184 and SII 3.190) record gifts of sheep and of gold to the temple of Tiruvūṟal by Kumaraṭi-naṅkai, the daughter of a *tevaṉār makaḷ* of this place; the gold is meant to provide offerings for the image of Kalikai-viṭaṅkar which Kumaraṭi-naṅkai has set up in the temple. In an inscription 30 years later, Kumaraṭi-naṅkai is herself described as a *tevaṉār makaḷ* of this temple and is mentioned as the mother of a donor who gives gold to provide offerings for the deity Kalikai-viṭaṅkar (SII 5.1366).

These three cases demonstrate that the daughter of a *tevaraṭiyāḷ* or a *tevaṉār makaḷ* could herself be a *tevaraṭiyāḷ* or a *tevaṉār makaḷ*, but beyond this the evidence, because it is so meager, raises more questions than it answers. Could a mother and daughter both be *tevaraṭiyār* at the same time, whereas *tevaṉār makaḷ*s only acquired this title after their mother's death? Or did Kumaraṭi-naṅkai, the daughter of a *tevaṉār makaḷ*, acquire *tevaṉār makaḷ* status herself not as a result of her mother's death but because she had made a major donation to the temple? Was it *necessary* for a *tevaṉār makaḷ* or a *tevaraṭiyāḷ* to have a mother who had this status or bore this term-title, in the same way that the *devadāsīs* of more recent times were invariably the daughters of *devadāsīs*?

I am inclined to answer this last question in the negative. First, the evidence for the inheritance of these term-titles is, as we have just seen, very slight, and this fits in with a general pattern in Chola society as a whole, in which titles seem to have been personally acquired rather than inherited. Second, temple women were very infrequently identified with reference to their parentage: only in 8 of the 221 inscriptions in which temple women are named do temple women who were not slaves mention their mothers. If temple woman status were dependent on descent from a woman who had this status, we would expect to see more frequent references to temple women's mothers. Possibly the fact that such references, when they do occur, date for the most part from the later Chola period indicates that temple woman status increasingly became hereditary, but we must look at further evidence before coming to this conclusion.

If temple women did not usually inherit titles from their mothers, they may nonetheless have acquired, hereditarily, responsibilities and privileges in the temple. In the early Chola period, there are only two cases in which temple women seem to have had hereditary associations with the temple—and both are somewhat ambiguous. The earlier of the two is a tenth-century inscription from South Arcot district, dated in the reign of a Rashtrakuta king, which granted to a woman and her *vaṟkattār* a plot of land as property for her use (*bhogam*) in exchange for her undertaking to provide dancing at festivals (SII 26.391). The word *vaṟkattār* can be understood either as "those belonging to her lineage" or as "those belonging to her group" (MTL 3504, 3518, 3557).[25] The second inscription is from the end of Rajaraja I's reign (A.D. 1014) and records the establishment of 400 *taḷicceri peṇṭukaḷ* at the Rājarājeśvara temple in Tanjavur (SII 2.66). This inscription specifies that the share (*paṅku*) of produce and the responsibility of performing service (*paṇi*) assigned to each woman should, when she died or moved elsewhere, be transferred to her nearest relative (*aṭutta muṟai*) or, if such a person was not suitable (*yogyar*), to someone who was qualified, chosen either by the near relative or by the group (of *taḷicceri peṇṭukaḷ*) from among their number. Here we do see inheritance of the right to temple service, but the principle of heredity is qualified by the insistence on fitness for the position.[26]

In the later Chola period, ten inscriptions from six temples indicate the establishment of hereditary links to the temple for temple women. All of these inscriptions date from the thirteenth century and all describe deals—the exchange of gifts to the temple for service rights or honors. Three of the six temples where such arrangements were made are in Chingleput district: there are three inscriptions from the Vaiṣṇava temple in Uttaramerur (ALB 8,177; ARE 180 and 183 of 1923), two from the Śaiva temple in Tiruppulivanam (ARE 210 and 211 of 1923), and one from the Vaiṣṇava temple in Tiruppukkuli (ARE 179 of 1916). These inscriptions all record gifts made by women to the temple and grants to them and their descendents of various privileges, including the right to receive consecrated food offerings and the right to wave the flywhisk before the deity in festival processions. Of the other three temples where deals for hereditary rights were made by temple women, one is also in the northern region—an inscription from North Arcot district (ARE 29 of 1940–41) recording the grant of the first house in the temple quarter (*tirumaṭaiviḷākam*) and precedence in festival ritual to a woman and her descendents, in consideration of her gift of gold to the temple. At the other end of Tamilnadu, in Kanyakumari district, two inscriptions from Cholapuram describe the grant of consecrated food and other honors to a *tevaraṭiyāḷ* and her descendents (*santāṉa-praveśam*), after gifts were made by her and by her older brother (KK 255 = TAS 6.16 and KK 256 = TAS 6.15). Only one of the ten inscriptions of the later Chola period comes from the core Chola region: it records the gift of several images by a *tevaraṭiyāḷ* of the temple and the grant to her and her *vaṟkattār* of the privilege of participating in morning and festival rituals (NK 134).

The picture we get from these inscriptions, then, is that temple women only rarely established hereditary relationships with the temple. This is consistent with the finding that emerged earlier in this chapter that there were not, in the Chola period, "traditions," stretching from one generation to the next, of temple women's association with particular temples. If we consider the numbers of inscriptions that mention hereditary association with the temple as a proportion of all inscriptions that show temple women filling service or responsibility functions in the temple, making deals, or receiving food or honors from the temple—all of which might be hereditary relationships, and which seem to have become so in more recent times—we find that 4 percent of such relationships are said to be hereditary in the early Chola period (two of fifty-four) and 12 percent are said to be hereditary in the later period (ten of eighty-two). Thus there does seem to be an increase in the thirteenth century in the extent to which women's connections with the temple became hereditary, but most such associations were not hereditary and those that were, in the later period, were established as a consequence of donations to the temple.

If the great majority of temple women's hereditary relationships with the temple were the result of deals, the situation for their male counterparts was markedly different. None of the hereditary links established by men involved the exchange of gifts to the temple for privileges in the temple. The hereditary relationships of men were for the most part temple service positions or occasionally responsibility functions. However, hereditary relationships are rarely mentioned in Chola period inscriptions for either temple women or temple men.[27]

Because inscriptions record the establishment of new arrangements, rather than describing ordinary procedures, it is possible that the common, routine practice in the Chola period was inheritance of temple service positions. But this seems unlikely, given that the inscriptions refer to a variety of ways, apart from inheritance, in which a position might be acquired—for example, through a gift, through purchase from another individual, as the result of a deal, or as *strīdhana* (i.e., by a man from his father-in-law)—and a variety of qualifications, apart from heredity, for the right to perform temple service, such as experience or knowledge, place of residence, or some other principle of succession.[28] Furthermore, in the many inscriptions that record the creation of new positions or the appointment of new people to fill existing positions, not only is the position rarely defined as hereditary but also the person newly granted the position, whether male or female, is scarcely ever described as having hereditary qualifications to fill it.[29] During the Chola period, heredity was in a some cases a factor in the process through which rights, responsibilities, and privileges in the temple were acquired, but for temple women, as well as for other temple servants, this factor was not nearly as important as it was to become in later times.

Temple Women's Families

In the twenty-fourth year of the reign of the emperor of the three worlds, Śrī Kulottuṅkacoḻatevar,

for [the god] Tiruttāntoṉṟicuramutaiya nāyaṉār, Lord of Caṇpai alias Virarācentirapuram, in Vāṇakoppāṭi, on the north bank of the Peṇṇai [River], in Irācarācavaḷanāṭu,

I, Aḻakiyaperumāḷ, the daughter of Puṇṇiyañceytāḷ—a temple woman (*tevaraṭiyāḷ*) in the temple of [the god] Tiruvekampamuṭaiyār who is the Lord of holy Kāñcipuram, and the female companion (*aṇukki*) of Malaiyamāṉ Aḻakiyāṉ Ākāracūraṉ alias Irācagampirac-cetiyarāyar of Kiḷiyūr—

gave land [whose boundaries are described] to this deity, to provide for festival expenses for the procession on the holy day of Tiruppuraṭṭāti.

May this [endowment] last for as long as the sun and the moon shall shine. Whosoever tampers with this [grant] is considered to have commited sin on the banks of the Gaṅgā and at Kumari, to be one who will enter the lowest of the seven hells, and to have given his wife to a *paṟaiyaṉ*. May the *paṉmāheśvarar* protect this [grant].

—SII 22.87: this inscription was engraved in A.D. 1202 on the south wall of the central shrine of the Jambunātha temple in Jambai, South Arcot district.

Although there is little evidence in the Chola period inscriptions that the status of temple woman or the roles that temple women played were passed hereditarily from mother to daughter, the inscriptions do mention family relationships in which temple women were involved, as we see in the preceding record and others translated earlier in this chapter. An examination of these relationships will help to further illuminate the character of temple women's identities in the Chola period.

The first thing that must be said about family relationships is that they seem quite incidental to the identities of most temple women, especially in comparison to the centrality of hometowns. We have seen that 71 percent of the Chola period inscriptions that name temple women identify them in terms of their links to a deity, a temple, or a place (table 5.1). In table 5.2, we see that only 11 percent of these inscriptions identify women through family relationships.[30] The deemphasis on kinship connections is particularly striking when we contrast temple women with other kinds of women. In table 5.2, we see that only palace women and Jain religious women were as rarely identified in terms of links to kin and that most other women were identified with reference to a family member—most frequently, their husbands.[31] For most women, kinship connections were central to the definition of their social identities, in the same way that relationship with a sacred place was at the core of temple women's identities; and if family relationships played a minor role for temple women, associations with hometowns were rarely as significant for other kinds of women.[32]

In only 25 of the 221 inscriptions in which temple women are named are they identified in terms of family relationships. In 16, or two-thirds of these, they were described as the daughters of women. Fourteen of the 16 are inscriptions from the later Chola period, suggesting that tracing kinship through the mother was increasingly a feature of temple women's family organization. Or this rise may be correlated with the increase in references to slavery: 8 of the 16 inscriptions describe women who have been given or sold to the temple as slaves. In several of these inscriptions, family groups that were headed by women (occasionally including their sons, as well as their daughters and granddaughters) became slaves of the temple. Of the other 8 inscriptions, in which temple women who were not slaves are identified as the daughters of women, 6 are from the three northern districts of Tamilnadu. We may find an indication here that female-focused kinship patterns for temple women were emerging in the later Chola period, particularly in this area.

Although a number of inscriptions identify temple women as the daughters of women, in only one case is a temple woman described as the daughter of a man (NK 157).[33] In this inscription, which, being fragmentary, is somewhat ambiguous, it appears that the daughters of a man of the village, a *veḷḷāḷaṉ*, were sold to the temple. There are just two other inscriptions in which temple women are identified with reference to their blood relationship with a man. In one (SII 22.141), a woman described as the mother of a *veḷḷāḷaṉ* is given as a slave to the temple. In the other (KK 255 = TAS 6.16),

Table 5.2 Family identifications for women of different types

	Family-identified	Female relative		Male relative		
		Mother	Other	Husband	Father	Other
Temple women						
n = 221	25 (11%)	16 (7%)	0	6 (3%)	1 (.5%)	2 (1%)
Palace women						
n = 95	0	0	0	0	0	0
Queens						
n = 198	154 (78%)	3 (1.5%)	0	131 (66%)	42 (21%)	19 (10%)
Jain religious women						
n = 29	2 (7%)	0	0	1 (3%)	1 (3%)	0
Nonroyal, Nontemple women (in 8 study areas)						
Brahmans						
n = 79	71 (90%)	1 (1%)	1 (1%)	63 (80%)	3 (4%)	11 (14%)
Non-Brahmans						
n = 110	65 (59%)	3 (3%)	2 (2%)	39 (35%)	13 (12%)	12 (11%)

The symbol n = the number of inscriptions in which individuals, of each type, are *named*.

a *tevaraṭiyāḷ* is identified as the sister of a man who made a donation to the temple and thereby procured some temple privileges for her.

Six inscriptions identify temple women as wives. Since the status of the temple woman as a woman without human marital ties is considered to be such a central feature of her character in recent ethnography and analysis, we should examine these inscriptions in some detail. Three of these inscriptions have been presented in chapter 2, in the discussion of whether the category of temple women overlapped with other categories of women. These three inscriptions refer to two women, both of whom are described as *tevaṉār makaḷs* and *teviyār* ("wives" and "queens")—in one case, of Piḷḷai Ceramāṉar, presumably a prince of the Chera dynasty of Kerala (SII 13.153 and 154), and in the other, of the great Chola ruler Rajaraja I (ARE 385 of 1924). These inscriptions are all from Tiruchirappalli district and are dated in the tenth or early eleventh century.

Two other inscriptions, both dated in the eleventh century (or, in one case, perhaps the early twelfth century), refer to temple women as *akamuṭaiyāḷ*, "wives." In one, from Tiruvorriyur in Chingleput district, a female donor named Caturaṉ Caturi is identified as a *tevaraṭiyāḷ* of the Lord of Tiruvorriyur, as well as someone's wife (ARE 147 of 1912). In the other, from South Arcot district, a woman who made a donation to a Jain temple is described both as a *tevar makaḷ* and as the wife of a *tevaraṭiyār* of the temple precincts (*tirumaṭaiviḷākam*) (SITI 28). Finally, a thirteenth-century inscription from Tanjavur district refers to a stonemason, his wife, and their four sons as servants of the *maṭha* that had bought them (ARE 409 of 1925). This inscription resembles the matrilineal slave inscriptions already discussed, except that here the family head, an artisan, is a man.

We see in these references to temple women as wives a range of different circumstances, but the chronological distribution may indicate a changing notion of the nature of their status. Perhaps in the early Chola period, when inscriptions refer to queens as temple women, and in the middle Chola period, when two inscriptions describe temple women as *akamuṭaiyāḷs*, there was a variety of conceptions about the character of the temple woman—perhaps including Jain-influenced conceptions—and in some of these, marriage and temple woman status were not incompatible. It is possible that only in the later Chola period did a more consistent definition of the temple woman as unmarried begin to take shape—except in the case in which the temple woman had become the property of the temple as the wife of a male slave.

In addition to the handful of inscriptions that describe temple women as wives, there are two cases in which, as we have seen in chapter 2, the categories of temple women and of palace women overlap and temple women are represented in terms of relationships with men who were neither their husbands nor their kin. In one of these inscriptions (ARE 560 of 1921) the precise nature of this relationship is obscure: the *tevaraṭiyār* Āyuṭainācci, mentioned as the mother of a man who made a donation, is described as a member of the *parivāram* of an anonymous *kāṇiyuṭaiyār* (*kāṇi*-owner). In the other of the two inscriptions (SII 22.87—the preceding translation), a record of the late eleventh century, Puṇṇiyañceytāḷ is described both as the *aṇukki* of a Malaiyamāṉ chief and as one of the *tevaraṭiyār* of the temple of Lord Tiruvekampam in Kanchipuram. Puṇṇiyañceytāḷ's daughter appears also to be the daughter of the Malaiyamāṉ chief—judging from the similarity of their names—and this inscription records her gift to a temple in the region where her father held power, 100 kilometers from Kanchipuram (see Orr 1997).

Puṇṇiyañceytāḷ's situation seems similar to that of the temple women of the early and middle Chola periods who are described as wives. Her liaison with a man is evidently not inconsistent with her status as a temple woman. Nor is it incidental to the definition of her social identity, as the relationship between the temple women of more recent times and their patrons seems to have been.[34] The way in which the identity of temple woman is presented in the inscriptions of the Chola period, in the case of Puṇṇiyañceytāḷ and the temple women who are described as wives, is similar to the way in which other married women are identified through their relationships with their fathers, as well as with their husbands.[35] It would appear that a woman's identity as a temple woman was no more in conflict with her status as wife than another woman's identity as a daughter would be. This parallel, as well as the very fact that there were temple women who were the wives of men, points to a fundamental difference between Chola period temple women and the *devadāsīs* of the early twentieth century. The identity of these *devadāsīs* as wives of God is linked to a ritual of dedication that resembles the marriage ceremony and is regarded as wholly incompatible with marriage to a mortal man. There is no evidence that temple women underwent such a marriage to God in the Chola period or even in the following period of Vijayanagara rule; the earliest reference I have found to a dedication ritual for temple women that involves marriage to the temple deity dates from the seventeenth century and is contained in a palm-leaf manuscript from the Suchindram temple in Kanyakumari district (Pillay 1953, 281–82). If the identity of the temple woman in recent history was tied to her status as the wife of God—ever auspicious because her husband was immortal—this was not the case for her counterpart of earlier times.[36]

Temple women in the Chola period were not commonly identified with reference to their relatives; they appear, in fact, more frequently in the identifications of other individuals. Whereas only twenty-five temple women are described as the daughters or wives or sisters of other people, in forty-six inscriptions, or about 20 percent of all the inscriptions in which temple women are named, temple women are mentioned in the context of identifying another person; that is, other people describe themselves as the daughters, sons, or sisters of temple women. This reinforces the idea that some Chola period temple women were a part of—indeed, were the heads of—female-focused family groups. There are thirty inscriptions in which women identify themselves as the daughters of temple women and another eight in which men are described as the sons or grandsons of temple women. This type of identification indicates, first, that temple women had children and, second, that their children, at least some of the time, traced their descent through their mothers. In none of these thirty-eight inscriptions do we find mention of the father's name or of the paternal line. In addition, there are also six other inscriptions in which an individual is identified as the sister of a temple woman, one in which she is said to be a temple woman's mother, and one in which the individual is described as a temple woman's brother. Thus the relationship most often referred to—in 83 percent of the cases in which temple women are mentioned as relatives—is the maternal one.

All but three of the forty-six inscriptions that refer to temple women in the identification of other individuals use either the term *tevaṉār makaḷ* or *tevaraṭiyāḷ*. The consistent use of one or the other indicates that these terms designated a particular status—a high status, which donors and others who identified themselves through their relationship to temple women, were eager to highlight. Temple women are mentioned in the identification of other people relatively more frequently in the northern districts of Tamilnadu, particularly in North Arcot district; in Tanjavur district and in the southern districts this kind of reference is quite rare. This pattern of identification is found throughout the Chola period but most commonly in the last subperiod. Also, it is only in the last subperiod that we find inscriptions in which men describe themselves as the sons, grandsons, or brothers of temple women.

A few of these temple women and their sons seem to be linked to the *kaikkoḷar* community. In inscriptions of the early Chola period, the term *kaikkoḷar* refers to men who were members of groups associated with the Chola court; these men are described as members of the "select (*terinta*) *kaikkoḷar*," of "palace establishments" (*veḷams*), or of "armies" (*paṭais*) and were active as donors, particularly in Tanjavur and South Arcot districts. The later identity of the *kaikkoḷar* as weavers only begins to be evident in the thirteenth century (Ramaswamy 1985, 14–15). It is at this same time, in the last part of the Chola period and increasingly in subsequent centuries, that *kaikkoḷar* came to have important administrative functions and ritual status in various temples, particularly in northern Tamilnadu.[37] And also—in the thirteenth century and in the north—we begin to see connections between *kaikkoḷar* and temple women.

Two inscriptions mention a woman named A̲ramuṭaiyāḷ, the mother of a man who made donations both to the temple at Tiruvannamalai in North Arcot district and to the temple at Tiruvennainallur in South Arcot district. In the record from Tiruvannamalai, dated A.D. 1237, A̲ramuṭaiyāḷ is described as one of the *kaikkoḷar* of the temple of the Lord of Tiruvennainallur (SII 8.91). In the record from Tiruvennainallur, dated A.D. 1249, she is said to be one of the *tevaraṭiyār* of the Lord of that place (SII 12.150). These inscriptions, together with others of the late Chola period, indicate that at a few of the temples in the northern part of Tamilnadu, some temple women or their male kin were members of the *kaikkoḷar* community.[38] Tiruvennainallur is one of the places where we find evidence of temple privileges being granted to *kaikkoḷar* in the thirteenth and subsequent centuries. As for the other temple that A̲ramuṭaiyāḷ's son endowed—Tiruvannamalai—here, too, there seems to have been an association between *kaikkoḷar* and temple women dating back to the late Chola period. This is suggested in a thirteenth-century inscription (SII 8.120), which records the benefactions of the son of one of the twenty-four *tevaraṭiyār* of Tiruvannamalai; among his gifts to the temple to which his mother belonged was a shrine dedicated to the god Piḷḷaiyār (Gaṇeśa) for the *kaikkoḷar* to worship in. If we assume that he was constructing a shrine for the benefit of members of his own community, this is a case in which the son of a temple woman may be identified as a *kaikkoḷar*.[39]

Such links between temple women and *kaikkoḷar* became much more strongly articulated in recent South Indian history: *kaikkoḷar* girls were dedicated as *devadāsīs*, some male *kaikkoḷar* were musicians and dance teachers (*naṭṭuvar*) rather than weavers, there were liaisons between temple women and wealthy *kaikkoḷar*, and the children of temple women occasionally married *kaikkoḷar* (Thurston and Rangachari 1909, 2:127–28, 138; 3:37–40; Mines 1984, 28–29, 31, 46). Some of these relationships appear to have antecedants in the late Chola period, at least in certain temple towns of northern Tamilnadu, and are linked to an increasing visibility of men as members of temple women's families.

The identification of people, particularly men, as the relatives of temple women and the identification of temple women as the daughters of women indicate a female-focused family pattern, which is especially in evidence in the northern part of Tamilnadu and in the last century of the Chola period. The reckoning of kinship through the maternal line and the acknowledgement of maternity were at no point in the Chola period common features of temple women's families, but they are features that are encountered considerably more frequently among temple women than among other types of women. The children of palace women in some cases traced their lineage through their mothers, but the recognition of palace women as progenitors in Chola period inscriptions is less than half as common as is the case for temple women.[40]

Temple women's identities, unlike those of most other women, were not defined by marriage or male lineage. In this respect, Chola period temple women resemble the *devadāsīs* of the nineteenth and twentieth centuries[41] but differ from the several matrilineal communities of South India. These communities include groups of Tamilnadu and of Kerala that follow the matrilineal and matrilocal *marumakkatāyam* system; groups in Karnataka who practice the *aḷiya-santāna* system (in which descent is reckoned through the daughters of the family to sons-in-law); and groups in Karnataka and Andhra Pradesh who have adopted the *basavi* system (known as *illaṭumu* in Telugu), dedicating unmarried daughters to the temple when there are no sons in the family—the dedicated daughter bears sons who belong to her father's lineage.[42] The existence of matrilineality among these various South Indian groups has led some scholars to the conclusion that the earliest family structure in South India was matrilocal and matrilineal and that the social organization of temple women, among other groups, is a survival of kinship patterns that were much more pervasive in ancient times (Ehrenfels 1941, 16–17, 105; Hutton 1963, 160–63; Bhattacharyya 1971, 65–66; Nandi 1974, 72–73).

Apart from the problem of finding evidence of matrilineality in ancient South India,[43] this idea is misleading insofar as it obscures the very major differences between temple women of the Chola and modern periods and women in other South Indian matrilineal systems. These latter systems do reckon lineage in the female line but are at the same time predicated on marriage as a primary kinship link (Schneider and Gough 1962, 5 and passim; Dumont 1983, 128–33). Also, in many of these matrilineal systems, women's brothers play a key role in the kinship and power structure of the family, as, for example, in the *marumakkatāyam* pattern of Kerala (Sreedhara Menon 1979, 88). In some of the other matrilineal systems—notably the *basavi*, *aḷiya-santāna*, and *illaṭumu* patterns—there is such an emphasis on the continuity of the paternal line (that of the woman's father) that we might well identify these systems as essentially patrilineal.[44] But in the Chola period inscriptions that describe temple women there is a dearth of husbands, brothers, and fathers.

It seems likely that the kinship structure of South Indian temple women, with its deemphasis on marriage or male lineage, developed quite independently of other South Indian matrilineal systems, including the *basavi* system. The practice of reckoning descent through the mother's line, which seems to emerge in the later Chola period, was important in the social arrangements of later South Indian temple women. But neither in the Chola period nor in its subsequent development was the kinship organization of South Indian temple women a matrilineal system in the strict sense.[45]

The ways in which Chola period inscriptions identify temple women allow us to see which elements were unique to them and which were shared with other people in the world in which they lived, as well as which elements were peripheral and which were central to their status as temple women. At the core of their identities was a relationship with a sacred place, particularly understood in terms of a relationship with the deity of a specific shrine in the Tamil country; this relationship is represented as part of temple women's identities consistently throughout the Chola period. This fact, as well as the way in which the relationship was described and the roles of those who were related to the deity or the temple, distinguishes temple women from temple men. The emphasis on relationship with a sacred place also marks temple women as very different from other women, for whom kinship relations were the primary source of identity. Temple women rarely defined themselves through kinship connections, but when they did, these tended to be female-focused family links.

When we can discern anything about them, the families of temple women, especially in the northern part of the Tamil country and the later Chola period, seem often to have been headed by women. This kind of family arrangement must not, however, be considered a full-blown matrilineal system for many reasons—the most important of which is that there is little evidence that temple women's families were organized around any system. Nor were temple women's relationships with temples established or arranged in the precise, formal, and consistent patterns we associate with the *devadāsīs* of recent history. Chola period temple women did not have long-standing traditions of temple service at particular temples, and they did not acquire their position and status through birth or through a fixed ceremonial procedure of initiation or ritual marriage to the temple deity. There is little to suggest that in the Chola period there was a uniform definition of what the temple woman "community" was or a common conception about what being a temple woman "meant." The only notion that was perhaps shared—and is reflected in several of the ways in which temple women were referred to, named, and identified—is that of the "daughter of God," but even in this case, the reflections are faint and deflect in several directions. The relationship to the temple that was integral to who temple women were was not arrived at through the implementation of a singular, overarching institutional, ritual, or symbolic system but was, instead, realized in unique and individual ways by many particular temple women.

SIX

Conclusions

The Temple Woman of Medieval Tamilnadu

In the preceding chapters, I have examined various aspects of the character and activities of temple women in the Chola period. It is now time to discover what the whole picture looks like, to see what emerges when all the pieces of the puzzle are assembled.

Temple women constituted a social category that was distinct: they clearly were different, for example, from palace women or from ordinary family women. At the same time, however, the boundaries of this group were not rigidly circumscribed, and at no point during the Chola period do we find that the identity of the temple woman was defined by heredity or membership in a particular caste or community, by professional skill, or by ritual function. What did seem to be a defining feature of this group of women was that their identities were bound up with a particular place; that is, their most important connections were with a temple, a deity, or a village. This relationship was much more significant in temple women's self-definition than were the functions in the temple or the family relations with which they were involved. Temple women were not concentrated at particular sacred sites. Although several were associated with the town of Kanchipuram, the places where temple women were based were numerous and widespread throughout the Tamil country, and were most often smaller-sized temples rather than the largest and most famous religious centers. Nor were temple women usually linked to royal capitals or courts; Rajaraja's effort to establish hundreds of temple women at the temple of Tanjavur was exceptional, extravagant—and ultimately unsuccessful.

The importance of temple women's relationships with a temple, a god, or a place was expressed not only in the ways they identified themselves but also in the terms applied to them in Chola period inscriptions. These terms had such meanings as "devotee of God" (*tevaraṭiyār*), "daughter of God" (*tevaṉār makaḷ*), and "woman of the temple" (*taḷiyilār, patiyilār*). They did not identify temple women with reference to sectarian affiliations but underscored the connection between temple women and a particular locale, and the deity of that place. These terms were also nonfunctional: Chola period temple women were not referred to as "dancers" or by other terms that indicated ritual or professional functions. Indeed, even apart from the terms used, there is little evidence in the inscriptions that temple women had important roles to play in the ritual and administrative life of the temple. In the Chola period, the services that temple women performed appear to have been optional, occasional, and nonessential. Women's functions in the temple were vaguely defined and usually unskilled; in some cases temple women were assigned menial tasks, for which they were relatively poorly remunerated, and in other cases they had honorary functions, for which they received no remuneration at all. No tasks were exclusively female, and many forms of involvement in temple affairs, including almost all responsibility functions, appear to have been closed to women.

Temple women's relationships with the temple were secured not as a consequence of ritual function or professional skill—nor through inheritance or ceremonies of initiation or "marriage" to the temple deity—but through their donations. According to the testimony of the Chola period inscriptions, making gifts to the temple was the single most important role for temple women. In this regard, they were very different from temple men; and the character of their donations also marked them as different from other donors. Temple women endowed temples in their hometowns to an unusually high degree, and they patronized medium-sized temples rather than those that were more popularly supported. Unlike such donors as royal women, who appear to have followed one another's example and focused on a relatively small number of temples, temple women's patronage was diffuse and individualistic. They used donations as a way to forge and strengthen connections with the temple in their locality, connections that were critical to their status and identities as temple women.

There is a rapid rise in the number of temple women whose activities are recorded in inscriptions of the twelfth and thirteenth centuries, especially in the far northern and southern regions of Tamilnadu. Their rising public presence contrasts with the dramatic decline in the number of inscriptional references to other kinds of women. The increase in the visibility of temple women between the early and later Chola periods is directly linked to their increasing activity as donors, particularly as patrons of their home temples. There are also, in the later Chola period, more and more frequent references to temple authorities in the records of temple women's gifts. These changes indicate that temple women were increasingly active in securing relationships with local temples.

This increase in temple women's initiative and involvement in creating links to the temple is also demonstrated by the emergence in the later Chola period of the explicit mention of temple women's deals with the temple—the exchange of a donation for certain rights or privileges. The deals negotiated by temple women resulted in the enhancement of a relationship already established with the temple. As a consequence of their deals, they more often acquired honors in the temple—for example, the privilege of proximity to the deity—than a "position" or regular support from the temple. Their direct negotiations with temple and village authorities involved them in a type of transaction with the temple that we do not see in the case of any other kinds of donors or temple servants in the Chola period.

Whereas temple women in the later Chola period were increasingly in evidence as donors and as makers of deals, we see a declining involvement of temple women in responsibility functions, despite the fact that more and more men are described in inscriptions of the later period as performing such functions. Temple service functions for temple women are mentioned with approximately the same frequency throughout the whole of the Chola period, although there are signs that some temple women may have become more functionally specialized in the later Chola period—apparently displacing men as festival dancers. But this period also sees a rise in the numbers of temple women who were given as slaves to the temple and who performed menial functions. We have no evidence that temple women were increasingly engaged in temple service, and of the relatively few temple women who did have roles in the ritual or administrative life of the temple, many seem to have been involved in tasks that, increasingly, had more of the nature of honors than of skilled functions.

In the later Chola period, there were more temple women and more well-defined relations between temples and temple women than in the early Chola period. The idea of the temple woman seems to take a firmer shape. The three definitional features of the temple woman outlined in chapter 2 coincide with one another more frequently in the later Chola period than they did in the earlier period. There is a shift away from the term *tevaṉār makaḷ*, "daughter of God," toward greater use of *tevaraṭiyār*, "devotee of God," to refer to the increasingly cohesive social category of temple women. The term *tevaraṭiyār* is used more and more exclusively and consistently for temple women as individuals rather than for "devotees" in general. A further indication that the category of temple woman was becoming more well defined may be found in the fact that there is an increase in the last part of the Chola period in the number of temple women who identified themselves with reference to their mothers and in the number of other people who identified themselves with reference to a *tevaraṭiyār* mother. The emerging evidence, especially in the northern parts of Tamilnadu, for such matrilineal kinship reckoning suggests the beginnings of a family-based definition of temple women's identities, within the framework of the female-focused family, which came to be characteristic of the *devadāsī* of later times. Another development of the late Chola period and the northern region of Tamilnadu, which was to have significance for the evolution of the community of temple women in the post-Chola era, is the indication that some temple women were associated with the *kaikkoḷar*, or weaving community.

But even in the later Chola period, the primary focus for temple women's identities continued to be a connection with a particular sacred place rather than with family, caste, community, profession, or function. This connection became in the later Chola period increasingly defined with specific reference to the temple (*koyil*) rather than the deity or the town. And the temple women who made links with the temple increasingly received individual recognition. The relationship between temple women and temples became not only more specific in the course of the Chola period but also much stronger and deeper—as the number of temple women increased, their efforts to forge relationships with temples intensified and their identity became more firmly defined.

Politics and Place, Margins and Centers

We have discovered in the course of this study that temple women were most in evidence and most active in the periods and regions in which Chola power and influence were least felt: in the later Chola period, in the northern and southern regions of Tamilnadu, where inscriptions were dated in the reigns of non-Chola kings, and at smaller temples that did not attract much royal attention. It is ironic that the case long held to be the *locus classicus* for the medieval South Indian *devadāsī* phenomenon—Rajaraja I's establishment of 400 temple women at his great temple in Tanjavur—turns out to be something of an aberration in terms of the time and place of its occurrence: at the beginning of the eleventh century, in the heart of the Chola territory, and at a large royal temple. Indeed, this unusual royal gesture did not have the effect of encouraging the continuing presence, activity, or support of temple women, either at the Rājarājeśvara temple or elsewhere. Instead, temple women flourished in places and periods in which local politics were strong and the Chola king's presence and authority were weak. They acquired position and status through their individual efforts rather than by royal fiat.

The activity through which temple women established relationships with the temple was donation, and a great deal of this donative activity—and virtually all of the deals negotiated by temple women—took place outside of the sphere of Chola influence. What was it about the peripheral temple—removed from the Chola region and from royal Chola interest, distant from imperial centers and different from the most famous sacred sites—that attracted temple women? These temples provided local centers around which networks of ritual, economic, and social transactions took shape. The role of temples as local centers became increasingly important in the course of the Chola period, except where royal involvement compromised the temple's autonomy and weakened local political and economic arrangements.[1] Temple-based networks and the institutions at their core came to have more and more complex and well-defined structures through which interactions took place, status was accorded and acknowledged, and roles were assigned. A large number, and an increasing number, of individuals became participants in these networks, and among these people were temple women. As the networks developed—in various ways at different temples and different localities—there were certain contexts that evidently afforded temple women more opportunities than others. Temples that were well established but not the largest, wealthiest, and most famous, in localities where they had a significant role to play in economic and political dynamics, seem to have frequently offered temple women possibilities for involvement in temple life.

In this section, I examine the character of this involvement in terms of its location, that is within the structure of the temple itself and within the network spreading outward from this center. This examination provides the foundation for a more general discussion of "woman's place" in religious institutions.

We see in the Chola period the increasing elaboration of Hindu temples as institutions, the development of their hierarchies and bureaucracies, and their increasing penetration of local economies and politics. Max Weber ([1922] 1964, 60–61) has described this kind of development in the structure of religious communities as "routinization," a process through which stability and economic support are secured for religious functions, such as preaching and worship, and for those who perform them. The performers of these religious services become more and more a well-defined group, monopolizing the privileges associated with their religious functions and having increasingly impersonal and formalized relations with other members of the community. Routinization frequently involves the replacement of a relatively simple organizational structure based on "charismatic" authority with an administrative system based on "rational-legal" authority. The most highly developed of these systems are bureaucracies, which according to Weber have the following features: (1) clear differentiation of responsibilities among officials, (2) hierarchical arrangement of offices, (3) technical criteria of recruitment, and (4) impersonal norms governing relations among officials (W. Scott 1987, 25, 40–41).

These characteristics correspond to those that have been used to define institutions by modern sociologists, and I use the terms "institutionalization" and "bureaucratization" interchangeably for the process by which organizations come to increasingly possess these features.[2] Hindu temples, in the course of the Chola period, can be said to be undergoing bureaucratization, at least with respect to the first three of Weber's four characteristics. The last characteristic implies the separation of personal from official rights and relationships; in this regard, the Chola period temple system resembles more closely Weber's "traditional" authority structure, where there is little separation between the personal and the public and where privileges, property, and position belong to a person rather than to an office (W. Scott 1987, 40–42).

The "routinization of charisma" and the processes of bureaucratization are described by Weber largely with reference to "prophetic" religions, a category that does not include Hinduism. But Weber points out that similar processes occur when religious communities grow up under the leadership of priests, and he also refers to the "prophetic" function of reformers within Hinduism (Weber [1922] 1964, 60–61, 78). Thus Hinduism, like other religions, was prone to "a decline or petrifaction of prophecy," in which increasing systematization was accompanied by popularization and ritualization. In Weber's view, these developments, which entailed compromising with traditional lay practices and adulterating an earlier, original religious vision and doctrine, were motivated especially by the desire of priests to aggrandize their status and income. Hinduism, for example, "constantly betrayed a growing tendency to slide over into magic, or in any case into a semimagical sacramental soteriology" ([1922] 1964, 77–79).

There has been very little theoretical work subsequent to Weber's on the evolution of religious institutions. Weber's model seems to remain the best available for our understanding of these processes. Unfortunately, we have also retained, to a large extent, Weber's legacy of a negative valuation of the impact on religious organizations of bureaucratization and of accommodation to the needs of lay followers. This negative judgment is widespread and is shared by many students of Indian religious and social history. Bureaucratization may be considered to produce organizations that are too complex, too rigid, too impersonal, too inefficient, and too inaccessible to outsiders (Whetten 1987, 341–43); or interactions between the organization and its "clients," growing out of the institution's accommodation to the surrounding community, may be viewed negatively both for the economic drain the religious organization represents for the laity and for the dissipation of the original and unitary purpose of the organization.[3]

Ivan Strenski has urged a reassessment of this type of negative view in the scholarly analysis of the bureaucratization and "domestication" of the Buddhist *saṅgha* (monastic order) in the course of its development in ancient India. He points to the fact that donations to the *saṅgha* are recirculated in the community, in a system of "generalized exchange," and emphasizes the idea that the increase of economic and political interest focused on the *saṅgha* is a natural and normal development rather than a deviation from Buddhism's purpose (1983, 463–66, 471, 475; see also Silber 1995, 201–2, 217–18). In more general terms, Eisenstadt (1968, 412–16) has described the positive benefits of institutionalization and "institutional entrepreneurship"—social integration, efficiency, and support for the survival of a society—arising as a result of the establishment, through institutions, of systems of exchange between entrepreneurs and other members of society.

When we look at the consequences of institutionalization in Chola period temples, the assessments of Strenski and Eisenstadt appear to be more applicable than Weber's. Interactions between the institution and the community that involved exchange, such as those emphasized by Strenski and Eisenstadt, seem to have resulted in the mutual benefit of temple and locality in both economic and political terms. The temple was at the center of an economic network that encouraged trade, investment, and agricultural expansion. The exchange system worked well on a political level because the temple provided opportunities for the expression of religious values and relationships with the deity, involving notions of status, that were widely shared. Temple authorities were not concerned with "popularizing" or accommodating local religious peculiarities because—from the very beginning of the Chola period—temples had been strongly localized and the pattern of temple ritual had shared much with popular practice. The processes of bureacratization in the course of the Chola period did not close off the temple to interaction with the outside community but seemed in fact to have had the opposite effect. This means that core religious values associated with the *bhakti* ideology of inclusivism and universalism did not deteriorate with increasing bureacratization but were effectively expressed, as the temple continued to involve a wide range of types of people in its activities.

At the same time, the processes of bureaucratization—differentiation, hierarchy, and definition of eligibility—restricted and limited the extent of this involvement. We have seen several examples of how, within the temple organization, high-status or new professional groups began to dominate in certain temple functions, such as gardening and hymn singing, displacing the former performers of these tasks, who came from a variety of groups. We even saw temple women taking over a function that had not, earlier, been so exclusively theirs—the duty of dancing at festivals. And those various and vaguely defined groups of "honored devotees" who had in the early Chola period been fed or supported by the temple or had had responsibility for temple affairs, became more and more explicitly identified, either as (male) individuals or as members of specific sectarian groups.[4]

But even at the end of the Chola period, arrangements within the temple cannot be characterized as highly stratified or rigidly organized around distinctions of sex, caste, or community.[5] The institutional developments in the Chola period temple did not wholly conform to Weber's model of bureaucratization: because involvement in the organization was frequently defined with reference to a particular person rather than to an office, personal negotiation and individual initiative kept open the possibility of functioning within or on the borders of the system, even as other forces tended toward restrictions within and exclusion from the structure of the temple. Temple women were among those who took advantage of this state of affairs.

I have argued that temple women were not at the center of the temple organization, either in terms of its ritual or its administrative arrangements. Yet temple women were able, by acting as donors, to establish relationships with the temple and to position themselves within its structure. Their situation was, from one point of view, marginal. There were certain key roles that men had—as priests or drummers or temple managers, for example—from which women seem to have been categorically excluded. But we misunderstand the medieval South Indian temple if we regard its institutional structure or its religious purpose as emanating entirely from these core functions. If we locate temple women on the margins of the system, we must recognize that the margins were very broad, densely populated, and extremely important in shaping the form and the significance of the temple.

Among the many people who also had positions on these broad borders were the men who, in increasing numbers, performed responsibility functions of an honorary character. Many of these men were not temple servants or functionaries but acted as witnesses or signatories in arrangements made by the temple as a way of acquiring status in and recognition from the temple. Other figures whom we might locate in the borderlands were the countless donors, including temple women and other women, whose gifts supported—and, in some cases, helped create—the forms of ritual, the objects of worship, and the physical fabric of the shrine, which together made up the reality of each particular temple in the Tamil country. Through their gifts, donors acquired religious merit and public recognition, but they also became real participants in temple life, engaged in a religious activity that was, in fact, not marginal at all but central to the very existence and the reason for existence of the temple.[6]

Rather than seeing these actors, including temple women, as figures on the edge or on the outside of the structure of the temple, it may be more useful to visualize them as traversing the broad borderlands between the institutional core—where certain temple servants and temple authorities had more or less clearly defined roles deemed critical to the functioning of the temple—and the surrounding society. Although temple women were not very numerous in comparison to the many other people crossing through this territory, they appear to have had a unique style in their journeying. First, they started out closer to the institutional center than many of these others, and through their gift giving they succeeded in securing positions closer still to the temple core—far more than other donors in the Chola period. Their gifts not only brought them recognition by the temple but also confirmed their status as temple women. In some cases this status was reinforced by the assignment of duties that they were to perform in the temple, which more often had the character of privileges than of service positions. Temple women, more than other donors and with increasing frequency, made donations to their home temples, thereby forging links with local temple authorities and thus solidifying their connection to a particular sacred place.

The individual and local nature of temple women's associations with the temple also distinguished them from other sojourners in the institutional borderlands of the temple—both from other donors and from men who performed responsibility functions. Whereas these others may have made gifts and forged connections in locations removed from their home base, temple women's associations were highly localized. Members of other groups of people—royal women, merchants, lords, and others—had much more opportunity for mobility and interaction with one another than did temple women. Not only were temple women few in number, but also they were isolated from one another. It does not appear that in the Chola period they constituted a class any more than they did a caste.

Individual temple women, nonetheless, seem to have been able in the course of the Chola period to carve out an identity that allowed them to continue and even enhance their involvement in temple life, whereas most other women were progressively being edged off the margins of the temple structure as their donations declined. Queens and palace women disappeared most rapidly and completely from the inscriptional record, whereas the decline in visibility of other non-Brahman women was somewhat less precipitous. Brahman women continued throughout the Chola period to be mentioned in inscriptions and to act as donors; their economic autonomy, however, was compromised, as their property transactions were increasingly negotiated through male relatives who acted as their agents (*mutukaṇs*).[7] Temple women present a contrast to all these types of women insofar as their public visibility, activity in all kinds of roles, and participation in the life of the temple increased in the course of the Chola period.

In Weber's model of the development of religious institutions, the exclusion of women from roles within the organization is regarded as the natural accompaniment of the "routinization and regimentation of community relationships" associated with bureaucratization and the shift from "charismatic" to "rational-legal" authority structures ([1922] 1964, 104–5). But other scholars question whether this is an inevitable development and explore the possibility that reasons other than structural ones explain this kind of change (Schussler Fiorenza 1983, 77–80, 82–83, 286–87; Gold 1985, 80–81). One of the contexts in the history of Christianity in which we see a major decline in women's engagement with religious institutions is medieval Europe, beginning in about the ninth century in France and several centuries later in England. In the early Middle Ages, when much of western Europe had yet to come under Christian influence, women's participation and patronage were actively solicited by churchmen. In this "frontier" situation, royal women, wealthy women, and noblewomen were able to establish themselves in positions of considerable power, notably as abbesses of convents, often with authority over monks, as well as nuns, and with influence at high levels in the ecclesiastical hierarchy (Stafford 1983, 123–25, 193; Gold 1985, 77–78; Wemple 1987, 132, 138, 149; Schulenburg 1988, 105–11; 1989, 217–21).

The rapid decline in the subsequent period of women's power and participation in the church has been blamed in part on increasing bureaucratization (Stuard 1987, 158–59; Schulenberg 1988, 119–20) but there are a number of other factors that seem to be as much or more responsible for the decline in women's religious activity: (1) new economic arrangements and strategies within the family that resulted in the curtailment of women's property rights (Stuard 1987, 163–69; Schulenberg 1989, 233–34); (2) efforts by the church to free itself from lay influence and to institute reforms, including the establishment of new clerical roles and relations with society that marked differences between monks and nuns and reduced support for female religious communities (Schulenberg 1988, 114–17; 1989, 224–29, 236–37); and (3) the reassertion of a dualistic (and misogynist) religious ideology of gender (Gold 1985, 81; Stuard 1987, 164–66).

This development in medieval western Europe provides an interesting parallel to the situation in medieval South India. There are important differences between the two: for example, South Indian Hinduism did not have formal roles, equivalent to those of nun or abbess, for women within its religious institutions; temple-based Hinduism was more securely established in early medieval Tamilnadu than was Christianity in France or England; and there was no central authority in Hinduism, like the pope, which could formulate policy or institute reform. Another important difference is that in India, some women—temple women—continued to play public roles in religious contexts. It is, nonetheless, worth exploring whether some of the forces that had a negative impact on European women's participation in religious life may also have been experienced by women in India, thus suggesting reasons for the declining visibility of nontemple women and the continuing presence of temple women in the temple milieu of medieval Tamilnadu.

Of the three factors influencing women's circumstances in the medieval Christian church—economic changes that affected women's property rights; increasing autonomy of religious institutions from lay control; and an ideology justifying the restriction of women's religious roles—the one that seems to have least relevance to the South Indian context is the second. Indeed, I have argued that the temple of medieval Tamilnadu was encircled by an ever-broadening zone in which lay and religious interests and identities overlapped. It may be, however, that by the end of the Chola period, there was increasing competition for position within this zone, which hindered women's participation; the increasing prominence of sectarian groups and the proliferation of individual men involved with responsibility functions suggest this possibility.

Economic factors seem to have been most significant in determining the different trajectories of men and of women (temple women and other women) in the extent of their involvement with the temple.[8] Although many women had access to wealth, this access was restricted in various ways, and for most women circumscribed within the structure of marriage. Women apparently did not have control over their *strīdhana* property, which was instead transferred by their fathers to their husbands. Women seem to have acquired rights to household and, in some cases, personal wealth through marriage rather than through inheritance. We have too little information about these arrangements to state definitely that they were increasingly limiting women's access to wealth, but it does appear that in the course of the Chola period there was greater and greater consolidation of local control over property and more clearly differentiated and specified property rights (see, e.g., Heitzman 1987a, 54–58). Thus economic power might well have become concentrated in the hands of male heads of households, and control over wealth increasingly defined in terms of the rights of individual men—and not women. Temple women, being unmarried, were free from the economic limitations that marriage imposed on other women, and their economic autonomy allowed them to continue to act as temple patrons, whereas other women's donative activity was curtailed.

The third factor under consideration is religious ideology: were ideas about gender revived or developed and utilized in medieval South India, as they were in medieval western Europe, as a way to restrict women's access to roles in religious institutions? We cannot find in the inscriptions any evidence for such a development. Nor does the Tamil religious literature contemporary with the inscriptions suggest that women were, because of their nature or circumstances, less qualified than men to participate in religious life.[9] There may be a tendency in the Chola period inscriptions toward identifying women increasingly as wives, but marriage did not by definition preclude religious activity for either men or women.[10] Nor—if we can point to the increasing presence of shrines for the consorts of Śiva and Viṣṇu and the elaboration of a theology of complementarity between male and female divinity as indications of an emerging religious ideology of marriage—were these ideas mobilized to *enhance* the possibilities of women's participation in religious life. The figure of the consort goddess, increasingly visible in the course of the Chola period, did not provide a paradigm that was pressed into service as legitimation for women's presence in the temple.[11] It could have done so, but it did not, and the only reason that we find this in the least surprising is because the identity of the temple woman as we know her from more recent times seems to be so strongly predicated on this model.

Without recourse to such ideas—drawing in some cases, instead, on the concept of a father-daughter relationship rather than a husband-wife bond—Chola period temple women built up a place for themselves within the broad borders of the temple structure. Their individual intiative and personal negotiations allowed them to make connections with the temple in a manner that was distinctive to them. Their activities in making deals and thereby obtaining rights—in some cases hereditary rights—to perform services and receive honors anticipate relationships that were to become much more common in later times. That temple women were quick to take advantage of the opportunities presented by the processes of temple institutionalization and interaction with the locality meant that they were well positioned with respect to subsequent developments. The status they garnered and the situation they occupied in the temple in the late Chola period allowed them in the following centuries to have a continuing role in the life of the temple, eventually establishing themselves in hereditary positions as specialists in dance. They were thus able to accomplish something that later participants in the system of deals and honors could not, that is, to move from a location in the border area of the institution to a position quite close to the inside of the ritual and institutional structure of the temple.

From the Chola Period Temple Woman to the Twentieth-Century *Devadāsī*

How does this study of the Chola period temple woman contribute to our understanding of temple women in general and the roles of women in Indian religion and society? What is the relationship between the temple women of the Chola period and those of other, more recent periods? To begin to answer these questions, I return to the ideas currently prevalent about temple women, outlined in the first chapter, to reassess their value in the light of the present study. These understandings of temple women, the products of recent historical experience and of scholarship on twentieth-century temple women, were divided into four themes: (1) the notion that there is a pan-Indian and transhistorical *devadāsī* "phenomenon"; (2) ideas about the degeneration of the *devadāsī* institution; (3) the concept of the *devadāsī* as passive victim or as a pawn or token in the political or ritual schemes of priests and kings; and (4) the understanding of the *devadāsī*'s persona as primarily bound up in her identity as a woman, whether with reference to her sexuality or to her representation of feminine principles of auspiciousness or power (*śakti*).

My findings clearly challenge the first of these themes—the assumption of the universality and consistency of the *devadāsī* phenomenon. Even within the confines of the period and the region I have studied, there are significant geographical variations and changes through time in the situation and activities of temple women. And it is obvious that the temple women of medieval Tamilnadu are in many significant respects unlike their counterparts of the early twentieth century. The three factors of hereditary eligibility, professional skill, and temple dedication that seem to define the *devadāsīs* of recent times are not characteristic of Chola period temple women even in the thirteenth century. In the 600 years that followed the Chola period, the circumstances, identities, and activities of South Indian temple women continued to change.

The findings of the present study also suggest that we must be cautious in our assessment of the relations between temple women and other types of women, in assuming identity, similarity, or functional or structural parallels. For example, although temple women in certain times and places (sixteenth-century Vijayanagara or twentieth-century Puri) may have had much in common with women of the royal court, temple women in the Chola period were quite distinct from palace women. Or if certain Chola period temple women seem to have been involved in a kinship pattern that was in some sense matrilineal, it is of a rather different sort than the pattern that has been described for *basavis* or for South Indian matrilineal communities. Or if temple women in recent times ought to be understood primarily as ritualists, those in the Chola period do not seem to be so defined. In this study I have described the temple women of a particular period and a particular region: they are different from other kinds of women in their own time and place, and they are different from the temple women of other times and places. Our understanding of temple women is best served by attending to the particularities of each of the various groups of temple women—and other women—whom we may be able to study, rather than by dissolving the distinctions among them. Our understanding of the social and religious roles of Indian women in general can only increase if we discard the notion that what women do, where they are situated, and what they "mean" are everywhere and always the same.

Considering the second theme, the issue of the "degeneration" of the *devadāsī* institution, my findings do not support the notion that temple women in medieval South India suffered a decline in status or a degradation of their functions inside or outside the temple. On the contrary, temple women were increasingly active and acquired greater and greater public recognition in the course of the Chola period. Their identities and status seem more secure and well defined at the end of the period than in the earlier Chola period. We cannot, of course, ignore the fact that there was a growing number of temple women who had the status of slaves. Nor can we deny that temple women were restricted in their access to various activities of the temple, perhaps increasingly so, and that their ritual functions appear to have been, in the Chola period, inessential and marginal to temple life. But in their efforts to establish a presence in the temple, they were not attempting to compete with their male counterparts in acquiring positions central to the functioning of the temple; the situation they created for themselves was uniquely theirs and was one that allowed them to remain implicated in South Indian temple life for centuries to come.

The third theme relates to the extent to which temple women had agency in the processes that defined their identities and shaped their lives. From what we have discovered of Chola period temple women, it is clear that it was not through the manipulation of royal or priestly figures, nor as the result of impersonal bureaucratic forces or ideological or ritual necessity, that they acquired their status as temple women and whatever roles may have accompanied this status. Instead, their own initiatives and efforts were of primary importance, notably their activities as donors. Chola kings played virtually no role in arranging for the establishment or support of temple women. In the whole corpus of Chola period inscriptions that refer to temple women, the famous installation of 400 temple women by Rajaraja I at the Tanjavur temple emerges as a singular and idiosyncratic event. Apart from this one grand royal gesture, the temple women of Tamilnadu prospered in precisely those areas where Chola influence was minimal. Much more common than connections with the royal court were temple women's links with temple authorities. But temple authorities did not recruit women to serve in the temple. Instead, the association of temple women with the temple was the product of their own initiative. Developments within temples as institutions—the processes of increasing bureaucratization and interaction with the surrounding community—provided a context in which links could be forged, but it was temple women who seized the opportunity to make these links. Temple women were active, not passive, in shaping their situation, but the form their actions took was very different from the approach of men who sought status or position within the structure of the temple.

This fact is central to our reconsideration of the last of the four themes: the question of whether, in the Chola period, temple women's identities as women were fundamental to the significance of their presence and function in the temple. My answer to this question is yes, but for reasons entirely different from those that have been forwarded in the case of twentieth-century temple women. The specifically feminine identity of the *devadāsī* of recent times has been argued for with reference to temple women's sexual activity or to their ritual significance, deriving from their "marriage" to the temple deity or their representation of female divinity or divine energy. Chola period temple women were clearly sexually active, given the references to their children in the inscriptions, but there is no hint that their sexual activity was significant to their identities or to their roles in the temple. With respect to the idea that temple women were identified as the wives of God or that they symbolized female divinity, we have seen that neither the terms applied to Chola period temple women nor their names nor their relationships with the temple and the deity it enshrined indicate that such feminine personas contributed to the definition of their status as temple women. But if these feminine qualities or identities were irrelevant to Chola period temple women, their positions and roles were nonetheless uniquely feminine in that the types of relations they established with the temple and the manner in which these relations were established were different from those of men. By using patronage as a means of forging associations with the temple and acquiring recognition, status, rights, and privileges from the temple, temple women were in fact pioneering an approach to relationship with the temple that became much more widespread—and no longer exclusively "feminine"—in the post-Chola period.

As a result of this reconsideration of the assumptions, descriptions, and analyses embodied in the four themes characteristic of recent understandings of temple women, I think it is clear that the ideas represented by the first two must be rejected: temple women in all times and places in India's history have not had the same identities, activities, or significance, nor has "the *devadāsī* institution" degenerated over time. Concerning the other two themes—ideas about the passivity or victimization of temple women and the symbolic significance of their sexuality or association with divine feminine power—my study leads me to the conclusion that these ideas are not relevant to or meaningful for Chola period temple women. Because my rejection of these ideas puts me at odds with those reformers, officials, and scholars who have been concerned with temple women in the modern period, I will attempt to see whether our positions might be reconciled by examining the historical processes through which the Chola period temple woman may have been transformed into the *devadāsī* of the twentieth century.

Certainly the political and social changes that took place in Tamilnadu after 1300 produced a dramatically different context within which such a transformation could have occurred.[12] In the post-Chola period, political structures take an entirely new shape. At the local level, power and economic resources became concentrated in the hands of chiefs, *nāyakas*, or "little kings"—some of whom came from outside the Tamil country. These figures were arrayed under the authority and control, at least nominally, of a greater sovereign; most of these local rulers professed loyalty to the Vijayanagara throne. This type of political arrangement constituted a major departure from the system that had prevailed in the Tamil country during the Chola period. Also, from the fourteenth century onward, there were significant movements of people—migrations of groups within Tamilnadu and in-migration of new populations from outside the region—and the establishment of new patterns and centers of settlement. Accompanying the changes in the political and social situation were shifts in the sphere of religion. New deities became prominent, new systems of patronage took shape—in which royal donations came to be of increasing importance—and the character and the role of the temple was altered.[13]

I propose several possibilities for the ways in which these historical circumstances may have allowed or encouraged the production of an identity for South Indian temple women in line with the images and interpretations of the *devadāsī* found in recent scholarship. In the discussion that follows, I explore the developments of the post-Chola period with respect to two issues: (1) the emergence of the definition of the temple woman in terms of heredity and professional specialization; (2) the question of the ritual persona of the temple woman, her symbolization of a specifically feminine divinity or spiritual force, and her status as a passive instrument.

At the very end of the Chola period, the rights and duties of temple women were increasingly hereditary, there were more well-defined and formal arrangements for their support by the temple, and they seem to have dominated in the performance of festival dances. These developments constitute a change in comparison with the situation of temple women in the early Chola period, but we must be careful not to overstate their importance. Even by the end of the Chola period, very few temple women had these sorts of roles or relationships with the temple. Furthermore, there is little correlation among these elements: for example, temple women who were supported by the temple through permanent and well-defined arrangements were not necessarily assigned specific ritual functions; those who had roles as festival dancers did not occupy hereditary positions.

It is only in the post-Chola period that we find a body of inscriptions that indicates the coming together of some of these elements to produce a well-organized and well-supported system of female temple service in a number of temples in the southern, northern, and western regions of the Tamil country.[14] These inscriptions of the fourteenth to sixteenth centuries, dated in the reigns of Pandya and Vijayanagara rulers, specify precisely the order in which individual temple women were to serve in the temple, according to their rank or "turn" (*muṟai*, *aṭaivu*, *kuṭi*). Many of these inscriptions also record definite and permanent arrangements for the support of temple women, although they do not refer to the hereditary character of either service rights or support arrangements.[15]

Inscriptions of the post-Chola period indicate that temple service and relationships in which temple women received support from the temple were becoming central to their roles and identities. Of the Tamil inscriptions dating from 1300 to 1700 that refer to temple women, nearly three-quarters mention these types of association with the temple—and less than a quarter identify temple women as donors to the temple.[16] Many of these inscriptions, however, are extremely vague about the nature of the services to be performed by temple women, even as they spell out in great detail arrangements for support and the rank or order of precedence of individual women within the hierarchy of temple servants. Indeed, support, rank, and temple honors seem to have been intimately associated with one another—one temple woman in the fifteenth century, for example, was granted land and a house, the first "turn" (*mutal aṭaippu*), and the right to receive one of the garlands that had been offered to the deity (IPS 710)—whereas temple service as such was evidently a peripheral issue. The inscriptions do not provide evidence that temple women of the post-Chola period were increasingly establishing themselves in professional roles in the temple; on the contrary, the proportion of the inscriptions that indicate that temple women served as dancers and singers is actually *smaller* than that found in the Chola period.[17]

There are many fewer inscriptions in the fourteenth to seventeenth centuries than in the Chola period, and there are fewer inscriptions still after the end of the seventeenth century. After this point, we can no longer rely on these sources to provide information about temple women's roles and identities. It is significant that even at the end of the seventeenth century, when the epigraphical stream runs dry, the elements of hereditary right to temple service and professional specialization—which appear to be such central characteristics for temple women in the early twentieth century—have not yet become established. I believe that we can understand this puzzling fact by considering that there were two phases of change in political conditions in the Tamil country after the close of the Chola period; I propose that these two phases are tied to shifts in the nature of temple women's identities.

In the period of 1300 to 1700, a series of new kings, chiefs, and governors came to power in Tamilnadu. Many of these rulers had "foreign" or nonroyal origins and became involved with temple affairs as a means of establishing legitimacy in their new territories. The influx of wealth to the temple, because of their gifts, and the institution of new and more elaborate worship rituals, processions, and festivals had, on the one hand, the effect of preempting local patronage, including that of temple women and, on the other hand, the effect of encouraging an increasing concern with position and precedence in temple performances on the part of temple women, as well as others who were associated with the temple.

In the seventeenth century, political matters took another turn, as numerous new "warrior kings" gained preeminence in various parts of the Tamil country and as the Nayaka overlords became less concerned with their connections to the Vijayanagara throne in distant Karnataka and more preoccupied with their authority in the region (Dirks 1987, 43–54). Thus what Dirks calls the "old regime" was brought into being. Of course from our perspective this all looks rather new: the impact of these political rearrangements on the temple was a dramatic intensification of what had gone on in the preceding period, bringing into being "a new state-level culture of kingship and pious patronage," in which "the political sphere has successfully absorbed the sacred arena of temple and temple-deities" (Bayly 1989, 68; Narayana Rao, Shulman, and Subrahmanyam 1992, 58). Royal patronage promoted the accelerated growth of major temples and pilgrimage centers, and royal largesse became the source of temple service rights and temple honors. Royal display permeated the temple, and sacred ceremonies took place in the palace. Court musicians composed songs and choreographed dances for women to perform in the temple, and temple women sang and danced for the king.[18] It is in this context, in the course of the seventeenth and eighteenth centuries, that the temple woman as we know her in more recent times—with her skill in dance and with her hereditary right to support and temple privileges—came into being.

This chronological framework may also help us to understand the historical development of the second aspect of the contemporary *devadāsī*'s identity: her ritual persona, her representation of auspiciousness and female divine power, and her "instrumentality"—her being as a symbol rather than an agent. As we have seen, these features of temple women's status and roles are not in evidence in the Chola period. And in the centuries after 1300, there is little to suggest that these features were increasingly significant for temple women. We do not find, for instance, in the inscriptions of the post-Chola period, the emergence of the temple woman as ritualist; although many women were involved in temple service, there is no insistence on their performance of specific ritual tasks. Temple women are not described as participating—as did the *devadāsīs* of more recent times—in daily and festival rituals that enact the marriage and marital relations of god and goddess, although such rituals were certainly celebrated during this period.[19] Nor is there any hint in the inscriptions that temple women were dedicated through ceremonies in which they were symbolically "married" to the temple deity.

There is no evidence that the symbolic significance of temple women's roles was being amplified—but there is evidence that temple women's effective agency was being diminished. I have argued that such agency was exercised by temple women in the Chola period through their activity as donors, whereas men associated with the temple had a variety of other means through which they actively sought to gain influence and recognition. In the post-Chola period, temple women stopped making gifts to the temple, but they did not move into other roles—as temple functionaries, for example—in which they might have found the opportunity to exercise influence or to actively shape their circumstances. Instead, these temple women played passive roles, as the recipients of assignments of rank and property; we do not see them *using* their rank and property, as their predecessors had done. One way in which temple women's agency may have begun to be compromised is through their associations with other groups or communities. We see, at the end of the Chola period, the first indications of alliances between temple women and groups like the *kaikkoḷar*. Such alliances were increasingly a fact of life for temple women, producing community identities for them and, in some cases, resulting in the transfer of control over their lives to others, including men of their communities.

In the period of 1300 to 1700, many ideas and practices might have been utilized to form an identity for temple women centered around the representation of female divinity or to create a ritual role that capitalized on this symbolism. By this period, the great male gods Śiva and Viṣṇu were firmly paired with consort goddesses in temple iconography, ritual practice, and theology, and there was a continuing efflorescence of goddess imagery throughout the period. Many new festivals and worship services were established, providing contexts in which temple women's ritual roles might have been developed. But it is in the context of royal, not religious, ceremonial that we find women utilized for their symbolic value. According to Pamela Price's analysis of Vijayanagara court ritual, palace women represented the qualities—such as auspiciousness, material well-being, and fertility—"necessary to the successful maintenance of the kingdom"; royal ceremonies were "formal expressions of the personal political status of males," which demonstrated male control of female energy (1990, 595–97).[20] These ideas of the instrumental and symbolic function of women seem not, however, to have been transferred from the court to the temple—not, at any rate, until the advent of the "old regime."

In the seventeenth and eighteenth centuries, "temple and court . . . have merged," "[the god] holds court exactly like a Nāyaka king," and "the worlds of court and temple—in effect, now a single world—are populated by innumerable, crazed, lovesick women, dreaming only of the alluring divine king"; "courtesans and *devadāsīs* merge into a single role" (Narayana Rao, Shulman, and Subrahmanyam 1992, 185–89). If the Nayaka court had truly become so "feminized" and the Nayaka king had so successfully made over the temple deity in his own image, it is easy to understand how temple women (and palace women) could have acquired a secure place in the ritual life of the temple and occupied the symbolic role of goddess consort. This imaging of the activity of the king and the god in terms of generosity, pleasure, and consumption (*bhoga*)—including the enjoyment of women—also suggests the dominance of male subjectivity in the formulation of notions of women's significance in the temple and the palace.

It is interesting to consider the possibility that the idea of a conjugal relation between the temple woman and the deity springs not from the female devotional attitude but from the male sexual imagination. In fact, it remains mysterious how the concept of temple women as "wives of God"—and the ceremony that underwrites the concept—came to be established. Temple women themselves may well have had a hand in promoting the idea and the practice as a way to entrench their right to participate in temple ritual and to formalize their eligibility for support and privileges from the temple. But the honor of serving as the representative of the god's consort may have had a cost.

If we see evidence that women in the post-Chola period had increasingly instrumental significance, does this imply that women suffered a loss in power? Is the rise in the use of feminine symbolism correlated with a decline in women's agency and control over their situations? Given the concurrence of the rise in goddess imagery and the decline in the public representation of women that took place in the later Chola period, as well as an increasing feminine ritual presence in the post-Chola era coinciding with a decreasing agency in political, economic, and religious spheres, I am inclined to answer yes. Although the relationships between the power and freedom of human women, on the one hand, and "the feminine" in ritual and symbol, on the other, are complex and various, it seems to me quite certain that the identification in the last several centuries of temple women as the "wives of God" or as representatives of divine feminine forces has not empowered them in any effective, pragmatic sense.[21]

As the period of the "old regime" gives way to the colonial period, profound political, social, and religious changes were set in motion—which had implications for, among other things, the utilization of ritual and symbol and the status of women. In terms of the impact of colonial rule on the temple and on temple women, we find decreasing economic resources, increasing conservatism, and competition for position and privilege in the temple. Temples, subject to criticism by and interference from British colonial authorities, were put on the defensive. It is in this context, in the late colonial period, that the attention of reformers was directed toward temple women, and legislation was enacted that finally put an end to the existence of the *devadāsī*, as we have seen in chapter 1. For temple women and their supporters, for those who resisted changes to temple life or who sought to defend Hindu tradition, these developments had the effect of reinforcing the instrumental vision of the *devadāsī* as a figure of symbolic and ritual importance. For the reformers, this significance was denied, and temple women were, as Inden puts it, "patients, those who had to be variously pacified or punished, saved, reformed, or developed" (1990, 23). By the end, centuries after the close of the Chola period, it would seem that there was no acknowledgement of or opportunity for temple women's agency.

In this survey of the centuries from the end of the Chola period to the end of the colonial period, which concludes the present study, I have tried to chart the changes that occurred in the definition, functions, and character of temple women in South India and to suggest ways in which religious, social, and political developments may have helped to mold these changes. This survey underscores the idea that the temple woman, the *devadāsī*, is not a figure who exists outside of time. Temple women, in various parts of India and in various periods of Indian history, have found themselves in different situations and capable of different kinds of activities, just as the contexts in which they have lived and acted have been various. There are many temple women, including women who lived in very recent times, about whose lives we may be able to discover very little. But we are fortunate in having the opportunity to learn something of the identities and activities of Chola period temple women through the medieval Tamil inscriptions.

In this study, I have attempted to show how temple women in Tamilnadu have had a dynamic history within the Chola period itself and, as we have just seen, from the end of the thirteenth century to the present. This history is different from the one I expected to find. For one thing, the past is so very different from the present. The classic, beautiful Chola period temples are there, but it is difficult to find one's way through the rest of the landscape, around the unfamiliar contours of Chola period religious, social, and political life. A great deal more exploration remains to be done in this foreign territory before we will fully appreciate the significance of the history of temple women in this period. That this history needs to be interpreted in terms different from those that have been useful in understanding temple women in recent times is clear from the fact that the Chola period temple women are so different from their modern counterparts. They are not wives of the temple deity and they are not temple dancers.

The central aspect of temple women's identities in the Chola period was not linked to their activities in the temple nor to their ritual significance but was, instead, a matter of their relationship to the temple. But if, in the ritual context, the functions or activities of Chola period temple women were incidental to their identities, what these women *did* in the temple, their actions as donors, was vitally important to who they were. In the course of the Chola period, temple women, through their own initiative and effort, increasingly made a place for themselves as individuals within—or on the margins of—the temple community. It was through their own agency that they established and secured relationships with the temple, not as the consequence of heredity or as the result of ritual necessity or royal sponsorship. And through their actions, they shaped—and changed—the definition of what it was to be a temple woman.

Appendix I

Geographical and chronological distribution of Indian inscriptions relating to temple women

District	Before A.D. 850	A.D. 850–1300	After A.D. 1300	Date unknown	Total
Tamilnadu					
Tanjavur	—	75	4	2	81
Chingleput	—	57	13	3	73
South Arcot	—	33	8	5	46
Tiruchirappalli	—	32	18	3	53
North Arcot	—	27	15	1	43
Tirunelveli	—	26	21	2	49
Madurai	—	9	1	—	10
Kanyakumari	—	9	6	—	15
Chittoor	—	8	24	1	33
Malabar + Travancore	—	6	3	—	9
Ramnad	—	6	3	—	9
Coimbatore	—	5	4	—	9
Salem	—	1	1	—	2
?	—	—	1	—	1
Sri Lanka	1	5	—	—	6
Andhra Pradesh					
Godavari	1	7	1	3	12
Guntur	—	37	2	2	41
Vizagapatnam	—	6	31	2	39
Krishna	—	8	4	—	12

(continued)

District	Before A.D. 850	A.D. 850–1300	After A.D. 1300	Date unknown	Total
Ganjam	—	5	3	1	9
Nellore	—	8	3	3	14
West Godavari	—	5	—	1	6
Kurnool	—	—	1	—	1
?	—	3	—	1	4
Karnataka					
Kolar	—	5	3	—	8
Mysore	—	2	4	—	6
Bangalore	1	1	2	—	4
Bellary	—	7	—	—	7
South Kanara	—	1	1	1	3
Dharwar	—	16	1	—	17
Hassan	—	8	1	—	9
Hyderbad	—	7	1	—	8
Shimoga	—	6	1	—	7
Bijapur	1	6	—	—	7
Chitaldroog	—	3	—	—	3
Tumkur	—	2	1	—	3
Belgaum	—	1	—	—	1
Kadur	—	—	2	—	2
Northern India					
Rajasthan and Gujurat	—	4	—	—	4
Maharashtra	—	1	—	—	1
Orissa	—	4	1	—	5
Central India	—	1	—	—	1
Uttar Pradesh	1	1	—	—	2
Bengal and Bihar	—	3	—	—	3
Unknown provenance	—	—	7	1	8
Total:	5	457	192	32	686

Definitions of district boundaries are for the most part based on the usages of published editions of inscriptions, often reflecting pre-Independence political divisions (see also Sitaraman, Karashima, and Subbarayalu 1976; R. Singh 1971). Some of the "districts," especially those of the northern part of the subcontinent from which I have collected relatively few inscriptions, are very large geographic zones rather than districts in any official sense.

In grouping the South Indian districts into regions, I have followed the lead of the Indian government and classified them on the basis of dominant language. Because of differences between the language use of early medieval inscriptions and that of modern Indian society and because of the biases in my criteria for selecting inscriptions for inclusion in my database (e.g., favoring those written in Tamil), my "linguistic states" are rather different from present-day political units. I hope these differences—such as the incorporation of Kerala into Tamilnadu or the inclusion of Ganjam district in Andhra Pradesh and of Hyderabad in Karnataka—will cause neither offense nor confusion.

Appendix II

Geographical distribution of inscriptions in database, dataset, and corpus of Chola period inscriptions referring to temple women

District	Database	Dataset	Chola period temple women
Tamilnadu			
Tanjavur	259	254	75 (25%)
Chingleput	124	97	57 (19%)
South Arcot	123	102	33 (11%)
Tiruchirappalli	156	124	32 (11%)
North Arcot	99	77	27 (9%)
Tirunelveli	91	63	26 (9%)
Madurai	21	17	9 (3%)
Kanyakumari	25	16	9 (3%)
Chittoor	42	14	8 (3%)
Malabar + Travancore	27	22	6 (2%)
Ramnad	15	8	6 (2%)
Coimbatore	11	7	5 (2%)
Salem	4	2	1
Sri Lanka	8	2	2
Andhra Pradesh			
Godavari	25	1	1
Cuddupah	6	2	
Guntur	68		
Vizagapatnam	53		
Krishna	19		
Ganjam	18		

(*continued*)

District	Database	Dataset	Chola period temple women
Nellore	15		
West Godavari	12		
Kurnool	6		
Karnataka			
Kolar	14	8	5 (2%)
Mysore	10	1	1
Bangalore	6	1	1
Bellary	14	1	
South Kanara	4	1	
Dharwar	27		
Hassan	21		
Hyderabad	21		
Shimoga	20		
Bijapur	14		
Chitaldroog	8		
Tumkur	7		
Belgaum	2		
Coorg	2		
Northern India			
Rajasthan and Gujurat	10		
Maharashtra	7		
Orissa	5		
Central India	4		
Northeast (Assam)	4		
Uttar Pradesh	4		
Bengal and Bihar	3		
Northwest (Himachal Pradesh)	1		
Unknown provenance	22		
Total	1457	820	304 (100%)

See the notes to appendix I for an explanation of district and regional boundaries.

The database is made up of all the inscriptions I collected that I deemed potentially useful in understanding temple women.

The dataset is the subset of inscriptions in the database that fall inside the geographical and chronological parameters of this study: the inscriptions of the dataset are written in Tamil and date from the period A.D. 850–1300.

The corpus of Chola period inscriptions that refer to temple women (Chola period temple women) are those inscriptions in the dataset that refer directly to temple women, according to the definition in chapter 2. I have indicated the percentage of inscriptions that refer to temple women in each district when this percentage is 2 or more. So, for example, it can be seen that Tanjavur district contributed 25 percent of the total number of Chola period inscriptions that refer to temple women.

Appendix III

List of Chola period inscriptions referring to temple women

Reference	Location (district)	Date (A.D.)
SII 2.66	Tanjavur	1014
SII 3.15	Chittoor	1014
SII 3.38	Chingleput	1229?
SII 3.92	North Arcot	885
SII 3.94	Tanjavur	9th century?
SII 3.102	Tanjavur	931
SII 3.128	Chingleput	986
* SII 3.143 (chap. 4)	Chingleput	985
SII 3.158	Chingleput	973
SII 3.184	North Arcot	963
SII 3.190	North Arcot	966
SII 3.195	Chingleput	969
SII 3.209	Tanjavur	1098
SII 3.210	Tanjavur	1164
* SII 4.134 (chap. 5)	Chingleput	1118
* SII 4.223 (chap. 4)	South Arcot	1036
* SII 4.558 (chap. 4)	Chingleput	1235
SII 4.867	Chingleput	1045
SII 4.1246	Godavari	1113
SII 4.1388	Sri Lanka (country)	1070
SII 5.418	Tirunelveli	1257?
SII 5.430	Tirunelveli	1290?
* SII 5.520 (chap. 4)	Tanjavur	1050
* SII 5.701 (chap. 2)	Tanjavur	1124
* SII 5.705 (chap. 4)	Tanjavur	1142

(continued)

Reference	Location (district)	Date (A.D.)
SII 5.707	Tanjavur	1218
SII 5.716	Tanjavur	952
*SII 5.1360 (chap. 3)	Chingleput	1172
SII 5.1364	North Arcot	1014
SII 5.1366	North Arcot	996
SII 6.19	Tanjavur	1113
SII 6.59	Tanjavur	1267
SII 7.56	North Arcot	945
SII 7.97	North Arcot	1126
SII 7.147	South Arcot	1248?
SII 7.485	Tanjavur	1140
*SII 7.526 (chap. 1)	Tanjavur	872
SII 7.529	Tanjavur	9th century?
SII 7.785	South Arcot	1089
SII 8.66	North Arcot	1031
SII 8.83	North Arcot	1236
SII 8.91	North Arcot	1237
SII 8.116	North Arcot	1180
SII 8.120 = TAM 206	North Arcot	1264
SII 8.147	North Arcot	1210
SII 8.162	North Arcot	1143
*SII 8.228 (chap. 5)	Tanjavur	1158
SII 8.280	South Arcot	1185
*SII 8.333 (chap. 4)	South Arcot	1253?
SII 8.529	Chittoor	941
SII 8.678	Tiruchirappalli	1005
SII 12.85	Chingleput	888?
SII 12.150	South Arcot	1249
*SII 12.151 (chap. 3)	South Arcot	1250
SII 12.172	South Arcot	1254
SII 12.178	South Arcot	1256
SII 12.180	South Arcot	1256
SII 12.196	South Arcot	1258
SII 12.198	Chingleput	1259
SII 12.204	Chingleput	1260
SII 12.214	Chingleput	1262
SII 12.221	South Arcot	1265
SII 12.253	Tanjavur	13th century
*SII 13.88 (chap. 3)	Tiruchirappalli	875?
*SII 13.103 (chap. 5)	Tanjavur	953?
SII 13.153	Tiruchirappalli	955?
SII 13.154	Tiruchirappalli	955?
*SII 13.170 (chap. 4)	Tanjavur	992
SII 13.218	Tanjavur	10th century?
SII 14.18	Tirunelveli	10th century?
SII 14.40	Tirunelveli	9th century?
SII 14.74	Tirunelveli	10th century?
SII 14.83	Ramnad	10th century
*SII 14.132 (chap. 4)	Tirunelveli	1025
SII 14.178	Tirunelveli	11th century
SII 17.204	South Arcot	1099
SII 17.222	South Arcot	1001

(continued)

Reference	Location (district)	Date (A.D.)
SII 17.540	Tanjavur	1177
SII 17.541	Tanjavur	1219
SII 17.544	Tanjavur	1240
SII 17.588	Tanjavur	1168
SII 17.593	Tanjavur	12th century
SII 17.600	Tanjavur	1266
SII 17.606	Tanjavur	1119
SII 17.619	Tanjavur	939
SII 17.628	Tanjavur	1118
SII 19.92	Tanjavur	974?
SII 19.92A	Tanjavur	10th century?
SII 19.148	Tanjavur	10th century?
SII 19.228	Tanjavur	979?
*SII 19.283 (chap. 2)	South Arcot	10th century?
*SII 19.357 (chap. 4)	Tiruchirappalli	992
*SII 22.87 (chap. 5)	South Arcot	1094?
SII 22.141	South Arcot	1017
SII 22.147	South Arcot	1191?
*SII 22.153 (chap. 2)	South Arcot	1145
SII 23.47	Tanjavur	12th century
SII 23.100	Tirunelveli	1220
*SII 23.102 (chap. 3)	Tirunelveli	1220
SII 23.121	Tirunelveli	13th century?
SII 23.205	Tanjavur	943
SII 23.223	Tanjavur	10th century
SII 23.299	Tanjavur	1123
*SII 23.423 (chap. 5)	Madurai	13th century?
SII 23.428	Madurai	1270
SII 23.473	Tanjavur	1240
SII 26.323	Chingleput	1259
SII 26.391	South Arcot	957
SII 26.437	South Arcot	1213
IPS 97	Tiruchirappalli	1260
IPS 128	Tiruchirappalli	1132
*IPS 139 (chap. 4)	Tiruchirappalli	1168
IPS 150	Tiruchirappalli	1196
*IPS 152 (chap. 3)	Tiruchirappalli	1198
*IPS 162 (chap. 4)	Tiruchirappalli	1207
IPS 176	Tiruchirappalli	1218
IPS 223	Tiruchirappalli	1200?
IPS 319	Tiruchirappalli	1238
IPS 366	Tiruchirappalli	1265
IPS 367	Tiruchirappalli	1266
IPS 486	Tiruchirappalli	13th century?
SITI 28	South Arcot	12th century?
*SITI 118 (chap. 1)	North Arcot	1119
SITI 393	Chingleput	11th century?
SITI 444	Chingleput	1196
SITI 520	Chingleput	1235
SITI 537	Chingleput	1231
SITI 1009	Tanjavur	1266

(*continued*)

Reference	Location (district)	Date (A.D.)
NK 69	Tanjavur	1004
*NK 134 (chap. 1)	Tanjavur	1213
NK 139	Tanjavur	1213
NK 145	Tanjavur	1191
NK 157	Tanjavur	1201
TK 195	Tanjavur	1250?
KK 14	Kanyakumari	1127
KK 115 = TAS 1.14g	Kanyakumari	1042
KK 194 = TAS 8,34	Kanyakumari	1256
KK 255 = TAS 6.16	Kanyakumari	1253
*KK 256 = TAS 6.15 (chap. 3)	Kanyakumari	1252
TAS 1.1	Kanyakumari	866
TAS 1,289f	Travancore	1218
TAS 2.3	Travancore	12th century?
*TAS 5.24 (chap. 4)	Travancore	1168
TAS 6.14	Kanyakumari	1243
TAS 7.16	Kanyakumari	1264
TAS 8,32	Kanyakumari	1238
TAS 8,41–42	Malabar	961
TAS 8,43	Malabar	934
TAS 8,43–44	Malabar	10th century?
ESITA 19	Tirunelveli	1200/1248
ESITA 25	Tirunelveli	1243/1221
ESITA 28	Tirunelveli	1243/1221
ESITA 29	Tirunelveli	1243/1221
ESITA 42	Tirunelveli	13th century
ESITA 46	Tirunelveli	1243/1221
ALB 8, 177 (#10)	Chingleput	1216?
TAM 279	North Arcot	1281
TDI 1.4	Chittoor	10th century?
TDI 1.12	Chittoor	936
TDI 1.97	Chittoor	1235?
TDI 1.129	Chittoor	10th century?
EC 9.Hs143	Bangalore	1151?
EC 10.Bp38	Kolar	1280?
EC 10.Kl106	Kolar	1073?
EC 10.Kl108	Kolar	1072
EC 10.Kl121	Kolar	1225?
EC 10.Sd91	Kolar	1103
EC 14.Tn189	Mysore	1203
EZ 4.24	Sri Lanka (country)	1100?
EI 21.38	Chingleput	1069
ARE 163 of 1894	Tanjavur	1123
ARE 188 of 1908	Tanjavur	1249
ARE 117 of 1910	Tanjavur	909?
ARE 217 of 1910	Chingleput	13th century?
ARE 235 of 1910	Chingleput	1197?

(continued)

Reference	Location (district)	Date (A.D.)
ARE 277 of 1910	Chingleput	12th century?
ARE 284 of 1910	Chingleput	1265
ARE 296 of 1911	Tanjavur	1208
ARE 334 of 1911	Chingleput	1154?
ARE 336 of 1911	Chingleput	1161?
ARE 338 of 1911	Chingleput	1083
ARE 339 of 1911	Chingleput	1083
ARE 345 of 1911	Chingleput	1083
ARE 347 of 1911	Chingleput	1082
ARE 348 of 1911	Chingleput	1083
ARE 128 of 1912	Chingleput	11th century?
ARE 139 of 1912	Chingleput	1041
ARE 147 of 1912	Chingleput	1049
ARE 153 of 1912	Chingleput	1038
ARE 503 of 1912	Tiruchirappalli	1194
ARE 504 of 1912	Tiruchirappalli	13th century?
ARE 506 of 1912	Tiruchirappalli	1202
ARE 522 of 1912	Tiruchirappalli	1183
ARE 80 of 1913	Tanjavur	1176
ARE 439 of 1913	Salem	13th century
ARE 50 of 1914	Tanjavur	1157
ARE 332 of 1914	Tiruchirappalli	1251/1229
ARE 377 of 1914	Tiruchirappalli	1225
ARE 96 of 1915	Coimbatore	12th century?
ARE 111 of 1915	Coimbatore	12th century?
ARE 131 of 1915	Coimbatore	12th century?
ARE 179 of 1916	Chingleput	13th century?
ARE 468 of 1916	Tirunelveli	1251/1229
ARE 557 of 1916	Tirunelveli	1256/1300
ARE 223 of 1917	Tanjavur	1235
ARE 276 of 1917	Tanjavur	1011
ARE 16 of 1918	Tanjavur	1004
ARE 29 of 1918	Tanjavur	1061/1021
ARE 14 of 1919	South Arcot	1008
ARE 242 of 1919	North Arcot	1121
ARE 159 of 1920	Coimbatore	13th century?
ARE 168 of 1920	Coimbatore	1070
ARE 514 of 1920	Tanjavur	12th century
ARE 553 of 1920	South Arcot	10th century?
ARE 56 of 1921	Chingleput	1073
ARE 60 of 1921	Chingleput	1024?
ARE 66 of 1921	Chingleput	1029?
ARE 73 of 1921	Chingleput	1028?
ARE 211 of 1921	North Arcot	11th century
ARE 230 of 1921 •	North Arcot	1119
ARE 257 of 1921	North Arcot	997
ARE 258 of 1921	North Arcot	997
ARE 478 of 1921	South Arcot	1153?
ARE 560 of 1921	Tanjavur	1274
ARE 47 of 1922	South Arcot	1083
ARE 141 of 1922	Chittoor	1088
ARE 397 of 1922	Chingleput	989/999

(continued)

Reference	Location (district)	Date (A.D.)
ARE 180 of 1923	Chingleput	1219?
ARE 183 of 1923	Chingleput	1275?
ARE 210 of 1923	Chingleput	1265
ARE 211 of 1923	Chingleput	1258
ARE 33 of 1924	Ramnad	1195/1243
ARE 385 of 1924	Tiruchirappalli	1012
ARE 74 of 1925	Tanjavur	1184
ARE 76 of 1925	Tanjavur	12th century
ARE 111 of 1925	Tanjavur	943?
ARE 137 of 1925	Tanjavur	1103
ARE 152 of 1925	Tanjavur	1116
ARE 171 of 1925	Tanjavur	1184
ARE 409 of 1925	Tanjavur	1219
ARE 411 of 1925	Tanjavur	1189
ARE 90 of 1926	Tanjavur	1208
ARE 91 of 1926	Tanjavur	1198
ARE 94 of 1926	Tanjavur	1208
ARE 95 of 1926	Tanjavur	13th century
ARE 35 of 1927	Tirunelveli	1210/1258
ARE 36 of 1927	Tirunelveli	1210/1258
ARE 285 of 1927	Tanjavur	1148
ARE 326 of 1927	Tanjavur	1015
ARE 8 of 1928–29	Tirunelveli	1257?
ARE 24 of 1928–29	Ramnad	1241/1219
ARE 25 of 1928–29	Ramnad	1258/1302
ARE 26 of 1928–29	Ramnad	1272/1187
ARE 334 of 1928–29	Chingleput	1068?
ARE 350 of 1928–29	Chingleput	1223
ARE 107 of 1929–30	Chingleput	1164?
ARE 125 of 1929–30	Chingleput	1142?
ARE 179 of 1929–30	Chingleput	1160?
ARE 212 of 1929–30	Chingleput	1093?
ARE 214 of 1929–30	Chingleput	1154?
ARE 215 of 1929–30	Chingleput	1089?
ARE 219 of 1929–30	Chingleput	1089?
ARE 53 of 1932–33	Chingleput	1285/1259
ARE 230 of 1932–33	Tirunelveli	1257/1209
ARE 240 of 1932–33	Tirunelveli	1242/1220
ARE 241 of 1932–33	Tirunelveli	13th century?
ARE 242 of 1932–33	Tirunelveli	1253
ARE 100 of 1935–36	South Arcot	1184
ARE 190 of 1935–36	Ramnad	13th century
ARE 149 of 1936–37	Tiruchirappalli	948
ARE 90 of 1939–40	North Arcot	1272
ARE 95 of 1939–40	North Arcot	1278
ARE 389 of 1939–40	Tiruchirappalli	1243
ARE 29 of 1940–41	North Arcot	1231
ARE 132 of 1940–41	Chingleput	13th/14th century
ARE 143 of 1940–41	South Arcot	11th century?
ARE 144 of 1940–41	South Arcot	1079?
ARE 149 of 1940–41	South Arcot	1090?
ARE 160 of 1940–41	South Arcot	1094?

(*continued*)

Reference	Location (district)	Date (A.D.)
ARE 161 of 1940–41	South Arcot	1092?
ARE 176 of 1940–41	South Arcot	11th century?
ARE 242 of 1941–42	Madurai	1233/1255
ARE 179 of 1943–44	Chittoor	1160?
ARE 261 of 1943–44	Tiruchirappalli	938
ARE 58 of 1945–46	North Arcot	1295
ARE 300 of 1960–61	Tanjavur	1236
ARE 334 of 1960–61	Tiruchirappalli	12th century
ARE 340 of 1960–61	Tiruchirappalli	1135
ARE 234 of 1961–62	Chingleput	1045
ARE 340 of 1961–62	Madurai	12th century
ARE 352 of 1961–62	Madurai	13th century
ARE 434 of 1961–62	Tiruchirappalli	1139
ARE 435 of 1961–62	Tiruchirappalli	1142
ARE 471 of 1962–63	Madurai	13th century
ARE 502 of 1962–63	Madurai	1021
ARE 505 of 1962–63	Madurai	1030
ARE 588 of 1962–63	Tanjavur	1184
ARE 638 of 1962–63	Tiruchirappalli	13th century
ARE 250 of 1963–64	Madurai	12th century
ARE 275 of 1964–65	Tanjavur	10th century
ARE 232 of 1971–72	North Arcot	13th century
ARE 374 of 1972–73	Tirunelveli	1227?
ARE 207 of 1973–74	North Arcot	1208

An asterisk indicates that a translation of the inscription appears in this volume.

Notes

Notes to Chapter 1

1. Among the ethnographers and anthropologists who have provided accounts of the temple women of recent history are Shortt (1870), Fawcett (1890), Crooke [1896] 1974, 4:364–71), Francis (1904, 64–67) Nagam Aiya (1906, 383–85), Thurston and Rangachari (1909, 2:125–53), Russell [1916] 1975, 3:373–84), Enthoven [1920] 1975, 1:145–47 and 298, 3:70–72), and A. Srinivasan (1984, 75–91).

2. Legal, legislative, and public debates about the *devadāsīs* are represented or described by the following authors: Farquhar ([1914] 1967, 410–14), Mayo (1927, 47–50; 1929, 125–38), Oddie (1979, 102–109), A. Srinivasan (1983), and Jordan (1989 and 1993).

3. One of these sources is a Magadhi inscription (EI 10. Lüder's List 921) from the Jogimara cave in the Ramgarh hills of Madhya Pradesh, which has been variously dated as belonging to the third century B.C. or the first century A.D. (Nilakanta Sastri 1974, 174–76; D. Bhandarkar on EI 22.8). The text of this inscription is *sutanukā nāma | devadāsikyi | tām kāmayitha bālanaśeye | devadinne nāma | lūpadakhe* (Shekhar 1960, 104; Varadpande 1983, 54). It has been translated: "Sutanukā by name, *devadāsī*; the excellent among young men loved her, Devadinna by name, skilled in sculpture" (M. Boyer in the *Journal As. Ser.* X, 3, 484ff); or, alternatively: "Sutanukā by name, a *devadāsī*, made this resting place for girls. Devadinna by name, skilled in painting" (M. Bloch in the *Annual Report of the Archaeological Survey of India* 1903–4, 128–30) (cited by Shekhar 1960, 104; Chandra 1973, 45). If the first translation is correct, this inscription could be considered simply a particularly long-lived specimen of graffiti ("Devadinna loves Sutanukā"); the second translation would point to the character of the inscription as a record of a charitable donation, Sutanukā's sponsorship of the construction of a cave dwelling, which was perhaps decorated by Devadinna. In neither case does this inscription give us any evidence that the *devadāsī* Sutanukā was a temple woman, nor, as has also been

suggested by Nilakanta Sastri (1974, 175) and Varadpande (1983, 54), that she was a dancer or actress.

The second early occurrence of the term *devadāsī* is in the *Arthaśāstra*, the famous manual on statecraft composed perhaps as early as the fourth century B.C. or as late as the fourth century A.D. (Basham 1959, 79; Kangle 1965, 98; Trautmann 1971, 5–6). Here we read that the superintendant of yarns, one of the king's officials, could employ various kinds of women to produce yarn, including widows, maidens, women who have left their homes, prostitute "mothers," aged *rājadāsīs*, and *devadāsīs* whose service of attendance (*upasthāna*) had ceased (*Arthaśāstra* 23.2). Although this passage suggests that *devadāsīs* had some service function, it is not at all clear that their "attendance" was in the context of the temple rather than, for instance, the palace.

The third reference to the term *devadāsī* that appears to be quite early is found in some editions of Buddhaghoṣa's fifth-century *Sumaṅgalavilāsinī Dīghanikāya-Aṭṭhakathā*, in the commentary on the *Brahma-jāla-sūtra*. The *sūtra* lists various wrong means of livelihood, which are not practiced by the Buddha, including "obtaining oracular answers through divine interrogation (*devapañho*)" (verse 26). Buddhaghoṣa explains the meaning as "the Buddha does not interrogate the *devadāsī* (or *dāsī*) fallen under the spell of a god" (*devapañham ti devadāsīya* (or *dāsiya*) *sarīre devatam otāretvā pañhapucchanaṃ*, *Sumaṅgalavilāsinī Dīghanikāya-Aṭṭhakathā* 1(6).26; see notes by the editor, M. Tiwary, 1:15). Here we see the term *devadāsī* (or *dāsī*) applied to a woman who has no apparent connection with a temple but who is, rather, involved in religious practices associated with possession and prognostication.

Apart from these three references to *devadāsīs* from what we might consider the premedieval period, a passage from one of the Puranic texts, the *Brahmāṇḍa Purāṇa* (4.11), which may be as early as the fifth century, also uses this term. In this passage, *devadāsīs* are mentioned as one of the sexual partners prohibited to Brahmans, along with other kinds of *dāsīs* and various other categories of women. Here again there is no indication that the term *devadāsī* applies to temple women.

4. The term *devadāsī* occurs only in eight of the total of forty-nine Agamic references to temple women whose texts I have examined. The term is in several cases found as part of a compound with *gaṇikā* ("courtesan"). All eight of the Agamic references to *devadāsīs* occur in Vaiṣṇava texts (*Īśvara Saṃhitā*, *Śrīpraśna Saṃhitā*, *Sanatkumāra Saṃhitā*, *Vaikhānasāgama*). (See Orr 1994c, 115–16.)

5. *Agni Purāṇa* 211.72, *Śiva Purāṇa* Vāyuvīyasaṃhitā 25.41 (cited by Varadpande 1983, 51), *Bhaviṣya Purāṇa* 1.93.67 (quoted by Altekar 1959, 183), *Padma Purāṇa* Śriṣṭikhanda 52.97 (quoted by Varadpande 1983, 60), and possibly (according to Hazra 1958, 196) *Viṣṇudharmottara Purāṇa* 3.341 (but cf. Kramrisch's translation, where this passage does not exist). This last text is classified by some as a Pāñcarātra text (Inden 1985, 54), and therefore might be considered an Āgama rather than a Purāṇa.

6. The eighth-century Prakrit text *Kuvalayamālā*, a Jain text from Rajasthan, mentions that beautiful prostitutes (*vilāsinīs*) were singing and bearing umbrellas and flywhisks in the temples of Avanti (*Kuvalayamālā* 1:50.5–6). References to prostitutes worshiping and congregating at temples can also be found in Kālidāsa's *Meghadūta* (1.35); in the eighth-century *Kuṭṭanīmata* (742–43, 754–56, 799); in the eleventh-century *Śṛṅgāramañjarī Kathā* (Chandra 1973, 209); and in *Kathāsaritsāgara*, also of the eleventh century (trans. Tawney, 1:139, with Penzer's note). The eleventh-century *Samayamātṛkā* (2.85) seems also to refer to worship by prostitutes (cf. Sternbach 1942, 74a). Neither in this work (*Samayamātṛkā* 8.87; cf. Chandra 1973, 209) nor in *Kuṭṭanīmata* (*Kuṭṭanīmata* 663; cf. Chandra 1973, 209;

Shastri 1975, 86) is there any indication that prostitutes received support from the temple.

7. In the literature and memorial stones of Karnataka, beginning at least as early as the ninth century, there are references to dead heroes being greeted and attended by heavenly women, or "prostitutes of the gods" (*dēvagaṇikkeyar*) (EC 8.Sb 10; Settar and Kalaburgi 1982, 21–23). In the Tamil poems of the Āḻvārs and Nāyaṉmārs (particularly those of the later saints, of the eighth or ninth century) and in the twelfth-century Tamil work *Kaliṅkattupparaṇi*, which describes the Chola king's victories, there are further references to these celestial women (Orr and Young 1986, 28–32; Shulman 1985, 291; cf. also the eleventh-century lexicon *Piṅkalanikaṇṭu* 185).

8. I provide a full account and analysis of the Agamic portrayal of women's participation in temple life in Orr 1994c. In my work with Agamic materials, I have relied on the research and the preparation of editions and translations by N. R. Bhatt, Hélène Brunner, Gérard Colas, Bruno Dagens, Richard H. Davis, J. Gonda, T. Goudriaan, Seetha Padmanabhan, V. Raghavan, and H. Daniel Smith. For help in staying afloat in the vast ocean of Āgamas and in tracing references and locating texts, I am grateful for the special assistance I have received from Dr. S. S. Janaki of the Kuppuswami Sastri Research Institute, from the librarians and staff of the Institut français d'Indologie in Pondicherry and of the Adyar Library in Madras, and from Seetha Padmanabhan and H. Daniel Smith.

9. The seventh-century Chinese traveler Hiuen Tsang found female musicians at the temple of Multan in Sind (Watters [1904–5] 1973, 2:254). According to a series of Arabic and Persian accounts of the ninth to thirteenth centuries, based on the reports of Arab travelers, women, reputedly prostitutes, were in attendance and provided song and dance at Hindu temples in Sind and western India. (I am indebted to Derryl MacLean for providing me with relevant references and translations from the works of Ahmad b. Abi Ya'qub al-Ya'qubi, Ibn Rustah, Gardizi, al-Marwazi, and al-Maqdisi and from the *Chachnāmah*; see also Sachau [1888] 1971, 157.)

10. Marco Polo visited South India in the thirteenth century and reported that young women, before they married, served the temple deity with song and dance (Ponchiroli 1954, 192; Latham 1958, 270); sixteenth-century Portugese visitors to the South Indian kingdom of Vijayanagara described hereditary female temple service and the participation of dancing women, who were apparently temple women, in the religious and court life of the capital (Sewell [1900] 1962, 234, 253–61, 264, 275, 358–60).

11. The scholarly tradition of understanding Indian society, history, politics, and art—and Indian women—through abstract and ahistorical religious concepts, or social values undergirded by religious concepts, has been remarked on by a number of scholars (R. Sharma 1961, 113–14; Waghorne 1981, 146; 1994, 86–94; A. Srinivasan 1983, 77–78; 1984, 239–53, 296; Burghart 1985, 9–10; Dirks 1987, 3–4; Inden 1990, 55–58, 99–100; Prakash 1990, 391–94; Mitter 1992, 257–59, 263–67; Leavitt 1992, 29–30; Ludden 1993, 260–61).

12. Chattopadhyaya draws attention to the persistence of the idea of India's timelessness by quoting Madeleine Biardeau's *Hinduism: The Anthropology of a Civilization* (1989): "In spite of a sizeable collection of inscriptions on stones or on copper plates . . . the evidence scarcely enables us to reconstruct what one would call a history. . . . Change, when it does appear, is only superficial and always refers back to a normative foundation" (Chattopadhyaya 1994, 2–3). Other reflections on the origins, accuracy, and impact of this idea may be found in Stein (1969, 41–47), Dandekar (1978, 18, 36–37), A. Sharma (1980), Pollock (1989 and 1993, 104), Collins (1991), and Orr (1994a).

Said (1979, 97, 207–8) and Inden (1990, 22–23, 73) discuss the divesting of a people of history as an aspect of Orientalism. A number of scholars have drawn our attention to the problems of the label Orientalist (Clifford 1988, 259–75; Halbfass 1991, 9–13; O'Hanlon and Washbrook 1992, 155–67; Pollock 1993, 97–101). Although it is clear that "Orientalism" can all too quickly deteriorate into a term of abuse, the debate about Orientalism—and parallel discussions about androcentrism—have had, I believe, a positive effect in increasing scholarly self-consciousness and in encouraging on-the-ground studies as a balance to the more traditional abstract, textual, and philosophical approaches.

13. Out of the multitude of works on Hindu myth and symbol—too many to survey here—I would like to draw attention to the importance of the work on feminine symbolism by Babb (1970), C. M. Brown (1974), Kinsley (1975 and 1988), Tapper (1979), O'Flaherty (1980), Wadley (1980), Marglin (1982; 1985a; 1985b), Coburn (1984 and 1991), Obeyesekere (1984), and Erndl (1993). The reflections of some of these scholars, as well as others (Gross 1974, 158–59; Sanday 1981; Lakshmi 1982; Bynum 1985, 2–4, 9–12; Gold 1985, xviii-xix, 145; Das 1987, 59–64; Young 1987, 73–75), on the relations between feminine symbolism and women's experience have provided an increasingly sophisticated framework for analyzing the potential salience of these symbols for women. Another important area of scholarship that is relevant to our understanding of the significance of symbolic and ideological systems in India is the critical study of the ways in which those systems have been produced and the recognition of the coexistence of competing systems (Stein 1969, 54–55; Lingat 1973; Burghart 1985, 9–10; Pollock 1989).

14. Amrit Srinivasan discusses the impact of colonial and Indological perspectives on the contemporary study of Indian society and of temple women: "That these [empiricist and idealist] attitudes continue to influence scholarship even in a post-colonial context is rather surprising. . . . The *devadāsī* studied even today in terms of either of these intellectual streams would emerge as a civil, exploited 'class' or functionally integrated 'caste' . . . on the one hand, and as the embodiment of pan-Indian religious notions of *Sakti* or other such orthogenetic concepts, on the other" (1983, 77–78). Srinivasan's work (1984) has provided an alternative framework for understanding the social structure of the early twentieth-century *devadāsī* community. In addition, her analysis (1983) and that of Jordan (1989) are extremely helpful in demonstrating how our vision of the temple woman has come into being, through the interplay of political and social historical forces in the last 150 years. It is therefore somewhat odd to find both Srinivasan and Jordan, in their treatment of temple women in earlier South Indian history, resorting to abstract religious concepts—seeing temple women as symbols of the goddess-consort of the temple deity (A. Srinivasan 1984, 281–83) or as representations of the sacred, embodying a traditional Hindu worldview in which the sacred was immanent and intertwined with kingship (Jordan 1989, 73–74).

15. Basham (1961, 280–83), R. Sharma (1961, 106–7), and Mitter (1992, 257–59, 263–67) have discussed the idea of a history of degeneration and the timing of decline. As in the case of Indian nationalist histories, "regionalist" histories of South India have sometimes blamed foreign influences—infiltration by northern, Aryan, and Brahmanical interests—for having brought about the degeneration of the earlier, more egalitarian society of the Dravidian South (Jaiswal 1974; Lakshmi 1990). This position presents an interesting contrast to the view (promoted by the European Indologists who saw links between Indo-Aryan and European civilization) that

Aryan society and religion decayed as a result of contact with Dravidian culture (Inden 1990, 89, 117, 120–21; Mitter 1992, 257–59, 263–67).

16. According to Deyell, "certain of the putative elements of early medieval society, such as feudalization, decentralization, decline of trade and village self-sufficiency, have become virtual axioms of historic and economic texts" (1990, 3; see also Inden 1990, 72–73, 89, 117, 120–21, 185–88). Chattopadhyaya, citing a number of prominent Indian historians (including R. N. Nandi, D. N. Jha, R. S. Sharma, and N. R. Ray), challenges their belief that "feudalism" explains the changes that occurred in medieval Indian history, charging that the use of the term "feudalism" is often simply the reflection of the judgment that "decline" and political fragmentation have taken place rather than an explanation for historical processes (1994, 8–14, 36–37, 188–95). Descriptions of the deterioration of the political, economic, and social order are frequently coupled with the characterization of medieval art as decadent (D. Desai 1975; cf. Michell 1993).

17. We find examples of the depiction of women's status as declining—in India generally or in South India specifically—in the works of Altekar (1959), Nadarajah (1969), and Balasubramanian (1976). Uma Chakravarti (1989) provides a particularly cogent analysis of the nationalist political agendas that underwrote this vision of Indian women's history (see also R. Sharma 1961, 106–11; A. Srinivasan 1983, 85; Thapar 1987, 10; Sarkar 1992, 223–24).

18. The notion that the *devadāsī* system has, in one or the other of these two ways, degenerated over the course of time is extremely pervasive (see, e.g., Penzer 1924; Sinha and Basu 1933; S. Chatterjee 1945; Punekar and Rao 1962; Bonoff 1973; D. Desai 1975; Gaston 1980; Prasad 1983; Nair 1994).

19. Raheja and Gold (1994, 3–13) present a survey of the recent scholarship on Indian women that emphasizes their passivity. Feminist scholars, in their studies of women of the past or of women in other societies, have had to struggle with the tendency to see the women they study as victims rather than actors (Johansson 1976, 401; Schussler Fiorenza 1983, 85–86; Lerner 1986, 233–36; Mohanty 1988, 70–71, 79). One also encounters in contemporary scholarship the problem that women's agency is recognized only in contexts of challenge, overt resistance, or radical change (Haynes and Prakash 1991, 7–8; Tharu and Lalita 1991, 152) or that when non-Western women are perceived as exercising agency, the motives for their actions are presumed to be similar to those of women in the West (Abu-Lughod 1990, 323; Tharu and Lalita 1991, 154).

20. Among the recent analyses of the "uses" of Indian women in colonial, nationalist, and reformist representations of tradition are the important contributions of Ballhatchet (1980), Kishwar (1986), U. Chakravarti (1989), Mani (1989), I. Chatterjee (1990), O'Hanlon (1991 and 1994), Sarkar (1992), P. Chatterjee (1993), Price (1994), and J. Whitehead (1995). Particularly significant in the present context is Lata Mani's discussion of the ways in which both supporters and critics of the practice of *sati* denied agency to the women involved and represented them, even when they were seen as heroines, as puppets or victims.

21. Amrit Srinivasan (1983) and Kay Jordan (1989) have documented the process through which temple women became the focus of reform movements. The dichotomization of Indian womanhood into two images—the "traditional" woman, idealized in nineteenth-century nationalist discourse as chaste, self-sacrificing, dependent, and oriented toward the family, and her counterpart, the prostitute, dancing-girl, or *devadāsī*, who had economic autonomy and was not defined as a wife and mother—

is discused by Suleri (1992, 92–93); P. Chatterjee (1993, 126–32, 151–55); Nair (1994, 3164–65); Ramanujan, Narayana Rao, and Shulman (1994, 26–31) and J. Whitehead (1995).

22. These concerns are expressed, for example, by Katherine Mayo (1927, 47–50; 1929, 125–38; see also A. Srinivasan 1983, 80–82, 87; 1984, 111–12, 131–35; Jordan 1989, 113, 127f, 155f, 168f, 214–16, 260f). Judy Whitehead (1995) has shown how, in the eyes of Western reformers, age of consent and prostitution were perceived as medical problems, thus justifying state intervention and the implementation of various methods of control and treatment. The way in which British authorities, both in Britain and in India, treated prostitution as a medical issue has been described by Ballhatchett (1980) and Walkowitz (1980). The medicalization of the *devadāsī* issue is illustrated by the approaches of Katherine Mayo, an American woman, and Dr. Muthulakshmi Reddy, a South Indian woman who campaigned vigorously against *devadasī* dedication (Mayo 1927, 47; A. Srinivasan 1983, 76; 1985, 1874; Jordan 1989, 243–44, 247–48; Meduri 1996, 160–76).

23. I. Chatterjee (1990, 30) has discussed the lack of foundation for the lurid images of girls being kidnapped as a means of "recruiting" prostitutes in India. Several recent studies of prostitution in Southeast Asia have also challenged the notion that women are typically forced into prostitution against their will or forcibly taken from their families. This is not to deny that desperation and deception may be among the factors that make women choose to engage in prostitution. In the case of temple women, the studies of Marglin and Srinivasan on the family histories and kinship relations of surviving members of the *devadāsī* community indicate that girls adopted into *devadāsī* families were often closely related to the temple women who adopted them. Although in some cases, money was given by temple women to the parents of girls whom they adopted, we find no evidence from the nineteenth or twentieth centuries of girls being dedicated to temples against the will of their parents; indeed, parents seem frequently to have been eager to have their daughters so dedicated (see Thurston and Rangachari 1909, 2:143–52).

24. It is not difficult to demonstrate that in the case of Hindu temple women, as for other Oriental women, "the spectacle of subject women . . . could not but be exciting" for the colonial European male (Kabbani 1986, 80–81; see also 47–48; Said 1979, 207–8; Alloula 1986, 95). Two erotic fantasies that I have come across, without particularly wanting to, focus on the sexual experience of Englishmen with *devadāsīs*, and, although one is violently pornographic and the other merely titillating and rather silly, both depict the *devadasī* as a kind of sex slave (Mardaan 1967; Gogarty 1937, 53–55).

The focus on the sexuality of the *devadāsī* is part of a long-standing and widespread European male attitude toward the Orient that characterizes it as a realm of lascivious sensuality (Alloula 1986, 95; Kabbani 1986, 6). Even Katherine Mayo, who as a woman might be expected to have a somewhat different perspective from her male counterparts, is persuaded that the character and circumstances of the people of India are entirely determined by their obsession with sex and their sexual behavior (Mayo 1927, 16, 22–32; see also Burton 1992, 143–51). Suleri's analysis (1992, 92–93) of the way in which the sexuality and accomplishments of the "nautch-girl" represented the threat of "cultural contagion" feared by both male and female Anglo-Indians may help us to understand the Western reaction to the Indian woman as a sexual being.

25. This process was not an exclusively Indian phenomenon: in Western countries in this period, there are similar official and reformist efforts to identify and isolate

categories of people as prostitutes, deviants, and criminals (Walkowitz 1980; Hobson 1987; Foucault 1995, 251–56).

26. Our knowledge of prostitutes—even in recent history, but certainly in earlier times—is far too slight for us to speculate about whether there were in fact "traditional" communities or castes of prostitutes in India and about how colonialism may have changed their circumstances. In Indian literature, from a very early period, there are references to *veśyās* and *gaṇikās* ("prostitutes" and "courtesans"), but they are for the most part portrayed as ideal types or stock characters of various sorts, depending on the genre (e.g., as donors in Buddhist literature, as royal attendants in Epic literature, and as cultured beauties in Sanskrit drama). We know very little about what prostitution or concubinage actually entailed in various periods of Indian history or what relation there may be between the *veśyās* and *gaṇikās* of literature and the forms of prostitution encountered by (or created by) European colonists.

27. Such legislation was passed as early as 1909 in the princely state of Mysore and in 1930 in Travancore, another princely state. In Madras Presidency, which constituted the whole of South India except for the princely states and the dominions of the Nizam of Hyderabad, two pieces of legislation were destined to bring an end to the dedication of *devadāsīs*. In 1929, a bill was passed that effectively separated *devadāsīs*' rights to property from temple dedication and service. In 1947, a bill was passed that had orginally been proposed in 1937, banning *devadāsī* dedication. Such a bill was also passed in Bombay Presidency in 1934.

28. Even some of the early ethnographers (Shortt 1870, 187–88; Thurston and Rangachari, 1909, 2:124ff)—who were not reluctant to consider the *devadāsīs* prostitutes—reported that in the nineteenth century, these women frequently formed quite permanent sexual relationships and were not particularly promiscuous. The studies of Marglin (1985b) and A. Srinivasan (1984), based on interviews with surviving *devadāsīs*, indicate that their social and sexual arrangements had the character of long-term and noncommercial liaisons in the early part of the twentieth century as well. These studies, as well as other recent studies of temple women, emphasize the absence of exchange of money for sexual services and point out the opportunities that temple women had to acquire money through other means (Marglin 1980, 249; 1985b, 35, 41; A. Srinivasan 1984, 191–97; Kersenboom 1991, 144–47).

Srinivasan considers the use of the term "prostitute" for South Indian temple women in the nineteenth and twentieth centuries the result of the imposition of an "alien context of understanding," the application of "universalistic jargon essentially insensitive to socio-historical complexity" (A. Srinivasan 1983, 76, 96). The use of the label "prostitute" for temple women by the British was also linked to a condemnation of Hinduism, whose perceived abuses and excesses demonstrated the need for paternalistic British rule.

The information we have about women dedicated to temples in Tamilnadu and Orissa in recent history suggests that we might reconsider whether it is accurate to label them prostitutes. But the custom of dedicating women to temples, particularly temples of the goddess Yellammā, that prevails today in districts on the Karnataka-Maharashtra border, is more justifiably linked to prostitution. Most of the women so dedicated who remain in their home villages or reside near the shrine where they were dedicated are not prostitutes but contract relatively long-term liaisons with a patron or lover, who provides some support; they are rarely directly supported by the temple but do receive payments from temple priests and from the public for the performance of rituals and various other services, receive alms, and work as agricultural laborers (Assayag 1989, 361–63, 370; Shankar 1990, 104–8; Tarachand 1991, 62–68, 94–98, 102). Other women, especially Harijan women, who are persuaded by their families or by procurers to dedicate themselves to Yellammā, go to cities in Karnataka and Maharashtra to become prostitutes (Punekar and Rao 1962, 14–15, 78–84; Tarachand 1991, 111–13, 116–19). The manipulation and exploitation of Harijan women by this system has been fought against in recent years through local community organizing (Hankare 1981; Omvedt 1983; Jain 1985; Shankar 1990, 146–155). It seems clear that these *devadāsīs* are distinguishable from other types of temple women and that this distinction has been recognized for some time (Jordan 1989, 295–99; cf. Kersenboom 1987, 193, 195–97).

29. There is a passage in the *Mahānirvāṇatantra* that has been interpreted by some as referring to a temple woman in its mention of the *devaveśyā* (prostitute of the god) as one of the five kinds of *veśyās* along with the *rājaveśyā*, *nagarī*, *guptaveśyā*, and *brahmaveśyā*) who may represent female divine energy (*śakti*) in a particular Tantric ritual—which, presumably, involves the sexual union of the male adept with a female partner (Meyer 1952, 275). This text dates to the second half of the eighteenth century (Goudriaan and Gupta 1981, 98–99). Frédérique Marglin (1985b, 217–18) suggests, on the basis of information and texts provided by one of the priests of the Jagannatha temple, that the morning ritual performed by the *devadāsīs* can be interpreted as a Tantric ceremony, their dance symbolizing ritual sexual union as one of the five elements of esoteric Tantric rites.

30. Brunner (1990, 125–28) questions whether, in the Agamic system or in temple practice, there is evidence of the necessary linkages posited by Kersenboom among the *devadāsī*'s ritual activity, her auspiciousness, her sexuality, and her representation of the goddess. Very similar questions could be raised with reference to Marglin's interpretations.

31. This outline of the political history of the Chola period is based on Nilakanta Sastri (1955), Subbarayalu (1982, 266), and Heitzman (1997, 4–8). The division of the Chola period into four subperiods is a convention used by many of those who have provided basic tools for the study of inscriptions from this period (e.g., Sitaraman, Karashima, and Subbarayalu 1976; Karashima, Subbarayalu, and Matsui 1978) and is consequently adopted by those who base their analysis on these inscriptional sources. I have departed from the customary usage of this system of periodization only in my extension of the last subperiod for twenty years after the end of the Chola dynasty, up to A.D. 1300.

32. Sitaraman, Karashima, and Subbarayalu (1976, 88) counted Tamil inscriptions dated in the regnal years of Chola kings, and calculated that 3,543 such inscriptions had been published and about 7,000 were unpublished, amounting to a total of over 10,000 Tamil inscriptions of the Chola dynasty. More recently, Garbini (1993, 73) has arrived at the figure of 20,000 for all Tamil inscriptions, in all periods, published and unpublished. I estimate that the size of the corpus of Chola period inscriptions in Tamil that serve as the basis for my study is midway between these sets of figures, given that I am including for consideration not only inscriptions of the Chola dynasty but also all Tamil inscriptions dated between 850 and 1300 and that at virtually every South Indian site the great majority of extant inscriptions in Tamil belong to this period.

33. I am indebted to Dr. K. V. Ramesh, who as Chief Epigraphist at the time of my research in 1983–84, graciously granted me permission to consult the transcripts of unpublished inscriptions. More recently, the same courtesy and cooperation have been extended to me by the Director of Epigraphy, Dr. Madhav N. Katti, and by

Chief Epigraphist Dr. M. D. Sampath, for which I am extremely grateful. I also owe a debt of gratitude to James Heitzman, who has generously shared his notes on and translations of a number of unpublished inscriptions that I did not have the opportunity to read at the Chief Epigraphist's Office in Mysore.

34. In Tamilnadu the number of stone inscriptions declines after A.D. 1300, except at a few important temples. This development may be linked to shifting economic and political patterns. Perlin (1981, 276–77), discussing developments in the fourteenth and fifteenth centuries throughout India, describes a transition from extensive hegemony to intensive forms of rule, linking isolated nuclei of settlement. Stein (1989, 21–27), dealing specifically with Tamilnadu in the fourteenth century, points to the increasing concentration of resources in towns (including temple towns) and of power in the figure of the ruler. On political, economic, and religious transformations in the post-Chola period, see also Stein (1978b, 36–40); Granda (1984); Ludden (1985, 42–67); Dirks (1987, 34–36, 43–48); Karashima (1992); and Narayana Rao, Shulman, and Subrahmanyam (1992). Although her specific focus is on medieval Andhra Pradesh, Cynthia Talbot's (forthcoming, Chap. 1) discussion of the characteristics of the "age of inscriptions" is relevant to our understanding of developments in South India as a whole.

35. Religious texts that were used or produced in medieval Tamilnadu—including the Āḻvārs' and Nāyaṉmārs' poems and works composed by the Vaiṣṇava and Śaiva *ācāryas*—have been increasingly attracting scholarly attention, and thus I can mention only a few of the names of scholars whose pioneering efforts have opened up this important area of research and whose work is particularly relevant to the period of my study. Among these are John Carman, Norman Cutler, M. Dhavamony, M. A. Dorai Rangaswamy, Friedhelm Hardy, Dennis Hudson, Vasudha Narayanan, Walter Neeval, Indira Peterson, A. K. Ramanujan, David Shulman, K. Sivaraman, K. K. A. Venkatachari, Glenn Yocum, Katherine Young, and Kamil Zvelebil. Scholars working on Vaiṣṇava and Śaiva Agamic texts—some of whose names are listed in note 8—have also made important contributions to our understanding of religious life in medieval Tamilnadu. Although we are very far from being able to determine the precise relations between practice in Chola period temples and the prescriptions of the Āgamas, a number of the Agamic texts—texts apparently composed during the ninth to thirteenth centuries—show marks of having been influenced by features of South Indian practice (H. Smith 1975, 67ff; Gonda 1977, 55–56, 145–46; R. Davis 1991, 12–19; see also V. Raghavan's foreward to *Śrīpraśna Saṃhitā*; *Kāmikāgama* 1.4.438; *Īśvara Saṃhitā* 11.256).

36. Among those who have contributed significantly to our knowledge of medieval South Indian temple architecture and iconography are K. R. Srinivasan (1960), S. R. Balasubrahmanyam (1966, 1971, 1975, 1979), T. A. Gopinatha Rao [1916] (1971); K. V. Soundara Rajan (1972), and R. Champakalakshmi (1981b).

37. Inscriptions and images of Tīrthaṅkaras and Jain deities provide evidence of the flourishing of Jainism in Tamilnadu from the second century B.C. to the present. In the Chola period, Jain inscriptions are especially plentiful in North Arcot and Chingleput districts in the northern part of Tamilnadu; in South Arcot district in the "middle" country; in Madurai and Tirunelveli districts in the far south; and in the former Pudukkottai state, which lies within the Chola region but borders on the south (see Orr 1998). The material evidence for Buddhism in Tamilnadu is less abundant and more difficult to situate in time and space, but there are Buddhist images datable from the sixth century to the seventeenth century, which were produced in the Tamil country and which, in many cases, bear Tamil inscriptions. In addition to

the material evidence, there are a number of literary works composed in Tamil by Jain and Buddhist authors of the medieval period. A great deal of research remains to be done to elucidate the character and evolution of Jainism and Buddhism and the interactions among Jain, Buddhist, and Hindu traditions in Tamilnadu's history. Some of the work that has already been done, and collections of relevant textual, inscriptional, and art historical sources that have been made, include Gopinatha Rao (1915), Ramaswami Ayyangar (1922), Ramachandran (1934 and 1954), P. Desai (1957), Aiyappan and Srinivasan (1960), Champakalakshmi (1974 and 1978), A. Chakravarti (1974), Ramesh (1974), Nagaswamy (1975); Soundara Rajan (1975), K. Srinivasan (1975), A. Chatterjee (1978), Kandaswamy (1978 and 1981), Vasudeva Rao (1979), Vijayavenugopal (1979), Velu Pillai (1980), Krishnan (1981), Sivaramamurti (1983), Yocum (1983), Obeyesekere (1984), Ekambaranathan and Sivaprakasam (1987), Dehejia (1988), Richman (1988), Hikosaka (1989), Mahadevan (1995), Monius (1997), R. Davis (1998), Orr (1998, forthcoming a), and Peterson (1998). One of the most potentially productive directions for this investigation—an avenue that has as yet scarcely been ventured onto—lies in the coordination of epigraphic, literary, iconographic, and archeological evidence.

38. The earliest inscriptional reference to worship in Tamilnadu that I have encountered is the Pallankoyil Jain copper-plate grant of the mid–sixth century, written in Sanskrit and Tamil. Although unearthed in Tanjavur district, this inscription concerns an endowment of land made by the Pallava king Simhavarman to a Jain ascetic of Tiruparuttikkunru, or Jina Kanchi, in present-day Chingleput district. This gift was made to an ascetic to conduct worship (*pūjā*) for "the foremost of *jinas*, *jainas*, and *munis*" (T. Subramaniam 1958–59 = *PCM*, 1–32). The other early Jain inscriptions that record endowments for worship—dated on paleographic grounds to the seventh and eighth centuries—are stone inscriptions, frequently engraved at the bases of sculpted images of Tīrthaṅkaras and goddesses (*yakṣīs*) (Orr forthcoming a). The epigraphical evidence for the presence of Jainism in Tamilnadu before the sixth century is also in the form of stone inscriptions, but these are records that describe the gifts of rock-cut dwellings and "beds" for Jain monks, rather than gifts in support of worship.

The earliest material evidence for Buddhist worship in Tamilnadu is contemporary with the Jain evidence: several images of the Buddha, although they are not inscribed, are datable on stylistic grounds to the sixth century (Ramachandran 1954, No. 38; Dehejia 1988, 58). It is interesting that one of these Buddha images was found in Kanchipuram—the same locale associated with the earliest Jain and Hindu inscriptions relating to worship.

39. The Śaiva and Vaiṣṇava poet-saints describe the worship of the deity, in image form, with flowers, incense, lamps, water, drums, chanting and singing, music, food offerings, and anointing or bathing with sweet and fragrant pastes and liquids (Dorai Rangaswamy 1958, 1067–70; Kandiah 1973, 174–213; Hardy 1983, 288–90, 328–29). Earlier works of Tamil literature, dating from the fourth to seventh centuries A.D.—texts such as *Neṭunalvāṭai*, *Maturaikkāñci*, and *Paripāṭal*—refer to similar patterns of worship, involving flowers, incense, food offerings, music and dance, lights, drums, cloth, and umbrellas (see *Paripāṭal* 17; Kandiah 1973, 119–20, Hardy 1983, 140, 211–12).

40. *Āśvalāyana Gṛhya-sūtra* (4.7.10 and 4.8.1) mentions *āsana*, *arghya*, *gandha*, *mālya*, *dhūpa*, *dīpa*, and *acchādana* (seat, water, perfumes, flowers, incense, lights, and cloth) as services to be offered to Brahmans invited to a *śrāddha* (Kane 1930–62, 2:730). These elements are identical to those appearing in later texts—Āgamas,

Purāṇas, and various Agamic and Dharmaśāstra digests and compendia—in the descriptions of twelve, sixteen, eighteen, twenty-four, or thirty-six *upacāras* ("ways of service") to be offered to temple deities, which typically also include bathing or anointing (*snāna* or *abhiṣeka*) and food-offerings (*naivedya*) (see Kane 1930, 2:729–35, 5:34f.; Brunner 1963, 1:App. 7; Appadurai and Breckenridge 1976, 193, n. 5; R. Davis 1986, 223–33, 264–74, 317–35; *Śaivāgamaparibhāṣamañjarī* 4.78–86). The *Mahābhārata* (Anuśāsana parva 98) provides early evidence of the employment of such elements in Hindu worship; here we find references to the offering of flowers, incense, and lamps.

Early Mahāyāna Buddhist texts refer to worship with flowers, perfumes, incense, flags, banners, cloth, lamps, and music (Hardy 1983, 29–33), and there is inscriptional evidence of Buddhist worship of this character as early as the fifth and sixth centuries in western, central, and eastern India. For example, an inscription from Bagh, in Madhya Pradesh, mentions perfumes, flowers, incense, garlands, and food oblations (*gandha-puṣpa-dhūpa-mālya-balisatra*) as elements in the worship of the Buddha (fifth or sixth century; CII 4, 19–21, cited by Schopen 1990, 184); and at Valabhi in Gujurat, Buddhist worship involving perfumes, incense, flowers, lamps, and oils (*gandha-dhūpa-puṣpa-dīpa-taila*) is described in an early sixth-century inscription (JRAS 1895, 379–84, cited by Schopen 1990, 186). Also at Valabhi, in approximately the same period, there is an inscriptional reference to offerings made to a Hindu deity, Sūrya, in which very similar elements are involved—worship, bathing, perfumes, flowers, lamps, music, song, dance, and food oblations (*pūjā-snāpana-gandha-puṣpa-dīpa-vādya-gīta-nṛtya-balicharusātra*) (seventh century; EI 21.18).

41. Hardy's idea that elite Buddhist religious practice remained aloof from those forms of worship he considers part of a folk pattern is called into question by the work of Gregory Schopen (e.g., 1985; 1988–89).

42. Stein suggests that "non-Brahmans would presumably . . . have been denied access to many ritual performances involving Brahman functionaries. For one reason, the shrines of canonical deities during the early Chola period and most of the period of the great Cholas were located in the residential quarters of Brahman villages, thus non-Brahmans would have suffered restrictions of movement into these quarters" (1980, 232). Apart from the large-scale participation of non-Brahmans as patrons of temples, the involvement of non-Brahmans in ritual roles and the lack of emphasis that the inscriptions place on Brahmanical identities (see, e.g., Orr 1995a and 1995c) would argue against Stein's interpretation. Champakalakshmi (1981a, 421) and Kulke (1982, 249–50) have also questioned Stein's assumptions about the discontinuity between "Vedic" ("smarta," "sastric," "canonical") Brahmanical religion and localized folk religion in the Chola period.

43. Stein himself explains the emergence of a multitiered pattern of sectarian affiliation—based on loyalty to clan and local deities, to regional Śaiva and Vaiṣṇava temples, and to major temple centers and preceptor networks—within the context of developments of the post-Chola period, particularly in the fifteenth century and onward, when new dominant castes became prominent in various localities (Stein 1978b, 36–40). Fuller's (1988, 64–65) argument for the distinction between village "territorial" temples (dedicated to tutelary goddesses) and large "universal" temples (dedicated to Śiva or Viṣṇu) is, like Stein's, based on relatively late historical evidence and recent ethnography. Susan Bayly (1989, 40–41, 48, 55–58, 65–70) argues that even as late as the eighteenth century, "there were few hard and fast boundaries between the blood-taking 'demonic' beings and the remote 'Sanskritic' gods"

for many worshipers in Tamilnadu and that, instead of Brahmanical culture, it was the religious culture of groups migrating into the Tamil region, especially of warriors, that shaped the colonial and contemporary religious landscape.

Bayly (1989, 30–40) describes goddess worship as an important element of the warrior culture that came to be entrenched in Tamilnadu—in its "little kingdoms" and its villages—in the late precolonial period (see also Stein 1978b; Hiltebeitel 1988, 20–23, 44–45; 1991, 3–6, 367–69; Price 1996, 136–146). It is important to recognize that ethnographic accounts (like those of H. Whitehead 1921, as well as of more recent field-workers), describing South Indian village religion as focused on the worship of local goddesses, may be entirely irrelevant to our understanding of folk religion a thousand or more years earlier. Apart from the fact that the economic and social circumstances of villagers or tribal people would have been utterly transformed over the centuries, major religious changes would certainly have occurred, as much within the "little tradition" as within the elite tradition. Indeed, when we consider the literary and archeological evidence of the first half of the first millenium A.D., there is no foundation for the assumption that goddess worship was originally, or has been continuously, the dominant feature of folk religion in South India or that goddesses worshiped in early South Indian history resembled those of modern villages (K. Srinivasan 1960, 1–9, 21–35; Diehl 1964; Hart 1975, 21–50; Champakalakshmi 1975–76; Nagaswamy 1982, 4–18; Hardy 1983, 127–67).

44. Suresh Pillai (1968, 440–43) argues that at the great temple of Tanjavur, built by Rajaraja I at the beginning of the eleventh century, a conscious effort was made to absorb "local and independent goddesses." According to Stein (1980, 237–38) the emergence of shrines for consort goddesses in the later Chola period represents "an assimilation of folk conceptions of deity," the female deity being "then as now the major focus of village, clan and locality devotion" (see also Stein 1973; 1978b, 37–39, 44). David Shulman's analysis of Tamil temple myths (*sthalapurāṇa*s)—most of which were composed in the sixteenth and seventeenth centuries—shows the importance of the figure of the local goddess and of myths of her marriage within these traditions; Shulman concludes that these goddesses have long been identified with the soil, agriculture, and fertility in the Tamil country and that the mythic plot through which "the god may be drawn to the site by the goddess and be rooted there by marriage to her" reflects the historical priority of goddesses as objects of local worship (1980, 138–41).

45. Richard Davis (1998) develops the notion of a "shared religious culture" in which both Hindus and Jains of early medieval Tamilnadu participated. A number of other authors have recently questioned the extent to which sectarian identities and communities—Hindu, Muslim, Buddhist, and Jain —were salient in premodern India (Bayly 1989, 40; Kaviraj 1992, 25–26; Thapar 1992, 77, 84–85; Talbot 1995a; R. Davis 1997; Wagoner forthcoming). Although a great deal more research remains to be done to elucidate the situation in medieval Tamilnadu, I am inclined, on the basis of the inscriptional evidence, to consider that for most people in the Chola period, collective identities were "multiple and layered and fuzzy" (Kaviraj 1992, 25–26) and that the "Hindu" category or community was not particularly well defined or meaningful. Some preliminary efforts (Orr 1995a) to explore the salience of Śaiva and Vaiṣṇava identities in this period have led me to believe that these categories similarly lacked firm definitions or clear boundaries.

In the present description of the religious situation in the Chola period, I am focusing primarily on what we would consider "Hinduism" and "Jainism"—because of the availability of inscriptional materials in institutions associated with these traditions—but Buddhists and Muslims were also a part of the religious scene in this period. I have already mentioned the evidence for the Buddhist presence. Muslims resided in Tamilnadu, especially in trading centers on the coast, from the eighth or ninth century, and began to settle further inland during the thirteenth and fourteenth centuries (Bayly 1989, 77ff and 86ff).

46. The idea of a god enshrined in a temple as being equivalent to the human recipient of a gift has occasioned a good deal of discussion among the exegetes of Dharmaśāstra literature (Kane 1930–62, 2:157, 889, 915–16; Sontheimer 1964; Derrett 1968, 146–47, 484–88; Talbot 1988b, 154–57). This idea is clearly in evidence in Chola period inscriptions that record gifts not only to Hindu but also to Jain and Buddhist institutions. Similar ideas are expressed about the Buddha in early medieval texts and inscriptions from outside the Tamil country as well (Schopen 1990, 189–92; Collins 1992, 237).

47. Relevant Dharmaśāstra texts and examples of pre-Chola period religious giving—to Brahmans—can be found in *Manusmṛti* (11.1–6), *Yājñavalkya Smṛti* (13.317 and *Mitākṣara*), Kane (1930–62, 2:110ff, 842, 860–61), Gonda (1965, 198–229), and Dirks (1976, 141). In Dharmaśāstra and exegetical literature on religious gifts, building and endowing temples and making gifts to deities are considered *dāna* only in a secondary sense; complications arise because of the fact that there can be no acceptance of the gift by the donee (*pratigraha*) and because the donor does not necessarily divest himself or herself of future use of or interest in the gift (Kane 1930–62, 2:841–42, 910; Sontheimer 1964). As we have seen, however, in practice, donors believed that the donee (the deity) *did* in fact accept such a gift. This kind of gift is sometimes considered *pūrta*—a type of gift that, unlike gifts associated with Vedic sacrifice, can be made by women and *śūdras* (Kane 1930–62, 2:157, 889, 915–16; Talbot 1988b, 154–57). Indeed, whereas we see throughout medieval India the involvement of considerable numbers of women in the patronage of Jain, Buddhist, and Hindu institutions, gifts to Brahmans appear to be made exclusively by men.

In most scholarly discussions of gift giving in the Chola period, and particularly of royal patronage, an adequate distinction has not been made between gifts to temples and gifts to Brahmans (e.g., Stein 1980, 152–65, 357, 364; Shulman 1985, 28–33 and 37–39). In fact, we know very little about the support of Brahmans in the Chola period. Stein makes several suggestions about the way in which *brahmadeyas*—villages donated to Brahmans—came to be established in Tamilnadu. On the one hand, he indicates that local landholders were the sponsors of *brahmadeyas*, beginning as early as the seventh century (1980, 82–83, 166, 341); on the other, he points to kings as the patrons of Brahmans, emphasizing the importance of *brahmadeyas* as part of the ritual polity of the Chola kings and indicating that the establishment of *brahmadeyas* reached a peak during the rule of Rajaraja I (160, 339–40, 357, 363–65). Although several scholars have dealt briefly with the administrative structure and the distribution of *brahmadeyas* in Tamilnadu in the Chola period (Nilakanta Sastri 1955, 492–503; Hall 1980, 32–40; Tirumalai 1983; Karashima 1984, 36–40; Champakalakshmi forthcoming), we still lack detailed study of *brahmadeyas* and their origins in Tamilnadu of the type that has been undertaken for Karnataka by Dikshit (1964) and for Kerala by Veluthat (1978).

48. The activity of women—nuns, as well as laywomen—as patrons of Buddhist and Jain institutions is documented by Horner (1930, 317–61), N. Dutt (1973, 56–57), Hanumantha Rao (1973, 63–65), Ramesh (1974), Nagaraja Rao (1985), Schopen (1985 and 1988–89), Willis (1985, 73–77), Ekambaranathan and Sivaprakasan (1987), Nath (1987, 69–76), and U. Singh (1996).

49. A few examples in the corpus of Chola period inscriptions indicate expiation as a reason for making a gift, although these records seem for the most part to be describing public atonement for a social wrong (murder or assault), following the decision of local authorities, rather than an act of individual piety (see, e.g., Jha 1974, 215–16). I have come across no references to gifts being made as the consequence of a vow.

It has been suggested that gifts of lamps or gifts to support the perpetual fueling of lamps had funerary or memorial connotations, but I have not found evidence that this was the case in the Chola period temple milieu. Although the inscriptions do not provide details about how the many lamps donated to temples were actually used in ritual or what place they had in the temple, we may find a clue in the descriptions of daily worship in the Āgamas. For example, the *Kāmikāgama* outlines the evening ritual as follows: after the deity (Lord Śiva in the form of a *liṅga*) is bathed, fed, adorned, and entertained with song and dance, the priest "perfumes the sanctum with incense . . . [and] illuminates the sanctum on all sides with perpetual lamps, circular gateway lamps, trident lamps, lamp garlands, and various other kinds of lamps. . . . Gifts of cows, sesamum, gold, and grass and the like for cows are presented from offerings made by the local people. Then the night ceremony is performed, using many continually-burning lamps filled with oil and lit with good wicks" (R. Davis 1986, 326). This passage is interesting not only because it describes a ritual context for the use of lamps but also because it refers to gifts made—"by the local people"—to support the lamps; these gifts are remarkably similar to those (of cows, sheep, or gold for lamps) recorded in Chola period inscriptions. The idea that perpetual lamps were used for illumination in the temple, rather than as an element in *pūjā*, is put forward by Talbot (1988b, 144–45) with reference to the similar gifts recorded in Telugu inscriptions of the thirteenth century; she considers them "votive" offerings.

50. Among the Chola period inscriptions, only 25 (4 percent) of the 600 published inscriptions of the four study areas (see note 65) refer to the transfer of merit. Such references are much more common and more explicit in other regions and periods in Indian history. For example, Schopen has found a large number of Buddhist inscriptions that refer to the transfer of the merit from a donation; recipients of the merit are usually the donor's parents or "all beings" or both (1985, 31–43; see also 1991, 9–13). In the case of inscriptions of the Kakatiya period (thirteenth century) from Andhra, Talbot finds that fully half of all donative records refer to the transfer of merit; although in many of these records merit is transferred to the donor's family members, Talbot remarks on what is apparently a new phenomenon in this period of transferring merit to a political superior, the king and/or overlord of the donor (1988a, 195; 1988b, 32, 87; 1991, 333). Among Tamil inscriptions of the post-Chola period, there are frequent and explicit references to the transfer of merit: according to Karashima (1984, xxxii), "there are many Vijayanagara Tamil inscriptions with phrases such as 'for the merit (*puṇṇiyamāka*)' or 'for the health (*tiru mēnikku naṉṟāka*)' of the king or a *nāyaka*." In my area study of Chola period inscriptions, only one of the twenty-five donations that involve a transfer of merit refers to the king as the recipient of the merit of the gift (cf. Heitzman 1985, 319–20; 1987a, 41–42).

Another way in which inscriptions may refer to religious merit is in the context of the formulaic expressions that are on occasion appended to the record of a gift. These include imprecations against those who would obstruct the terms of the grant and phrases that describe the merit attaching to donors and to the protectors of endowments (see Pargiter 1912; Kane 1930–62, 2:861–63, 1271–77; T. Subramaniam 1957, 232–33). A very small proportion of Chola period inscriptions—only about 3 percent of the published inscriptions in the four study areas (see note 65)—include such expressions.

51. The idea that various groups of donors make gifts for different reasons is developed with reference to Sherpa communities in the Himalaya region by Ortner. She suggests that "small" people are motivated by the aim of "valorization"—social recognition and the right to participate in the social game—whereas "big" people make gifts with a view to "legitimation"—securing and maintaining positions of power (1989, 197).

52. Although I am here contrasting inscriptions and texts, inscriptions are, of course, texts of a certain type, as Steven Collins (1991, 1–2) has pointed out. The differences between inscriptions and other sorts of texts are perhaps most striking when inscriptions are compared with Hindu mythological, legal, and ritual texts. Other kinds of literature produced in South Asia—genealogies and chronicles, for example—may have much more in common with inscriptions (Stein 1969, 41–47; Pollock 1989; Collins 1991).

Gregory Schopen stands out as the most vocal proponent of the value of inscriptions for historical research and has, indeed, used these sources with fascinating results in the reconstruction of the history of Indian Buddhism (see, e.g., 1990 and 1991). Although I agree with much of what he has to say, I do not believe that the sharp dichotomy between the character of inscriptions and texts that he insists on is entirely valid. For example, he distinguishes inscriptions from literary sources on the basis of the idea that inscriptions were not meant to be circulated (1991, 1–2, n, 3). This idea does not seem to stand up very well in the case of Chola period inscriptions, whose contents were publicly circulated both in the sense of representing long-term publicity for a donor and in terms of the ceremonial use of the inscriptional text; for example, Stein (1980, 358) suggests that part of the inscribed text may have been read aloud as an element of the ritual of donation, and Heitzman (1995) discusses the role of witnesses, whose names are recorded in inscriptions, as participants in temple ceremonies of gift giving (see also Stein 1980, 360–61).

53. Padma Kaimal's studies of temple patronage and temple styles demonstrate clearly that the early Chola kings did not utilize an "incorporative" strategy, whereby their gifts to temples served to integrate their kingdoms politically or culturally; instead, early Chola temples were built and supported by local, diffuse, and nonroyal patronage (1988, 156–81; 1996, 33–40; cf. Younger 1995, 92–98, 130–36). Although in subsequent times we find a few grand examples of the sponsorship of temples by Chola kings—such as Rajaraja's construction of the Great Temple at Tanjavur at the beginning of the eleventh century and his son Rajendra's building efforts at Gangaikondacholapuram—the vast majority of gifts to temples continued to be made by people who had nothing to do with the Chola court. Royal interest in temples, and the efforts of chiefs and warriors to validate their rule through association with and patronage of temples, are not typical of the Chola period but become increasingly prevalent after 1300, in the Vijayanagar and Nayaka periods.

Although several authors have proposed that even before the Chola period the ritual life of South Indian temples was influenced by a royal model (V. Subramaniam 1980, 31, 35, 44, n. 40; Hardy 1983, 206–9, 225), we do not in fact see very many parallels between temple ceremony and symbolism and what we know of court life in the Chola period. Links between court and temple culture seem to have become especially close beginning in the sixteenth century, and the intermingling of royal and divine symbolism characterized the era of Nayaka rule and of the "little kingdoms" in Tamilnadu in the late precolonial period (Narayana Rao, Shulman, and Subrahmanyam 1992, 58, 88–90, 187–89; Waghorne 1994, 111).

54. This idea of the medieval feudal economy has been elaborated by D. D. Kosambi and R. S. Sharma primarily with reference to North Indian society. Kosambi 1969, 172–75, 196) blames priestly greed, ritualism, superstition encouraged by Brahmans, and the insularity of village society for the inhibition of the "growth of commodity production and hence of culture, beyond a certain level." According to Sharma (1965, 241–42), religious institutions were implicated in the feudalization process—which resulted in self-sufficient village economies, the decreased use of coins, and widespread subjugation of the peasantry—because the donation of land to temples and monasteries undermined agrarian and communal rights, and revenues from crafts and commerce were funneled into the coffers of these institutions.

This kind of analysis has been applied to developments in Tamilnadu in the Chola period and in the immediately preceding centuries by Sharma (1974, 178, 189) himself, by Jha, and by Narayanan and Veluthat. Jha (1974, 207, 212–13) maintains that cash donated to temples in the Chola period was converted into unproductive deposits, and thus did not circulate in the economy, and that the terms of land grants to temples tended to oppress the peasantry by increasing taxation. Narayanan and Veluthat consider early medieval temples to be centers for economic domination by Brahmans; in their view, temples were instrumental, in the course of the *bhakti* period—and as the result of *bhakti* ideology and practice—in establishing feudalism and a highly stratified society (Narayanan and Veluthat 1978, 45–58; Veluthat 1979, 188–91). The idea of a linkage between religious conceptions—in particular, the devotional attitude known as *bhakti*—and feudal relationships in the political and economic sphere has been formulated elsewhere: "In the early stages of Vaiṣṇavism, a sense of the devotee's lowliness is an essential ingredient of the concept of *bhakti*, and seems to reflect the ideology of the ruling classes. The ruling classes of the Gupta period express their *bhakti* to the god in an attitude of service, described as *dāsyabhāva* (the state of servitude) by later theologians" (Jaiswal 1967, 113). Hardy (1983, 460–62) argues that also in South India, the conception of relationship with the god Viṣṇu (or Kṛṣṇa)—and the idea of temple service—was shaped by "feudal" relations in Tamilnadu.

55. "The vast and growing wealth of the temples brought them into more and more intimate business relations with the neighbourhood" (Nilakanta Sastri 1955, 652). Appadorai (1936, 274–301), in his classic study of the economy of medieval South India, describes the variety of these relations—the role of the temple as employer, as landlord, as consumer, as lender, as depository, and as the supporter of handicrafts and land reclamation projects—concluding with an analysis of "the Temple as an agency in breaking the isolation and self-sufficiency of the village."

Various aspects of the temple's economic functions and relations in medieval South India are also treated by Stein (1960), Heitzman (1985, 227–40), and Ludden (1985, 33–34). Ludden, for example, describes the way in which the gifts of merchant guilds to temples might be used to establish a good local reputation and points out that "individual merchants could also cement trade links by grants from one to a temple in the locality of another, because the second man could then contract to supply the goods required for the endowed temple ceremony" (1985, 33).

56. The particular value of inscriptional sources for the reconstruction of women's history has been taken advantage of by a number of scholars who are working outside of the South Asian context. The task undertaken by scholars such as Brooten

(1982), Diakonoff (1986), Kraemer (1988), Lesko (1989), and Clark (1990), who have utilized inscriptions in their exploration of women's history and religious roles in ancient Egypt and western Asia and in the Greco-Roman world, is much more difficult than my own insofar as they must struggle with a very small number of inscriptional references to women. In some ways—particularly in terms of quantity—the inscriptional sources I am dealing with resemble more the kinds of records and archival sources being used in the reconstruction of medieval European women's history (e.g., by Gold 1985). In fact, it seems likely that Indian inscriptions were in many cases copies of documents in record offices (Stein 1980, 353; Inden 1990, 232).

57. Studies of the social history of the Chola period include the work of Appadorai (1936, 23–24, 313–18), Nilakanta Sastri (1955, 55–57), Arokiaswami (1956–57), Stein (1968 and 1980, 207–15), Jaiswal (1974), A. Swaminathan (1978), Kulke (1982), Karashima (1984), Heitzman (1985, 157–63), and Young and Orr (1988). The characterization I have given of society in the Chola period, where caste identities are not the critical factors of social organization, may also apply to later periods and to regions outside Tamilnadu—as is suggested by the work of Perlin (1981), Inden (1986), Dirks (1989), Talbot (1992), and Ludden (1993).

58. I discuss the identities and activities of Brahmans at the temples of Srirangam and Chidambaram in Orr 1995a and 1995c. The inscriptions provide several sorts of clues that people not referred to as *brāhmaṇas* may in fact be Brahmans: they may be described as residents of *brahmadeyas* (*akarams*, *caturvedimaṅgalas*), they may be members of Brahman "assemblies" (*sabhais*, *mulaparusais*), they may bear *gotras* as part of their names, or they may have wives who are referred to as their *brāhmaṇīs*. Some people are referred to as *śivabrāhmaṇas* in the inscriptions, but they tend not to be associated with any of these markers of Brahman identity; they are associated more closely with temple affairs, and it seems likely that they were "Brahmans" by initiation rather than by birth. As Yāmuna, the Śrīvaiṣṇava, alleges: "The Śaivas . . . say, 'merely by entering Consecration one becomes instantly a Brahmin'" (*Āgama Prāmāṇyam* 85, trans. van Buitenen, 71; see also Brunner 1964).

That such a thing was considered possible—although frowned on by the orthodox—and that the inscriptions lay so little stress on Brahman identity, bear witness to the fact that in Chola period society there was a very different notion of the nature and importance of the boundary between Brahman and non-Brahman than that which has been formed, in popular and scholarly circles, in more recent times in South India (Jaiswal 1974; see also Bayly 1989, 27, 48, 56–58, 65–70).

59. The inscriptions employ the spelling *veḷḷāḷa*, which I adopt here; in contemporary Tamil usage, the spelling is *vēḷāḷa* or *vēḷḷāḷa* (with long *e*). According to Susan Bayly, even in the eighteenth and early nineteenth centuries, "Vellala affiliation was as vague and uncertain as that of most other south Indian caste groups"; *veḷḷāḷa* identity was a source of prestige and thus "there were any number of groups who sought to claim Vellala status for themselves," including traders and petty cultivators, as well as large-scale landholders (1989, 411). Irschick (1994, 191–94, 200–1) discusses the processes through which, in the course of the nineteenth century, *veḷḷāḷa*s came to be identified as "authentic Dravidians" and the "original" cultivators of the land.

Among scholars, the argument for the antiquity of the *veḷḷāḷa* community, as a dominant and distinct social group in existence from the early part of the first millenium, seems to rest on the assumption that the term *vēḷir*, found in Tamil poetry of the Cankam period, means *veḷḷāḷas* or the chiefs of the *veḷḷāḷas* (Champakalakshmi 1975–76, 119–22; Subrahmanian 1966, 254, 280–81). The "Poruḷ" section of *Tolkāppiyam*, which dates from the fifth or sixth century, contains a passage (vv. 625–39) that outlines the occupations of *antaṇar, aracar, vaicikaṉ*, and *vēḷāṇmāntar*, and later commentators, as well as more recent scholars, have understood this passage as referring to Brahmans, kings, *vaiśya*s, and *veḷḷāḷas* (Kanakasabhai, cited by Jaiswal 1974, 130; Subrahmanian 1966, 258–59, 280). However, the term *vēḷāṇmāntar* is not necessarily the equivalent of *veḷḷāḷa*, and five centuries later the tenth-century lexicon *Piṅkalanikaṇṭu* does not consistently identify *veḷḷāḷas* as the "fourth caste" but informs us that this term is a synonym of both *vaiciyar* (Skt. *vaiśya*) and of *cūttirar* (Skt. *śūdra*) (*Piṅkalanikaṇṭu* 773 and 780). Another lexicon, *Tivākaram*, which is thought to be of slightly earlier date than *Piṅkalanikaṇṭu*, lists the six kinds of work of the *veḷḷāḷas*: agriculture, tending animals, trade, playing on musical instruments, spinning and weaving, and serving the twice-born (MTL, 3843–44). The references from these two lexicons suggest that neither a definition based on *varṇa* nor one based on occupation had become fixed by the beginning of the Chola period. This should be contrasted with Stein's (1980, 84, 448) characterization of the *veḷḷāḷas* of the early Chola period as being *sat* ("clean") *śūdras*, having a ritual status second only to that of Brahmans, and as firmly connected with cultivating the land and being, indeed, the dominant peasant group.

60. It has been suggested by some scholars that merchants were "outsiders" in Chola period society or in the communities that grew up around temples. Reiniche, for example, draws a sharp distinction between insider (agriculturalist) and outsider (merchant) donors at Tiruvannamalai, in North Arcot district: "le vrai sacrifiant se définit par rapport à la terre et l'ordre social tel qu'il doit être par rapport à la localité" (1985, 111). Stein (1980, 78–79, 84–89, 213–14, 227–29) contrasts craftsmen and merchants—regarded with suspicion in local politics, as they were landless, itinerant, urban, and Jain or Buddhist—with agriculturalists, whose ties to the land and to Brahmans and Hindu institutions were central to the creation and articulation of Chola period society, polity, and religion. These characterizations of merchants—and the dichotomies between merchant and agriculturalist, urban and rural, and heterodox and Hindu—do not appear to me to be borne out by the evidence of the inscriptions, which shows, in fact, that merchants were integrated into local society, active as patrons of local temples, and influential in local politics (see also Hall 1980, 4, 51–63, 190; 1981, 395–96, 400–1).

61. Given the relative paucity of evidence and the absence of detailed study of these phenomena, my characterization of Chola period society is somewhat conjectural. Others would present a different picture. Heitzman (1985, 157–63), for instance, considers that in the Chola period *paṟaiyar* "were practically if not legally attached to the lands and wills of the landowners and cultivators who controlled the land," in what amounted to a system of serfdom (see also Jha 1974 and Hanumanthan 1980). Other discussions of hierarchy in Chola period society and of changes that took place in the course of the period include those of Appadorai (1936, 23–24, 313–18), Nilakanta Sastri (1955, 555–57), Arokiaswami (1956–57), A. Swaminathan (1978), and Young and Orr (1988).

62. See Orr 1995a and 1995c for discussions of the administration of the temples at Srirangam and Chidambaram.

The word *māheśvara* (and its Tamil variants, e.g., *māhecuvarar*), is derived from the name of Śiva, Māheśvara, the Great Lord; *māheśvaras* are devotees of Śiva. In Chola period inscriptions, the word *māheśvara* is found most often with the prefix *pal* ("many, several, diverse"), reduced by *sandhi* to *paṉ*; the term *paṉmāheśvara* is used to denote a corporate group that oversaw the execution of the terms of a grant to a Śiva temple and undertook the protection (*rakṣai*) of the arrangements on an ongoing basis. The parallel term in grants to temples dedicated to Viṣṇu is *śrīvaiṣṇava*.

63. A thorough study of the evolution of South Indian *maṭhas* has not yet been undertaken, although some valuable and relevant information can be found in the works of Nilakanta Sastri (1955, 628–34, 650–52), Rajamanikkam (1962), Lorenzen (1972, 165–66), Gurumurthy (1979, 13–25, 70–73), Stein (1980, 230–41), Champakalakshmi (1981a, 421), Suthanthiran (1986), K. Swaminathan (1990, 117–22), Koppedrayer (1991), and Kulke (1993, 208–239). I plan to pursue this topic in detail; some of my preliminary findings have been presented in Orr 1994b, 1995a, and 1995c.

64. The discussions of human agency in history that have been particularly helpful to me are those of Ortner (1989, 11–18, 194–95, 198–99), Inden (1990, 18–19, 23–24, 26), Comaroff and Comaroff (1991, 8–9, 14–17, 28–29), and Bourdieu and Wacquant (1992, 106–109).

65. In my area studies I have read the Tamil texts of all the relevant published inscriptions from each of these four study areas, using as a guide *A Concordance of the Names in the Cōḻa Inscriptions* (Karashima, Subbarayalu, and Matsui 1978). The total number of inscriptions used in my area studies is 600; over 2,000 individuals are named in these inscriptions, 134 women and 1,893 men. The number of temple men named in these inscriptions, making up my "temple men" sample group, is 219—118 Brahmans and 101 non-Brahmans. Reliance on the *Concordance* has imposed certain limitations on the data in the area studies: the *Concordance* has been constructed only with reference to inscriptions published before 1975 and to those dated in the regnal year of a Chola king. Thus, for example, inscriptions from the very end of the period, after the fall of the Chola dynasty in 1279, would not be considered.

66. Excluding three very long inscriptions from the Rājarājeśvara temple in Tanjavur (SII 2.66, 2.94, and 2.95), this sample of "all women" consists of 577 women (79 of whom are temple women), out of a total of 8,373 individuals named (7 percent). As I have described in the previous note, the manner in which the *Concordance* has been compiled introduces certain particularities into this sample group. In addition, the lack of inclusion in the *Concordance* of information from inscriptions found in the far southern and western districts of Tamilnadu means that these regions are not represented in the sample group of "all women."

Notes to Chapter 2

1. Of the 134 references that exhibit feature a ("temple woman" terms), 22 (16 percent) also show feature b and 96 (72 percent) show feature c. The fact that the "temple woman" terms occur particularly frequently in conjunction with feature c—the mention of association with a particular temple—is perhaps due to the ease with which the most commonly used terms can be combined with the indicative prefix *i-* to produce such forms as *ittevaraṭiyāḷ* ("devotee of *this* god") and *ittevaṉār makaḷ* ("daughter of *this* god").

2. The following table shows the districts in which ten or more references were found, how many references there are, and the percentage of the total number of references in each district that refer to two or more of the definitional features.

	Number of references	Percentage with two or more features
Chingleput	22	68
North Arcot	19	84
South Arcot	24	71
Tiruchirappalli	21	62
Tanjavur	46	57
Tirunelveli	16	94
Madurai and Ramnad	10	80

3. The following table shows how much overlapping there is between definitional feature a ("temple woman" terms) and the other two features of the definition (b, functions in or support by the temple, or c, identification with reference to a specific temple or deity) in each of the four subperiods.

Percentage of a	*Also in b*	*Also in c*	*In either b or c*
Chola 1 (a = 19)	0	84	84
Chola 2 (a = 12)	8	58	67
Chola 3 (a = 35)	34	63	97
Chola 4 (a = 68)	13	79	87

4. In several places in this book I present information about queens, drawn in most cases from an earlier study of royal women's donative activities in the Chola period (Orr 1992). For that study, I collected 198 inscriptions that refer to queens, three-quarters of whom are Chola queens. I used the *Concordance* (Karashima, Subbarayalu, and Matsui 1978) as my primary guide in locating these inscriptions, which represent only a fraction of the total number of Chola period inscriptions that refer to queens. I have also examined the activities and identities of queens in a more recent study based on the detailed analysis of the representation of women in the inscriptions of eight study areas, dating from AD 700–1700 (Orr forthcoming b).

5. I have found women whom I would class as palace women in ninety-five Chola period inscriptions. The term *poki* (from Sanskrit *bhogi*) is used to refer to palace women in nine of these inscriptions, and this term probably ought to be translated "concubine." A sexual relationship may also be implied when the term *aṇukki* is applied to a palace woman, as it is in sixteen inscriptions, but this is not necessarily the case, given the use of the parallel male term *aṇukkaṉ* to denote a male "intimate" of the king, who may frequently hold titles of high rank (Heitzman 1985, 343–44 and 370, n. 56). The term most frequently used for palace women (in forty-one inscriptions) is *peṇṭāṭṭi*, a word formed by the addition to *peṇ* ("woman") of *āḷ* (a verbal root meaning "to rule, to receive, to control, to maintain," or a noun meaning "man, servant, slave, laborer") and the feminine ending *-ti* (MTL 254, 2858). This combination of words would seem to connote a woman in some way dependent on or subject to another. According to the *Tamil Lexicon*, the meaning of *peṇṭāṭṭi*, as it is found in Tamil literature, is "woman" or "wife," and we occasionally find this meaning in inscriptional usage, but more typically the term seems to mean "woman servant" or "attendant" and is most often applied to palace women.

In twenty-six inscriptions, palace women are associated with *veḷams*. *Veḷams* were palaces or royal establishments of various kinds in the capital, where numerous royal servants resided (Nilakanta Sastri 1955, 449–50; Heitzman 1985, 343–44). The identification of some of these *veḷams* as kitchen or bathing establishments gives us our only clue about what types of service and attendance palace women may have performed. Given the prominence of palace women in Chola period inscriptions as women of wealth and rank, it seems unlikely that they had menial functions. The palace establishments cannot be considered "harems," insofar as men as well as women were said to belong to the *veḷams* or *parivāras* of kings. Also it should be remembered that palace women were, in a quarter of all references to them, associated with queens.

That palace women had, on occasion, very high status is illustrated by the case of Paravai, the *aṇukki* of Rajendra I. Paravai made a number of very generous donations to several temples, one of which is recorded in SII 4.223 (translated in chapter 4), and on several occasions made such donations together with Rajendra or made endowments for his merit (Ponnusamy 1972, 26, 32–35, 51). Another indication of the power and position of palace women is the fact that we have records of several grants made by men who transferred the merit of their gifts to palace women (e.g., SII 23.356).

6. The term *koyiṟpiḷḷaikaḷ* is found not only in these inscriptions, in what appears to be a Jain context, but also in the Hindu *bhakti* literature of the same period. The Śaiva poet-saint Māṇikkavācakar, in his ninth-century poem *Tiruvempāvai*, gives a description of the early-morning activities of girls who were undertaking a vow, and refers to these young women as *kōyiṟpiṇāppiḷḷaikaḷ*, "female children of the temple" (*Tiruvācakam* 7.10). The internal evidence of the poem does not support the idea that these girls were attached to the temple in a formal sense (see Orr and Young 1986; cf. Hardy 1978, 138; 1983, 477; and Kersenboom 1987, 22–23), but a comparison of the inscriptional and literary use of this term clearly shows its lack of mooring to any particular sectarian milieu.

It is possible to identify as Jain the *koyil* referred to in one of the two inscriptions considered here because the inscription (SII 3.92) mentions, in addition to the *koyiṟpiḷḷaikaḷ*, individuals who are clearly Jain religious women, since they are termed *māṇākkiyār* and *kurattis*. In the case of the other inscription (SII 14.40), the identification of the *koyil* as Jain is not as certain but is suggested by the place where the inscription was found.

7. Jain *paḷḷis* combined several institutional functions, including cultic activities; education; monastic organization; and the provision of food and shelter for itinerant ascetics, teachers, and pilgrims. There is at least one case in which the term *paḷḷi* refers in inscriptional use to a Buddhist institution, but I have not come across such usage in what would be considered a Hindu context. The Hindu *maṭha*, however, as it developed in the course of the Chola period, bears a very close resemblance to the earlier Jain *paḷḷi* (Orr 1998 and forthcoming a).

8. Several authors have assumed that Pañcavaṉ-mātevi was a *tevaṉār makaḷ* in the sense of being the daughter of a human lord rather than the "daughter of God." According to Balambal, the *tevaṉār* in this case, the "Lord of Avanikantaṟpappuram," is a Paluvetturaiyar chief, who seems to have been related to several other Chola queens in addition to being Pañcavaṉ-mātevi's father (1976, 81–84; see also Balasubrahmanyam 1975, 43–44, 243ff, 270–71). Although there is certainly the possibility of admitting this interpretation—given the ambiguities of the term *tevaṉār makaḷ*, which will be discussed later in this chapter—the fact that the name of the temple deity is the Lord of Avanikantaṟpappuram and that the tenth-century *tevaṉār makaḷ*, Nakkaṉ Akkāranaṅkaiyār, is clearly identified as the daughter of the Lord of "this temple" (*ittaḷi*) suggests to me that Nakkaṉ Pañcavaṉ-mātevi had a similar status. It remains to be explained, however, why there is an overlap between queens and temple women *only* in the case of this one temple.

9. For the general characterization of *devadāsīs* as having been, throughout history, closely linked with kings and the royal court, see Gaston (1980, 69–73) and Jordan (1989, 61–72). The interpretations of the ritual significance of the *devadāsīs* that have been developed by Marglin and by Kersenboom depend in important respects on the notion of a ritual and artistic culture shared by temple and court (see, e.g., Marglin 1985b, 26, 117, 127, 143–5, 174–75, 182–83; Kersenboom 1987, 15–16, 27, 37–38, 47–48, 205–6), yet these authors acknowledge that in Orissa and in South India this culture did not begin to develop and involve the *devadāsī* until the seventeenth century (Marglin 1985b, 124–26, 130, 134; Kersenboom 1987, 64–65, 84, n. 299). Narayana Rao, Shulman, and Subrahmanyam (1992, 58, 183–89, 217) have recently provided a compelling description and analysis of the development of this culture in the South Indian Nayaka courts of the sixteenth and seventeenth centuries, where the symbolic domains of temple and palace were fused and "courtesans and *devadāsīs* merge[d] into a single role." On the importance of *devadāsīs* in the courts of the "little kings" of Pudukkottai and Ramnad, in nineteenth-century South India, see Waghorne (1994, 25, 63) and Price (1996, 35, 65–70).

10. There are two eleventh-century Tamil inscriptions from a goddess temple in Kolar district, in present-day Karnataka, that describe the support given to temple women—including twenty-four *tevaraṭiyār*, four *yokinikaḷ* (*yoginīs*), seven *peṇpiḷaikaḷ* (girls), a *kanniyā* (virgin), and a group of singers and dancers, some of whom may have been female—as part of the expenses for a festival (EC 10.Kl106d and Kl108). That this is the only case of a link between temple women and a Śākta temple in the Chola period indicates the distinction between the Chola period *devādasī* system and that which prevails in western Karnataka and Maharashtra today, where giris and young women are dedicated to goddess temples, particularly temples of the goddess Yellammā (see note 28 in chapter 1).

I have already discussed the three inscriptions in which women classified as temple women are said to receive support from Jain institutions; there is a fourth inscription (SITI 28) in which a *tevaṉār makaḷ* (who, interestingly, is identified as the wife of a *tevaraṭiyār*) acts as a donor to a Jain temple.

Some scholars have suggested that the conception of Śiva as paired with Śakti in Śaiva doctrine has encouraged a feminine presence in Śaiva temple ritual (Mohan Khokar, personal communication, 29 November 1983). Given that the idea of "coupleness" is equally well developed in the South Indian Vaiṣṇava tradition, where Śrī and Viṣṇu are the divine pair, it is not clear that the doctrinal differences are very great in this regard. It is worth noting, as well, that women are mentioned as participants in temple ritual just as frequently in the Vaiṣṇava Agamic texts, both Pāñcarātra and Vaikhānasa, as they are in the Śaiva Āgamas (Orr 1994c). Where differences between the Śaiva and Vaiṣṇava traditions in South India can be seen to have developed is in the organization of temple service and the structure of authority; for example, singing and accompanying gesture (*abhinaya*) came to be the province of Brahman men in Vaiṣṇava temples, whereas in Śaiva temples women and non-Brahman men took on these roles. But even with respect to institutional structures and women's place within them, differences between Śaiva and Vaiṣṇava temples are not very great (Orr 1995a).

11. The single exception I have come across is a reference to *dēvadāsīgaḷ* ("devotee" or "slave of God") in a Kannada inscription of the twelfth century (EC 7.Sh97), referring to women who received support in a Jain temple. The relationship between the terms *devadāsī* and *tevaraṭiyāḷ* will be discussed later in this chapter.

12. For the non-Tamil inscriptions, I have used a definition for temple women that is essentially the same as the one I have used for the Tamil inscriptions, except that there are no particular terms I consider to be definitional features. To locate and understand the contents of these non-Tamil inscriptions, I have relied on abstracts, summaries, translations, and secondary sources. In table 2.4, I classify some inscriptions from North India, Karnataka, and Andhra Pradesh as utilizing "other" terms for temple women simply because I was not able to find and read the original texts of these inscriptions, written in Sanskrit, Kannada, Telugu, and other languages.

13. The Kannada term *sūḷe* is clearly related to the Sanskrit *śūlā*, meaning "a harlot, prostitute" (MW, 1086). In inscriptions from Karnataka this term is usually used with reference to temple women, although there are a few cases where it is applied to the "concubine" of an important man, rather than the "prostitute" of the temple. The Tamil equivalent—*cūḷai* (*Piṅkalanikaṇṭu* 944)—is not commonly found even in literary usage and does not seem to appear at all in inscriptions.

14. In my study of women's ritual roles in the Śaiva and Vaiṣṇava Āgamas (Orr 1994c), I found that in about half of all the references to women's participation in temple services and celebrations, the women were referred to as prostitutes. The most commonly used term for "prostitute" in this context is *gaṇikā*, connoting a prostitute of beauty and culture, a "courtesan" (MW, 343; Sternbach 1965, 199–202, 206, 212–14; *Kāmasūtra* 1.3.20). As I have noted in Chapter 1, it is not clear in these Agamic references whether the women involved in temple rituals are really temple women—that is, women regularly employed in or formally connected to the temple—or whether the *gaṇikās* mentioned in the Āgamas as participating in temple ritual are prostitutes but not temple women.

Although the Āgamas seem to project the idea of the overlapping identities and ritual functions of temple women and prostitutes—and we find a few other stray hints of a connection in the accounts of Arab travelers to northwestern India and in Sanskrit literature, as we have seen in the first chapter—it is difficult to link this literary imaging of the temple prostitute with the situation revealed in the medieval inscriptions of Karnataka or elsewhere. The literary sources are scattered and extremely diverse in their dates, provenances, and genres. They paint several different types of portraits of female temple service, none of which emphasizes the prostitute image to the exclusion of other identities. There is little evidence connecting the Āgamas with ritual practice in medieval Karnataka. Finally, there is a lack of correspondance between the Agamic texts and the Kannada inscriptions in the "prostitute" terminology employed: we find the term *gaṇikā*, on the one hand, and the Sanskrit-derived *sūḷe*, on the other.

15. The supposition that *pātrās* were performers is based more on the meaning of the term itself than on the evidence of the inscriptions, which do not apply the term particularly to temple women with ritual tasks that involved song and dance. The inscriptions do not support the statement of Parasher and Naik that "the word *pātrā* is always used to describe only the dancing girls and singing girls" (1986, 66). These authors also seem to consider, with very little justification, that *pātrā* means "prostitute." After saying that this is a secondary meaning of *pātrā* that developed over time, they develop their argument that temple women in Karnataka *were* "courtesans of God" on the basis of the use of this term, along with *sūḷe*, in the Kannada inscriptions: "It is specifically noted in some of the inscriptions that the temple girls were meant for the enjoyment of the god. . . . Other instances extend this enjoyment to important personages of the temple. . . . The very meaning of the term *sūḷe* and *pātrā* . . . are indicative of this role" (1986, 66, 76–78).

16. *Tevaraṭiyār*, as a nonsectarian term, can be contrasted with a number of terms used in the North Indian devotional context, such as *parama-bhāgavata* and *parama-māheśvara*, denoting the devotees of Viṣṇu and Śiva, respectively (Jaiswal 1967, 159–60, 203–7; Pathak 1960, 1).

17. The idea that honor and reverence are to be offered to the feet of a deity or of a superior, senior, or holy person is widespread throughout India, but the expression of this concept and the exploitation of its symbolism are particularly important in Tamil devotional literature. Early examples are found in the Tamil poems *Tirumuṟukāṟṟuppaṭai* (4; 62–66; 250–52; 279) and *Paripāṭal* (5.77–80; 9.83– 85; 21.68–69), which may date from the sixth century (Kandiah 1973, 112–13; Zvelebil 1977, 252). In these two texts, the feet of the god Murukaṉ are sought as the object of worship and as refuge and goal; salvation is defined as the shade of his feet, and is longed for by all his devotees.

18. The Āḻvārs and Nāyaṉmārs do use "slave" imagery in describing their relationship to God. They call themselves and other devotees *toṇṭar* ("slaves") or *āṭceyvōm* ("we who have been made your slaves"—e.g., *Tiruppāvai* 29). They perform the labor of slaves (*aṭimai toḻil, akattaṭimai*) or "lowly service" (*kuṟṟēval*) as a way of worshiping God (*Periyatirumoḻi* 2.1.1; *Tēvāram* 7.9.6; 7.30.8; see also Orr and Young 1986, 28–32). They have been "enslaved" (*āṭkoḷ*) by God—although as Yocum (1982, 189) points out, *āṭkoḷ* could equally mean "possession" by God. The notion of slavery in its literal sense was not foreign to these poet-saints, but the range of meanings most central to their use of the term and the concept of *aṭiyaṉ* are those related to service and surrender to a supreme and sovereign power rather than those associated with slavery as a social institution.

19. A term related to (and frequently confused with) *aṭiyār*, which has the same honorific connotations and is often encountered in inscriptional contexts similar to the one just described, is *aṭikaḷmār*. Like *aṭiyār*, it is derived from the Tamil word for "foot" (*aṭi*) and may refer to the habit of devotees or ascetics of wandering on foot (Sethu Pillai 1974, 25). In inscriptional use, the term is first encountered in the southern district of Tirunelveli, in the sixth to eighth centuries, referring to Jain ascetics. Beginning in the eighth century, the term is used to refer to deities (e.g., in SII 2.99 and PCM 8); in the ninth century, it refers collectively to eminent religious Hindus, as well as Jains; and by the tenth century it is used more generally as an honorific title and as part of the names of notable people (Velu Pillai 1976, 55, 78n, 232–33, 462, 491n).

Minakshi (1977, 214; also Khokar 1979, 37; Sadasivan 1993, 38–40) identifies as female dancers the *aṭikaḷmār*—who, along with Brahmans, *brahmacārins* (Ta. *māṇis*) and temple servants (*paṇiceymakkaḷ*), were to be offered food during a festival—in a ninth-century Pallava inscription from Tanjore district (ARE 303 of 1901 = SII 7.525). This identification, however, seems rather doubtful. It is more likely that these *aṭikaḷmār* were honored devotees, as were the *aṭiyār* who were similarly offered food in early Chola period inscriptions.

20. Another development in the later Chola period inscriptions is the appearance of the term *aṭimai*, yet another word derived from the Tamil *aṭi* ("foot"). Although *aṭimai* is used by the *bhakti* poets, it is not found in inscriptional usage before the twelfth century. In inscriptions of the later Chola period, however, it becomes the term most commonly used to mean "slave"; it is encountered in that sense more frequently than is *aṭiyār* and does not seem to share with the term *aṭiyār* any ambiguity of meaning.

21. The use of women as personal or domestic servants, with the status of slaves, is documented from a very early period in the history of North India. *Dāsīs* were earlier and more frequently so employed than were their male counterparts, *dāsas* (R. Sharma 1980, 25–26, 50–52, 103–4). In the *Atharva Veda* and the *Brāhmaṇas*, the generosity of kings and chiefs who made gifts of *dāsīs* is praised (Macdonnell and Keith [1912] 1958, 1:356–58; Kane 1930–62, 2:837–39; Upadhyay 1974, 117–19; Thapar 1976, 39–41). Women who had the status of slaves, sometimes said to number in the hundreds, appear in early Buddhist texts, in the *Mahābhārata*, and in the Purāṇas as domestic servants and personal attendants to chiefs, rulers, priests, and Brahmans (Kane 1930–62, 2:182; Meyer 1952, 508–9; Chanana 1960, 46–52, 65–72, 127; R. Sharma 1980, 50). The occasional inscriptional references to *dāsīs*—found, for example, in tenth- and eleventh-century records from northwestern and central India and from the Deccan—depict them similarly, as anonymous, menial workers of low and dependent status (EI 1.41; HAS 5; Vogel 1911, 164–69).

The use of the term *dāsī* to signify "prostitute" is found in Sanskrit literature dating from the beginning of the Christian Era, in such texts as *Yājñavālkyasmṛti*, *Arthaśāstra*, and *Kāmasūtra* (Sternbach 1942, #34 and #68; 1965, 208; *Arthaśāstra* 1963, 183). That *dāsīs* were concubines or bore the children of their masters is clear from Vedic and early Buddhist literature; and the later *smṛti* literature deals in detail with the problem of the status of the *dāsīputra*, the son of the *dāsī* (Chanana 1960, 19–20; Mazumdar 1978, 112–15; U. Chakravarti 1983, 9). The social conditions and attitudes that made it possible to consider one's own *dāsīs* as sexually available seems to have led to the application of the word *dāsī* to other kinds of women who were sexually available, especially to common prostitutes rather than courtesans.

22. See *Pādatāḍitaka* and the other *Caturbhāṇī* plays in Ghosh's edition. Some Jain and Buddhist women with devotional *dāsī* names are mentioned in inscriptions: Jain nuns, disciples, and laywomen with the names Jīnadāsī and Arhadāsī appear in inscriptions from Mathura of the first or second century A.D. (A. Chatterjee 1978, 61–63); and a Buddhist woman named Saghadāsī ("devotee of the *saṅgha*") is referred to in an inscription from Amaravati in Andhra Pradesh, dating from the fourth century A.D. or earlier (EI 10 Lüder's List #1218).

In Chola period inscriptions, men bear names with devotional or sectarian (especially Vaiṣṇava) connotations, using the suffix *-dāsa* (Ta. *tācaṉ*, *tātar*): Śivadāsaṉ, Periyakoyildāsar, Nārāyaṇadāsaṉ, Śrīgopāladāsar, and Śrīvaiṣṇavadāsar (see Orr 1995c, 136, n. 29). I have located only a single example of a female name of this type, that of the palace woman Vaṉtoṇṭattāti, whose name means "devotee of the [Śaiva] saints" (ARE 520 of 1921). It seems that in Tamil usage, the significance of *dāsī* (Ta. *tāci*, *tāti*) is closely allied to the range of meanings this word conveys in Sanskrit, which hardly ever includes religious connotations. The word is very rarely found in Tamil inscriptions, and in medieval Tamil and Manipravala (mixed Tamil-Sanskrit) literature, it is used to mean "maidservant," "menial servant," or "prostitute" [*Cilappatikāram* 6.125; *Piṅkalanikaṇṭu* 936, 3625; *Āṟāyirappaṭi Kuruparampparā Prapāvam*, 54; *Divyasūricaritam* 6.28; *Kuruparamparā Prapāvam* (Hardy 1983, 475); *Cūṭāmaṇinikaṇṭu* (MTL, 1825)].

23. Inscriptions from Bengal and Orissa, of the twelfth and thirteenth centuries, extol the generosity of kings who donated hundreds of women to temples (EI 1.35; EI 6.17B; SII 6.1197), and the twelfth-century Kashmiri chronicle *Rājataraṅgiṇī* (1.151) describes similar royal endowments.

David Shulman (1985, 311) maintains that "Tamil literary tradition records many stories about *veśyā*s [prostitutes] in the Chola court," but it seems unlikely that these stories were composed in the Chola era itself. The courtly ethos of the Chola period is of a character markedly different from the royal style of both North India in the same era and Tamilnadu in subsequent times. The emphasis on military valor, the defeat of enemies, and territorial conquest in Chola court poetry and royal *praśastis* contrasts strikingly with the depiction of the king in terms of the erotic appeal and virility—and power over a slave or harem woman—that one finds elsewhere. As we have seen, references in Chola period inscriptions to palace women indicate their high status, and do not employ *dāsī* or "prostitute" terminology (see note 5).

24. Included in the figures for and the discussion of the term *tevaraṭiyār* are several other synonymous terms: *emperumāṉaṭiyār, tevaṭicci, āḻvāṉaṭiyāḷ, tirunamattaṭiyār*, and *tevaka aṭiyāḷ*. Their meanings are identical to *tevaraṭiyār*, and the chronological patterns of their distribution and application are similar to those of *tevaraṭiyār*. The total number of inscriptions (154) that refer to temple women (table 2.4) includes 8 that use the term *emperumāṉaṭiyār*, 3 that use *tevaṭicci*, and 1 each of the other three terms. The term *emperumāṉaṭiyār* replaces the *tevar* in *tevaraṭiyār* with *emperumāṉ* ("our Lord"), a name applied to the god Viṣṇu. Three of the 8 *emperumāṉaṭiyār* references are from the first subperiod and apply the term to a group of people, which may or may not have included women. Of the 5 remaining inscriptions, which date from the later Chola period, 4 apply the term *emperumāṉaṭiyār* to individual women. Two of these women were donors to the temple, one was the relative of a donor, and one (ARE 277 of 1910) was the mother of a woman who had attempted to sell the land rights assigned to her by the local Brahman assembly (*sabhai*) and was consequently fined. All 8 of the inscriptions that refer to *emperumāṉaṭiyār* are from the northern and middle regions of Tamilnadu; 4 come from Tirupati, the important Vaiṣṇava center in Chittoor district, in the far north of the Tamil country. After A.D. 1300 the term gained currency at Vaiṣṇava temples farther south, while it continued to be important in the north, particularly at Tirupati.

Another term that is equivalent to *tevaraṭiyāḷ* is *tevaṭicci*, found especially in inscriptions from Kerala, where the *aṭiyāḷ* of *tevaraṭiyāḷ* is replaced by *aṭicci*, a Tamil word meaning "devoted maidservant" (MTL, 2064), which exhibits a phonology characteristic of Malayalam. That *aṭicci* has the same meaning as *aṭiyāḷ* is strongly suggested by the use of *aṭicci* to refer to a woman who was the Chera queen's "retainer" (SII 14.150; Tirumalai 1980, 16). I do not agree with the view of M. G. S. Narayanan (1973, 46) that *tevaṭicci* is a translation of the Sanskrit *devadāsī*; I regard this term as the Kerala Tamil version of *tevaraṭiyāḷ*. The term is found in three Tamil inscriptions of the later Chola period from Travancore (the southern part of Kerala). In two (TAS 2.3 and TAS 5.1), the *tevaṭiccis* are described as temple servants; and in the third (TAS 1, 289–91), the *tevaṭicci* was a woman who acted as a patron of the temple.

In an inscription of the early twelfth century from Kanchipuram in Chingleput district, an *āḻvāṉaṭiyāḷ* is said to have made a donation to a Viṣṇu temple (SII 4.134). *Āḻvāṉ* or *āḻvār*, used especially by Vaiṣṇavas, means "lord" (in Chola period inscriptions, this term is more frequently used as a name of God than to refer to the Vaiṣṇava *bhakti* poet-saints); thus *āḻvāṉaṭiyāḷ* is equivalent to *tevaraṭiyāḷ*. A donor in a thirteenth-century inscription from Tanjavur district is described as the daughter of a woman who was one of the *tirunamattaṭiyār* of the temple (SII 23.473). This term means, literally, "devotee of the holy name." A thirteenth-century inscription from South Arcot records a donation made on behalf of the granddaughter of a *tevaka aṭiyāḷ*, a "devotee of the divine" (SII 26.437).

25. I have found only four inscriptions—one in each of the four subperiods—that use the term *tevaraṭiyār* to refer to an individual male. There are, in contrast, 121 inscriptions that apply the term to individual women: 4 in the first subperiod, 6 in the second, 43 in the third, and 68 in the last. Three inscriptions, dating from the second and third subperiods, make it clear that a group of *tevaraṭiyār* associated with temple service consists of women (EC 10.Kl106; EZ 4.24; SII 14.132).

26. See Orr 1994b, and note 62 in chapter 1, with references there.

27. We never find women referred to as members of any of these groups in Chola period inscriptions. What may be at issue here is the problem of initiation for women. Membership in these groups was probably the result either of sectarian initiation or priestly consecration. Women's lack of access to full initiation is indicated, often rather obliquely, in various Agamic texts. "The participation of women in worshiping Śiva, as these texts prescribe it, always requires a mediating male, either an initiated husband performing domestic *pūjā* or a consecrated priest administering temple worship" (R. Davis 1991, 40–41). The statement found in many Āgamas, both Śaiva and Vaiṣṇava, that women are eligible for *dīkṣā* (e.g., in *Jayākhya Saṃhitā* 16.2) is almost invariably qualified elsewhere in these texts: either women have access only to the lower rungs of the ladder of initiation (Dagens 1979, 29–30 and 72–73, n. 24, citing Śaiva Agamic commentaries and digests); there is a separate ladder for women (Gupta 1983, 71–73, citing the Vaiṣṇava *Jayākhya Saṃhitā* 16.61); or the rituals of initiation are modified for women, usually by eliminating *mantra*s (*Pauṣkara Saṃhitā* 27.123–146; R. Davis 1991, 40). In discussions of women's eligibility for *dīkṣā*, the Āgamas frequently class women together with *śūdras*, or with children and the old, sick, and feeble-minded.

28. I have found thirty-two inscriptions that use the terms *tevaṉār makaḷ* or *tevaṉār makaṉ* or variants such as *tevaṉār makkaḷ* ("children of God") or *mahādeva makaḷ* ("daughter of the Great God"). Twenty-two of these inscriptions refer to women and eight to men. In only two cases (where the gender-neutral *makkaḷ* is used or where the inscription is quite fragmentary) is it impossible to ascertain the sex of the people to whom the term is applied.

29. The clues in inscriptions that are helpful in determining whether a *tevaṉār* is a man or a god include: the information about whether the *tevaṉār* is the recipient of donations (in which case he is very probably a deity) or whether he is identified as someone's son or figures in another inscription as a donor (in which case we can assume he is a man); the use of the honorific plural forms *makaṉār* or *makaḷār* for "son" or "daughter," which are most often associated with human *tevaṉār* parentage; and the description of a *tevaṉār* as the lord of a *koyil* or *taḷi* (temple), which indicates his identity as a deity.

30. Another, later, example of this usage is a sixteenth-century inscription that records the order of the deity (the female saint Āṇṭāḷ worshiped as the consort of Viṣṇu), in which she addresses her command to "our son" (*nāṉ kumāraṉ*), apparently the king (SII 23.511). In the Chola period, we find a related expression in an inscription in which the king is referred to (by the god) as "our friend" (ARE 554 of 1904).

31. Four inscriptions refer to *tevaṉār makaḷs* at Tiruvidaimarudur (SII 19.92; SII 19.92A; SII 23.205; SII 23.223); three inscriptions refer to *tevaṉār makaḷs* (ARE 122 of 1931; SII 13.103; SII 19.148) and three to *tevaṉār makaṉs* (SII 5.619; SII 13.350; SII 19.361) at Tiruchatturai; and four inscriptions refer to *tevaṉār*

*makaḷ*s (SII 3.184; SII 3.190; SII 5.1364; SII 5.1366) and one to *tevaṉār makaṉs* (SII 5.1372) at Takkolam.

32. In A. Srinivasan's study of twentieth-century temple women in Tamilnadu, she states: "As a consequence of the fairly permanent, singular and public nature of the relationship between a *dasi* and her patron, it was absolutely clear who the father of her children was" (1984, 194).

33. On Tamil *bhakti* as an expression of romantic and erotic love, see Dorai Rangaswamy (1958, 1238–52), Ramanujan (1981), Hardy (1983), and Cutler (1987).

34. Little attention has been paid to the parent-child relationship as it is enunciated by the Āḻvārs and Nāyaṉmārs, although Lynn Ate's (1978) study of Periyāḻvār's *Tirumoḻi* explores the relationship in which the devotee plays the part of the parent. Most scholars have tended to consider that relationships in which the devotee takes a subordinate position to God are modeled on the master-servant relationship (Hardy 1983, 460–63; Radhakrishnan and Rajagopalan 1984, 211). The fact that the hierarchical relationship is so consistently read as a "feudal" rather than a "family" one may be a consequence of the scholarly use of the ancient Tamil literary categories of *akam* and *puṟam* ("interior" poetry of love and "public" poetry concerned with the exploits of chiefs and kings) or of Bengali Vaiṣṇava theological categories (*dāsya-bhāva*, *sākhya-bhāva*, *vātsalya-bhāva*, and *mādhurya-bhāva*) in interpreting the Tamil *bhakti* literature.

35. Some Tamil scholars interpret the infix *il* in the term *patiyilār* as a negative particle, so that the sense would be "ones not attached to a particular place (*pati*)" (K. K. A. Venkatachari, personal communication, May 1988) or even "ones without husbands (*patis*)" (P. Venkatesan, personal communication, January 1984). It seems to me, however, that at least in the inscriptional usage of the term, there are several arguments against these interpretations: (1) the presence of the shorter form of the term, *paṭiyār*, in several inscriptions, in one case (SII 5.520) used apparently interchangeably with *patiyilār*; (2) the parallelism with the term *taḷiyilār*, and the use of the term patiyilār to denote sex-nonspecific groups, both of which argue against the "husbandless" translation; (3) the fact that the *patiyilār* are in fact identified according to place, which argues against the "ones without a place" translation.

The terms with the *il* infix (*patiyilār* and *taḷiyilār*) are almost all found in inscriptions of the later Chola period, whereas those without the infix (*paṭiyār* and *taḷiyār*) are found only in the early period. This suggests that the forms with the infix evolved out of earlier usages, and thus reinforces the first point.

36. This inscription is the only place, to my knowledge, where we encounter the term *paṇimūppimār*. Despite the fact that the *Tamil Lexicon*, referring to this inscription, defines *paṇimūppimār* as "temple dancing-girls" (MTL, 2459), the term seems in fact to signify "senior female devotees"—*mūppi* meaning an "elderly woman," with connotations of respect or superiority (MTL, 3324), and *paṇi* meaning, among other things, "services to a deity as by a devotee; *toṇṭu* . . . bowing, reverencing" (MTL, 2457). *Paṇi* may also have the meaning of "work, service, trade; *toḻil*" and it may be possible to interpret *paṇimūppimār* as "senior female temple servants" in a more practical than devotional sense.

37. In addition to the twelve *patiyilār* who bear the title *talaikkoli*, there are seven other temple women with *talaikkoli* as part of their names who are not referred to by the term *patiyilār*. One, Nakkaṉ Piratamātevi *alias* Mumuṭicoḻat-talaikkoli, is named in the inscription (SII 19.283) that prefaces my discussion of the term *tevaṉār makaḷ*, and in two other inscriptions (SII 19.92A and SII 23.223) *tevaṉār makaḷs*

bear the title *talaikkoli*. There is one inscription that mentions two *taḷiyilār* with *talaikkoli* names (EC 10.Kl121), and two inscriptions in which temple women with *talaikkoli* names are not referred to by any "temple woman" terms.

38. The *talaikkōl* is described in *Cilappatikāram* as a staff that "was the central shaft of a splendid white umbrella captured in the battle-field from monarchs of great repute. It was covered over by purest *jāmbūnada* gold, its joints bedecked with nine gems. This staff represented Jayanta, Indra's son, and as such was worshipped in the palace of the protecting king of the white umbrella (the Cōḻa)" [Dikshitar 1978, 111 (*Cilappatikāram* 3.114ff); see also 374 (*Cilappatikāram* 28.98–99)].

The association between the *talaikkōl* as royal staff and *talaikkōl* as a title or honor bestowed on female dancers is illustrated in the description of the courtesan Mātavi's dance debut before the Chola king, in the third canto of *Cilappatikāram*. Before the dance recital, Mātavi bathed and adorned the *talaikkōl* and it was taken in procession on the back of the state elephant, accompanied by the king, his advisors, and the court poet. The court poet then placed it on the stage, and Mātavi, after making obeisance to the *talaikkōl*, performed a series of dances. At the end of her performance, the king, greatly impressed with her skill, gave her a leaf garland and 1,008 gold pieces, according to the prescribed rule (*viti-muṟai*), in recognition of her having "obtained the *talaikkōl*" in her dance debut (*Cilappatikāram* 3.160–62). Elsewhere in *Cilappatikāram*, we find other uses of the term *talaikkōl* to signify a mark of recognition: the *apsarā* Urvaśī, as a skilled dancer, is said to have obtained the position (*tāṉam*) of *talaikkōl* (*Cilappatikāram*, 3.3; Dikshitar 1978, 104), and a *talaikkōl arivai* ("*talaikkōl* girl") is mentioned as one of the inhabitants, among other singers and dancers, of the courtesan's quarter of Madurai (*Cilappatikāram* 14.154; MTL, 1774; cf. Dikshitar 1978, 234).

39. Separate subcategories of temple women, each assigned to perform particular ritual tasks, are mentioned in post-Chola period sources. According to one of the temple women interviewed by Kersenboom, there were traditionally six groups of *devadāsīs* at the temple in Tiruvarur, in Tanjavur district:

> 1. *patiyilār*—the oldest and most prestigious class of devadasis; 2. *Īśāna pattiṉiyār* ("wives of Īśāna"); 3. *tēvaraṭiyār* ("slaves of god", Skt. *devadāsī*); 4. *tattai* ("given one", Skt. *dattā*); 5. *alaṅkāra dāsī* ("ornamental dasi"); 6. *rudragaṇikā* ("courtesan of Rudra-Siva"). (Kersenboom 1987, 183)

The prestige of the first group was enhanced by the identification of Paravai, wife of the saint Cuntaramūrtti, as one of the *patiyilār* of the temple at Tiruvarur (Kersenboom 1987, 28). Each of these groups had certain ritual rights and responsibilities in the temple, although not all of the temple women of Tiruvarur to whom Kersenboom spoke agreed on what the precise arrangements and order of precedence had traditionally been (1987, 183–84).

The inscriptions of Tiruvarur do not provide evidence of such a classification or hierarchy among temple women, although there is a thirteenth-century inscription (SII 17.600) that mentions a female *patiyilār* as the seller of land in the area around the temple. This list of types of temple women resembles two other classification schemes: the organization of temple women at the Tiruvorriyur temple in Chingleput district into the groups *patiyilār*, *tevaraṭiyār*, and *isapattaḷiyilār* (= Skt. *ṛṣabha* or *vṛṣabha*, the bull vehicle of Śiva + *taḷiyilār*), according to the account of a series of fourteenth-century inscriptions (ARE 195 of 1912; ARE 208 of 1912; SITI 525), and the list of seven types of *devadāsīs* that is apparently mentioned for the first time by Thurston, in his *Castes and Tribes of Southern India*. Thurston himself claims that his list appears in "old Hindu works," and to a certain extent it resembles the classification of types of *dāsas* found in *smṛti* literature (e.g., *Manusmṛti* 8.415, cited in Chanana 1960, 114). I have never encountered such a list in the "old Hindu works" dealing with temple women that I have consulted. The seven classes of *devadāsīs* are

> (1) Dattā, or one who gives herself as a gift to a temple; (2) Vikrīta, or one who sells herself for the same purpose; (3) Bhritya, or one who offers herself as a temple servant for the prosperity of her family; (4) Bhakta, or one who joins a temple out of devotion; (5) Hrita, or one who is enticed away, and presented to a temple; (6) Alankāra, or one who, being well trained in her profession, and profusely decked, is presented to a temple by kings and noblemen; (7) Rudraganika or Gopika, who receive regular wages from a temple, and are employed to sing and dance. (Thurston and Rangachari 1909, 2:125)

Such classification schemes, where they existed in practice, seem to have been primarily of local relevance and, as both the fourteenth-century inscriptions from Tiruvorriyur and the conflicting accounts of Kersenboom's *devadāsī* informants attest, were frequently subject to contest and negotiation and would therefore have been unlikely to remain fixed over time.

Notes to Chapter 3

1. In my survey of donations made in the four study areas, most are the equivalent in value of an endowment for one or two perpetual lamps. The range of values is from the equivalent of half a lamp to six or eight lamps—assuming that a perpetual lamp could be supported by 400 to 500 *kuḻis* of land, 15 to 20 *kaḻañcus* of gold, 25 to 30 cows, or 90 to 96 sheep.

Many of the gifts of queens, princes, and other members of the royal family fall into this range. But in the case of certain individuals and certain periods of Chola dynastic rule, royal gifts were of considerably more value. Donations made by Queen Cempiyaṉ Mahādevi in the late tenth century, for instance, included the sponsorship of the rebuilding in stone of numerous temples and substantial gifts of land and vessels and ornaments of gold and silver; in the early eleventh century, Rajaraja I's queens gave large amounts of gold, land, and precious ornaments. Chola kings were not involved in temple donations, on either a small or large scale, as extensively or as early as were queens; temple patronage by Chola kings, reflected in the inscriptions only from the time of Rajaraja I, involved gifts of the value and type of Cempiyaṉ Mahādevi's, or royal orders that redirected land revenues to the temple.

2. In the area studies, I have used *A Concordance of the Names in the Cōḻa Inscriptions* (Karashima, Subbarayalu, and Matsui 1978) as a general guide but have constructed the group of temple men on the basis of my own examination of the Tamil texts of all the published inscriptions from the four study areas, rather than relying on the *Concordance*'s classification of individuals as "religious." Of the 219 temple men, 118 are Brahmans and 101 are non-Brahmans. Almost half of these men are referred to in the inscriptions of one of the four study areas, Kumbakonam taluk in Tanjavur district, and three-quarters are named in the inscriptions of the later Chola period; they are particularly numerous in the inscriptions of the third subperiod.

3. Two of the temple men described as donors are mentioned in inscriptions from Kanchipuram taluk in Chingleput district, dating from the third subperiod, and the third temple man appears in an inscription of the last subperiod from Kumbakonam

taluk in Tanjavur district. That these references all come from the later Chola period is consistent with the distribution of named temple men in general, in the four study areas, but it may also indicate a broader pattern in which temple men's gift giving, meager as it is in any case, is more characteristic of the later Chola period and the post-Chola period (see Orr 1999).

The very small proportion of temple men who acted as temple patrons may be contrasted not only with comparable figures for temple women but also with the gift giving of Jain religious men. Forty-six percent of the Tamil inscriptions that refer to men associated with Jain institutions or identified as Jain teachers describe them as donors; most of them are mentioned in inscriptions of the eighth and ninth centuries as the sponsors of Jain images (Orr 1998 and 1999).

4. For analyses of the representation of women and their activities, including their donations, in Tamil inscriptions of the Chola and post-Chola period (the eighth through seventeenth centuries) see Orr 1999 and forthcoming b. Talbot's (1991, 1994, 1995b, forthcoming) work provides parallels from Andhra, using medieval Telugu inscriptions as the basis for discussions of the character of women's lives and behavior. Balambal (1976), Spencer (1983), Orr (1992), and Kaimal (1996) examine the special role of queens as temple patrons in Tamilnadu during the Chola period.

5. The group of "women in general" in the area study includes temple women; especially in the fourth subperiod, when references to nontemple women decline, there is considerable overlap between the two groups. Were we to remove the temple women named as donors in the four study areas from the group of women in general, the decline in the donative activity of this group would be even more precipitous.

6. The changing relations between donors and the institutions they endowed in medieval Tamilnadu are paralleled to some extent by those that have been reconstructed by scholars of early Christianity. In both cases the potential for women to acquire influence through their patronage may have been particularly curtailed.

In the second and third centuries A.D., authority in Christian communities was increasingly vested in local officers and clergy who were men (Schussler Fiorenza 1983, 77–83, 286–87; Clark 1990, 253–54). At the same time, Christian leaders sought and received patronage for the activities of these communities from their members, including women. In discussing the solicitation of donations from wealthy women, Bobertz (1992, 9) describes the "delicate interplay between the obvious need for such patronage within the Christian community and the ways in which [ecclesiastical authorities] would attempt specifically to limit the expected perogatives, status and honor, emerging from such acts." Roman customs and practices of patronage gave rise to certain expectations about the kind of recognition and influence that could be acquired through gifts. One way in which these expectations were frustrated in the case of donations to the Christian churches, as their institutional structures evolved, was in the patron's loss of control over the use of the wealth donated, which went into the hands of the bishop and clergy; this development reduced the authority and influence that wealthy women had earlier been able to exercise in the church (Schussler Fiorenza 1983, 287–88; Bobertz 1992, 13–14).

That patronage of Christian institutions did not decline despite these limitations—as patronage of Hindu temples seems to have done in some regions and among some groups of donors—may be due to the success of church authorities in linking patronage with the concepts of atonement and salvation. In addition, the Christian women who continued to act as donors seem in many cases to have been ascetics—virgins or widows (Clark 1990, 254, 260, 263–64; Bobertz 1992, 11). Although such women, who may in some cases have become leaders of women's monastic communities, are quite different from the Hindu temple women I have studied, it is perhaps significant that in both Christian and Hindu contexts the women who remained visible as donors were "religious" women of some sort—and husbandless—rather than family women.

7. In an earlier study (Orr 1992) of 161 records of queens' gifts to temples, I found that they concentrated their donative activities in Tanjavur district (where 52 percent of queens' gifts were made); numerous donations (28 percent of their gifts) were also made in neighboring Tiruchirappalli district. Palace women show a similar pattern of temple patronage, although their gifts are somewhat less concentrated in the core Chola region and are found further afield than the donations of queens: of 76 inscriptions that record palace women's gifts, 42 percent are to temples in Tanjavur district and 17 percent are found in Tiruchirappalli district; proportionately more of their gifts than those of queens are found in South Arcot district (17 percent) and in Chingleput district (7 percent), to the north of the core Chola region.

8. Of the 128 records of gifts of temple women, 27 percent are from Chingleput district; 21 percent from Tanjavur district; 16 percent from Tiruchirappalli district; 12 percent from South Arcot district; 8 percent from Tirunelveli district; 5 percent from Madurai district; 3 percent from Kanyakumari district; 2 percent each from North Arcot and Coimbatore districts; and 1 inscription (1 percent) each from Chittoor, Ramnad, Travancore, Salem, Mysore, and Bangalore districts.

9. In Tanjavur district, queens made 85 gifts to 29 different temples, producing an average of almost 3 gifts per temple, and in Tiruchirappalli district, the 46 gifts that queens made at 13 temples produces an average of 3.5 gifts per temple (Orr 1992). Looking at the sample of queens as a whole, we find that they gave on the average 2.6 gifts per temple. In contrast, temple women's gifts rise above the average of 2 per temple only in Chingleput district in the north (35 gifts to 14 temples, or 2.5 gifts per temple) and in Tirunelveli district in the south (11 gifts to 4 temples, or 2.75 gifts per temple). Perhaps the concentration of donations by temple women at specific temples in these two regions was encouraged by conditions prevailing, and opportunities arising, outside the core Chola region. Overall, in all districts, temple women made 133 gifts to 73 places, an average of 1.8 gifts per temple.

The patterns of concentration of donations for palace women are quite different than for queens; in fact, palace women seem to exhibit even less of a group effort than do temple women. In the three districts where most of their gifts were made, we find in Tanjavur district that palace women made 32 gifts to 23 different temples (an average of 1.4 gifts per temple), in Tiruchirappalli district they made 14 gifts to 10 temples (1.4 gifts per temple), and in South Arcot district they made 13 gifts to 12 temples (1.1 gifts per temple). The average overall, in all districts, is about 1.3 gifts per temple. These findings demonstrate that palace women typically did not follow one another's example in their choice of temples to endow. It can be shown, however, that they frequently followed the lead of queens (and that queens on occasion followed their lead); thus palace women did participate in the donative consortium of royal women (see Orr 1992).

10. This literature does not consider women to be autonomous or independent social beings. Several of the authors of and commentators on the Dharmaśāstras maintain that a woman married by one of the "recommended" forms of marriage is subsumed into her husband's identity, insofar as she assumes her husband's *gotra* at the time of marriage (Kane 1930–62, 2: 466–67). The Dharmaśāstra texts are in accord in defining the patrilineal family structure in terms of a husband's primacy

in bestowing identity on (and in having "possession" of) his wife's offspring (e.g., *Manusmṛti* 9.27–56, 332–37).

Access to economic resources is linked in the normative literature to the capacity to engage in religious activity. The Mīmāṃsā philosopher Śabara informs us that a woman can participate in sacrificial ritual only in partnership with, and in a subsidiary role to, her husband; she, herself, cannot act as the sponsor of the sacrifice because she owns no property independently of her husband (*Śabara-bhāṣya* 6.1.6ff; see also Leslie 1989, 41–43, 110–15; Jamison 1996, 16–18, 36–38, 194–95). Manu also says that "there is no separate yajña for women (independently of the husband) nor vrata (vows) nor fasts (without his consent)" (*Manusmṛti* 5.155, trans. Kane 1930–62, 2: 558–59). In Manu's discussion of the disposition and inheritance of women's property (*strīdhana*), his list of the types of property a woman may possess consists essentially of gifts bestowed by her husband at or after the time of her marriage or by her brother, mother, or father (*Manusmṛti* 9.194). As Mukund (1992) points out, there appears to be no obligation on the part of anyone—her husband or her natal family—to necessarily provide a woman with property of her own. Although there is much variation among the authors of the Dharmaśāstras on the issue of women's inheritance from her natal family, whenever it exists it is never equivalent to the inheritance of her brothers and is frequently absent altogether in the case of a married woman.

11. Elsewhere (Orr 1994c; 1999; and forthcoming b) I provide a more detailed comparison of the evidence of medieval Tamil inscriptions with normative textual prescriptions that relate to women's access to wealth and capacity to engage in religious activity. Talbot's findings, based on her analysis of Telugu inscriptions of the Kakatiya period (A.D. 1175–1325) in Andhra Pradesh, are similar to mine: she finds that 15 percent of the individual endowments recorded in inscriptions were made by women, and concludes that "women possessed considerable personal property and were able to alienate that property as individuals in their own right. The view of women's property rights and influence which we gain from the Kakatiya period corpus of inscriptions thus seems to contradict the submissive and dispossessed image of women which commonly appears in the brahmanical legal literature" (1988b, 213).

12. In this discussion, I am treating the ownership, donation, buying, and selling of property as unambiguous and straightforward concepts and actions, but this is something of a misrepresentation. Especially with regard to rights over, control of, and transactions involving land, property relations in medieval South India were extremely complex, frequently involving several types of claims on property by different individuals or groups (see Granda 1984, 85–157, 207–31; Heitzman 1985, 117–84, 444–66; Talbot 1988b, 135–38).

13. In a study of eight study-areas, I have found that out of close to 500 women named in inscriptions of the eighth through thirteenth centuries, 31 percent are represented as owning land; this proportion rises from 27 percent in the tenth and eleventh centuries to 42 percent in the twelfth and thirteenth centuries (Orr forthcoming b). These figures do not necessarily mean that women acquired greater access to land in the course of the Chola period, but may simply indicate that women were affected by the general trend for inscriptions to provide increasingly detailed specifications of individual land rights (Heitzman 1987a, 57). In either case, it is clear that women were acknowledged as having such rights throughout the whole of the Chola period, even if they were represented as landowners less often than men.

14. I have found that about half of the women described in twelfth- and thirteenth-century inscriptions as acquiring, possessing, or disposing of land were Brahmans and that temple women were, in the thirteenth century, also prominent (Orr forthcoming b).

The *Concordance* lists the names of fifteen women who are identified in the Chola inscriptions as land sellers; of these, twelve are Brahman women. Brahman men also loom large as landholders: 70 percent of male land sellers or landowners mentioned in inscriptions of the four study areas are Brahmans.

15. In my examination of eight study areas, I found no references to *mutukaṇs* or other agents negotiating women's property transactions in the eighth and ninth centuries, three such references dating from the tenth and eleventh centuries (when sixty-nine women were mentioned as the purchasers, sellers, owners, or donors of land), thirty-three such references in the twelfth and thirteenth centuries (when a total of seventy-eight women were involved in land transactions), and only one reference after A.D. 1300 (Orr forthcoming b).

16. Even when a woman's *strīdhana* was under her husband's control, she might not relinquish all interest in this property. Lalitha (1986) refers to a Chola period inscription (ARE 39 of 1925) that records a husband's compensation to his wife for having spent her *strīdhana*.

17. In the Dharmaśāstras and later legal literature, *strīdhana* is clearly described as property under a woman's personal control, which may be preferentially inherited by her daughters rather than her sons (Tambiah 1973, 85–90). The source of the differences between this conception of *strīdhana* and that in medieval Tamilnadu and other South Indian contexts has been a matter of debate between Derrett and Tambiah. I am inclined to agree with Derrett's description of the property rights of women in traditional South India—that *citaṉam* was property brought by a woman to her marriage, which became subject to her husband's control, and that a wife had a major share in the couple's or family's joint estate both during her husband's life and at his death (1968, 412–13). It is probable that I agree with Derrett's view because we are using, in part, the same set of inscriptional records as evidence. Tambiah has taken exception to Derrett's notion of the "non-Aryan family." In Tambiah's view, the organization of the South Indian and Sinhalese households, which Derrett considers examplary of this "non-Aryan family," is not of independent origin but derives from a classical pan-Indian pattern; that the conception of *strīdhana* in South India seems to deviate from the ideas put forward by the Dharmaśāstras, is, according to Tambiah (1973, 90–91), the result of a separate evolution rather than a distinct origin.

18. Several other inscriptions refer to the inheritance of rights or responsibilities by sons-in-law (SII 2.66; SII 3.210; SII 22.235) or brothers-in-law (SII 5.579). The transfer of wealth from a man to his son-in-law or from a man to his sister's son is found in other South Indian inheritance systems, including the *aḷiya-santāna* pattern of Karnataka, the *marumakkatāyam* pattern of Kerala, or the *illaṭumu* pattern of Andhra Pradesh (Hutton 1963, 70, 160–61, 167; Bhattacharyya 1971, 84–86; Derrett 1968, 407–9). In matrilateral cross-cousin marriage, which is a preferred form of marriage in Tamilnadu, Karnataka, and elsewhere in South India (see Trautmann 1981; Chekki 1974, 79–83), a man's sister's son and his son-in-law are often the same person, and a man transferring his wealth through his daughter to his son-in-law effectively keeps the property in the family.

There is more inscriptional evidence in medieval Karnataka than in Tamilnadu that suggests that women directly inherited wealth. Several inscriptions of the tenth to thirteenth centuries record the inheritance of women's property by women (EC 9.Cr 59; EI 29, 203–9), the inheritance from men by women when there were no male heirs (EC 1.52), or the inheritance by both a daughter and a son (EC 6.Mu 24).

19. For example, there is a record of the donation made by a woman (probably a widow) of income from her husband's property (SII 13.281B). I have found three inscriptions that seem to refer to the rights of widows to inherit their husbands' property (ARE 429 and 538 of 1918; ARE 258 of 1926; see ARE 1919, Part II, para. 19; Lalitha 1986). In two other inscriptions (SII 12.199; EI 21.27), women are held liable for the fines or taxes incurred by their sons or husbands.

20. Temple women in the nineteenth and twentieth centuries inherited wealth from their mothers. According to early ethnographers, South Indian temple women bequeathed their property either equally to sons and daughters (Thurston and Rangachari 1909, 2:127) or preferentially to their daughters (Shortt 1870, 185, 187). Later anthropological study of South Indian temple women indicates that ancestral land (including the land and house that were the service allotment, or *maniam*, associated with the right to serve in the temple), as well as gold and jewelery, was inherited by the daughter of a temple woman who had herself been dedicated as a *devadāsī*; other wealth that had been acquired by a temple woman in the course of her life was usually willed only to her daughters, although in theory her sons and daughters were equal heirs (A. Srinivasan 1984, 188–92). Outside of South India, inheritance by the daughters of temple women seems also to have been the rule in recent history (Crooke 1896, 2:381–82; Marglin 1985b, 83).

21. Apart from temple and royal support, the *devadāsīs* of Puri whom Marglin studied received gifts at pilgrim houses, where *devadāsīs* were invited to receive *pūjā* from the pilgrims and to sing and dance (Marglin 1985b, 35, 41). In South India, similarly, temple women until recently received support from royal courts and from private individuals in exchange for the performance of song, dance, and ritual functions (Kersenboom 1991, 144–47). The income of South Indian temple women in recent times came from various sources: revenue from the lands assigned by the temple as service tenure, payment for dancing at marriages, and gifts from patrons and "fans"; these earnings were quite substantial and allowed the *devadāsī* not only to support a large household but also to occasionally spend money on herself or make a charitable endowment in her own name (A. Srinivasan 1984, 196–97).

The fact that temple women were economically independent of men, holding property in their own name, was regarded as problematic within the context of nineteenth- and early twentieth-century conceptualizations of female respectability and was one of the factors that fueled the *devadāsī* abolition movement. Among men of the *devadāsī* community in South India, both economic self-interest and the desire to have their sisters and daughters conform to the reinvented "traditional" norms of Hindu womanhood impelled them to campaign for the eradication of the system that allowed *devadāsī* women to have economic autonomy (A. Srinivasan 1985, 1873–74; Nair 1994, 3161–65). The respectable woman, according to the new definitions being framed, could not be economically independent; a woman who acquired wealth of her own must be a prostitute (O'Hanlon 1994, 58–59). This view is based on the notion that the Dharmaśāstras represent a real social system, that property is actually entirely under the control of men, and that the only way a woman can have access to property is through her (sexual) relationship with a man. It is striking that this view, in connection with the temple women of past or more recent history, is so persistent, even among authors who are aware that the branding of *devadāsīs* as prostitutes was a politically motivated gesture (Parasher-Sen 1993, 252–57; Nair 1994, 3161 and 3165).

22. Palace women represent something of an intermediate case. On the one hand, they resemble temple women insofar as they are not defined by marriage. On the other hand, they resemble other women with respect to the decline—in fact, disappearance—of their activities as recorded in inscriptions of the later Chola period. Although the palace woman was not married, her situation was similar to the wife's and unlike the temple woman's insofar as she was socially defined by a connection with an individual rather than an institution. This type of social definition would have had the same kind of economic ramifications for palace women as it did for wives. In the case of the palace woman, her primary connection would be with a king, a queen, or a chief, or with a retinue (*parivāram*) or palace establishment (*veḷam*) associated with a particular royal figure. This connection was certainly a source of status and was also probably an important source of wealth for these women, who may have received housing, food, and clothing from royal establishments and who probably received gifts from their patrons as well. But it was a limited and particular connection. The queen or king whom the palace woman served might die, or the palace woman might fall out of favor. In this regard, the group of palace women, considered as a whole, may have been much less economically secure than most other women, who were in any case supported through a marriage *system.*

23. For descriptions of the relationship between donations and the acquisition of temple honors in the post-Chola period, see Stein (1960, 171–73); Appadurai and Breckenridge (1976, 197–98); Granda (1984, 139, 199–200); and Breckenridge (1986, 28–29, 36–38).

24. One rarely finds the term *prasāda* used to denote cooked food in this context and never the equivalent term *mariyātai* ("leavings"), which in later usage came to denote honors in general (Appadurai and Breckenridge 1976, 197–98).

According to certain Śaiva Āgamas and to the Śaiva Siddhānta tradition, food and other substances that have been offlered to Śiva are deemed too pure to be distributed among or consumed by his worshipers (Brunner 1969; R. Davis 1986, 234–39). It is well known that South Indian Śaiva temples today distribute sacred ash as *prasāda*, in contrast to Vaiṣṇava temples, where consecrated food is received by devotees as a temple honor. Despite Agamic proscriptions, however, food offered to Lord Śiva is taken by officiating priests in contemporary Tamilnadu (Fuller 1984, 14; Breckenridge 1986, 30). In the Chola period, as seen particularly in inscriptions of the later Chola period, food offered to the deity in Śaiva temples was consumed by donors, temple servants, and worshipers, although this was not a very common practice (Orr 1994b).

The mention in the inscription at the beginning of this section of the privilege of receiving the *parivaṭṭam*, the head-cloth of the temple deity, is one of very few such references in the Chola period. In the Vijayanagara and subsequent periods, this became a much-coveted honor and one that was frequently bestowed on temple women (see, e.g., Kersenboom 1987, 34, 142–43). Apart from the translated inscription, I have found only one other Chola period reference to the privilege of receiving the *parivaṭṭam*—in which the *śivabrāhmaṇas* of a temple in Mayuram in Tanjavur district were granted this honor (SII 23.372).

25. This is a late Chola period inscription from the great Vaiṣṇava temple at Srirangam, describing the donation of a gold ornament by the wife of a *śrīvaiṣṇava* in the temple, in return for which she received the right to a "livelihood" (*jivanam*) of consecrated food (*prasāda*) (SII 24.163).

26. Even if we count the receipt of cooked food (*coṟu*) from the temple as a form of payment, rather than a ritual honor, and combine cases in which temple

women received *coṟu* in exchange for their gifts with cases in which they received more obvious forms of support (such as a house or the right to a share in the income from temple property), we find that only six of the twenty-one records of temple women's deals—less than a third—describe such support as the only "return" on the deal. In four other inscriptions, temple women receive both some form of support and the right to perform a particular service as a temple honor. The remaining eleven inscriptions—over half of the records of temple women's deals—represent them as receiving only ritual privileges, without material compensation of any kind, in exchange for their gifts. In contrast, in the inscriptions that describe deals made by men, two-thirds (four out of six) refer only to the receipt of support (a house or rights in temple property).

27. In contrast, only one of the records of temple women's exchanges of gifts for temple honors mentions the involvement of a king—a Telugu Coda ruler, who sanctioned the temple woman's gift to the temple. The fact that these records have so little reference to royal figures and that they are located in areas where Chola authority was relatively weak suggests that temple honors in South India were not originally or fundamentally predicated on the generosity and prestige of the king, as has been maintained, for example, by Nicholas Dirks (1976, 152; 1987, 289). Royal resources and authority had little to do with the system of temple honors as it began to emerge in the later part of the Chola period; it was in the post-Chola period that upstart warrior rulers and local "little kings" became increasingly implicated in and central to the system (Breckenridge 1986, 28–29; Bayly 1989, 44 and 68; Price 1996, 109–10).

28. There are indications in present-day Tamilnadu of a similar method of transferring rights: a professional male temple musician (a member of the *periyamēḷam*) would on occasion marry his daughter to one of his star pupils, presumably thereby transferring his right to temple service as *strīdhana* or making his son-in-law his successor (A. Srinivasan 1984, 217–18). This kind of transfer, for male temple servants who had hereditary positions in both the Chola period and in recent history, might have been resorted to when there was no son with the proper qualifications. For women in the *devadāsī* communities studied by Srinivasan, whose right to serve in the temple was, like that of the male temple musicians, hereditary, there had to be a different strategy for finding a successor when there were no suitable daughters because marriage was out of the question for women dedicated to temple service (i.e., a *devadāsī* could not have her daughter-in-law as a successor); in these cases, a girl would be adopted (A. Srinivasan 1984, 207 and 236, n. 43).

Because the hereditary principle was not as strongly articulated in the Chola period with reference to temple service rights, we should not assume that the situation in the Chola period exactly parallels that of recent South India. Nonetheless, given the Chola period references to inheritance by sons-in-law, there may have been some similarities. Perhaps in the later Chola period, when temple women began to acquire hereditary temple honors by making deals, they on occasion adopted daughters as their successors when they had no natural daughters. In fact, in terms of time and place—toward the end of the Chola period and in the northern part of Tamilnadu—we find a coincidence between the establishment of these hereditary temple privileges and the emergence of a system of maternal descent among temple women.

29. A thirteenth-century inscription from Salem district, dated in the reign of a Pandya king, records the redistribution of worship rights in a temple when a woman was ordered to sell her privileges (apparently to pay for temple jewels she was

thought to have stolen), which were then bought by other temple servants (ARE 439 of 1913). The second inscription, from Chingleput district and again dated in the reign of a Pandya king, seems to record the prohibition of such a sale by a temple woman (ARE 277 of 1910). In this case, the daughter of an *emperumāṉaṭiyār* was in possession of land rights that had been granted by the *sabhai* (local assembly of Brahmans), but she was fined by the *sabhai* when she sold these rights on her daughter's behalf; the land in question was in the end purchased by the temple authorities.

30. The relationship between a temple woman and her locality, temple, or deity, which I am indicating here as genitive ("of this village," "of the temple," or "of this god"), is most often expressed in the Chola period inscriptions with no indication of a case relationship, or when a case ending is found, it is the locative. So, typically, we find such constructions as "Name-of-place-*ūr tevaṉār makaḷ*," "Name-of-temple-*koyil tevaraṭiyāḷ*," or "Name-of-god-*uṭaiyār tevaraṭiyāḷ*," in which the words *ūr* ("village"), *koyil* ("temple"), or *uṭaiyār* ("lord") will not be declined with a case ending. We might think of these phrases as compound forms: "the daughter (*makaḷ*) of the god (*tevaṉār*) of Such-and-such-*ūr*," "the devotee (*aṭiyāḷ*) of the Lord (*tevar*) of the temple Such-and-such," or "the devotee of the Great Lord (*uṭaiyār tevar*) So-and-so." Or we may simply consider that the case endings have been omitted, something that is a fairly regular feature of inscriptional Tamil, as it is of the literary Tamil of the Āḻvārs and Nāyaṉmārs of several centuries earlier (Zvelebil and Vacek 1970, 16). Sometimes we will find a word in one of these phrases in an "oblique" form, that is, the form it would take before case endings, but with the endings themselves absent (e.g., two words for "town"—*puram* and *nagaram*—may appear as *purattu* and *nagarattu*, and *īśvaram*, "lord," may appear as *īśvarattu*). The occasional use of the locative case in hometown identifiers takes the form *koyilil* ("in the temple") *tevaraṭiyāḷ*. In a few cases we also see the future adjectival participle of the verb *iru* ("to live, dwell") incorporated into these identifiers, for example, in the expression *tirumaṭaiviḷākam irukkum tevaraṭiyār*, "the *tevaraṭiyār* who dwell in the temple precincts."

Although some researchers have treated hometown identifiers of this type as part of the personal name of an individual (Heitzman 1995 and his concordance; cf. Karashima, Subbarayalu, and Matsui 1978), this does not seem appropriate in the case of temple women, for whom the hometown identifier is typically not incorporated into the name but syntactically distinct.

31. Of the 304 Chola period inscriptions that refer to temple women, there are 222 in which the portion of the inscription is available which might contain a reference to a temple woman's hometown. One hundred and twenty-nine, or 58 percent, of these identify temple women in terms of the village, temple, or deity with which they are associated. In contrast, for women in general in the Chola period, I have found that only 12 percent are identified with reference to hometowns in an analysis of inscriptions from eight study areas (Orr forthcoming b).

32. There are only four relatively famous temples that received gifts from temple women who were associated with other temples: the temple at Tiruvalisvaram in Tirunelveli district and the temples at Udaiyargudi, Elavanasur, and Tiruvamattur, all in South Arcot district.

33. These five study areas are those used by James Heitzman (1985), and the data on donations made in diffierent locales were drawn from the concordance of names he has very generously made available to me, supplemented by information from the *Concordance* of Karashima, Subbarayalu, and Matsui (1978). Talbot's

(1988a, forthcoming) work on religious endowments in medieval Andhra Pradesh provides the inspiration for this typology.

The method for coding places used by Karashima and his colleagues and by Heitzman, which I adopt here and throughout this work, allows me to consider that temple towns are roughly equivalent to temples. In other words, the units coded as distinct towns or villages are quite small and in most instances contain only a single temple where inscriptions are found. The term "temple town" is, in fact, rather misleading because in almost all cases these places are much too small to be considered towns.

34. For example, the classification of Kudumiyamalai in Pudukkottai (Kulattur and Alangudi taluks) as a type I temple town reflects the fact that this place received by far more donations than any other temple town in the study area. In absolute terms, however, the fifty-five donations made at Kudumiyamalai are only half the number made at Srirangam, in Tiruchirappalli taluk, which is classified as a type II temple. Factors that affect the classification of any given temple town include the numbers of donations made in each study area (see Table 3.4) and the number of temples of various types in each study area.

35. The gifts of temple women in the five study areas are distributed as follows:

Kumbakonam taluk (Tanjavur district):
Tiruvidaimarudur (type II), five gifts
Tirupurambiyam (type III), one gift
Kuhur (type III), one gift
Tiruvalanjuli (type III), one gift
One "small" (type IV) temple, one gift
Total: nine gifts

Kulattur and Alangudi taluks (Pudukkottai/Tiruchirappalli district):
Kudumiyamalai (type I), two gifts
Tirukkattalai (type III), one gift
Four "small" (type IV) temples, four gifts
Total: seven gifts

Tirukkoyilur taluk (South Arcot district):
Elavanasur (type III), two gifts by temple women
Tiruvennainallur (type III), one gift
One "small" (type IV) temple, one gift
Total: four gifts

Tiruchirappalli taluk (Tiruchirappalli district):
Tiruverumbur (type III), one gift
Uyyakkondar (type III), one gift
Allur (type III), one gift
Total: three gifts

Tirutturaipundi taluk (Tanjavur district):
Vedaranyam (type I), one gift
Total: one gift

36. Cynthia Talbot (1988b, 241–46, 281), in her analysis of temple patronage in medieval Andhra Pradesh, finds that women typically made gifts to major temples rather than smaller, local ones, and she suggests that religious considerations were impor-

tant in the choice of which temples to patronize. This is similar to the pattern we see here for donations made by women—except temple women—in medieval Tamilnadu.

37. Three other inscriptions record the *receipt* of the merit of a gift by a temple woman or by her relative: the donation of a woman for the merit of a *tevaraṭiyār* (possibly her daughter?), the gift of the chief Gaṇḍagopālaṉ for the merit of a *tevaraṭiyāḷ*'s sister, and a donation made by a Brahman (*paṭṭar*) on behalf of the daughter and granddaughter of a temple woman (SII 14.18; SITI 537; SII 26.437).

38. In the corpus of inscriptions of the Kakatiya period in Andhra Pradesh, Talbot (1991, 334–35) has found that a quarter of donations were made as "multiple acts," recorded together with the gifts of others, and that a considerable number of these appear to have had the purpose of reinforcing links between political subordinates and their overlords.

39. Of the other six instances in which temple women's gifts were recorded together with those of others, in two cases temple women gave gifts along with palace women (ARE 73 of 1921; SII 8.678), and in four inscriptions temple women are mentioned as being codonors with men. In none of these latter cases does the joint character of the donation seem to be particularly significant. In two of the four inscriptions that mention men as codonors with temple women, the temple women appear to have bought the land they are donating from the men; thus a whole parcel of land is jointly given to the temple by the codonors (IPS 97; SII 17.540). In another inscription (SII 3.38), temple women are listed among a large number of various types of donors, including men. The fourth inscription describes gifts made by both a *tevaraṭiyāḷ* and a palace man (*paṇimakaṉ*) (ARE 147 of 1912).

40. The figures for other donors cited here are based on my examination of the texts of inscriptions from the four study areas. Temple authorities include *tāṉattār*, *śivabrāhmaṇas*, *māheśvaras*, *śrīvaiṣṇavas*, supervisors (*kaṇkāṇi ceyvār*), managers (*śrīkāriyam ceyvār*), and accountants (*kaṇakkar*). By village authorities I mean such individuals and groups as *sabhaiyār*, *ūrār*, *nakarattār*, and *nāṭṭār*.

41. The proportion of donative records in the four study areas that mention temple authorities rises from 11 percent in the first subperiod to 39 percent in the last; for temple women, the shift is from 14 percent to 67 percent.

Notes to Chapter 4

1. Of the fifty-nine set-up grants I collected, fifteen, or about a quarter, were sponsored by Chola queens or kings. Most of the inscriptions that record set-up grants date from the tenth and eleventh centuries.

2. At the great temples of Srirangam, dedicated to Viṣṇu, and Chidambaram, dedicated to Śiva, inscriptional references to gardeners vastly outnumber those to priests; the inscriptions at both these places suggest that by the late Chola period, the temples were entirely surrounded by flower gardens and groves, which provided materials essential for worship (Orr 1995a and 1995c).

3. In many ways, there is remarkable continuity in the types of activities that took place in temples in Tamilnadu from the mid-Pallava period, or the early *bhakti* period (about the seventh century), up to the end of the Chola period (the thirteenth century). One of the very few innovations in temple ritual during this time is the emergence of hymn singing as an important element in temple liturgy in the tenth century. Katherine Young and I have argued that hymns were not a formal part of temple ritual during the *bhakti* period itself (Orr and Young 1986, 39–40). Before the early tenth century, there is just a single inscription (SII 3.43), variously dated

to the mid-ninth or even mid-eighth century (Balasubrahmanyam 1975, 77), that refers to the singing of hymns (*tiruppatiyam*) in the temple.

4. In many cases the individuals or groups provided with support by the temple would not have been temple servants but "honored devotees." Within the group of fifty-eight inscriptions that refer to "support only" for temple women, twenty-two are references to the offering of food to *tevaraṭiyār* and others (who can be identified as definitely female in only a few cases). It is unlikely that these people would have had ritual, administrative, or other functions in the temple.

5. The figures in this table for temple women are different from those in tables 3.1 and 4.2. Whereas the latter provide the numbers of *inscriptions* that represent temple women in various roles, table 4.3 enumerates *individuals* mentioned by name. In the 304 Chola period inscriptions that refer to temple women, there are 238 named temple women. I have used this method of presentation in table 4.3 so that temple women could be compared with temple men. To locate temple men in the four study areas, I used the *Concordance of the Names in the Cōḻa Inscriptions* of Karashima, Subbarayalu, and Matsui (1978) as a guide, although in addition to the men whom these authors classify as "religious," I have included a number of others whom I have determined, on the basis of my reading of the inscriptions, were in fact temple men—having functions in the temple, receiving support from the temple, or being identified as "of the temple." Of the 1,893 men named in the inscriptions of the study areas, I have classified 219 as temple men. See note 65 in chapter 1 and notes 2 and 3 in chapter 3 for further information about this group of temple men and about my method of carrying out the area studies.

6. Another point of contrast is that although a number of inscriptions record arrangements for the support of individual temple women without referring to any particular service functions they are to perform, this is extremely rare in the case of temple men. The only context in which we commonly find "support only" arrangements for men, without specification of concommitant duties, is in provisions made for the feeding of devotees, Brahmans, *māheśvaras*, and so on. In the Chola period, in contrast to later times, inscriptions that record such arrangements virtually never specify the individual identities of those who are to be offered food in the temple (Orr 1994b and 1995b).

7. The tending relationship that temple Brahmans entered into was similar to that of temple women, although Brahmans are much more frequently described in this role—being charged with providing a regular return on temple resources entrusted to them (see, e.g., Heitzman 1985, 137–38; 177, n. 32). The extent to which they may themselves have profited from such arrangements is not clear, but it is possible that both Brahmans and temple women were being provided with support by the temple through this system. The tending relationships of shepherds are of a somewhat different character because these people were not temple men but had simply entered into an investment contract with the temple. It has been suggested, however, that at Tanjavur and elsewhere in South India this kind of arrangement made shepherds (or agriculturalists) into temple servants, who may in some cases have eventually taken on other temple duties (Spencer 1968, 279 and 292; Talbot 1988b, 184–85, 284; 1991, 331).

8. In the Jain context in medieval Tamilnadu, we find a parallel situation. Of the 104 inscriptions that refer to Jain "religious men," 13 (or 12 percent) describe them as being in charge of the administration of endowments or of institutions, such as Jain *paḷḷis*. None of the 29 inscriptions that refer to Jain "religious women" mention their involvement in such responsibility functions (Orr 1998).

9. Although here I am primarily concerned with how temple men—the male counterparts of temple women—secured status through their involvement in responsibility functions, men who had more secular identities were also engaged in temple business, evidently with similar interests in the positive effect on their reputation that this activity might have. In his study of intermediate authorities, or "lords," in the Chola period, James Heitzman argues that "the most important means for determining the relative power or influence of different titled lords was the holding of public ceremonies that become 'political contests' for demonstrating the extent and commitment of each lord's following, his gentility, and his generosity. The typical style of 'administration' in this system was the public meeting or court where resource transfers took place according to stylized ritual prescriptions" (1997, 225). Heitzman (1997, 206–16) provides several concrete examples of individual men whose public activity, "multidimensional" exercise of influence, and "ramified contacts" included extensive involvement in temple affairs.

10. Saskia Kersenboom's work is particularly noteworthy in this regard. The interest of Frédérique Marglin, of Anne-Marie Gaston, and of Avanthi Meduri in the study of *devadāsīs* was inspired by their own experience and training in Indian classical dance. Amrit Srinivasan—although she does not consider the *devadāsī*'s dance in terms of its ritual importance, as do Kersenboom and Marglin—focuses her analysis of temple women in recent South Indian history, and the organization of their community, on their professional status as dancers. Khokar (1983), Srinivasan (1983), and Meduri (1996) have documented the evolution of the dance traditions of the *devadāsī* after the advent, early in the twentieth century, of the campaign to prevent the dedication of temple women.

11. Song and dance are occasionally included by the Āgamas and other ritual handbooks among the eight, sixteen, twenty-one, or thirty-two *upacāras* ("ways of service" or "rites of adoration") offered in daily ritual to the deity (Kane 1930–62, 2:729–30; Brunner-Lachaux 1963, App. VII; Appadurai and Breckenridge 1976, 193; R. Davis 1986, 265–74, 317–18). But none of these sources gives the impression that the performance of song and dance is a ritual necessity; these texts characteristically present a number of different options for the conduct of daily worship, and if song and dance are mentioned at all, it is in the context of worship done in the most elaborate fashion. Most of the references to dance in the Āgamas appear in descriptions of festival celebrations rather than of daily ritual, but even at festivals, dance is not represented as a ritual necessity. Furthermore, the Āgamas provide very little specification of *what* dances were to be performed, in either daily or festival worship (cf. V. Subramaniam 1980, 36; Viswanathan n.d.). Were dance performances regarded as ritually significant, they would have been given more detailed treatment; instead, the Āgamas usually refer to dance in only the vaguest terms—as *nṛttagītavādya* ("dance, song, and instrumental music") or *śuddhanṛtta* ("pure dance"). (See Orr 1994c; Gorringe 1998.)

12. In discussing the temple arts of the Chola period, Kersenboom mentions the term *cāntikkūttu* but spells it with a short *a* and gives a derivation from Sanskrit *sandhi*; she speculates that this may be a variant of *navasandhi kautvam*, a dance performed by the *devadāsīs* of Tamilnadu in more recent times which honors the deities of the nine cardinal points (*sandhis*) (1987, 29; see also Janaki 1988, 167–175; Meduri 1996, 41–42; Viswanathan n.d.). Although we frequently encounter the word *canti* (with a short *a*) in Chola period inscriptions, usually designating the three times of day (*sandhyas*)—morning, noon, and evening—when worship was offered to the deity, the word *cānti* when combined with *kūttu* is consistently spelled with a long *a*.

13. The interpretation of *kūtti kāl* to mean "prostitute tax" may be argued on the basis of the fact that the word *kūtti* has the meaning of "prostitute" in later Tamil usage (MTL, 1071) and the hypothesis that a tax on prostitutes existed in medieval South Indian society. It is, however, difficult to support the idea that in the Chola period inscriptions *kūtti* means "prostitute." On the one hand, *kūtti* did not have this meaning in the Cankam and *bhakti* literature of preceding periods, and in inscriptional usage, *kūtti* and the parallel male term *kūttaṉ* appear in contexts in which the meaning of "dancer" is quite clear. Kūttaṉ, one of the names of Śiva in Tamilnadu, is also very common as a male given name. The idea that there was, in medieval South India, a tax on prostitutes is suggested by T. N. Subramaniam in his glossary in *South Indian Temple Inscriptions*, Volume 3, in reference to the terms *mukampārvai* and *kaṇṇāṭi*, which both mean "looking glass" (1957, xxiv, xxxix; cf. Gopalan and Subbarayalu 1967, 432, who define *mukampārvai* as a "customary present at the time of seeing a superior person"). Even if Subramaniam's interpretation of these terms is correct, they do not appear in Tamil inscriptions before the fourteenth century, fully three centuries after the references to *kūtti kāl* that are being considered here. A tax on dancers, on the other hand, is quite conceivable: we find parallels in three thirteenth-century inscriptions (SII 1.78; SII 17.564; SII 17.568) that refer to taxes on drummers (*uvaccaṉ kāl* or *uvaccaṉ perkkaṭamai*).

14. It is possible that *cāntikkūttar* as professional dancers may have been inheritors of an older bardic or indigenous Tamil tradition (Kersenboom 1987, 57, 151). But professional singers and dancers, male or female, were not generally referred to as *kūttar* or *kūttikaḷ* in the literature of the early Cankam period. The masculine forms *kūttaṉ* and *kūttar* are used in the *Poruḷ* section of the Tamil grammar *Tolkāppiyam* (which may date from around the fifth century A.D.) to refer to bards and minstrels as characters in literature (e.g., *Tolkāppiyam* 88, 148, 191, 491). In *Cilappatikāram* and *Maṇimēkalai* (probably of a still later date), the term *kūttu* is used to refer to the art of dance (e.g., *Cilappatikāram* 3.12, 13, and 19), and masculine *kūttar* and feminine *kūttikaḷ* are frequently used to designate dancers, singers, or actors (e.g., *Cilappatikāram* 5.50; 14.156; 26.106 and 228; 28.165; *Maṇimēkalai* 12.51; 18.6 and 35; 28.47). In the devotional poems of the Āḻvārs and Nāyaṉmārs (sixth to ninth centuries), *kūttu* most often refers to the dance of a god—Kṛṣṇa or, especially, Śiva (Orr and Young 1986, 50–54).

Another theory is that the term *cāntikkūttu* refers to classical as opposed to popular dance (Khokar 1979, 64; Kothari 1979, 23). In this case, the Chola period *cāntikkūttar* may have been developing new dance forms, perhaps under the influence of northern Indian classical dance and drama traditions. That these influences were present in Tamilnadu in this period is clear from the fact that there are so many reflections of the *Nāṭya Śāstra* in the descriptions of dance in *Cilappatikāram*, a Tamil work composed before Chola times.

Cāntikkūttu was performed at temple festivals. Other festival dances mentioned in Chola period inscriptions include *cākkaikkūttu*, which was performed by both men and women (ARE 65 of 1914; ARE 120 of 1925; ARE 8 of 1929; ARE 160 of 1941; SII 19.171), and *āriyakkūttu*, performed by men (ARE 120 of 1925; SII 3.202).

15. Singing and dancing at festivals, along with other forms of participation in festival observances, are also the most prominent ritual roles for women sanctioned by the Agamic texts (Orr 1994c). These roles are mentioned with particular frequency in the Pāñcarātra texts *Śrīpraśna Saṃhitā* and *Iśvara Saṃhitā*, both of which reflect practices particular to medieval South India (such as the use of Tamil hymns as part of temple liturgy). I suspect, therefore, that the Agamic imaging of the temple woman

as a festival performer has been, at least in part, influenced by the actual increase in the middle of the Chola period in women's involvement with festival dance.

16. These temple women of the later Chola period may be contrasted with a woman mentioned in an earlier (tenth-century) inscription (SII 26.391), who did have the capacity to transfer her rights hereditarily. She was granted land by the temple to support her as a festival dancer, and her descendents (*vaṟkattār*) were to continue to serve as dancers and to use the land.

17. Only one of the thirteen Chola period references to *naṭṭuvar* that I have found (SII 23.306) explicitly mentions the *naṭṭuvaṉ*'s connection with dance, but the term is clearly derived from Sanskrit *nāṭ*, "to dance" (MTL 2136–37; MW 525). Terms like this one, related to Sanskrit *naṭa*, *nāṭya*, or *nṛt*, are not at all common in Tamil inscriptions. Apart from *naṭṭuvaṉ*, the only other term of this type that I have found is *naṭṭiyāṭṭar*, which is probably a compound of Tamil *naṭṭiyam* ("dancing, acting," from Sanskrit *nāṭya*) and *āṭṭar* ("dancers," from Tamil *āṭu*). Two early Chola period inscriptions from Tiruchirappalli district (SII 8.659 and 698) mention *naṭṭiyāṭṭar* as owners of land. Terms of this type were much more widely used to refer to dancers outside of Tamilnadu. I have found the terms *naṭa*, *nartaka*, *nartakī*, *nṛtyantī*, or *nṛttāṅganā* in ten non-Tamil inscriptions, dating before A.D. 1300, from various parts of India including Karnataka and Andhra Pradesh. In seven of the ten references, the dancers were women. None of the female performers of dance in Chola period inscriptions is referred to by such terms.

That we find in the Tamil inscriptions *kūttu*-based terminology for "dancers" and *naṭa*-based language for "dance masters" may indicate the presence of two different dance traditions—an indigenous *kūttu* tradition, performed by professionals not linked to the temple, and a northern-influenced *nāṭya* tradition (see note 14). Each of these two traditions may have had its own group of professional specialists; if *cāntikkūttu* skills belonged to both women and men (although, as we have seen, *cāntikkūttar* with the title *ācāriya*, "teacher," were all men), *nāṭya* expertise seems to have been monopolized by men, by the *naṭṭuvar*.

18. In six of the thirteen inscriptions that refer to *naṭṭuvar*, they are listed together with temple women and other temple servants and described as receiving support from or acting as functionaries in the temple. But there is no indication of any special connection between *naṭṭuvar* and temple women, unless we consider significant the fact that *naṭṭuvar* and temple women are frequently in close proximity in the lists given in the inscriptions.

19. The renowned Tamil poet Kampaṉ, who lived during the later Chola period, was a member of the *uvaccar* community. His preeminent status as the author of the Tamil Rāmāyaṇa contrasts with the obscure and peripheral position of the later Ōcchar.

Another community of drummers, the *paṟaiyar*—whose anglicized name "pariah" is synonymous with "outcaste"— also experienced a drastic decline in status. The *paṟai* (the drum)—which features prominently in Cankam and *bhakti* literature—is frequently mentioned in Chola period inscriptions as an element in temple performances. But *paṟaiyar* did not serve as temple drummers. There are three contexts in which we find references to *paṟaiyar*: (1) in inscriptions, particularly from Tanjavur district, where there is the mention of *paṟaicceris*, which were evidently separate areas within villages where *paṟaiyar* resided; (2) in the imprecations of later Chola period inscriptions, which sometimes warn that those who overturn the terms of an endowment will have sunk to the level of a man who gives his wife to a *paṟaiyar*; and (3) in at least a handful of inscriptions (all from outside Tanjavur district) in which *paṟaiyar* appear as temple patrons and thus as people with economic resources and a legitimate public presence. I disagree with Heitzman, who considers that in the Chola period *paṟaiyar* "were practically if not legally attached to the lands and wills of the landowners and cultivators who controlled the land" (1985, 160; see also Jha 1974 and Hanumanthan 1980). *Paṟaiyar* in the Chola period ceased playing the ritual and professional roles they had in an earlier age—having been, perhaps, displaced by the *uvaccar*—but they were not yet entirely identified with the degraded and serflike status they were to acquire in later times (see also Appadorai 1936, 23–24, 313–18; Nilakanta Sastri 1955, 555–57; Arokiaswami 1956–57; K. Swaminathan 1978).

20. *Naṭṭuvar* may have competed with *uvaccar*, as well as with *cāntikkūttar*, for the role of dance teacher in the temple. That drummers, and the *uvaccar* themselves, were connected as teachers to temple women is suggested by Thurston's report that in Chingleput district, in the early twentieth century, the Ōcchar "act as dancing-masters to Devadāsīs, and are sometimes called Naṭṭuvaṉ" (Thurston and Rangachari 1909, 5: 419). In Tamilnadu in the last hundred years, most temple women have been trained in dance by *naṭṭuvaṉār*, men who belonged to the *ciṉṉamēḷam*, the male wing of the *devadāsī* community. The *ciṉṉamēḷam* is one section of the *mēḷakkāraṉ* "caste" group, which also includes the *periyamēḷam* (*nagaswaram*-players). Male members of the *ciṉṉamēḷam* might remain in their sisters' households and serve as musical accompanists (especially drummers) for the *devadāsīs* or establish themselves as dance teachers to the *devadāsīs* (*naṭṭuvaṉār*) (Thurston and Rangachari 1909, 2: 127–28; 5:59–60; Pillay 1953, 248; A. Srinivasan 1984, 198–226; cf. the *naṭṭuvaṉār* interviewed by Milton Singer 1972, 177, who emphatically denied any connection with *devadāsīs*).

The earliest inscriptional reference to *mēḷakkārar*, *ciṉṉamēḷam*, or *periyamēḷam* that I have encountered is an inscription of A.D. 1603 from South Arcot district that mentions *tevaraṭiyār* and *mēḷakkārar* (SITI 31).

21. Out of the thirteen inscriptions that mention *viṇṇappañ ceyvār* that I have located, six apply the term to men and none to women.

22. In the preceding discussion of dance, I have considered two inscriptions that refer to groups of "dancers" (*āṭiṉār*) and "singers" (*pāṭiṉār*). The term used for "singers" is based on the Tamil verb *pāṭu*. We cannot, however, determine whether these singers were male or female.

23. In the twelve inscriptions I have found that refer to the singing of *Tiruvāymoḻi*, this responsibility was assigned to men in four cases, to groups of singers whose sex was not apparent in eight cases, but in no case to singers who were clearly women.

24. On the one hand, we find in a thirteenth-century record (SII 7.118) from North Arcot district a list of communities swearing loyalty to their ruler: *pāṇar* are grouped with low-status groups like *paṟaiyar*, *veṭar* (hunters), and *iruḷar* (tribals) at the end of the list (*uvaccar*, interestingly, are listed toward the beginning, together with shepherds and *śivabrāhmaṇas*). On the other hand, in the same period—but much to the south, in Madurai district—we find an inscription (ARE 476 of 1963) that confirms the land rights (*kārāṇmai*) of a *pāṇaṉ* who is mentioned by name, which suggests a relatively high social and economic standing for this individual. The only other reference to *pāṇar* that I have found is from the second sub-period, in the long inscription from the Rājarājeśvara temple at Tanjavur (SII 2.66), where three (or perhaps four) *pāṇar* are mentioned by name and assigned shares as support from the temple. It is impossible to know what roles these *pāṇar* were meant to play in the temple, but it is perhaps significant that they are listed with artisans (carpenters, goldsmiths, etc.) rather than with the musicians mentioned earlier in the inscription. There is no indi-

cation of a connection between the *pāṇar* of the Tanjavur temple and the large group of temple women—*taḷicceri peṇṭukal*—named in this inscription.

25. The stories of the recovery, setting to music, and establishment of a professional group for the performance of the hymns are very similar in the Śaiva and Vaiṣṇava traditions, and both refer to events that are supposed to have taken place in the tenth or eleventh century (see Cutler 1987, 44–50). The Śaiva tale is found in Umāpati's *Tirumuṟaikaṇṭa Purāṇam* (fourteenth century), and the story of the Vaiṣṇava canon is told in *Kōyil Oḻuku* (which was compiled between the twelfth and the eighteenth centuries). In both traditions, a particular community or family is given the special responsibility of performing the hymns. It seems likely that these stories were used to legitimize the rights of those people who had succeeded in acquiring the role of singing hymns in the course of the Chola period.

26. In the first stanza of the Tamil poem *Tirupporcuṇṇam*, by the ninth-century Śaiva poet Māṇikkavācakar, women are called to the temple to make offerings, beautify the temple, sing praises, and take up flywhisks (*kavaris*) (*Tiruvācakam* 9.1; see Orr and Young 1986). In an early Chola period inscription from Tanjavur district, the *cāmarai* is mentioned as one of the marks of nobility bestowed by the king on a feudatory, along with an hereditary title, an army of elephants, palanquin (*civikai*), and so on (SII 3.89).

27. In the only passage in the Āgamas that I have found that specifically refers to the bearing of flywhisks, men perform this activity (*Īśvara Saṃhitā* 11.308–9). In the chronicle of the Srirangam temple, *Kōyil Oḻuku*, bearing flywhisks is described as a task performed both by male temple servants (*kaikkōḷar*) and by temple women (*emperumāṉaṭiyār*) (*Kōyil Oḻuku*, 94).

28. In addition to the three inscriptions considered here that use the term *kavarippiṇā* for women who perform flywhisk service, four other inscriptions use this term in other contexts (e.g., identifying a female donor as a *kavarippiṇā* or indicating support from the temple for *kavarippiṇās*). All seven inscriptions date from the mid-tenth to the mid-eleventh century; the term falls out of use in the later Chola period.

29. Tewari, in his study of royal attendants, says of *chauri* (*cāmarā*) bearers, as they are depicted in Sanskrit literature, "in comparison to the *chauris* they were holding and waving over the kings, specific references to them are few and far between"—whereas in artistic representations, "there is hardly an illustration of a *chauri* bearer in Indian art which does not present her as elegant, seductive and full of youth" (1987, 54–55).

30. There is more emphasis in Agamic texts than in Chola period inscriptions on women's involvement in temple festivals. But frequently the texts describe women as only one type of festival participant, out of several possible candidates. For instance, the *Sanatkumāra Saṃhitā* says that either a *devadāsī* or an *ācārya* ("teacher") should act as leader in the offerings to the directions during the *bhūtabali* ritual preparatory to the celebration of a festival (*Sanatkumāra Saṃhitā* Śivarātra 2.9.42). And in a number of Agamic references, *devadāsīs* are listed with other sorts of people, suggesting that the point of the text is to be inclusive of, rather than insistent on, the participation of such women along with other members of the temple or village community. In a festival procession described by *Īśvara Saṃhitā* (11.207), for example, the participants include not only *gaṇikādevadāsīs* but also townspeople, Brahmans, and so on. The *Parama Saṃhitā* (22.18–19) says that *gaṇikādevadāsikās*, artisans (*śilpins*), and servants (*sevakas*) should be brought together for a festival procession. It seems that functions associated with festival celebrations need not necessarily be performed by women or by a special class of female temple servants (see Orr 1994c).

31. On the basis of her interviews with South Indian informants and her study of recent commentaries on ritual texts, Kersenboom has concluded that "the most important task of the devadasi . . . was to remove evil influences from the deity [through her participation in the daily *dīpārādhanā* ("lamp-worship") ritual]. Her special qualification of being ever-auspicious (*nityasumaṅgalī*) made her more suited to this task than any of the ritual personnel" (1987, 119; see also 60–61 and 112–13).

There is, however, little textual or inscriptional evidence to support the idea that this interpretation is relevant to premodern South India. Although the Āgamas contain more references than do Chola period inscriptions to temple women's involvement with lamp service, these references are not extremely abundant, nor do they insist that temple women are preeminently qualified to perform this ritual function. I have found eight references in the Āgamas to temple women performing this function (out of a total of fifty-three references in the Āgamas to women's involvement in temple ritual), and three of these references clearly indicate that the employment of a woman in this ritual task was optional. For instance, the Śaiva text *Ajitāgama* (3.23.6) says that either the temple women of Śiva (*rudrayātanayoṣit*) or male assistants (*paricāraka*) might bring plates for lamps in the daily lamp-offering service. We find very similar mentions of alternative ritual performers—to bear lamps in procession or to participate in the daily lamp-waving (*nīrājana*) ceremony—in two Vaikhānasa texts, the *Vaikhānasāgama* (29.5) and *Bhṛgu Prakīrṇādhikāra* (Goudriaan 1970, 202; see Orr 1994c).

32. There are many references in the Sanskrit Epics and in Indian Buddhist literature to enormous numbers of women in the train of kings (Chanana 1960, 123–28). Although this aspect of the kingly persona is not particularly pronounced for kings in the Chola period in South India—less so, I would argue, than Shulman (1985, 303–39) has led us to believe—there is no question that the courts of Chola period kings included many palace women. That some of these women were, at least nominally, associated with personal attendance on the king is suggested by their identification as belonging in some cases to the *mañcaṉattār veḷam*, the "palace of the ceremonial bath" (e.g., SII 8.678; SII 22.27).

33. It is tempting to consider that the term *kambhada suḷeyār*, "pillar prostitutes," applied to temple women in medieval inscriptions from Karnataka, may reflect a similar, ornamental function for these temple women, whose roles, in addition to bearing flywhisks on occasion, were unspecified (Parasher and Naik 1986, 67). In a Tamil text of the post-Chola period—*Kōyil Oḻuku*, the chronicle of the temple of Srirangam—there is a suggestion of the ornamental character of temple women's services. The first of the duties assigned to temple women (*emperumāṉaṭiyār*) in this text seems to involve no ritual action at all but simply standing in the presence of the deity: "One [of the *emperumāṉaṭiyār*] would bathe herself, at dawn, and adorning herself, go to the temple and stand well in sight of the God." The text goes on to specify other tasks assigned to temple women, which involved bringing plates of incense and pots and dancing (*Kōyil Oḻuku*, 95–96).

Marglin (1985b) and Kersenboom (1987) have analyzed in detail the significance of temple women's roles as attendants in temple and palace ceremonies in more recent history. In their view, temple women who performed these services were not merely ornamental but served a critical function as representatives of auspiciousness, whose ritual actions were necessary for the protection and prosperity of temple and palace affairs. Given that in the Chola period temple women were engaged in attendance in the temple only occasionally—and in the king's palace, not at all—it does not seem that this interpretation of their ritual functions is very useful here.

The ornamental may, of course, be auspicious, but the question is whether this ornamental auspiciousness should be considered a ritual necessity or not.

34. The inscriptions do not provide any direct evidence of the character of women's domestic ritual, but there are some hints in Tamil literature. Hardy cites several references to the use of lamps in the worship performed by women in Cankam poems (*Neṭunalvāṭai* and *Maturaikkāñci*) which he dates to the second to fourth centuries A.D.: "Girls . . . light the wicks immersed in oil of the 'lights made of iron,' scatter rice and flowers, and worship"; "carrying many things, holding bright lamps in front and boiled rice . . . women undergoing a difficult pregnancy worship with devotion" (1983, 140). The ninth-century work by the Vaiṣṇava poet-saint Āṇṭāḷ, *Nācciyār Tirumoḻi*, describes women's creation of auspicious designs and other preparations that were part of the performance of a vow (*Nācciyār Tirumoḻi* 1.1; see Orr and Young 1986).

35. In the Śaiva devotional poems, there are references to the plaiting of garlands as one of the tasks of the devotees (*Tiruvācakam* 5.14) or of the Brahmans who worship Śiva (*Tēvāram* 7.30.3). The Vaiṣṇava poet-saints Toṇṭaraṭippoṭi and Periyāḻvār, both of whom were Brahmans, tended gardens and supplied garlands to the Lord, according to hagiographical accounts (Govindacharya 1982, 3, 22). Since there appears to be no evidence of their engagement in these activities in the poems themselves, it may be that the hagiographers of these two Āḻvārs were inspired by developments of the late Chola and post-Chola periods.

36. At the Vaiṣṇava temple of Srirangam, where a large number of inscriptions concern arrangements for the provision of flowers to the temple, we find in later Chola period inscriptions the responsibility for gardening assigned not only to laborers (*āḷs*) but also very frequently to *nampis* and *dāsanampis*, *śrīvaiṣṇavas*, and even *jīyar* (Orr 1995c). These figures, who are very often referred to by name, were individuals with high status in the corps of temple personnel or the sectarian community. At some temples, however, gardening and garland making continued to be treated as tasks for menial laborers even in the later Chola period. We can see this pattern at the great Śaiva temple of Chidambaram, where the gardeners mentioned in inscriptions of the twelfth and thirteenth centuries are all anonymous groups of *kuṭikaḷ* (Orr 1995a).

37. The *Bhāgavata Purāṇa* (XI.11.39) exhorts the devotees of Kṛṣṇa to sweep, wash, plaster, and decorate the floor of his shrine. We find references in the early Tamil Śaiva text *Tirumantiram* (1444, 1447) to the duty of the devotee to erect temples and to clean them (Narayana Ayyar 1974, 253–54). There are many passages in the Tamil poems of both Śaiva and Vaiṣṇava poet-saints that describe the cleaning of the floor of the temple as an act of worship appropriate to the ideal devotee (see, e.g., *Tiruvācakam* 5.14; *Tiruvāymoḻi* 10.2.7; Dorai Rangaswamy 1958, 1070; Orr and Young 1986).

38. It is interesting that there is no inscriptional evidence from the Chola period for women's involvement in pounding powders and pastes for adorning images, despite the several textual references to women's participation in this activity as part of festival observances. There are two such references in the Sanskrit Āgamas of the Vaiṣṇava Pāñcarātra tradition (*Śrīpraśna Saṃhitā* 34.74–75 and *Aniruddha Saṃhitā* 21.63). In Tamil devotional literature, an entire poem is built around the description of women pounding powder for a festival, the *Tirupporcuṇṇam* ("Gold-dust Song") in *Tiruvācakam*, composed by the ninth-century Śaiva poet-saint Māṇikkavācakar (see Orr and Young 1986). K. K. Pillay describes the involvement of temple women in this activity at the Suchindram temple, in the far south, in recent times: as part of fes-

tival observances, the ceremonial powdering of gold dust along with turmeric, to be smeared over the images, is done "by the Otuvar (chorist) and the Devadasi (of the 1st Kudi) together. . . . The pestle is held both by the Otuvar and the Devadasi during the pounding process . . . [and] both the persons sing a particular hymn from Manikkavacaga's Tiruvacagam" (1953, 228).

39. Five inscriptions refer to temple women who bear marks (in four cases the *triśūla*, Śiva's trident) indicating that they belong to a temple or a god. In four of the inscriptions (ARE 230 of 1921; ARE 141 of 1922; ARE 94 of 1926; EZ 4.24), these women appear to have been slaves; and in the fifth (ARE 537 of 1922), "those marked with the trident" seem to be temple servants or devotees in general, rather than temple slaves (ARE para. 19 of 1922; Nilakanta Sastri 1955, 556, 564, n. 43; Balasubrahmanyam 1975, 76; 1979, 53). In three inscriptions, we are able to learn the identity of the person who marked the temple women: in two cases, the person who gave the women to the temple, and in one case—in which slaves were purchased to work in a *maṭha*—the temple authorities.

Because of its association with the status of being, literally, a slave and because of the apparent lack of a ritual context in which the marking or branding occured, it is doubtful whether this practice is connected either with the South Indian *bhakti* and the Agamic sectarian traditions of marking, sometimes associated with rites of initiation (Hardy 1978, 134; Kingsbury and Phillips 1921, 39; Jaiswal 1967, 143–44), or with the ceremony of dedication performed by South Indian temple women in recent times, which was called "branding" (Ta. *muttirai*, from Skt. *mudrā*) and which involved the impression of a sectarian mark on the body of the dedicated *devadāsī* (Kersenboom 1987, 188; Viswanathan n.d., 57–58).

40. Fifteen of the twenty-two inscriptions that refer to slaves are from Tanjavur district.

41. The term used for "work" or "service" in this expression is *paṇi*, a word with very strong devotional connotations in the earlier Tamil *bhakti* literature. In the poems of both the Āḻvārs and Nāyaṉmārs, we frequently come across descriptions of the ideal devotee as one who performs service (*paṇicey*) for God (e.g., Māṇikkavācakar's *Tiruvācakam* 7.9, 10.12, 13.9, 27.5, 40.10, etc.; Cuntarar's *Tēvāram* 7.77.4; Nammāḻvār's *Tiruvāymoḻi* 1.10.11; Periyāḻvār's *Tirumoḻi* 5.3.3).

42. A much later record, dating from A.D. 1867, from the Suchindram temple at the southern tip of Tamilnadu, mentions three types of roles in outlining the duties of temple women: they were responsible for dancing and singing on various occasions; for the attendance functions of bearing lamps and flywhisks; and for the menial tasks of sweeping and cleaning the temple courtyard and shrines, washing the vessels used in worship, and clearing up after the offering of food to Brahmans (Pillay 1953, 283–85).

43. Of the seven inscriptions in the fourth subperiod that record deals made by temple women which resulted in temple service positions, three mention that support was provided by the temple. Of eight inscriptions from this subperiod that mention female slaves with temple service functions, only one describes arrangements for support.

44. The idea that all forms of *kāṇi* involved position, as well as property, is emphasized by Heitzman (1986, 11), who puts forward the notion of the "conditional nature of all property, dependent on the performance of public, social obligations"; by Karashima (1984, 26–27, 175, 196, n. 33), who stresses the idea that *kāṇi* and *mirāsi* were not only rights to land but also rights to privilege and power; and by Granda (1984, 122, 184), whose analysis of property relations in the post-

Chola period leads him to say that land rights "adhered to individuals like some personality trait," involving status as much as property.

45. In my analysis of religious *kāṇis* I am not distinguishing between village service *kāṇis* connected with temple duties (e.g., the grant of a *kāṇi* to a dancer or an artisan for service to the temple) and eleemosynary *kāṇis* (*brahmadeyas* and *devadānas*) that benefited temple servants. The distinction between the service tenure and the eleemosynary tenure was perhaps first made in Anglo-Indian law and does not seem to reflect any real functional division between types of temple service (Presler 1987, 77, 87). In the scholarly literature, Appadorai (1936, 164) and Nilakanta Sastri (1955, 570) make this distinction, and their lead is followed by later historians (Heitzman 1985, 135–37; Dirks 1987, 426–32).

Heitzman (personal communication) has suggested that *jivanam*, understood as a revenue grant allocated from public funds ordinarily collected as taxes (the "upper" share of produce from a piece of land), is different in source from *kāṇi* or *bhogam* (rights to the "lower" share). He distinguishes *brahmadeyas* and *devadānas* from *kāṇis* on the same basis.

Peter Granda (1984, 89–110, 219–23) provides a very comprehensive discussion of *kāṇi* and of the transmission of temple rights and land rights in the post-Chola period.

46. The notion of a share was in some instances closely linked to the concept of *kāṇi*. At times the term *paṅku* ("share") seems synonymous with *kāṇi* (e.g., SII 8.644); in other cases a specific service *kāṇi* might be divided into shares or days, distributed through the course of a month. In the present analysis, share arrangements are those in which various temple servants and temple expenses were assigned fixed amounts of income (in paddy or gold) out of the total revenues of the temple. A good example is provided by the long Tanjavur inscription (SII 2.66), in which each of the 400 *taḷicceri peṇṭukaḷ* was assigned one share (*paṅku*), defined as the amount of paddy (100 *kalam*) that 1 *veli* of land would produce; other temple servants were also assigned one share (e.g., the supervisor of the *taḷicceri peṇṭukaḷ*, the conch blower, and the goldsmith) or variously assigned a half or three-quarter share (some of the *uvaccar*, singers, carpenters, and barbers), two shares (*naṭṭuvar* and temple accountants), and so forth.

47. Every one of the seven inscriptions that refer to the *kāṇi* of a temple woman gives her name, and not one mentions arrangements for the support of other temple servants. Of the twenty-five inscriptions in which *kāṇi*-like arrangements are made for temple women, only four mention arrangements made with other temple servants and all but nine refer to the temple women by name. In contrast, twenty-three of the twenty-six inscriptions that describe share arrangements for temple women also specify allotments for other temple servants, and twenty of these inscriptions refer to temple women as members of an anonymous group (e.g., as *tevaraṭiyār*, or singing women).

48. In a few cases, temple women and other temple servants were paid with cooked rice (*coṟu*). Although payment in consecrated food (*prasāda*) and honors based on the distribution of consecrated food may have become very important in the post-Chola period, this does not seem to have been the case in the Chola period. See note 24 in chapter 3.

49. In my calculations of the value of the various kinds of property referred to in Chola period inscriptions, I have relied on the analyses of economics and mensuration undertaken by Appadorai (1936, 258–64, 701–32, 769f, 782–85, 796–810), K. Chatterjee (1940, 160–61), Nilakanta Sastri (1955, 557–62, 585–88, 613–24), Pandeya (1984, 144–45), and Heitzman (1985, 241–42, 510–12).

50. Of these twenty-two inscriptions, two are dated in the first subperiod, six in the second subperiod, four in the third subperiod, and ten in the fourth subperiod.

51. Ramaswamy (1989, 92, 94, 98) cites several Chola period inscriptions as evidence for her conclusion that in general women in early South India were paid less than men for domestic and agricultural labor. I have not found such a discrepancy in the case of temple service because women and men were not assigned to the same tasks within a single inscription or within a group of inscriptions from the same locale and period.

52. The term *cēri* has a wide range of meanings in Tamil literary and inscriptional usage. It may mean village, hamlet, suburb, district, or street, and it frequently denotes the quarter where a particular caste or professional group resides (MTL, 1636; SII 2.4 and 2.5; Gros 1968, 204, n. 38; Sethu Pillai 1974, 55; Karashima 1984, 46–48).

53. Amrit Srinivasan (1984, 148–56) describes the spatial organization of the area around the South Indian temple in recent history, highlighting the way in which the assignment of houses to temple women and allied groups near the east side of the temple and near the residences of the temple Brahmans served to demonstrate and enhance their "pure" or "high" status. Studies of the temples at Suchindram and Uttaramerur bear out Srinivasan's account to some degree (Pillay 1953, 10 and plan 2 "Sucindram in the time of Balamartanda Varma, 1729–1758 A.D."; Gros and Nagaswamy 1970, 124–27 and the map "Uttaramērūr: la ville moderne"). In the Chola period, however, we see diffierent patterns of habitation and land use around temples: residences were not densely clustered around the temple and much of the agrarian landscape was preserved in the process of "temple urbanization" (Heitzman 1987b). It appears that it is primarily in the post-Chola period—particularly at a few major temples that were renovated in this period (e.g., the Mīnākṣī temple at Madurai)—that we see the systematic application of the ideal model of the *mandala*, prescribed in Śilpaśāstra texts, to the organization of the streets and residences around the temple; in these cases there is a more orderly pattern of hierarchy "from the center outward" (J. Smith 1976, 31–36; see also B. Dutt 1925, 142–64; Reiniche 1985, 77–81, 85–91, 109, 112).

There are frequent references in inscriptions from Karnataka, dated in the eleventh to thirteenth centuries, to the housing of temple women, apparently in the vicinity of the temple; these districts are called *sūḷegeris*.

54. For the notion of a close connection between temple women and kings, see note 9 in chapter 3. The idea that *kāṇis* (or in more recent times, *ināms* and *māṉiyams*) have their ultimate source in royal largesse has been argued—or simply assumed—by British administrators, temple personnel, and many historians. Karashima (1984, 179–80), for example, has suggested that the *mirāsi* rights that the British attempted to deal with in the nineteenth century had their genesis in royal grants in the Chola period. Stein takes issue with the notion put forward by Nilakanta Sastri and other historians that rights to land rested ultimately in the state, and he traces this concept to colonial British interests rather than early South Indian practice: "Assuming the politic fiction that the government was landlord, the British claimed the right to a substantial portion of produce" (1980, 192). Heitzman (1985, 118–19, 144)—although he, like Stein, notes the vested interest of the British in the concept of universal royal possession of land—seems to support the idea that in fact in the Chola period *kāṇi* was understood as having its source in the universal lordship of the ruler, at least "conceptually," however irrelevant this "concept" might have been at the local level (1985, 141–42, 144, 164). Dirks (1987, 125–26, 128–29, 410–11) emphasizes strongly

the idea that *ināms* and *kāṇis* were, at least "in cultural terms" or "ideally," grants from the king—just as temple honors ultimately depended on royal prestige and largesse (Dirks 1976, 152; 1987, 289).

I am not persuaded that in the Chola period *kāṇis* "conceptually" or "ideally" derived from the king. It is true that in the colonial and modern periods, South Indian temple servants have upheld the view that their rights originated in royal grants (Fuller 1984, 91–92). This claim may not so much reflect ancient historical circumstances (or even "concepts"), however, as it does more recent changes: it has, for instance, been argued that profound alterations in the definition of *ināms* and in the relations between temple servants and the temple were the consequence of the policies of nineteenth-century British administrators (especially those in the Board of Revenue), who took too literally the idea that the state was the source of *ināms* (Appadurai 1981, 140–41; Fuller 1984, 94; Presler 1987, 77–81).

55. Neither royal sponsorship nor hereditary temple service arrangements were typical of the Chola period, but there seems to be a correlation between arrangements of support that were established by royal authority and those that were hereditary. This is not the case for temple women—there being so few instances of royal involvement with their support arrangements and, in addition, so few instances when their relationships with the temple were hereditary—but among temple men, it appears that a substantial proportion of royally sanctioned arrangements were hereditary and that a substantial proportion of hereditary arrangements were authorized by the king.

56. The arrangements for the support for temple women in medieval Tamilnadu may be compared with those in the same period in Karnataka, where, according to Parasher and Naik (1986, 70–77), temple women were largely patronized by members of the ruling family and of the top levels of the feudal hierarchy. The analysis of the types of donors responsible for establishing temple women in the temples of Karnataka serves as the starting point for the argument that these temples found both their material and their ideological basis in the feudal, hierarchical political order of the period. The power relations and ethos that were thus absorbed into the temple milieu had, according to Parasher and Naik, its effect on temple women, in their ritual tasks (modeled on royal ceremony), their standing in the hierarchy of temple servants, and the expectation that they were available for the "enjoyment" of those who held positions at the top of the various power structures—gods, Brahmans, kings, or members of the elite. If Parasher and Naik are correct about the sources of support for temple women in medieval Karnataka, the differences from the situation in Tamilnadu are very striking: it would appear that temple women in Tamilnadu depended to a much greater degree on local support—and on their own initiative—in securing their positions as temple servants.

57. The only possible exception that I can discover is that of the female singers (*naṅkaimār kāntarpikaḷ*) mentioned in a tenth-century inscription from Malabar district (TAS 8,43), whose role was (presumably) relatively professional, essential, skilled, and associated with proximity to the deity, in addition to being well paid. The only right-hand attribute in this case is the inscription's complete lack of specification of the actual tasks of these singers—an omission that may put in doubt some of the left-hand characteristics we have assumed.

58. These four inscriptions include three from the second subperiod (ARE 128 and 153 of 1912; SII 14.132) and one from the late thirteenth century (ARE 26 of 1928–29). In two of these inscriptions, it is not even entirely clear that the temple women involved did have functions in the temple.

Notes to Chapter 5

1. Apart from *tevar* and *tevaṉār*, various other terms for "god" or "lord" appear in the god identifiers of temple women. The word *nāyaṉār*, which has a Sanskrit root, is found only in the fourth subperiod. The Tamil word *uṭaiyār* (literally, "possessor") and the Sanskrit word *īśvara* and its Tamil equivalents are found in god identifiers throughout the Chola period. Sometimes we find a multiplication of words that mean "lord," of Tamil or Sanskrit origin, in the name of god, as in the following expressions: *tiruvekampaṉ uṭaiyār mahādeva makaḷ*, the daughter of the "Lord Great Lord" Tiruvekampaṉ (ARE 139 of 1912); *tiruvakattīcuram uṭaiyār tirunamattaṭiyār*, the *aṭiyār* of the holy name (*tirunamam*) of the "Lord Lord" of the holy shrine (*tiruvakam*) (SII 23.473); and *tirupokaṉuṭaiyanāyaṉār tevaraṭiyār*, the *aṭiyār* of "Lord Lord Lord" Tirupokaṉ (ARE 132 of 1940–41).

2. One of the few examples of this kind of identification in inscriptions of the early Chola period is the reference in the Tanjavur inscription (SII 2.66), which dates from the beginning of the second subperiod, to temple women as *taḷicceri peṇṭukaḷ*, "women of the temple district." In table 5.1, this inscription is classified as one which refers to temple women in terms of a temple identifier because all 400 women settled around the Rājarājeśvara temple are identified as *taḷicceri peṇṭukaḷ*, but each one also has an individual hometown identity. Of the 395 women listed in this inscription whose origins can be determined, 126 (32 percent) are god-identified (particularly with reference to their association with a deity termed *īśvara*), 97 (25 percent) are temple-identified (the term *taḷi* overwhelmingly predominates), and 146 (37 percent) are described as being of particular villages or towns; for 26 women (7 percent), it is, for various reasons, impossible to determine whether they are primarily associated with a temple or with a place. It is interesting that within the idiom and context of this inscription, proportionately more temple women are represented in terms of their connections with temples and places than is found generally in inscriptions of the second subperiod. Because I have, at the outset of this study, warned against the dangers of extrapolating from a single inscription—and this single inscription, in particular—it would be appropriate only to look at the ways in which this inscription may corroborate patterns discerned from the analysis of the corpus of inscriptions as a whole: I think it is fair to say that we see here a confirmation of the fact that place identifications were more important for temple women in the second subperiod than they were at other times. Table 5.1 indicates that this is the case not only for temple women but also for temple men.

The Tanjavur inscription also confirms that in the early Chola period temple women were much more likely than temple men to be hometown-identified at all. Whereas every one of the *taḷicceri peṇṭukaḷ* of the Tanjavur temple is identified by her place of origin, only a third of the men are described in such terms. Of the 101 men named and provided for in the inscription—most of whom are musicians, singers, or artisans—19 belong to a military or palace retinue, 8 are from a particular town, and 6 are from one or the other of Tanjavur's temples.

3. See note 65 in chapter 1 for information about the area study of temple men. In table 5.1, the numbers of inscriptions, rather than of individuals, are given. There are 219 temple men, who are mentioned in 109 inscriptions. In the row of figures for the second subperiod, the numbers of inscriptions that refer to men by god identifiers, temple identifiers, and place identifiers add up to more than the figure given for the hometown total because some of the inscriptions name several different types of men using different kinds of identifiers.

4. The ancient Cankam literature mentions Kanchi as the site of a shrine. Both the Āḻvārs and the Nāyaṉmārs praise this place in their devotional poems, composed in the sixth to ninth centuries. Kanchipuram is one of the three places, along with Srirangam and Tirupati, that the great fourteenth-century Vaiṣṇava *ācārya* Vedāntadeśika considered ideal as the dwelling place for a true devotee (Young 1978, 33).

5. None of the *taḷicceri peṇṭukaḷ* hails from faraway Kanchipuram; all fifty-four of the towns mentioned in the inscription as the hometowns of these women are in the core Chola region of Tanjavur and Tiruchirappalli districts. Forty-six *taḷicceri peṇṭukaḷ* came to the Tanjavur temple from Tiruvarur (seventeen are described as being from the town or from the Periyataḷicceri—"great temple district"—and the rest from one of five temples), thirty-one were from Palaiyaru (four from the town or a district within the town and the rest from one of five temples), twenty-one were from four temples in Niyamam, twenty were from three temples in Ambar, nineteen were from Tiruvaiyaru (ten from the town and nine from Lokamahādevi-Īśvara temple), eighteen were from four temples in the town of Tanjavur itself, seventeen were from Tiruvidaimarudur, and sixteen were from Ayirattali (three from Mallīśvara temple and the rest from the town). I have been able to identify all but fifteen of the fifty-four towns and villages given as hometowns of the *taḷicceri peṇṭukaḷ* by the Tanjavur inscription (SII 2.66). In this task I was aided by the previous research of Hultzsch, the editor of the inscription, and of Spencer (1969), Subbarayalu (1973), and Heitzman (1985, 280, 284, 508–29); especially valuable was the information on locations of places mentioned in inscriptions from the Tanjavur temple on which Heitzman based his mapping of the transactional network of the temple (1985, 252–311; 1991) and which he very kindly made available to me.

6. It is interesting that the use of the terms *tevaṉār makaḷ* and *tevaṉār makaṉ* is associated with a number of these places—particularly Tiruvidaimarudur, Tiruchatturai, and Takkolam but also Tiruvarur, Melappaluvur, and Kanchipuram (see note 31 in chapter 2).

7. Apart from the Tanjavur inscription, 238 temple women are named in Chola period inscriptions. Eleven bore the name of the Chidambaram temple. All but 2 of the 11 are mentioned in inscriptions of the last subperiod.

8. That temple women from specific temples do not characteristically bear the name of that temple, or its god is also demonstrated by the Tanjavur inscription (SII 2.66), which conveniently provides a long list of names and hometowns of temple women. Of the 383 names of *taḷicceri peṇṭukaḷ* discernible in this list, 62 incorporate place-names or the names of temple deities. As was the case in the whole corpus of Chola period inscriptions, the most prominent place-name in the names of these temple women is Chidambaram, which occurs in 12 instances. None of the *taḷicceri peṇṭukaḷ* transferred to Tanjavur were from the temple of Chidambaram. Eight women were named for the shrine or the deity of Tiruvaiyaru, but only 1 actually came from Tiruvaiyaru. Six women were named for Tiruvarur, but only 1 had Tiruvarur as her hometown. These 2 women, 1 from Tiruvaiyaru and 1 from Tiruvarur, are the only 2 of the 383 *taḷicceri peṇṭukaḷ* whose names and hometowns correspond.

Apart from these two *taḷicceri peṇṭukaḷ*, and the woman named Kāñcipura-naṅkai whose mother belonged to a temple in Kanchipuram, I have found only three other temple women whose names reflect a linkage to a place that is attested to in some other way: Tiruvūṟal-naṅkai was a *tevaṉār makaḷ* mentioned in three inscriptions of the late tenth and early eleventh centuries as the mother of several donors to the temple of Tiruvūṟal at Takkolam (ARE 257 and 258 of 1921; SII 5.1364); Cāṇi Oṟṟiāḻvi, who made a gift to the temple of the god Tiru Oṟṟiyūr Uṭaiyār in the twelfth century, is described as a *tevaraṭiyāḷ* of this temple (SII 5.1360—translated in chapter 3); and Tiruvaṇṇāmalai-māṇikkam, a *tevaraṭiyāḷ* of Tiruvannamalai, is mentioned as the mother of a donor to the temple in a thirteenth-century record at this place (SII 8.120).

9. Heitzman (1995) actually treats all place-names, even without the suffix *uṭaiyār*, as indicative of an individual's association with that place. In the context of his focus on a particular category of individuals who "control the flow of resources in a village environment" and who in fact typically do bear the title *uṭaiyār*, "usually connected with a place name," this treatment of the significance of place-names as part of personal names seems to work. But I would suggest that for other sorts of people who figure in the Chola period inscriptions—and particularly women—place-names have other meanings.

Even when the suffix *uṭaiyār* is present, there may be problems of interpretation. The authors of *A Concordance of the Names in the Cōḻa Inscriptions* distinguish between names of the form "village-*uṭaiyār*" and those of the form "sacred place-*uṭaiyār*"—except when the name of the sacred place ends in *-ūr* or some other termination that identifies it as a village or a town. "Unless the village which precedes the title is a holy place such as Tiruchirrambalam, this combination of a village name and *udaiyan* in a personal name seems to indicate that the person has the ownership of some land in the village" (Karashima, Subbarayalu, and Matsui 1978, xlvi). Perhaps what is behind this distinction is the idea that a "sacred place-*uṭaiyār*" name may well be interpreted as a deity's name (e.g., Tiruciṟṟampalam-uṭaiyār is the "Lord of Tiruciṟṟampalam").

10. The *Concordance* lists about 200 personal names that incorporate the name of Chidambaram or its central shrine (Tiruciṟṟampalam, Tillai, Ampalam, or Poṉṉampalam), and three-quarters are from the later Chola period, particularly the third subperiod. It is difficult to know precisely why these names suddenly began to enjoy popularity in the middle of the Chola period. One of the puzzling aspects of this issue is that the temple itself did not enjoy popularity, in the sense of attracting numerous patrons, until the thirteenth century, 100 years later (Orr 1995a).

11. Of the 238 temple women named in the inscriptional corpus as a whole (excluding the Tanjavur inscription), 40 bear goddess-names.

12. The use of goddess-names among the *taḷicceri peṇṭukaḷ* listed in the Tanjavur inscription (SII 2.66) also illustrates this point. Despite the fact that the Rājarājeśvara temple is dedicated to Śiva, more of these women bear Vaiṣṇava goddess-names (particularly Tiru, which is the Tamil form of Śrī) than Śaiva goddess-names (e.g., Umai and Mātevi). Of the 383 *taḷicceri peṇṭukaḷ* whose names are discernible, 33 have goddess-names.

13. The names Tukkai and Catti were borne by men whose names appear in Chola period inscriptions. Medieval Tamil inscriptions on Buddhist images record that these images were donated by women with the Hindu goddess-names Umai and Tukkai (Orr 1999). The only goddess-names used by temple women that are not widely shared among other types of people are those Tamil goddess-names that end in *nācciyār*. These are especially common among temple women in the last subperiod, when there is also an increasing use of the term *nācciyār* to refer to the goddesses worshiped in Hindu temples (Orr forthcoming a). But even *nācciyār* names are not borne exclusively by temple women.

14. Nakkaṉ is clearly a name and not, as some have concluded, a term that means "girl," "our sister," or "temple dancer" (EI 2, 278; Kersenboom 1987, 75, n.135).

15. Apart from the *taḷicceri peṇṭukaḷ*, twenty-one temple women have the name Nakkaṉ.

16. In the four study areas, nineteen women are described in inscriptions as being the daughters of men. Although in two cases there is some resemblance between the fathers' and daughters' names, in none of these inscriptions do we see the incorporation of the male name of the father as an element in the daughter's personal name. Having read through a large number of Chola period inscriptions that refer to women, I have been able to find only a handful of cases in which a woman bears her father's name. Heitzman (1995) has suggested that women sometimes took their husband's name, but I have not found any inscriptions in which this is the case.

Paternity seems something of a nonissue for temple women, as we see later in this chapter; when temple women or their offspring refer to their parentage, it is their mothers who are named. Nor do temple women or their sons or daughters incorporate their mothers' names into their own personal names. Only in one case, in thirteenth-century Tirunelveli district, do we see this kind of usage: Cempoṉ Tiyāki alias Vīrapattira-naṅkai, identified as the daughter of the *tevaraṭiyāḷ* Ampattāḷ in one inscription (ESITA 42) is referred to as Ampattāḷ Cempoṉ alias Tiyāki alias Vīrapattira-naṅkai in another (ESITA 28).

17. This is quite a difflerent idea from that advanced by Subbarayalu, who maintains that the reason the *taḷicceri peṇṭukaḷ* of Tanjavur temple were all named Nakkaṉ was that they were ignorant of their true paternity and so took the god enshrined in the temple as their adoptive father (1976, Chap. 7).

18. That these women's acquisition of the name Nakkaṉ would have been regarded as an honor is obscured by the interpretation of Suresh Pillai (1968, 439, 445–46), who holds Rajaraja I responsible for the "forcible naming pattern" of the *taḷicceri peṇṭukaḷ*. According to Suresh Pillai, giving all these women the name of the god Śiva was part of Rajaraja's project to establish a "canonical," Brahmanical religion in place of earlier indigenous cults focused on local gods and goddesses. This account is not very convincing, given the fact that Nakkaṉ was a name already in wide use at the time of Rajaraja's reign and that the worship of the great god Śiva had been established in Tamilnadu for many centuries.

19. Nineteen temple women bore the title *talaikkoli* as part of their names. See note 37 in chapter 2.

20. In Telugu inscriptions of the thirteenth and fourteenth centuries temple women are referred to by the term *māṇikamu* or *māṇikya* or named Māṇikama (Iswara Dutt 1967, 233; Talbot 1988b, 107–8). The term or title *māṇikkam* seems to be associated in the later South Indian *devadāsī* tradition with the task of waving auspicious lamps (*kumpālatti*) (Dirks 1987, 130; Kersenboom 1987, 28, 65–66). In the late nineteenth century, the feminine form of the word, *māṇikkattāḷ*, was considered to be synonymous with *devadāsī* (Thurston and Rangachari 1909, 4:451; Waghorne 1994, 217). In inscriptions of the post-Chola period, temple women frequently have the name Māṇikkattāḷ, as well as Māṇikkam.

21. We find in the Vaiṣṇava Āgamas the idea that a name received at the time of religious initiation should reflect the name of the deity of the sectarian tradition (Rangachari 1931, 35–36; Gonda 1965, 402; H. Smith 1975, 80–81). According to one early Pāñcarātra text, the *Jayākhya Saṃhitā*, the initiated person should be given a name connected with Viṣṇu, and it should convey the sense of "lordship" or "own-

ership" (Jaiswal 1967, 142). In contemporary South Indian Śaiva practice, the first of the series of initiations that priests undergo, which qualifies them to serve in the temple, centers on the ritual of naming (Fuller 1985, 111). In the ceremonies of dedication of *devadāsīs* in recent history, there are several elements that suggest sectarian initiation, notably the branding of the temple woman's body with the mark of the deity she is to serve (A. Srinivasan 1984, 174–77; Kersenboom 1987, 188–89, 191; Viswanathan n.d., 20–23, 57–58; cf. Jaiswal 1967, 142–44).

Magdalen Gorringe's recent (1998) translation and analysis of a section of the Śaiva *Kāmikāgama* centers on its description of the initiation (*dīkṣā*) of temple women (*rudragaṇikās*). This ceremony involves touching their heads with a rod (*daṇḍa*) and bestowing on them the title Daṇḍinī as part of their names (1998, 32–33, 35). Gorringe remarks that it is possible "that *Daṇḍinī* is a Sanskritisation of the Tamil *Talaikkōlli*" found as part of the names of temple women in the inscriptions (1998, 33 n. 161).

22. A fifteenth-century inscription from Pudukkottai, in Tiruchirappalli district, records the grant to the temple woman (*tevaṭimai*) Uṭaiyammai the title Nalutikkamvenṟa-māṇikkam and the right to perform certain services (IPS 814). In the following century, there is a record from Tirunelveli district, dated A.D. 1557, describing the grant of temple privileges and the title Periyanāṭṭu-māṇikkam to A̱lakuṭanāṭumperumāḷ Paḷḷiyaṟai-nācciyār (ARE 86 of 1927). And an inscription of A.D. 1614, from Nedungunam in North Arcot district, records the grant to Muttu, the daughter of a *tevaraṭiyāḷ*, of land and the title Vicaiyarākuva-māṇikkam (SII 17.762).

23. Heitzman notes the "remarkable continuity in dominant property relations expressed in the Chola period until the early colonial period," arguing that British colonial administrators of the late eighteenth century "found embedded in the Persian term *mirās* . . . the same body of property relations extant in the eleventh century" (1986, 20). But according to other scholars, "the complex of local revenue privileges connoted by the term *mirās* was poorly understood by the British and its meaning was radically transformed" (Appadurai 1981, 141). By the beginning of the nineteenth century, because of the urbanization of temple lands in South India, "the usage of the term *mirās* to describe various rights in the temple had lost all connection with the rural model of privileged shares of agricultural resources. Instead, it had come to encode the arguments of individuals and families both to hereditary claims on temple jobs and the perquisites and shares in the divine leavings attached to these jobs" (1981, 142). The increasing involvement of the colonial government in local and temple afflairs in the nineteenth century produced a situation of intense competition and conflict over these rights (1981, 142–48). Fuller (1984, 110) similarly argues the probability "that the British, keen to discover, record and codify the ancient hereditary rights that they thought were ubiquitous in India, were partly responsible for the contemporary insistence on their vital importance." In Irschick's (1994, 100–14) view, the formulation of the *mirāsi* system in Tamilnadu, accompanied by the production of texts that legitimized the claims of various groups to their "traditional" rights, was a collaborative efflort between the British colonizers and their Indian subjects.

24. Heitzman's study of local "lords" ("intermediary authorities") mentioned in Chola period inscriptions indicates an absence of the inheritance of honorific titles and even of positions and estates. "In the Tamil records the native place is important for intermediary authorities, but territoriality is not the only source of their political influence and is thus rarely paraded in the inscriptions. It is the combina-

tion of a base of operations, high titles, and ritual largesse in different sacred sites that constantly recurs in the activities of all these individuals. . . . The titles naturally changed from person to person, and even for the same individual, as his relationship to his superiors changed and as he accomplished different tasks during his lifetime" (1995, 93–94).

In thirteenth-century inscriptions from Andhra Pradesh, Talbot has similarly found that "status titles," even those apparently indicative of occupation, were not passed on from father to son and therefore seem to be "to some degree connected with the person's achievements" rather than with status due to birth (1988b, 193–95). Talbot concludes that in comparison with more recent South Indian society, with its caste-based structure of hierarchy, "class and rank was much more fluid during that time, since there appears to have been a fair degree of social mobility" (1988b, 198; see also Talbot 1992).

25. The term *vaṟkattār* commonly appears in Chola period inscriptions, spelled in a variety of ways (*vaṟkkattār*, *vaṟggattār*). It is formed from the Tamil *vaṟkam* (*vaṟkkam*, *vaṟukkam*), which is derived from the Sanskrit *varga*. This term is found throughout the whole Chola period but seems to be especially used in the early Chola period for non-Brahman male temple servants (singers, dancers, and drummers). In a number of these cases, as in the inscription being discussed here, the term may with as much justification be translated "group" or "troupe" as "descendents." I have assumed, however, that this term is indicative of hereditary descent. In most cases, I have assumed the same for the term *vaḻi*. *Vaḻi* can mean "descendants" or "family lineage" but also a nonhereditary succession (*paramparai*) (MTL 3542–43). Another term used particularly in later Chola period inscriptions is *vaṅśattar*, from the Grantha *vaṅśam* (Tamil *vamican*), derived from the Sanskrit *vaṃśa* (MTL, 3494). This term, meaning "those of ones lineage, family," is less ambiguous than *vaṟkkattār* or *vaḻi* in indicating kinship connections through the generations.

26. Precisely the same qualification of the principle of heredity is seen in the case of the forty-eight male *piṭārar* appointed to sing hymns at Tanjavur temple (SII 2.65). For the *taḷicceri peṇṭukaḷ*, it is difficult to know what might constitute "fitness" because the nature of the service these women were to perform in the temple is entirely unspecified.

It seems clear that the 400 *taḷicceri peṇṭukaḷ* positions established by Rajaraja I did not in fact become permanent hereditary positions because nothing is later heard of temple women from this temple. This is probably the case for other temple personnel of the Tanjavur temple as well. Very few inscriptions appear at this temple in the years following Rajaraja I's death (Balasubrahmanyam 1975, 87), and it is surely significant that fewer than 50 years later we find a record at the temple of an arrangement made to give a *cāntikkūttaṉ* and his *vaṟggattār* a daily allowance of paddy to perform a play or dance (*nāṭakam*) in the temple (SII 2.67H). Had Rajaraja's extensive establishment of temple personnel—including various kinds of performers—survived even two generations, we would not expect such an "outside" professional to be hired.

27. It is perhaps especially surprising to find so few indications in the Chola period inscriptions of hereditary relationships with the temple for priests or other Brahman temple servants, given that priestly temple service in modern South India appears to be entirely hereditary in character (Fuller 1984, 81–86; Reiniche 1989, 77–93) and that a number of the medieval ritual handbooks, the Āgamas, mention hereditary qualification for temple service. Several of the Śaiva Āgamas and Vaikhānasa Āgamas emphasize that those who offer public worship (i.e., priests)

must be born into a particular lineage (Bhatt n.d., 8–15, 18). According to Brunner, for the Ādiśaivas—those devotees of Śiva who alone are eligible to worship on behalf of others—"il s'agit bien d'une filiation physique, les textes sont clairs sur ce point" (1964, 457). She points out that Ādiśaivas are unique in this regard because other worshipers attain their status by initiation (*dīkṣā*) and take on the "family" of the *guru* who initiates them; she quotes *Kāmikāgama*: "le *gotra* [des *Ādiśaiva*] ne s'obtient pas par la *dīkṣā*, mais par la naissance" (1964, 469, n. 18). Some of the Pāñcaratra Āgamas, of the Vaiṣṇava tradition, lay down similar restrictions: the *Īśvara Saṃhitā* (21.511–58) specifies that only those descended from Śāṇḍilya are eligible for the initiation that allows an individual to perform worship for others (H. Smith 1975, 80–81).

Neither in my examination of the group of Chola period inscriptions that refer to temple men nor in my detailed study of inscriptions from Srirangam and Chidambaram temples up to the early fourteenth century (Orr 1995a and 1995c) have I found any emphasis on the lineage (physical or spiritual) of those who fill priestly positions. My conclusion that Brahman, as well as non-Brahman, temple service became hereditary relatively late in South Indian history contrasts with the view that such hereditary connections with the temple are quite ancient. Hardy, for example, believes there is evidence in the poems of the early Āḻvārs that "may well mean . . . 'professional/hereditary temple service'" (1983, 289–90) and finds in Periyāḻvār's poems references to "institutionalized Brahman temple service" (1983, 403). Not only the Chola inscriptional record of some centuries later than the period of the early Āḻvārs, but also the internal evidence of the *bhakti* poems themselves argue against Hardy's conclusions (see Orr and Young 1986).

28. We have seen that at Rājarājeśvara temple in Tanjavur, the position of both female and male temple servants—*taḷicceri peṇṭukaḷ* or the *piṭārar* appointed to sing hymns—was to be inherited by a "near relative" but only if this person were fit for the position (SII 2.65 and 2.66; see note 26). In several other inscriptions of the early Chola period, Brahman or non-Brahman men were appointed to temple service positions on the basis of their experience or knowledge (e.g., SII 2.25; SII 3.128). In other cases, again from the early Chola period, Brahman or non-Brahman men were considered to have eligibility or responsibility for the performance of some task in the temple because of where they lived, not their family origins (SII 2.69; SII 2.70; SII 3.128).

A few inscriptions use the term *talaimāṟu* ("substitute, replacement"—literally "head-change"), which suggests a nonhereditary succession of responsibility for temple duties. One of these, an eleventh-century Chola inscription from Sri Lanka (SII 4.1388), names seven female *tevaraṭiyār*, along with several male *uvaccar* (drummers) and priests, as being responsible for overseeing a grant for perpetual lamps in the temple; after them, their replacements (*talaimāṟu*) were to continue to ensure that the lamps were lit. Tirumalai suggests that this inscription indicates a system of rotation of temple personnel, and he contrasts the system of succession indicated by this inscription from Sri Lanka with the system he considers usual in Tamilnadu in this period: it "allows for replacements or substitution, a procedure which is not ordinarily noticeable in the arrangements made in the mainland temples where the responsibility descended on the lineal successors (*vaṟgattār*) in the male-agnate line" (1982, 16). As we have seen, there is little evidence that a hereditary system was common on the "mainland." And there are several examples from Tamilnadu, from the early Chola period, of succession on the basis of "substitution," particularly among *uvaccar* (SII 2.66; SII 12.114).

In some Chola period inscriptions, the term *muṟai* conveys the idea of the rotation among several groups of the privilege or responsibility to perform temple services. This term is, however, somewhat ambiguous because it can mean either "relative" or "turn by which work is done" (MTL 3299–3300). It seems to have the former meaning in several mid-Chola period inscriptions (including SII 2.66), but more frequently, especially in references to temple women of the later Chola and post-Chola periods, *muṟai* evidently denotes a group of people who are not necessarily related to one another or a position in the rotation of duties (see, e.g., Fuller 1984, 81). In the inscription translated at the beginning of this section, *muṟai* has this latter sense.

29. In the case of temple women, only two inscriptions provide the least indication that family or lineage may have been significant in the grant of a position in or support from the temple. Both of these inscriptions are from Madurai district in the far south and are dated in the thirteenth century, in the reigns of Pandya kings: in one, land and a house site are granted to the daughter of a *tevaraṭiyāḷ* by the Pandya king (ARE 242 of 1941–42); in the other, land is granted as the property (*kāṇi*) of the daughter of a *tevaraṭiyāḷ*, apparently by a local lord or chief (SII 23.428). In neither case is the property received by the *tevaraṭiyāḷ*'s daughter associated with any function or service in the temple, nor is the daughter identified as being of the temple, so it is actually rather difficult to regard these inscriptions as demonstrating that being a *tevaraṭiyāḷ*'s daughter constituted a "qualification" for a temple position.

30. In table 5.1, where types of hometown identifications are presented, the figure for the total number of inscriptions in which temple women are named is given as 168, whereas in table 5.2 it is 221. The difference arises from the fact that, because of the state of preservation of the inscriptions, references to temple women's family relationships are found more frequently than references to their hometowns.

31. To provide figures for groups with which temple women might be compared, in table 5.2 I have drawn from a number of my studies. For information about the groups of palace women and queens, see notes 4 and 5 in chapter 2. Figures for Jain religious women come from Orr 1998. Because I particularly examine women's family relationships in Orr forthcoming b, I have drawn on the research I did for that article to provide figures for the groups of Brahman and non-Brahman women who are named in inscriptions of *eight* study areas—the four that are the base of the area studies in this volume (Kanchipuram taluk in Chingleput district, Tirukkoyilur taluk in South Arcot district, Kumbakonam taluk in Tanjavur district, and Kulattur taluk in Tiruchirappalli district) and four others (Chidambaram taluk in South Arcot district, Tiruchirappalli taluk in Tiruchirappalli district, Madurai and Melur taluks in Madurai district, and Ambasamudram and Kovilpatti taluks in Tirunelveli district).

32. My survey of the ways in which women are identified in inscriptions of the eight study areas, in the period of the eighth to the seventeenth centuries, shows that although close to 40 percent of temple women were identified with reference to a hometown, this was the case for only 5 percent of nontemple women (Orr forthcoming b).

33. In medieval Andhra, the situation was quite diffierent: temple women were most often identified with reference to their fathers (Talbot 1994).

34. The *devadāsīs* of recent history frequently contracted long-term liaisons with prominent and wealthy men, but their status was entirely independent of these connections and their families were autonomous and female-centered (A. Srinivasan 1984, 194–98; Marglin 1985b, 79–82).

35. In the tenth, eleventh, and twelfth centuries at least one in every ten women whose name appears in the inscriptions was identified with reference to more than one relative, most frequently her husband and her father (Orr forthcoming b).

36. The Āgamas make no mention of initiation rituals modeled on marriage for temple women (Brunner 1990, 125; Gorringe 1998), and the commentary on the Śaiva *Kāmikāgama* by Sadyojātaśivācārya, cited by Kersenboom (1987, 186–87), that does describe a ceremony of initiation resembling in some ways the *devadāsī* "marriage" ritual is of uncertain date and authenticity. Marco Polo, who is supposed to have visited South India in the late thirteenth century, observed that young women serve the deity in the temple "until they take husbands" (Latham 1958, 270).

The ritual of marriage to the temple deity is understood by the temple women of recent times, as well as by those who have studied them, to be the defining feature of *devadāsī* status, and, in large part, recent efforts to interpret their significance (by, for example, Marglin, Srinivasan, Kersenboom, and Meduri) hinge on this feature of the "making" of a *devadāsī*. Symbolically, according to these interpretations, it is marriage to the god that makes a woman ever-auspicious (*nityasumaṅgalī*), because she will never be widowed, and that transforms her into a representative of the goddess or of the god's power (*śakti*), because she has become the consort of the deity. Socially, this marriage sets her apart from other women as a sexually active but "celibate" (unmarried) woman. In ritual and occupational terms, the marriage signifies her initiation into the role of servant to a particular deity. Economically, it confers prestige that allows access to material advantage and artistic patronage.

There are several problems with the understanding that the temple woman's dedication ritual is fundamentally a rite of marriage. First, this is not the form of initiation into temple service universally practiced, even in recent times, nor does this form of initiation always have the same significance. In Travancore, at the beginning of the twentieth century, none of the Malayali *dāsīs* and only a few of the Tamil *dāsīs* were married to the temple deity (Nagam Aiya 1906, 384). In about the same period among temple women of the former Mysore state, it appears that the right to temple service was acquired through a kind of professional initiation rather than through a marriage ceremony (Kersenboom 1987, 200–1 n. 50; Antze n.d., 6–7). In another variation, it seems that some *devadāsīs* in Tamilnadu who had been dedicated to the temple also, later in life, married men of their community (A. Srinivasan 1984, 157).

Second, there is the problem of the sex of the marriage partners. For example, at the Jagannātha temple at Puri in Orissa, precisely the same ceremony of "tying the cloth" (*sāḍhi bandhana*) is performed for Brahman and non-Brahman male temple servants as for *devadāsīs*; the latter consider this ritual to bring about their marriage to Lord Jagannātha (Marglin 1985b, 67–72). Are the male temple servants, having undergone the same dedication ritual, also married to the male deity? Also problematic is the argument that the various kinds of women "married" to goddesses (such as Yellammā, in western Karnataka) have thereby attained a status equivalent to that of women who are dedicated as temple servants through marriage to male deities (Kersenboom 1987, 192–93, 196–97—on dedication to Yellammā, see note 28 in chapter 1; Punekar and Rao 1962, 3; Hankare 1981, 30; Shankar 1990, 99–102)).

The stress on marriage as the central ceremony in the acquisition of temple woman status for *devadāsīs* in recent times has obscured the fact that becoming a temple woman was a process involving participation in various rituals, with many local variations and with complex symbolism that cannot be reduced simply to "marriage." In addition to ceremonies with the form or significance of marriage, rituals associated with coming of age, with sectarian initiation, and with professional development were also essential to the shaping of a temple woman's identity.

In accounts of the experience of South Indian temple women in recent history, there are two rituals that suggest marriage: *poṭṭukkaṭṭutal* or *tālikaṭṭutal* and the ceremony called *caṭaṅku* or *muttirai*, which usually takes place several years later. The first, *poṭṭukkaṭṭutal* or *tālikaṭṭutal*, involves tying a *poṭṭu* or a *tāli*. A *poṭṭu* is a gold ornament in the form of a cup or disc (MTL, 2914), and the *tāli* is the "central piece of a neck ornament solemnly tied by the bridegroom around the bride's neck as marriage-badge" (MTL, 1848). For temple women, then, the *poṭṭu* is a type of *tāli*. Possibly its use by temple women of Tamilnadu has been influenced by the customs of Andhra Pradesh. According to the *Tamil Lexicon*, the *poṭṭuk-karukalmaṇi* is "a string of black beads and discs . . . used by Telugus as a marriage badge" (MTL, 2914–15). The Telugu influence has been important in the dance and music traditions of Tamil *devadāsīs* for the last several hundred years. Although the link between *tāli* tying and marriage is very strong, there are aspects of this ritual that have the character of a coming-of-age ceremony (a *saṃskāra* equivalent to the *upanayana* performed for twice-born boys) or of a sectarian initiation (*dīkṣā*) (A. Srinivasan 1984, 171; Kersenboom 1987, 186–87, 200–1, n. 50; see also Thurston and Rangachari 1909, 2:143–44; Pillay 1953, 281–82; Lincoln 1981, 9, 116, n. 10; Allen 1982, 189–92; Vergati 1982; Young 1987, 69).

The second ritual that resembles marriage is the ceremony called *caṭaṅku* or *muttirai*, occurring several years after the *poṭṭu* tying, in which the *devadāsī* is "married" to a sword (*kaṭṭāri*) as a symbol of the deity. The *caṭaṅku* ceremony for South Indian *devadāsīs* obviously has a number of elements that mark it as a ritual of marriage, but its primary significance seems to be initiation into a ritual and professional role in the temple; it is frequently combined with the *devadāsī*'s first dance performance in the temple (A. Srinivasan 1984, 174–77; Kersenboom 1987, 188–89). There are also elements in the *cātaṅku* ceremony that suggest sectarian initiation (*dīkṣā*), notably the branding of the temple woman's body with the mark (*muttirai* = Skt. *mudrā*) of Śiva, Viṣṇu, or Murukaṉ (A. Srinivasan 1984, 174–77; Kersenboom 1987, 188–89, 191; Viswanathan n.d., 20–23, 57–58; cf. Jaiswal 1967, 142–44).

In addition to the *tāli*-tying and *caṭaṅku* or *muttirai* rituals, with their multivalent symbolisms, South Indian *devadāsīs* in recent times also took part in a series of professional life-cycle rituals considered necessary in becoming temple women. These rituals include *sātaka pūcai* (commencement of training), *kaccai pūcai* (bestowing of anklets), and *araṅkēṟṟam* (first formal performance) (A. Srinivasan 1984, 172–73, 175–76; Kersenboom 1987, 190–92). These rituals highlight the *devadāsī*'s relationship with her dance teacher (*naṭṭuvaṉār*) rather than her association with a temple, sectarian community, or deity.

37. *Kaikkoḷar* participated in temple ritual and had administrative responsibilities at temples in Kanchipuram, Manimangalam, and Tiruvorriyur in Chingleput district (Ramaswamy 1985, 54–55, 105–6); in Tiruvennainallur, Tirukkoyilur, and various other temple towns in South Arcot district (Ramaswamy 1985, 55, 105); in Tiruvannamalai and Devikapuram in North Arcot district (Karashima 1984, 159; Reiniche 1989, 110–11); at Tirupati in Chittoor district (Ramaswamy 1985, 106–7, 113); and at Srirangam (Ramaswamy 1985, 113; *Kōyil Oḻuku*, 94–95) and Kudumiyamalai (IPS 190; IPS 367) in Tiruchirappalli district. Most of the evidence for this ritual rec-

ognition of the *kaikkoḷar* comes from the post-Chola period. It is possible that this recognition was linked to the fact that *kaikkoḷar* were quite active as temple patrons (Mines 1984, 47; Ramaswamy 1985, 41–46, 96–99).

In addition to their administrative responsibilities, *kaikkoḷar* may have acted as temple servants in other ways: according to literary sources and caste traditions, a section of the *kaikkoḷar* community (called *poṉṉampala-kūttar* or *nāyaṉār*) were "temple minstrels," among whom the twelfth-century poet Oṭṭakūttar is a caste hero of the *kaikkoḷar* to this day (Mines 1984, 11; Ramaswamy 1985, 56). The only hint in Chola period inscriptions of the *kaikkoḷar*'s role as temple singer comes from Tiruvennainallur in South Arcot district (ARE 437 of 1921). This inscription, which seems to date from the thirteenth century, describes a conflict about the right to recite Tēvāram hymns in festival processions—a conflict that resulted in the death of a *kaikkoḷar*, who was given posthumous honors (see Ramaswamy 1985, 59). It is not clear in this case, however, whether hymn singing should be considered a professional ritual task or a temple honor. I have come across no other reference to *kaikkoḷar*'s singing even in the inscriptions of the post- Chola period. Temple support for *kaikkoḷar*, occasionally referred to in inscriptions from Chola and subsequent periods, seems to have been provided in exchange for the *kaikkoḷar*'s work as weavers of cloth for the temple (Ramaswamy 1985, 50–51, 101–3). There is, however, one reference to the term *poṉṉampala-kūttar* in a fourteenth-century inscription from Chingleput district, which mentions that this group, along with the *kaikkoḷar*, were responsible for arbitration in the case of a theft from the temple (SII 5.479).

I have not found any evidence that *kaikkoḷar* were dance teachers, although Amrit Srinivasan claims there are "various inscriptions of the thirteenth century which associate *Kaikōḷar* men with the *dāsīs*, in the role of dance *gurus*" (1984, 235, n. 39).

38. One other Chola period inscription that seems to indicate the identity of *tevaraṭiyār* and *kaikkoḷar* is a record probably dating from the twelfth or thirteenth century from Iluppur in Tiruchirappalli district, which refers to a man as both a *tevaraṭiyār* and one of the *kaikkoḷa-mutāliyār* (ARE 292 of 1943–44).

Two other Chola period inscriptions, both from the thirteenth century, may further indicate the link between temple women and *kaikkoḷar*, but these give no information about the character of the connection, only mentioning the two jointly. In one of these inscriptions, *kaikkoḷar* and temple women are described as purchasing house sites from the temple at Tiruvanakkoyil in Chingleput district (ARE 284 of 1910). In the other, *kaikkola-mutālikaḷ*, *tevaraṭiyār*, and the temple managers (*tāṉattār*) are said to have taken charge of a particular transaction at a temple in Tiruchirappalli district (ARE 638 of 1962–63). Such joint references become more numerous in the fourteenth to sixteenth centuries (see, e.g., ARE 117 of 1918; ARE 110 and 490 of 1921; ARE 277 and 292 of 1928–29; EC 9.Bn66; SII 1.87; SII 22.241; TDI 1.108).

In the post-Chola period, there is also more explicit evidence for the identity of temple women and *kaikkoḷar*: a temple woman of Kudumiyamalai in Tiruchirappalli district is referred to as a *kaikkoḷar* in an inscription of the Vijayanagara period (IPS 367); two fifteenth-century inscriptions from North Arcot district describe groups of *kaikkoḷar* who indentured themselves to the temple, the women undertaking to perform *tevaraṭiyār* services and the men to perform *kaikkoḷar* duties (ARE 278 and 279 of 1977–78); a temple *kaikkoḷaṉ*'s sister is depicted as a temple woman in another fifteenth-century inscription from North Arcot district (SITI 128); and a sixteenth-century inscription from Tirupati describes a temple woman as a *kaikkoḷar* (TDI 5.9).

It is worth noting that virtually all of the post-Chola inscriptions that link *kaikkoḷar* and temple women come from the northern districts of Chingleput, Chittoor, South Arcot, and North Arcot—the same region where we find the few indications of connection between the two groups during the Chola period.

39. Reiniche is, in my opinion, rather too definite about the links between *kaikkoḷar* and temple women at Tiruvannamalai and elsewhere. She says, "Les danseuses du temple de Tiruvannamalai étaient issues de la caste des Kaikkōḷar (des tisserands), un fait, confirmé par les inscriptions, qui n'est pas absolument général au Tamilnad . . . mais qui se retrouve en un certain nombre de lieux saints (dont, semble-t-il, Kañcipuram . . .)" (1989, 110).

Certainly for the Chola period, there seems in fact to be very scant inscriptional evidence that temple women came from the *kaikkoḷar* caste. If a few bits of such evidence begin to appear at the very end of the period, these may signal a changing state of affairs rather than a situation that had prevailed earlier in the temples of Tamilnadu.

40. Seven inscriptions out of a total of ninety-five that name palace women mention them in the context of identifying their daughters or sons. In one case, a man is identified as the son of King Rajendra's *aṇukki*; in the other six inscriptions, women are identified as the daughters of palace women, who are variously termed *peṇṭāṭṭis*, *veḷam* women, or *pokiyār*. Although the sons and daughters of palace women may well have been the offspring of the kings or chiefs in whose courts their mothers resided (as I have suggested in the case of the inscription translated at the beginning of this section), the inscriptions are silent on the subject of their paternity. This is not the case when people are identified as the sons or daughters of queens; there are no inscriptions in which queens are mentioned as ancesters or mothers apart from their royal husbands. We find a few inscriptions in which women identify themselves as the relatives of queens—as the mother (SII 12.85; SII 13.304; SII 19.77) or the younger sister (SII 5.524) of a Chola queen. This is, of course, understandable in that a queen would be a person of high rank, and thus a family connection to such a person would be a source of pride. Such references do not indicate a system of reckoning kinship through the female line.

We might expect prostitutes to be a category of women who were involved in female-focused kinship structures. In such works of Tamil literature as *Cilappatikāram* and *Maṇimēkalai* we are presented with the image of the courtesan family as a family of women, in which the courtesan's lineage and profession are passed from mother to daughter. Unfortunately, there is no information in Chola period inscriptions about prostitutes. From another period and another part of India, we do have a scrap of inscriptional evidence that supports the notion that prostitutes reckoned descent through their mothers: in an early inscription from Mathura, a courtesan (*gaṇikā*) is described as being the daughter of another courtesan, Loṇa Śobhikā (EI 10 Lüder's List 102; Nath 1987, 75; see also EI 33.51—D. C. Sircar, "Note on Ratnagiri Plates of Sōmavaṃśī Karṇa").

41. On the family arrangements of *devadāsīs* in recent history, see Thurston and Rangachari (1909, 2:127, 144–45, 147–49), A. Srinivasan (1984, 191–98), and Marglin (1985b, 79–82).

42. The most famous among the communities who practice the *marumakkatāyam* system are the Nayars (Schneider and Gough 1962; Dumont 1983). There are a number of ethnographic accounts of the women known as *basavis*. A *basavi*, instead of joining her husband's lineage and bearing children for his family, bore children who inherited her father's name and wealth, and she and her sons performed

funeral and memorial services for her father and his ancestors (Fawcett 1890; Francis 1904, 66–67; Thurston and Rangachari 1909, 2:135–36, 150–51; Srinivas 1942, 177–83). The *basavi* can be understood as equivalent to the "appointed daughter," the *putrikāputra* mentioned in the Dharmaśāstras and Epics, who may legitimately fill the role of a son if a family has only daughters (Kane 1930, 2:435–36, 3:647–59; *Mahābhārata*, Anuśāsana parvan 44–45).

A system parallel to the *basavi* system was current in Andhra Pradesh (Derrett 1968, 112, 407–9) and, until recently, in Tamilnadu as well: "An only child . . . who happened to be a daughter could 'dedicate' herself to the local deity and accept either one patron or lovers . . . in order to produce children for her family. This prevented family ancestral property from being dispersed. Dedication to god and to the temple therefore . . . was 'only in name' as the girl was brought back to her own house to further her own interests, economic and familial." (A. Srinivasan 1984, 181).

Kersenboom considers the *basavi* to be, like the temple woman, a type of *nityasumaṅgalī* (ever-auspicious woman) or "ritual woman" (1987, 194–95, 206). Despite the similarities in the ceremony of dedication that *basavis* and temple women of recent history underwent—which took the form of "marriage" to a deity—its motives seem to be entirely difflerent in the two cases. In contrast to the temple woman, the dedication of a *basavi* was not considered an initiation into the status of temple servant or professional performer (Thurston and Rangachari 1909, 2:135; Srinivas 1942, 178–78, 183).

43. Lemercinier (1979, 480) suggests that there is evidence in the Cankam literature of a matrilineal kinship structure in Kerala, although most students of Kerala's social history believe that matrilineal systems did not come into vogue until at least a thousand years later; there is evidence of a matrilineal and matrilocal *marumakkatāyam* system in Kerala in literature of the twelfth century and later periods (Mathew 1979, 60–65; Sreedhara Menon 1979, 41, 83–92).

It is also in the medieval period that we find hints of the emergence of matrilineality in other parts of South India. I have shown that in Tamilnadu, beginning in the thirteenth century, lineage was traced through the maternal line by some communities. There is very little inscriptional evidence of any sort of matrilineal practice before this period; were matrilineality in fact a feature of earlier Tamil society, it appears to have died out by the early medieval period. In Karnataka, there are inscriptions of the ninth and tenth centuries that mention *basavis* (Nandi 1974, 72–73) and other inscriptions of the tenth to fifteenth centuries that refer to the system of reckoning descent or corporate family responsibility through the daughters of the family to sons-in-law (*aḷiya-santāna*) (EC 6.Koppa 51 and 53; EC 7.Shimoga 102; EC 8.Sagar 100 and 104; EC 8.Sb 13).

44. Dumont (1983, 128–33) makes this point about the essentially patrilineal character of the *basavi* system and applies it further to the situation of Nayar women in Kerala, for whom the *tāli* tying, understood as a primary marriage, is "a way of inserting 'maternal' institutions [matrilineal inheritance] into a 'paternal' sociological milieu."

45. Amrit Srinivasan (1984, 194–95, 198), in her study of the social organization of families of temple women in the Tamilnadu of recent history, indicates that fathers were not acknowledged, that brothers lacked authority, and that sons were not likely to carry forward the family name. *Devadāsī* households were strongly matrifocal, although the fact that certain brothers or sons of *devadāsīs* established themselves independently of their female relatives as dance teachers (*naṭṭuvaṉār*), becoming the gurus of other *devadāsīs*, produced a "dichotomous" power structure in the *devadāsī* community as a whole (1984, 191–92, 196–97, 199–200, 235, n. 38).

The temple women of Orissa have a family structure similar to that of the *devadāsīs* of South India. Marglin's analysis of the kinship and marriage patterns and of the rituals performed for ancestors in the *devadāsī* community of Puri led her to the conclusion that "it seems as though male filiation is minimized almost to the point of non-existence, both for the men and for the women" (1985b, 79–82). Although men and women of this community honor almost exclusively female ancestors of the female line, Marglin argues that this system is not truly a matrilineal one, insofar as the female lineage is in large part established through *adoption* (especially by the *devadāsī*'s adoption of her brother's daughters) rather than through the continuation of the maternal bloodline (1985b, 79–81, 84–85).

Notes for Chapter 6

1. The increasing importance of the temple as a local center is signaled by the "growing withdrawal of temple supervisory responsibility from local assemblies and the bestowal of administrative autonomy upon full-time temple priests and employees" (Hall 1981, 408). In Hall's view, temple authorities gained greater control as the result of royal intervention in temple affairs. I believe, however, that this process took place even (and perhaps especially) at places where there was little or no royal interest, because such interest seems in many cases to have had the effect of short-circuiting links between the temple and the surrounding community. For example, at Tiruvidaimarudur in Tanjavur district, the involvement of the Chola ruler and his officers in temple affairs discouraged local donations (Heitzman 1995). Elsewhere, for example at Tanjavur and Srirangam, extensive royal patronage of temples appears to have substantially weakened local political and economic networks (Hall 1980, 200–1; Orr 1995c).

2. For example, Hoult (1969, 165–66) describes an institution as a process or an association that is (a) highly organized (i.e., there is a careful specification of the roles and role relationships of those involved), (b) highly systematized (i.e., there is a careful specification of what can and should be done by those involved), and (c) highly stable (i.e., relative to any given group or process, there is no dependence on the presence of any particular individuals). Institutionalization is the process whereby associations or procedures become increasingly organized, systematized, and stabilized.

3. We have seen in chapter 1 how the characterization of the medieval period in India in terms of feudalism and decadence is linked to notions of priestly greed and of a self-serving perversion of an earlier religious vision in order to attract and accomodate the masses (e.g., by Kosambi 1969, 172–73, 196, and R. Sharma, 1974, 187–89; see notes 16 and 54 in chapter 1).

The view that temple Brahmans are somehow degenerate—in performing worship for others and accepting payment for that service—is not confined to historians inspired by Weber or Marx but is shared by Hindus themselves. The ambiguous status of the Brahman as temple priest has been a point of debate and curiosity for at least a thousand years in South India (see Neevel 1977, 30–37; Appadurai 1983; Fuller 1984, 49–71).

4. Asceticism, associated with the development of *maṭhas* as centers for the transmission of both the Śaiva and Śrīvaiṣṇava sectarian traditions, was another element that arose in the processes of differentiation, hierarchy, and definition of eligibility in South Indian religious organizations. This development seems, however, to be more a feature of the post-Chola period (Orr 1994b; 1995b; 1995c).

5. For example, in my examination of the organization of temple life at Srirangam and Chidambaram, I have found that there was very little emphasis on Brahmanical identity, that there is no evidence of fixed connections between roles in the temple and membership in particular groups, and that there was a diffusion of claims to specific types of authority and status among various individuals and types of temple functionaries (Orr 1995a; 1995c). Women, however, particularly at Srirangam, were almost entirely absent from temple affairs, indicating perhaps that certain aspects of bureaucratization were more pervasive and exclusionary at these large and important temples than elsewhere in the Tamil country.

6. I have argued elsewhere for a reconsideration of the significance of religious patronage in Indian religions: instead of regarding gift giving as auxiliary to more fundamental or "virtuoso" religious activity, I suggest that it is a form of religious behavior that is religiously significant in its own right, as well as a public religious activity that in practice may be more widespread than any other. Because there is a great deal of evidence that women have been extensively engaged in donative activity—as is clear from the present study—I conclude that women cannot be regarded as marginal to public religious life (Orr 1999).

7. I do not want to give the impression that the economic and social situation of women was in decline from the beginning of the Chola period onward. The story is very much more complex. There is, for instance, ample evidence that women in the late Chola period had the right to possess and dispose of land in their own names and that they participated in political arrangements. Furthermore, some of the indications of limitations on women's authority, autonomy, and access to property that are characteristic of the later Chola period (such as the identification of women as wives and the mention of *mutukaṇs*) are less in evidence or disappear entirely in the post-Chola period (Orr 1997; forthcoming b).

8. These factors may be the most important ones in Europe, as well. In precisely the same period that I am considering here—the twelfth and thirteenth centuries (the later part of the Chola period)—we see in Europe an intimate connection between changing marriage and family arrangements and the decline of women's control over property and capacity to act as patrons of religious institutions. In this period in Europe, an increased emphasis on patrilineality, primogeniture, and the indivisibility of patrimony, loss of women's control over their dowries, increases in the amount of dowry, and the encouragement of widow remarriage all contributed to the change in women's economic position and religious activity (Stuard 1987, 160–68; Schulenberg 1988, 120; 1989, 234).

9. The Sanskrit Āgamas, some of which may have been composed or compiled in Tamilnadu during the Chola period, do raise obstacles to women's participation in religious life, evidently on the grounds that women are innately impure or of weak moral character (Orr 1994c, 120–25).

10. In note 4, I have remarked that asceticism was not a major feature in defining eligibility to perform religious functions during the Chola period. Although the ascetic sectarian leader was to become an increasingly important figure in the Śaiva Siddhānta tradition, there continued to be functions (such as that of temple priest) for which marriage was a requirement and sectarian communities (notably, the Śrīvaiṣṇavas) for whom householdership was the norm (Fuller 1984, 30–32; V. Narayanan 1990; Orr 1994c, 121; Olivelle 1995, 17–26; Young 1995, 182).

11. Another religious model, and a model of "marriage," that seems *not* to have had relevance to the position of women within the temple structure is the concept of relationship between the devotee and God as parallel to that between the female

beloved and the male lover (see note 33 in chapter 2). In Āṇṭāḷ's devotional verses of the ninth century and in the hagiographies and *sthalapurāṇas* of the late Chola period, there are explicit references to the idea of a human woman, a saint or princess, marrying the divine Lord. But how does the marriage of a human woman to a divine husband transform her? In South Indian myth and hagiography, a woman who marries a god is understood either to be a human incarnation of the divine consort of the deity or to attain divine status through her marriage, but she dies or disappears by merging into the image of the god (*Kōyil Oḻuku*, 5–6; Shulman 1980, 155–66; Harman 1989b, 44–54, 115–26, 146–63; Young 1995; forthcoming; see also H. Whitehead 1921, 20–22; O'Flaherty 1980, 67–71, 125–26). In other words, we do not find a model here for human women being transformed through marriage into goddesses while continuing to dwell in the world, a devotional paradigm, which if it had had relevance in the Chola period might have legitimized temple women's roles.

It is important to note that the woman, saint or devotee, who rejects human marriage to more fully devote herself to God does not necessarily take on the persona of the wife of her Lord. An example of another alternative, presented in the twelfth-century Tamil hagiography *Periya Purāṇam*, is Kāraikkāl Ammaiyār, who, once released from marriage to a human husband, took on the form of a skeletal demon to attend on Lord Śiva. Other possible female devotional careers and roles found in various non-Tamil traditions are mentioned by Kinsley (1980), Feldhaus (1982), and Ramanujan (1982). Particularly important in the context of devotion to Kṛṣṇa is the model of the *illicit* love afflair with God, which is an extramarital relationship.

12. I rely for information about conditions in the post-Chola period on Mahalingam (1940); Perlin (1981, 276–77, 288–93), Granda (1984), Karashima (1984, 164–65; 1992, 1–3, 16–17), Dirks (1987, 34–36, 43–48), Stein (1989, 21–27), Bayly (1989, 21–30), and Wagoner (1993).

13. For the impact of changing political and social arrangements in the post-Chola period on religious practices and religious institutions, see Breckenridge (1986), Bayly (1989), Narayana Rao, Shulman, and Subrahmanyam (1992), Orr (1995b), Talbot (1995a), Price (1996), R. Davis (1997), and Wagoner (forthcoming).

14. Nine sets of post-Chola period Tamil inscriptions provide details of the organization of groups of temple women. When several inscriptions are included in a set, they record changes in arrangements or in personnel. For example, a series of fourteenth-century inscriptions from Tiruvorriyur in Chingleput district describe alterations in the course of 30 years in the assignment of tasks to several groups of temple women, termed *patiyilār*, *tevaraṭiyār*, and *iṣapattaḷiyilār* (ARE 195 and 208 of 1912; SITI 525; see note 39 in chapter 2). The tasks include sweeping and smearing the temple precincts; carrying lamps, ash, and flowers; cleaning the rice used for offerings; fanning the deity; and singing and dancing.

Among the other inscriptions that outline specific arrangements of duties or precedence for temple women is another record from the northern part of Tamilnadu—a fifteenth-century inscription from North Arcot district (ARE 280 of 1977–78)—and an inscription from Kolar district, in the west, dated in the fourteenth century (EC 10.Ml 21). Three inscriptions come from Tiruchirappalli district, dated in the reigns of Pandya or Vijayanagara rulers (IPS 621; IPS 781; IPS 814). There are two sets of sixteenth-century inscriptions from the southern district of Tirunelveli (ARE 384, 388, 396 of 1916; and ARE 604, 605, 606 of 1916), and another inscription from the south, a fourteenth-century inscription from Kanyakumari district (KK 303). It is noteworthy that there are no inscriptions of this type from Tanjavur or South Arcot district.

15. Inscriptions of the post-Chola period provide little indication that temple women's positions were becoming increasingly hereditary. In chapter 5, we saw that the proportion of inscriptions that indicated that temple women had hereditary relationships with the temple, of those inscriptions that might possibly have done so, rose from 4 percent in the early Chola period to 12 percent in the later Chola period. This proportion goes up only very slightly, to 14 percent, in inscriptions that refer to temple women that date from 1300 to 1700.

16. I have found 128 such inscriptions: 70 percent mention temple women's performance of service functions or indicate that they received support from the temple, and 17 percent record their gifts to the temple.

17. Eight percent of the inscriptions dating from 1300 to 1700 that refer to temple women describe them as performing songs or dances in the temple. This proportion in the Chola period is 12 percent (see table 4.2).

18. These developments of the seventeenth and eighteenth centuries—which are all too frequently considered to be characteristic of the whole of the "precolonial" period in South India—are described by Appadurai and Breckenridge (1976), Dirks (1987, 43–54, 117–30, 285–89), Bayly (1989, 44–47, 55–58, 65–70), Narayana Rao, Shulman, and Subrahmanyam (1992, 88–90, 180–88), Ramanujan, Narayana Rao, and Shulman (1994), Waghorne (1994, 111), and Price (1996, 109–110). Obviously, in this period, one must take into consideration the additional factor of colonial influences on the political and religious arrangements of Indian rulers and Indian temples, but this goes well beyond the scope of the present study (see Appadurai 1981, 105–211; Dirks 1987, 358–83; Presler 1987; note 23 in chapter 5). The overlapping of the spheres of temple and court, from the seventeenth century onward, has been briefly dealt with in an earlier chapter (see note 9 in chapter 2), as has the establishment in the eighteenth and nineteenth centuries of the *devadāsī*'s dance repertoire (see chapter 4).

19. Recent ethnographic studies indicate that participation in such rituals was an important component of the ritual activity of *devadāsīs* in this century; see Lembezat (1953, 83, 93–96), Marglin (1985b, 99, 190, 198, 256–63), and Kersenboom (1987, 115, 136–39, 145–49, 159–62).

20. On women in the Vijayanagara court, see also Sewell ([1900] 1962, 234, 253–60, 275–77, 358–63), Kersenboom (1987, 35–38), and Hiebert (1992). The idea that women in a royal court may act as representatives of the king's attributes or possessions or the divine supports of his sovereignty—as *śakti*, as auspiciousness and good fortune, or as embodied goddesses—is found in a variety of other ritual and textual contexts (Herman 1979, 63–69, 138–49; Marglin 1981, 159–61, 178–79; Shulman 1985, 303–7, 331–32; Gupta and Gombrich 1986, 127, 132–34).

21. Some analyses of relationships between "the feminine" in divine and human realms in Indian religious thought find that the acknowledgement of human women's embodiment of divine force is closely linked to the restriction and subordination of women. Feminine divine power (*śakti*), when it is a force belonging to and used by human women (rather than an attribute of male sovereignty or divinity—see the preceding note), is frequently understood as arising from women's self-sacrifice and endurance, and its efficacy is a result of its being strictly controlled, through chastity and marriage, and channeled toward selfless ends (Babb 1970; Tapper 1979; Egnor 1980; Wadley 1980; Robinson 1985, 199–209; Young 1987, 94–96). As C. S. Lakshmi (1982) points out, this is an odd sort of power, whose existence and utility depends on self-abnegation.

Bibliography

Primary Sources: Inscriptions in Tamil and Other Languages

ALB Krishna Aiyangar, A. N. "Inscriptions of Uttaramerūr." *Adyar Library Bulletin* 7 (1943):79–88, 186–191, 259–266; 8 (1944):93–99, 177–82; 9 (1945):13–15, 94–98.

ARE *Annual Reports on Indian Epigraphy*. 1905–78. Delhi: Manager of Publications. Transcripts of the inscriptions abstracted in the ARE were graciously made available to me at the Office of the Chief Epigraphist, Archaeological Survey of India, Mysore.

EC *Epigraphia Carnatica*. 1889–1955. Madras/Bangalore/Mangalore/Mysore.

EI *Epigraphia Indica*. 1892–. Calcutta/Delhi: Director General, Archaeological Survey of India.

ESITA Swaminathan, K. D. 1990. *Early South Indian Temple Architecture: Study of Tiruvāliśvaram Inscriptions*. Trivandrum: CBH Publications.

EZ *Epigraphia Zeylanica*. 1912–. London: Oxford University Press for Government of Ceylon, Archaeological Survey of Ceylon.

HAS *Hyderabad Archaeological Series* 1915–56. Hyderabad: Nizam's Government.

IPS *Inscriptions (Texts) of the Pudukkottai State Arranged According to Dynasties*. 1929. Pudukkottai.

KK *Ka<u>nn</u>iyakumāri kalveṭṭukkaḷ*. 1972. Ed. Naṭa<u>n</u> Kācināta<u>n</u>. Madras: Tamil Nadu State Department of Archaeology.

NK *Na<u>nn</u>ilam kalveṭṭukkaḷ*. 1979–80. 3 vols. Ed. Ā. Patmāvati. Madras: Tamil Nadu State Department of Archaeology.

PCM *Thirty Pallava Copper-plates (prior to 1000 A.D.) (Pallavar ceppēṭukaḷ muppatu)*. 1966. Ed. Ti. Nā. Cuppiramaṇiya<u>n</u>. Madras: Tami<u>l</u> Varalā<u>rr</u>uk ka<u>l</u>akam.

SII *South Indian Inscriptions*. 1891–1990. vols. 2–26. Delhi: Director-General, Archaeological Survey of India.

SITI *South Indian Temple Inscriptions.* 1953–57. Ed. T. N. Subrahmaniam. Madras: Government Oriental Manuscripts Library.
TAM *Tirvannamalai: A Śaiva Sacred Complex of South India.* 1990. Vols. 1.1 and 1.2: *Inscriptions*, intro. ed. trans. P. R. Srinivasan. Institut français de Pondichéry.
TAS *Travancore Archaeological Series.* 1910–38. Vols. 1–8. Trivandrum.
TDI *Tirupati Devasthanam Inscriptions.* 1931–37. Vols. 1–6. Madras.
TK *Tiruttuṟaippūṇṭi kalveṭṭukkaḷ.* 1978. Ed. Rā Nākacāmi. Madras: Tamil Nadu State Department of Archaeology.

Primary Sources: Literature in Tamil, Sanskrit, Pali, and Prakrit

Āgama Prāmāṇyam, Yāmuna. Sanskrit text and English trans. J. A. B. van Buitenen. 1971. Madras: Ramanuja Research Society.
Agni Purāṇam: A Prose English Translation. M. N. Dutt. 1967. 2 vols. Varanasi: Chowkhamba Sanskrit Series Office.
Ajitāgama. Sanskrit text ed. N. R. Bhatt. 1964, 1967, 1991. 3 vols. Pondichéry: Institut français d'Indologie.
Aniruddha Saṃhitā. Sree Anirudha Saṃhitā: One of Divyasaṃhitā in Pancharātra. Sanskrit text ed. A. Sreenivasa Iyengar. 1956. Mysore.
Āṟāyirappaṭi Kuruparamparā Prapāvam. Maṇipravāla text. n.d. Trichy: S. Kiruṣṇasvāmi Ayyaṅkār.
Arthaśāstra, Kauṭilya. *The Kauṭilīya Arthaśāstra.* Sanskrit text (part 1—1960) and English trans. with critical and explanatory notes (part 2—1963) R. P. Kangle. Bombay: University of Bombay.
Bhāgavata Purāṇa. Śrīmad-Bhāgavatam. English trans. N. Raghunathan. 1976. 2 vols. Madras: Vigheswara Publishing House.
Brahmāṇḍa Purāṇa. Sanskrit text. 1914. Bombay: Sri Venkatesvara Press.
Brahmāṇḍa Purāṇa, Part 4. English trans. Ganesh Vasudeo Tagore. 1984. *Ancient Indian Tradition and Mythology*, Vol. 25. Delhi: Motlilal Banarsidass.
Cilappatikāram, Ilaṅkō Aṭikaḷ. Tamil text. Tañcāvūr: Tamiḻp palkalaik kaḻakam.
The Cilappatikaram. English trans. with intro. and notes V. R. Ramachandra Dikshitar. 1978. Madras: South India Saiva Siddhanta Works Publishing Society.
Divyasūricaritam, Garuḍa Vāhana. Sanskrit text ed. T. A. Sampath Kumaracharya and K. K. A. Venkatachari. n.d. Bombay: Ananthacarya Research Institute.
Īśvara Saṃhitā. Sanskrit text ed. P. B. Ananthacarya Swami. 1921. Conjeevaram: Author.
Jayākhya Saṃhitā. Sanskrit text ed. Embar Krishnamacharya. 1967. Gaekwad's Oriental Series No. 54. Baroda: Oriental Institute.
Kāmasūtra, Vātsyāyana. *The Kāmasūtra by Śrī Vātsyāyana Muni with the Commentary of Jayamaṅgala of Yashodhar.* Sanskrit text ed. Sri Gosvami Damodar Shastri. 1929. Benares: Chowkhamba Sanskrit Series Office.
The Kama Sutra of Vatsyayana. English trans. Sir Richard F. Burton. 1964. New York: Dutton.
Kāmikāgama, Part 1. Sanskrit (Grantha) text ed. Ci. Cuvāmināta Civācāriyar. 1977. Madras: Teṉṉintiya arccakar caṅkam.
Kāmikāgama. English trans. of "Rules for Daily Worship" Richard H. Davis. 1986. "Ritual in an Oscillating Universe," App. II. Ph.D. dissertation, University of Chicago.

Kathāsaritsāgara, Somadeva. English trans. C. H. Tawney. 1968. *The Ocean of Story*. Ed. N. M. Penzer. 10 vols. Delhi: Motilal Banarsidass.

Kōyil O̱luku. Kōil O̱lugu: The Chronicle of the Srīrangam Temple with Historical Notes. English trans. V. N. Hari Rao. 1961. Madras: Rochouse and Sons.

Kuṭṭanīmata, Dāmodara Gupta. Sanskrit text ed. Madhusudan Kaul. 1944. Calcutta: Royal Asiatic Society.

Kuṭṭanīmata. The Art of the Temptress; Translation of the 1200–year-old Sanskrit Classic, the Kuttni Mahatmyam. English trans. B. P. L. Bedi. 1968. Bombay: Pearl Publications.

Kuvalayamālā, Uddyotana. Prakrit text. *Kuvalayamālā Kathā*, Ratnabrabha. Sanskrit text ed. A. N. Upadhye. 1959 and 1970. 2 vols. Bombay: Bhāratīya Vidyā Bhavan.

Mahābhārata. English trans. Pratap Chandra Roy. n.d. 12 vols. Calcutta: Oriental Publishing Co.

Maṇimēkalai. Tamil text with commentary by Po. Vē. Cōmacuntaraṉār. 1975. Madras: South India Saiva Siddhanta Works Publishing Society.

Manusmṛti. The Laws of Manu. English trans. G. Buhler. [1886] 1988. *Sacred Books of the East*, Vol. 25. Delhi: Motilal Banarsidass.

Maturaikkāñci. Tamil text and English trans. J. V. Chelliah. [1946] 1985. *Pattupāṭṭu: Ten Tamil Idylls*. Tanjavur: Tamil University.

Meghadūta, Kālidāsa. *The Cloud Messanger*. Sanskrit text and English trans. Franklin and Eleanor Edgerton. 1964. Ann Arbor: University of Michigan Press.

Nācciyār Tirumoḻi, Āṇṭāḷ. Tamil text. 1971. *Nalāyira Tivviyap Pirapāntam*. Madras: V. N. Tēvanātaṉ

Nāṭya Śāstra, Bharata Muni. Sanskrit text ed. Manomohan Ghosh. 1956. Calcutta: Asiatic Society.

Nāṭyaśāstra. English trans. Manomohan Ghosh. 1961. Calcutta: Asiatic Society.

Pādatāḍikata, Syāmilaka. English trans. Manomohan Ghosh. 1975. *Glimpses of Sexual Life in Nanda-Maurya India: Translation of the Caturbhāṇī Together with a Critical Edition of the Text*. Calcutta: Manisha Granthalaya.

Parama Saṃhitā. Sanskrit text and English trans. S. Krishnaswami Aiyangar. 1940. Gaekwad Oriental Series No. 86. Baroda: Oriental Institute.

Paripāṭal. Tamil with French trans., intro., and notes François Gros. 1968. Pondichéry: Institut français d'Indologie.

Pauṣkara Saṃhitā. Sanskrit text ed. His Holiness Sree Yatiraja Sampathkumara Ramanuja Muni of Melkote. 1934. Bangalore: A. Srinivasa Aiyangar and M. C. Thirumalachariar.

Periya Purāṇam, Cekkiḻar. *Tiruttoṇṭar Mākkatai*: Tamil text ed. Pa. Irāmanāta Pillai. 1977. Madras: South India Saiva Siddhanta Works Publishing Society.

Periya Puranam. Condensed English version G. Vanmikanathan. 1985. Madras: Sri Ramakrishna Math.

Periyatirumoḻi, Tirumaṅkai Āḻvār. Tamil text. 1971. *Nalāyira Tivviyap Pirapāntam*. 1971. Madras: V. N. Tēvanātaṉ.

Piṅkalanikaṇṭu, Piṅkala Muṉivar. Tamil text. 1968. Madras: South India Saiva Siddhanta Works Publishing Society.

Rājataraṅgiṇī, Kalhaṇa. English trans. Ranjit Sitaram Pandit. 1977. New Delhi: Sahitya Akademi.

Śabara-bhāṣya (on Jaimini's *Mīmāṃsā sūtra*s). 1973–74. Trans. Ganganatha Jha. Baroda: Oriental Institute.

Śaivāgamaparibhāṣāmañjarī, Vedajñāna. Sanskrit text and French trans. Bruno Dagens. 1979. *Le Florilège de la doctrine Śivaïte*. Pondichéry: Institut français d'Indologie.

Samayamātṛkā, Kṣemendra. Sanskrit text ed. Paṇḍit Durgāprasād and Kāśīnāth Pāṇdurang Parab. 1925. 2nd ed. Bombay: Nirnaya Sagar Press.

Sanatkumāra Saṃhitā. Sanskrit text ed. Pandit V. Krishnamacharya. 1969. Madras: Adyar Library.

Śrīpraśna Saṃhitā. Sanskrit text ed. Seetha Padmanabhan. 1969. Foreword by V. Raghavan. Tirupati: Kendriya Sanskrit Vidyapeetha.

Sumaṅgalavilāsinī Dighanikāya-Aṭṭhakathā, Buddhaghoṣa. Pali text ed. Mahesh Tiwary. 1974. Vol. 1. Nalanda: Nava Nalanda Mahavihara.

Tēvāram, Ñānacampantar, Appar, and Cuntarar. Tamil text ed. T. V. Gopal Iyer and François Gros. 1984–85. 2 vols. Pondichéry: Institut français d'Indologie.

Tirumoḻi, Periyāḻvār. Tamil text. 1971. *Nalāyira Tivviyap Pirapāntam*. Madras: V. N. Tēvanātaṉ.

Tirumoḻi. English trans. selected poems Lynn M. Ate. 1978. "Periyāḻvār's Tirumoḻi: A Bala-Kṛṣṇa Text from the Devotional Period in Tamil Literature." Ph.D. dissertation University of Wisconsin, Madison.

Tirumuṟaikaṇṭa Purāṇam, Umāpati Civācāriyar. Tamil text. 1967. Tarumapuram: Tarumaiyātīṉam.

Tirumuṟukāṟṟuppaṭai. Tamil text and English trans. J. V. Chelliah. [1946] 1985. *Pattupāṭṭu: Ten Tamil Idylls*. Tanjavur: Tamil University.

Tiruppāvai, Āṇṭāḷ. Tamil text. 1971. *Nalāyira Tivviyap Pirapāntam*. Madras: V. N. Tēvanātaṉ.

Tiruppāvai. Un Texte Tamoul de Dévotion Vishnouite: Le Tiruppāvai d'Āṇṭāḷ. Tamil text and French trans. Jean Filliozat. 1972. Pondichéry: Institut français d'Indologie.

Tiruvācakam, Māṇikkavācakar. Tamil text with English trans. G. U. Pope. [1900] 1970. *The Tiruvāçagam or "Sacred Utterances" of the Tamil Poet, Saint, and Sage Māṇikka-vāçagar*. Madras: University of Madras.

Tiruvāymoḻi, Nammāḻvār. Tamil text. 1971. *Nalāyira Tivviyap Pirapāntam*. Madras: V. N. Tēvanātaṉ.

Tiruvāymoḻi. Selected English trans. A. K. Ramanujan. 1981. *Hymns for the Drowning: Poems for Viṣṇu by Nammāḻvār*. Princeton: Princeton University Press.

Tolkāppiyam, Ilampūraṇar. Tamil text. 1982. Madras: South India Saiva Siddhanta Works Publishing Society.

Tolkāppiyam. Tholkāppiyam (in English) with Critical Studies. S. Ilakkuvanār. 1963. Madurai: Kuṟaḷ Neṟi Publishing House.

Vaikhānasāgama, Marīci. Sanskrit text ed. K. Sāmbaśiva Sāstrī. 1935. Trivandrum: Government Press.

Viṣṇudharmottara Purāṇa. English trans. S. Kramrisch. 1928. *The Vishnudharmottara (Part III): A Treatise on Indian Painting and Image-making*, 2nd ed. Calcutta: Calcutta University Press.

Yajñavālkyasmṛti. Sanskrit text ed. Adolf Friedrich Stenzler. 1849. *Yajñavālkya's Gesetzbuch: Sanskrit und Deutsch*. Berlin/London: Williams & Norgate.

Yajñavalkya Smriti with the Commentary of Vijñāneśvara Called The Mitākṣara, Book 1. English trans. Srisa Chandra Vidyarnava. [1918] 1974. *Sacred Books of the Hindus*, Vol. 21. New York: AMS Press.

Secondary Sources and Reference Works

Abu-Lughod, Lila. 1990. "The Romance of Resistance: Tracing Transformations of Power through Bedouin Women." In *Beyond the Second Sex: New Directions in the Anthropology of Gender*, ed. P. R. Sanday and R. G. Goodenough. Philadelphia: University of Pennsylvania Press.

Agesthialingom, S., and S. V. Shanmugam. 1970. *The Language of Tamil Inscriptions 1250–1350 A.D.* Annamalainagar: Annamalai University.

Aiyappan, A., and P. R. Srinivasan. 1960. *Story of Buddhism with Special Reference to South India.* Publication on the occasion of the Buddha Jayanti celebration and exhibition. Madras: Government of Madras.

Alayev, L. B. 1985. "Methods of Studying Epigraphy as a Historical Source." In *Indus Valley to Mekong Delta: Explorations in Epigraphy*, ed. Noboru Karashima. Madras: New Era Publications.

Allen, Michael. 1982. "Girl's Prepuberty Rites amongst the Newars of the Kathmandu Valley." In *Women in India and Nepal*, ed. M. Allen and S. N. Mukherjee. Canberra: Australian National University.

Alloula, Malek. 1986. *The Colonial Harem*, trans. Myrna Godzich and Wlad Godzich, intro. Barbara Harlow. Minneapolis: University of Minnesota Press.

Altekar, A. S. 1959. *The Position of Women in Hindu Civilization: From Prehistoric Times to the Present Day*, 2nd ed. Delhi: Motilal Banarsidass.

Anandhi, S. 1991. "Representing Devadasis: 'Dasigal Mosavalai' as a Radical Text." *Economic and Political Weekly* 26/11–12 (Annual No.):739–46.

Antze, Rosemary Jeanes. n.d. "Approaching the Life and Role of a Mysore Court Dancer." Unpublished paper.

Appadorai, A. 1936. *Economic Conditions in Southern Indian (1000–1500 A.D.)*, 2 vols. Madras: University of Madras.

Appadurai, Arjun. 1981. *Worship and Conflict under Colonial Rule: A South Indian Case.* Cambridge: Cambridge University Press.

———. 1983. "The Puzzling Status of Brahman Temple Priests in Hindu India." *South Asian Anthropologist* 4:43–52.

Appadurai, Arjun, and Carol Appadurai Breckenridge. 1976. "The South Indian Temple: Authority, Honour and Redistribution." *Contributions to Indian Sociology*, 10:187–211.

Arokiaswami, M. 1956–57. "Social Developments under the Imperial Cōḷas." *Transactions of the Archaeological Society of South India*, 1–7.

Assayag, Jackie. 1989. "Women-Goddess, Women-Distress: Yellamma goddess' devotees in South India (Karnataka)." *Man in India* 69:359–73.

Ate, Lynn M. 1978. "Periyāḻvār's *Tirumoḻi*: A Bala-Kṛṣṇa Text from the Devotional Period in Tamil Literature." Ph.D. dissertation, University of Wisconsin, Madison.

Babb, Lawrence A. 1970. "Marriage and Malevolence: The Uses of Sexual Opposition in a Hindu Pantheon." *Ethnology* 9:37–48.

Balambal, V. 1976. "Great Women of Chola Dynasty." *Journal of Tamil Studies* 10:71–88.

Balasubrahmanyam, S. R. 1966. *Early Chola Art*, Part I. London: Asian Publishing House.

———. 1971. *Early Chola Temples.* Bombay: Orient Longman.

———. 1975. *Middle Chola Temples.* New Delhi: Thomson Press.

———. 1979. *Later Chola Temples.* New Delhi: Mudgala Trust.

Balasubramanian, C. 1976. *The Status of Women in Tamilnadu during the Sangam Age*. Madras: University of Madras.

Ballhatchett, Kenneth. 1980. *Race, Sex and Class under the Raj: Imperial Attitudes and Policies and Their Critics, 1793–1905*. London: Weidenfeld & Nicolson, 1980.

Basham, A. L. 1959. *The Wonder That Was India*. New York: Grove Press.

———. 1961. "Modern Historians of Ancient India." In *Historians of India, Pakistan and Ceylon*, ed. C. H. Philips. London: Oxford University Press.

Bayly, Susan. 1989. *Saints, Goddesses and Kings: Muslims and Christians in South Indian Society 1700–1900*. Cambridge: Cambridge University Press.

Bhatt, N. R. n.d. "What Is Sivagama?" Pamphlet.

Bhattacharyya, N. N. 1971. *Indian Mother Goddess*. Calcutta: Indian Studies Past and Present.

Bird, Phyllis. 1989. "'To Play the Harlot': An Inquiry into an Old Testament Metaphor." In *Gender and Difference in Ancient Israel*. Minneapolis: Fortress Press.

Bobertz, Charles A. 1992. "Almsgiving as Patronage: The Role of Patroness in Pre-Constantinian Christianity." Paper presented at the Annual Meeting of the American Academy of Religion, San Francisco.

Bock, Gisela. 1989. "Women's History and Gender History: Aspects of an International Debate." *Gender and History* 1:7–30.

Bonoff, Lisa Ann. 1973. "The Devadāsīs." M.A. thesis, University of California, Los Angeles.

Bourdieu, Pierre. 1977. *Outline of a Theory of Practice*. Cambridge: Cambridge University Press.

Bourdieu, Pierre, and Loic J. D. Wacquant. 1992. *An Invitation to Reflexive Sociology*. Chicago: University of Chicago Press.

Breckenridge, Carol Appadurai. 1978. "From Protector to Litigant—Changing Relations between Hindu Temples and the Rājā of Ramnad." In *South Indian Temples: An Analytical Reconsideration*, ed. Burton Stein. New Delhi: Vikas Publishing House.

———. 1986. "Food, Politics and Pilgrimage in South India, 1350–1650 A.D." In *Food, Society, and Culture*, ed. R. S. Khare and M. S. A. Rao. Durham, N.C.: Carolina Academic Press.

Brooten, Bernadette J. 1982. *Women Leaders in the Ancient Synagogue: Inscriptional Evidence and Background Issues*. Chico, Cal.: Scholars Press.

Brown, C. MacKenzie. 1974. *God as Mother: A Feminine Theology in India: An Historical and Theological Study of the Brahmavaivarta Purāṇa*. Hartford, Vt.: Claude Stark.

Brown, Charles Philip, with revisions by M. Venkata Ratnam et al. 1985. *Dictionary Telugu English*. New Delhi: Asian Educational Services.

Brunner, Hélène. 1963 and 1968. *Somaśambhupaddhati*, première (*Le rituel quotidien*) et deuxième (*Rituels occasionnels*) parties. Pondichéry: Institut français d'Indologie.

———. 1964. "Les catégories sociales védiques dans le śivaïsme du Sud." *Journal asiatique* 252:451–72.

———. 1969. "De la consommation du *nirmālya* de Śiva." *Journal asiatique* 257: 213–63.

———. 1990. Review of Saskia Kersenboom-Story, *Nityasumaṅgalī*. *Indo-Iranian Journal* 33:121–139.

Burghart, Richard. 1985. "Introduction: Theoretical Approaches in the Anthropology of South Asia." In *Indian Religion*, ed. Richard Burghart and Audrey Cantlie. London: Curzon Press; New York: St. Martin's Press.
Burton, Antoinette M. 1992. "The White Woman's Burden: British Feminists and 'The Indian Woman,' 1865–1915." In *Western Women and Imperialism: Complicity and Resistance*, ed. N. Chaudhuri and M. Strobel. Bloomington: Indiana University Press.
Bynum, Caroline Walker. 1985. "Introduction: The Complexity of Symbols." In *Gender and Religion: On the Complexity of Symbols*, ed. C. W. Bynum, S. Harrell, and P. Richman. Boston: Beacon Press.
Carman, John B. 1974. *The Theology of Rāmānuja: An Essay in Interreligious Understanding*. New Haven, CT.: Yale University Press.
Chakravarti, A. 1974. *Jaina Literature in Tamil*. New Delhi: Bhāratīya Jñānapīṭha.
Chakravarti, Uma. 1983. "The Myth of the Golden Age of Equality—Women Slaves in Ancient India." *Manushi* 3/6:8–12, 15. The material in this article is also found in "Of *Dasas* and *Karmakaras*: Servile Labour in Ancient India." In *Chains of Servitude: Bondage and Slavery in India*, ed. Utsa Patnaik and Manjari Dingwaney. Madras: Sangam Books, 1985.
———. 1989. "Whatever Happened to the Vedic *Dasi*? Orientalism, Nationalism, and a Script for the Past." In *Recasting Women: Essays in Colonial History*, ed. K. Sangari and S.Vaid. New Delhi: Kali for Women.
Champakalakshmi, R. 1974. "South India." In *Jaina Art and Architecture*, Vol. I, Chap. 9, ed. A. Ghosh. New Delhi: Bhāratīya Jñānapīṭha.
———. 1975–76. "Archaeology and Tamil Literary Tradition." *Puratattva*. Bulletin of the Indian Archaeological Society 8:110–22.
———. 1978. "Religious Conflict in the Tamil Country: A Re-appraisal of Epigraphic Evidence." *Journal of the Epigraphical Society of India* 5:69–81.
———. 1981a. "Peasant State and Society in Medieval South India: A Review Article." *Indian Economic and Social History Review* 18:411–26.
———. 1981b. *Vaiṣṇava Iconography in the Tamil Country*. New Delhi: Orient Longman.
———. forthcoming. "Re-Appraisal of a Brahmanical Institution: The Brahmadeya and its Ramifications in Early Medieval South India." In *New Horizons in South Indian Studies: Papers in Honor of Noboru Karashima*, ed. Kenneth R. Hall. New Delhi: Oxford University Press.
Chanana, Dev Raj. 1960. *Slavery in Ancient India as Depicted in Pali and Sanskrit Texts*. New Delhi: People's Publishing House.
Chandra, Moti. 1973. *The World of Courtesans*. Delhi: Vikas Publishing House.
Chatterjee, A. K. 1978. *A Comprehensive History of Jainism (up to 1000 A.D.)*. Calcutta: Firma KLM.
Chatterjee, Indrani. 1990. "Refracted Reality: The 1935 Calcutta Police Survey of Prostitutes." *Manushi* 57:26–36.
Chatterjee, Kumudranjan. 1940. "Temple Offerings and Temple Grants in South India." Paper presented to the Fourth Indian History Congress.
Chatterjee, Partha. 1993. *The Nation and Its Fragments: Colonial and Postcolonial Histories*. Princeton, NJ: Princeton University Press.
Chatterjee, Santosh. 1945. *Devadasi (Temple Dancer)*. Calcutta: Book House.
Chattopadhyaya, Brajadulal. 1990. *Aspects of Rural Settlements and Rural Society in Early Medieval India*. Calcutta: Centre for Studies in Social Sciences/K. P. Bagchi & Co.

———. 1994. *The Making of Early Medieval India*. Delhi: Oxford University Press.
Chekki, Danesh A. 1974. *Modernization and Kin Network*. Leiden: E. J. Brill.
Clark, Elizabeth A. 1990. "Patrons, Not Priests: Gender and Power in Late Ancient Christianity." *Gender and History* 2:253–73.
Clifford, James. 1988. *The Predicament of Culture: Twentieth-Century Ethnography, Literature and Art*. Cambridge, Mass.: Harvard University Press.
Clothey, Fred W. 1978. *The Many Faces of Murukaṉ: The History and Meaning of a South Indian God*. The Hague: Mouton.
Coburn, Thomas B. 1984. *Devī-māhātmya: The Crystallization of the Goddess Tradition*, Delhi: Motilal Banarsidass.
———. 1991. *Encountering the Goddess: A Translation of the Devī-māhātmya and a Study of Its Interpretation*. Albany: State University of New York Press.
Colas, Gérard. 1984. "Présentation et analyse de la Marīci-saṃhitā." *Journal asiatique*, 272, 343–68.
Collins, Steven. 1991. "Historiography in the Pali Tradition." Paper presented at the Annual Meeting of the American Academy of Religion, Kansas City.
———. 1992. "*Nirvāṇa*, Time, and Narrative." *History of Religions* 32:215–46.
Comaroff, Jean, and John Comaroff. 1991. *Of Revelation and Revolution: Christianity, Colonialism, and Consciousness in South Africa*, Vol. 1. Chicago: University of Chicago Press.
Crooke, W. (1896) 1974. *The Tribes and Castes of the North West Province and Oudh*. Delhi: Cosmo Publications.
Cutler, Norman. 1987. *Songs of Experience: The Poetics of Tamil Devotion*. Bloomington: Indiana University Press.
Dagens, Bruno, ed. and trans. 1979. *Le Florilège de la doctrine Śivaïte: Śaivāgamaparibhāṣāmañjarī de Vedajñāna*. Pondichéry: Institut français d'Indologie.
Dandekar, R. N. 1978. *Recent Trends in Indology*. Poona: Bhandarkar Oriental Research Institute.
Das, Veena. 1987. "On Female Body and Sexuality." *Contributions to Indian Sociology* n.s., 21:57–66.
Davis, Natalie Zemon. 1995. *Women on the Margins: Three Seventeenth-century Lives*. Cambridge, Mass.: Harvard University Press.
Davis, Richard H. 1986. "Ritual in an Oscillating Universe." Ph.D. dissertation, University of Chicago.
———. 1991. *Ritual in an Oscillating Universe: Worshiping Śiva in Medieval India*. Princeton, N.J.: Princeton University Press.
———. 1997. *Lives of Indian Images*. Princeton, N.J.: Princeton University Press.
———. 1998. "The Story of the Disappearing Jains: Retelling the Śaiva-Jain Encounter in Medieval South India." In *Open Boundaries: Jain Communities and Cultures in Indian History*, ed. John E. Cort. Albany: State University of New York Press.
Dehejia, Vidya. 1988. "The Persistence of Buddhism in Tamilnadu." *Marg* 39/4:53–74.
Derrett, J. Duncan M. 1968. *Religion, Law and the State in India*. New York: Free Press.
Desai, Devangana. 1975. *Erotic Sculpture of India: A Socio-cultural Survey*. New Delhi: Tata McGraw Hill.
Desai, Pandurang B. 1957. *Jainism in South India*. Sholapur: Jaina Saṃskṛti Saṃrakshaka Sangha.
Deyell, John S. 1990. *Living without Silver: The Monetary History of Early Medieval North India*. Delhi: Oxford University Press.

Dhavamony, Mariasusai. 1971. *Love of God According to Śaiva Siddhānta.* London: Oxford University Press.

Diakonoff, I. M. 1986. "Women in Old Babylonia Not under Patriarchal Authority." *Journal of the Economic and Social History of the Orient* 29:225–38.

Diehl, C. G. 1964. "The Goddess of Forests in Tamil Literature." *Tamil Culture* 11:308–16.

Dikshit, G. S. 1964. *Local Self-Government in Mediaeval Karnataka.* Dharwar: Karnatak University.

Dikshitar, V. R. Ramachandra, trans. 1978. *The Cilappatikaram.* Madras: South India Saiva Siddhanta Works Publishing Society.

Dirks, Nicholas B. 1976. "Political Authority and Structural Change in Early South Indian History." *Indian Economic and Social History Review* 13(2):125–57.

———. 1987. *The Hollow Crown: Ethnohistory of an Indian Kingdom.* Cambridge: Cambridge University Press.

Dorai Rangaswamy, M. A. 1958. *The Religion and Philosophy of Tēvāram: With Special Reference to Nampi Ārūrar (Sundarar)*, 2 vols. Madras: University of Madras.

Dumont, Louis. 1983. *Affinity as a Value: Marriage Alliance in South India, with Comparative Essays on Australia.* Chicago: University of Chicago Press.

Dutt, Binode Behari. 1925. *Town-planning in Ancient India.* Calcutta: Thacker, Spink & Co.

Dutt, Nalinaksha. 1973. *Mahayana Buddhism.* Calcutta: Firma K. L. Mukhopadhyay.

Egnor, Margaret. 1980. "On the Meaning of Śakti to Women in Tamil Nadu." In *The Powers of Tamil Women*, ed. Susan S. Wadley. Syracuse, N.Y.: Maxwell School, Syracuse University.

Ehrenfels, Baron Omar Rolf. 1941. *Mother-Right in India.* Hyderabad: Government Central Press.

Eisenstadt, Shmuel N. 1968. "Social Institutions." In *International Encyclopedia of the Social Sciences*, vol. 14, ed. David L. Sills. New York: Macmillan.

Ekambaranathan, A., and C. K. Sivaprakasam. 1987. *Jaina Inscriptions in Tamilnadu (A Topographical List).* Madras: Research Foundation for Jainology.

Enthoven, R. E. [1920] 1975. *The Tribes and Castes of Bombay.* Delhi: Cosmo Publications.

Erndl, Kathleen M. 1993. *Victory to the Mother: The Hindu Goddess of Northwest India in Myth, Ritual and Symbol.* New York: Oxford University Press.

Farquhar, J. N. [1914] 1967. *Modern Religious Movements in India.* Delhi: Munshiram Manoharlal.

Fawcett, Fred. 1890. "On Basivis: Women Who, through Dedication to a Deity, Assume Masculine Privileges." *Journal of the Anthropological Society of Bombay* 2:322–53.

Feldhaus, Anne. 1982. "Bahiṇā Bāī: Wife and Saint." *Journal of the American Academy of Religion* 50:591–604.

Fisher, Eugene J. 1976. "Cultic Prostitution in the Ancient Near East? A Reassessment." *Biblical Theology Bulletin* 6:225–36.

Folkert, Kendall W. 1989. "Jain Religious Life at Ancient Mathurā: The Heritage of Late Victorian Interpretation." In *Mathurā: The Cultural Heritage*, ed. Doris Meth Srinivasan. New Delhi: American Institute of Indian Studies.

Foucault, Michel. 1995. *Discipline and Punish: The Birth of the Prison*, trans. Alan Sheridan. New York: Vintage Books.

Francis, W. 1904. *Madras District Gazetteers: Bellary*. Madras: Government Press.

Frazer, James George. 1957. *The Golden Bough: A Study in Magic and Religion*, abridged ed. London: Macmillan.

Fuller, C. J. 1984. *Servants of the Goddess: The Priests of a South Indian Temple*. Cambridge: Cambridge University Press.

———. 1985. "Initiation and Consecration: Priestly Rituals in a South Indian Temple." In *Indian Religion*, ed. Richard Burghart and Audrey Cantlie. London: Curzon Press; New York: St. Martin's Press.

———. 1988. "The Hindu Temple and Indian Society." In *Temple in Society*, ed. Michael V. Fox. Winona Lake, Minn.: Eisenbrauns.

Garbini, Riccardo. 1993. "Software Development in Epigraphy: Some Preliminary Remarks." *Journal of the Epigraphical Society of India* 19:63–79.

Gaston, Anne-Marie. 1980. "The Place of Indian Classical Dance in Traditional Indian Culture." In *The Sacred and the Secular in India's Performing Arts*, ed. V. Subramaniam. New Delhi: Ashish Publishing House.

Gaur, Albertine. 1963. "Les Danses Sacrées en Inde." In *Les Danses Sacrées*. Sources Orientales VI. Paris: Seuil.

Gogarty, Oliver St. John. 1937. *As I Was Going down Sackville Street: A Phantasy in Fact*. London: Rich & Cowan.

Gold, Penny Schine. 1985. *The Lady and the Virgin: Image, Attitude, and Experience in Twelfth-century France*. Chicago: University of Chicago Press.

Gonda, J. 1961. "Ascetics and Courtesans." *Adyar Library Bulletin* 25:78–102.

———. 1965. *Change and Continuity in Indian Religions*. The Hague: Mouton.

———. 1977. *Medieval Religious Literature in Sanskrit*. Wiesbaden: Otto Harrassowitz.

Gopalan, R., and Y. Subbarayalu. 1967. "Glossary." In *South Indian Polity*, 2nd ed., T. V. Mahalingam. Madras: University of Madras.

Gopinatha Rao, T. A. 1915. "Bauddha Vestiges in Kāñchīpura." *Indian Antiquary* 44:127–29.

———. [1916] 1971. *Elements of Hindu Iconography*, 2 vols. Varanasi: Indological Book House.

Gordon, Stewart N. 1969. "Scarf and Sword: Thugs, Marauders, and State-formation in 18th Century Malwa." *Indian Economic and Social History Review* 6:403–29.

Gorringe, Magdalen. 1998. "'Daughters of Rudra': The Devadasi Institution considered in the Light of a Southern Śaivāgama, with Special Reference to the Process of Initiation." M. Phil. thesis, Oxford.

Goudriaan, T. 1970. "Vaikhānasa Daily Worship According to the Handbooks of Atri, Bhṛgu, Kāśyapa, and Marīci." *Indo-Iranian Journal* 12:1–215.

Goudriaan, Teun, and Sanjukta Gupta. 1981. *Hindu Tantric and Śākta Literature*. Wiesbaden: Harrassowitz.

Gough, Kathleen. 1981. *Rural Society in Southeast India*. Cambridge: Cambridge University Press.

Govindacharya, Alkondavilli. 1982. *The Holy Lives of the Azhvars or the Dravida Saints*. Bombay: Ananthacharya Indological Research Institute.

Granda, Peter August. 1984. "Property Rights and Land Control in Tamil Nadu: 1350–1600." Ph.D. dissertation, University of Michigan, Ann Arbor.

Gros, François, trans. 1968. *Le Paripāṭal*. Pondichéry: Institut français d'Indologie.

Gros, François, and R. Nagaswamy. 1970. *Uttaramērūr: Légendes, Histoire, Monuments*. Pondichéry: Institut français d'Indologie.

Gross, Rita. 1974. "Methodological Remarks on the Study of Women in Religion: Review, Criticism and Redefinition." In *Women and Religion*, rev. ed., ed. J. Plaskow and J. A. Romero. Missoula, Mont.: Scholars Press.

———. 1977. "Androcentrism and Androgyny in the Methodology of History of Religions." In *Beyond Androcentrism: New Essays on Women and Religon*, ed. Rita M. Gross. Missoula, Mont.: Scholars Press.

———. 1987. "Tribal Religions: Aboriginal Australians." In *Women in World Religions*, ed. Arvind Sharma. Albany: State University of New York Press.

Gupta, Sanjukta. 1983. "The Changing Pattern of Pāñcarātra Initiation: A Case Study in the Reinterpretation of Ritual." In *Selected Studies on Ritual in the Indian Religions: Essays to D. J. Holus*, ed. Ria Kloppenborg. Leiden: Brill.

Gupta, Sanjukta, and Richard Gombrich. 1986. "Kings, Power and the Goddess." *South Asia Research*. 6/2:123–38.

Gurukkal, Rajan. 1979. "Proliferation and Consolidation of the Temple-centred Social Hierarchy in the Cera Period." *Journal of Kerala Studies*, 6:333–46.

Gurumurthy, S. 1979. *Education in South India (Ancient and Medieval Periods)*. Madras: New Era Publications.

Hackett, Jo Ann. 1989. "Can a Sexist Model Liberate Us? Ancient Near Eastern 'Fertility' Goddesses." *Journal of Feminist Studies in Religion* 5:65–76.

Halbfass, Wilhelm. 1991. *Tradition and Reflection: Explorations in Indian Thought*. Albany: State University of New York Press.

Hall, Kenneth R. 1980. *Trade and Statecraft in the Age of Cōḷas*. New Delhi: Abhinav Publications.

———. 1981. "Peasant State and Society in Chola Times: A View from the Tiruvidaimarudur Urban Complex." *Indian Economic and Social History Review* 18:393–410.

Hankare, P. D. 1981. "Devdasis Organize." *Manushi* 7:29–30.

Hanumantha Rao, B. S. L. 1973. *Religion in Āndhra*. Guntur: Hanumantha Rao.

Hanumanthan, K. R. 1980. "The Social Status of the Paṟaiyas as Revealed from Inscriptions." *Journal of the Epigraphical Society of India* 7:12–17.

Hardy, Friedhelm. 1978. "Ideology and Cultural Contexts of the Śrīvaiṣṇava Temple." In *South Indian Temples: An Analytic Reconsideration*, ed. Burton Stein. New Delhi: Vikas Publishing House.

———. 1983. *Viraha-Bhakti: The Early History of Kṛṣṇa Devotion in South India*. Delhi: Oxford University Press.

Harman, William P. 1989a. "Sacred Marriage in the Study of Religion: A Perspective from India on a Concept that Grew out of the Ancient Near East." *Religion* 19:353–76.

———. 1989b. *The Sacred Marriage of a Hindu Goddess*. Bloomington: Indiana University Press.

Hart, George L. III. 1975. *The Poems of Ancient Tamil: Their Milieu and Their Sanskrit Counterparts*. Berkeley: University of California Press.

Haynes, Douglas, and Gyan Prakash. 1991. "Introduction: The Entanglement of Power and Resistance." In *Contesting Power: Resistance and Everyday Social Relations in South Asia*, ed. D. Haynes and G. Prakash. Delhi: Oxford University Press.

Hazra, R. C. 1958. *Studies in the Upapurāṇas*, Vol. 1. Calcutta: Sanskrit College.

———. 1975. *Studies in the Purāṇic Records on Hindu Rites and Customs*. Delhi: Motilal Banarsidass.

Heitzman, (E.) James. 1985. "Gifts of Power: Temples, Politics and Economy in Medieval South India." Ph.D. dissertation, University of Pennsylvania, Philadelphia.

———. 1986. "Property Relations in Early South India." Paper presented to the Mid-Atlantic Regional Conference of the Association for Asian Studies, Newark, Del.

———. 1987a. "State Formation in South India, 850–1280." *Indian Economic and Social History Review* 24:35–61.

———. 1987b. "Temple Urbanism in Medieval South India." *Journal of Asian Studies* 46:791–826.

———. 1991. "Ritual Polity and Economy: The Transactional Network of an Imperial Temple in Medieval South India." *Journal of the Economic and Social History of the Orient* 34:23–54.

———. 1995. "Networks of Social Control in Early South India." *Journal of Asian and African Studies* 50:73–109.

———. 1997 *Gifts of Power: Lordship in an Early Indian State* Delhi: Oxford University Press.

———. forthcoming. "Urbanization and Political Economy in Early South India: Kanchipuram during the Chola Period." In *New Horizons in South Indian Studies: Papers in Honor of Noboru Karashima*, ed. Kenneth R. Hall. New Delhi: Oxford University Press.

Herman, Phyllis Kaplan. 1979. "Ideal Kingship and the Feminine Power: A Study of the Depiction of *Rāmarājya* in theVālmīki *Rāmāyaṇa*." Ph.D. dissertation, University of California, Los Angeles.

Hiebert, Julie H. 1992. "The Vijayanagara Court Poetesses." Paper presented at the Annual Meeting of the Association for Asian Studies, Washington, DC.

Hikosaka, Shu. 1989. *Buddhism in Tamil Nadu: A New Perspective*. Madras: Institute of Asian Studies.

Hiltebeitel, Alf. 1988. *The Cult of Draupadī, Vol. 1: Mythologies: From Gingee to Kurukṣetra*. Chicago: University of Chicago.

———. 1991. *The Cult of Draupadī, Vol. 2: On Hindu Ritual and the Goddess*. Chicago: University of Chicago.

Hobson, Barbara Meil. 1987. *Uneasy Virtue: The Politics of Prostitution and the American Reform Tradition*. New York: Basic Books.

Horner, I. B. [1930] 1975. *Women under Primitive Buddhism*. Delhi: Motilal Banarsidass.

Hoult, Thomas Ford. 1969. *Dictionary of Modern Sociology*. Totowa, N.J.: Littlefield, Adams.

Hutton, J. H. 1963. *Caste in India*, 4th ed. Bombay/London: Oxford University Press.

Inden, Ronald. 1985. "The Temple and the Hindu Chain of Being." In *L'espace du Temple I: Espaces, Itinéraires, Médiations*, ed. Jean-Claude Galey. Paris: Éditions de l'École des Hautes Études en Sciences Sociales. *Puruṣārtha* 8: 53–73.

———. 1986. "Orientalist Constructions of India." *Modern Asian Studies* 20: 401–46.

———. 1990. *Imagining India*. Cambridge, Mass.: Blackwell.

Index des mots de la littérature tamoule ancienne, 3 vols. 1967–70. Pondichéry: Institut français d'Indologie.

Irschick, Eugene F. 1994. *Dialogue and History: Constructing South India, 1795–1895*. Berkeley: University of California Press.

Iswara Dutt, Kunduri. 1967. *Inscriptional Glossary of Andhra Pradesh*. Hyderabad: Andhra Pradesh Sahitya Akademi.

Jagadeesan, N. 1967. "The Araiyar." *Bulletin of the Institute of Traditional Cultures*, Part 1, 46–52.
Jain, Chakresh. 1985, June 9. "Devadasis: Maids of God . . . and Men." *Express Magazine*.
Jaiswal, Suvira. 1967. *Origin and Development of Vaiṣṇavism*. Delhi: Munshiram Manoharlal.
———. 1974. "Studies in the Social Structure of the Early Tamils." In *Indian Society: Historical Probings, in Memory of D. D. Kosambi*, ed. R. S. Sharma with Vivekanand Jha. New Delhi: People's Publishing House.
Jamison, Stephanie W. 1996. *Sacrificed Wife, Sacrificer's Wife: Women, Ritual, and Hospitality in Ancient India*. New York: Oxford University Press.
Janaki, S. S. 1988. "Dhvaja-Stambha (Critical Account of its Structural and Ritualistic Detail)." In *Śiva Temple and Temple Rituals*, ed. S. S. Janaki. Madras: Kuppuswami Sastri Research Institute.
Jha, D. N. 1974. "Temples as Landed Magnates in Early Medieval South India (c. A.D. 700–1300)." In *Indian Society: Historical Probings*. New Delhi: People's Publishing House.
Johansson, Sheila Ryan. 1976. "'Herstory' As History: A New Field or Another Fad?" In *Liberating Women's History: Theoretical and Critical Essays*, ed. Berenice A. Carroll. Urbana: University of Illinois Press.
Jordan, Kay Kirkpatrick. 1989. "From Sacred Servant to Profane Prostitute: A Study of the Changing Legal Status of the *Devadāsīs*, 1857–1947." Ph.D. dissertation, University of Iowa, Iowa City.
———. 1993. "Devadāsī Reform: Driving the Priestesses or the Prostitutes Out of Hindu Temples?" In *Religion and Law in Independent India*, ed. Robert D. Baird. Delhi: Manohar.
Kabbani, Rana. 1986. *Europe's Myths of Orient*. Bloomington: Indiana University Press.
Kailasapathy, K. 1968. *Tamil Heroic Poetry*. London: Oxford/Clarendon Press.
Kaimal, Padma A. 1988. "Stone Portrait Sculpture at Pallava and Early Cōḻa Temples: Kings, Patrons and Individual Identity." Ph.D. dissertation, University of California, Berkeley.
———. 1996. "Early Cōḻa Kings and 'Early Cōḻa Temples': Art and the Evolution of Kingship." *Artibus Asiae* 56/1–2: 33–66.
Kandaswamy, S. N. 1978. *Buddhism as Expounded in Manimekalai*. Annamalainagar: Annamalai University.
———. 1981. "Jainistic and Buddhistic Literature." In *Literary Heritage of the Tamils*, ed. S. V. Subramanian and N. Ghadigachalam. Madras: International Institute of Tamil Studies.
Kandiah, Arumugam. 1973. "A Critical Study of Early Tamil Śaiva Bhakti Literature with Specific Reference to *Tēvāram*." Ph.D. dissertation, University of London.
Kane, P. V. 1930–62. *History of Dharmaśāstra*, 5 vols. Poona: Bhandarkar Oriental Research Institute.
Kangle, R. P. 1965. *The Kauṭilīya Arthaśāstra, Part 3: A Study*. Bombay: University of Bombay.
Kannabiran, Kalpana. 1995. "Judiciary, Social Reform and Debate on 'Religious Prostitution' in Colonial India." *Economic and Political Weekly* 30/43:WS59–WS69.
Karashima, Noboru. 1984. *South Indian History and Society: Studies from Inscriptions A.D. 850–1800*. Delhi: Oxford University Press.

———. 1992. *Towards a New Formation: South Indian Society under Vijayanagar Rule*. Delhi: Oxford University Press.

———. 1996. "Response" to panel on South Indian Epigraphic Studies in Honor of Professor Noboru Karashima, presented at the Annual Meeting of the Association of Asian Studies, Honolulu.

Karashima, Noburu, Y. Subbarayalu, and Toru Matsui. 1978. *A Concordance of the Names in the Cōḻa Inscriptions*, 3 vols. Madurai: Sarvodaya Ilakkiya Pannai.

Kaviraj, Sudipta. 1992. "The Imaginary Institution of India." In *Subaltern Studies VII*, ed. Partha Chatterjee and Gyanendra Pandey. Delhi: Oxford University Press.

Kelly-Gadol, Joan. 1976. "The Social Relations of the Sexes: Methodological Implications of Women's History." *Signs* 1/4:809–823.

Kersenboom, Saskia C. 1981. "Viṟali (Possible Sources of the Dēvadāsī Tradition in the Tamil Bardic Period)." *Journal of Tamil Studies* 19:19–41.

———. 1987. *Nityasumaṅgalī: Devadasi Tradition in South India*. Delhi: Motilal Banarsidass.

———. 1991. "The Traditional Repertoire of the Tiruttaṇi Temple Dancers." In *Roles and Rituals for Hindu Women*, ed. Julia Leslie. Rutherford, N.J.: Fairleigh Dickinson University Press.

Khokar, Mohan. 1979. *Traditions of Indian Classical Dance*. Delhi: Clarion Books.

———. 1983, January 16. "The Greatest Step in Bharatanatyam." *Sunday Statesman*.

Kingsbury, F., and G. E. Phillips. 1921. *Hymns of the Tamil Śaivite Saints*. Calcutta: Association Press.

Kinsley, David R. 1975. *The Sword and the Flute*. Berkeley: University of California Press.

———. 1980. "Devotion as an Alternative to Marriage in the Lives of Some Hindu Women Devotees." *Journal of Asian and African Studies* 15:83–93.

———. 1988. *Hindu Goddesses: Visions of the Divine Feminine in the Hindu Religious Tradition*. Berkeley: University of California Press.

Kishwar, Madhu. 1986. "The Daughters of Aryavarta." *Indian Economic and Social History Review* 23:151–86.

Kopf, David. 1993. "Dancing 'Virgin,' Sexual Slave, Divine Courtesan or Celestial Dancer: In Search of the Historic *Devadāsī*." In *Bharata Nāṭyam in Cultural Perspective*, ed. George Kliger. New Delhi: Manohar.

Koppedrayer, K. I. 1991. "Are Śūdras Entitled to Ride in the Palanquin?" *Contributions to Indian Sociology* 25:191–210.

Kosambi, D. D. 1969. *Ancient India: A History of Its Culture and Civilization*. New York: Meridian Books.

Kothari, Sunil. 1979. "History: Roots, Growth and Revival," "Natya: Bhagavata Mela Nataka," "Kuravanji: Dance Drama," and "Mysore School of Bharata Natyam." In special issue on Bharata Natyam, *Marg* 32/3.

Kraemer, Ross S., ed. 1988. *Maenads, Martyrs, Matrons, Monastics: A Sourcebook on Women's Religions in the Greco-Roman World*. Minneapolis, Minn.: Fortress Press.

Krishnan, K. G. 1981. "Jaina Monuments of Tamil Nadu." In *Studies in South Indian History and Epigraphy*. Madras: New Era Publications.

Kulke, Hermann. 1982. "Fragmentation and Segmentation Versus Integration? Reflections on the Concepts of Indian Feudalism and the Segmentary State in Indian History." *Studies in History* 4:237–63.

———. 1993. *Kings and Cults: State Formation and Legitimation in India and Southeast Asia*. New Delhi: Manohar.

Lakshmi, C. S. 1982, November 6. "Up the Drumstick Tree." Review of *The Powers of Tamil Women*, ed. Susan Wadley. *Economic and Political Weekly* 17/45: 1815–17.

———. 1990, October 20–29. "Mother, Mother-Community and Mother-Politics in Tamil Nadu." *Economic and Political Weekly*, WS72–WS83.

Lalitha, R. 1986. "The Economic Status of Women under the Imperial Cholas." In *Essays in Indian History and Culture*, ed. Y. Krishnan. New Delhi: Indian History and Culture Society.

Latham, Ronald, trans. 1958. *The Travels of Marco Polo*. Harmondsworth: Penguin.

Leavitt, John. 1992. "Cultural Holism in the Anthropology of South Asia: The Challenge of Regional Traditions." *Contributions to Indian Sociology* 26/1:3–49.

Lembezat, B. 1953. "Karikal Amméar: Patronne de la ville de Karikal." *Revue de l'Histoire des Religions* 144:78–99.

Lemercinier, Geneviève. 1979. "Kinship Relationships and Religious Symbolism among the Clans of Kerala during the Sangam Period (First Century A.C.)." *Social Compass* 26:461–89.

Lerner, Gerda. 1986. *The Creation of Patriarchy*. New York: Oxford University Press.

Lesko, Barbara S., ed. 1989. *Women's Earliest Records: From Ancient Egypt and Western Asia*. Proceedings of the Conference on Women in the Ancient Near East, Brown University, Providence, R.I., 1987. Atlanta, Ga.: Scholars Press.

Leslie, I. Julia. 1989. *The Perfect Wife: The Orthodox Hindu Woman According to the Strīdharmapaddhati of Tryambakayajvan*. Delhi: Oxford University Press.

Lincoln, Bruce. 1981. *Emerging from the Chrysalis: Studies in Rituals of Women's Initiation*. Cambridge, Mass.: Harvard University Press.

Lingat, Robert. 1973. *The Classical Law of India*, trans. J. Duncan M. Derrett. Berkeley: University of California Press.

Lorenzen, David N. 1972. *The Kāpālikas and Kālāmukhas*. Berkeley: University of California Press.

Ludden, David. 1985. *Peasant History in South India*. Princeton, N.J.: Princeton University Press.

———. 1993. "Orientalist Empiricism: Transformations of Colonial Knowledge." In *Orientalism and the Postcolonial Predicament*, ed. C. Breckenridge and P. van der Veer. Philadelphia: University of Pennsylvania.

Macdonell, A. A., and A. B. Keith. [1912] 1958. *Vedic Index of Names and Subjects*. Varanasi: Motilal Banarsidass.

Mahadevan, Iravatham. 1995. "From Orality to Literacy: The Case of the Tamil Society." *Studies in History* 11/2:173–88.

Mahalingam, T. V. 1940. *Administration and Social Life under Vijayanagar*. Madras: University of Madras.

———. 1967. *South Indian Polity*, 2nd ed. Madras: University of Madras.

Mani, Lata. 1989. "Contentious Traditions: The Debate on *Sati* in Colonial India." In *Recasting Women: Essays in Colonial History*, ed. K. Sangari and S. Vaid. New Delhi: Kali for Women.

Mankodi, Kirit L. 1966. "A Note on Ancient Indian Sacred Prostitution." *Journal of the Oriental Institute* 15:479–87.

Mardaan, Ataullah. 1967. *Deva Dasi*. North Hollywood, Cal.: Brandon House.

Marglin, Frédérique Apffel. 1980. "Wives of the God-King: The Rituals of Hindu Temple Courtesans." Ph.D. dissertation, Brandeis University, Boston.

———. 1981. "Kings and Wives: The Separation of Status and Royal Power." *Contributions to Indian Sociology* 15:155–81.

———. 1982. "Types of Sexual Union and Their Implicit Meanings." In *The Divine Consort: Rādhā and the Goddesses of India*, ed. J. S. Hawley and D. M. Wulff. Berkeley, Cal.: Berkeley Religious Studies Series.

———. 1985a. "Female Sexuality in the Hindu World." In *Immaculate and Powerful: The Female in Sacred Image and Social Reality,* ed. C. W. Atkinson, C. H. Buchanan, and M. R. Miles. Boston: Beacon Press.

———. 1985b. *Wives of the God-King: The Rituals of the Devadāsīs of Puri*. Delhi: Oxford University Press.

———. 1987. "Hierodouleia." In *The Encyclopedia of Religion*, ed. M. Eliade. New York: Macmillan.

Mathew, K. S. 1979. *Society in Medieval Malabar: A Study Based on Vadakkair Pāṭṭukaḷ*. Kottayam: Jaffe Books.

Mayo, Katherine. 1927. *Mother India*. New York: Blue Ribbon Books.

———. 1929. *Slaves of the Gods*. New York: Harcourt, Brace.

Mazumdar, B. P. 1978. "*Dasiputras* in Ancient and Early Medieval India." *Quarterly Review of Historical Studies* (Calcutta) 18/2:114ff.

Meduri, Avanthi. 1996. "Nation, Woman, Representation: The Sutured History of the Devadasi and her Dance." Ph.D. dissertation, New York University.

Meyer, Johann Jakob. 1952. *Sexual Life in Ancient India*. London: Routledge & Kegan Paul.

Michell, George. 1993. "Reflections on Vijayanagara." *South Asia* 16:15–32.

Minakshi, C. (1938) 1977. *Administration and Social Life under the Pallavas*. Madras: University of Madras.

Mines, Mattison. 1984. *The Warrior Merchants: Textiles, Trade and Territory in South India*. Cambridge: Cambridge University Press.

Mitter, Partha. 1992. *Much Maligned Monsters: A History of European Reactions to Indian Art*. Chicago: University of Chicago Press.

Mohanty, Chandra. 1988. "Under Western Eyes: Feminist Scholarship and Colonial Discourses." *Feminist Review* 30:61–88. Published in somewhat altered form in *Third World Women and the Politics of Feminism*, ed. C. T. Mohanty, A. Russo, and L. Torres. Bloomington: Indiana University Press, 1991.

Monier-Williams, Monier. [1883] 1974. *Religious Thought and Life in India* (*Vedism, Brāhmanism and Hindūism*). New Delhi: Oriental Books Reprint Corp.

Monius, Anne E. 1997. "In Search of 'Tamil Buddhism': Language, Literary Culture, and Religious Community in Tamil-speaking South India." Ph.D. dissertation, Harvard University, Boston.

MTL. *Tamil Lexicon*, 6 vols. [1927–35] 1982. Madras: University of Madras.

Mukund, Kanakalatha. 1992. "Turmeric Land: Women's Property Rights in Tamil Society since Early Medieval Times." *Economic and Political Weekly* 27/17: WS2–WS6.

MW. Monier-Williams, Monier. [1899] 1979. *A Sanskrit-English Dictionary*, new ed. Oxford: Oxford University Press.

Nadarajah, Devapoopathy. 1969. *Women in Tamil Society: The Classical Period.* Kuala Lumpur: University of Malaya.

Nagam Aiya, V. 1906. *Travancore State Manual*, vol. 2. India District Gazetteers. Trivandrum: Travancore Government Press.

Nagaraja Rao, M. S. 1985. "Brāhmī Inscriptions and Their Bearing on the Great Stūpa at Sannati." In *Indian Epigraphy: Its Bearing on the History of Art*, ed.

Frederick M. Asher and G. S. Gai. New Delhi: Oxford & IBH Publishing Co./ American Institute of Indian Studies.
Nagarkar, B. B. 1893. "The Work of Social Reform in India." In *The World's Parliament of Religions*, Vol. 1, ed. John Henry Barrows. Chicago: Parliament Publishing Company.
Nagaswamy, R. 1975. "Jaina Art and Architecture under the Pallavas." In *Aspects of Jaina Art and Architecture*, ed. U. P. Shah and M. A. Dhaky. Ahmedabad: L.D. Institute of Indology.
———. 1982. *Tantric Cult of South India*. Delhi: Agam Kala Prakashan.
Nair, Janaki. 1994, Decenber 10. "The Devadasi, Dharma and the State." *Economic and Political Weekly*, 3157–67.
Nandi, Ramendra Nath. 1973. *Religious Institutions and Cults in the Deccan (c. A.D. 600– A.D. 1000)*. Delhi: Motilal Banarsidass.
———. 1974. "Family and Inheritance in Early South India." *Proceedings of the Thirty-fifth Indian History Congress*, 72–77.
Narayana Ayyar, C. V. 1974. *Origin and Early History of Śaivism in South India*. Madras: University of Madras.
Narayana Rao, V., David Shulman, and Sanjay Subrahmanyam. 1992. *Symbols of Substance: Court and State in Nāyaka Period Tamil Nadu*. Delhi: Oxford University Press.
Narayanan, M. G. S. 1973. *Aspects of Aryanization in Kerala*. Trivandrum: Kerala Historical Society.
Narayanan, M. G. S., and Kesavan Veluthat. 1978. "Bhakti Movement in South India." In *Indian Movements: Some Aspects of Dissent, Protest and Reform*, ed. S. C. Malik. Simla: Institute of Advanced Study.
———. 1990. "'Renunciation' in Saffron and White Robes." In *Monastic Life in the Christian and Hindu Traditions: A Comparative Study*, ed. Austin B. Creel and Vasudha Narayanan. Lewiston, N.Y.: Edwin Mellen Press.
Nath, Vijay. 1987. *Dāna: Gift System in Ancient India (c. 600 B.C.–c. A.D. 300)*. Delhi: Munshiram Manoharlal.
Nayar, Nancy Ann. 1992. *Poetry as Theology: The Śrīvaiṣṇava Stotra in the Age of Rāmānuja*. Wiesbaden: Otto Harrasowitz.
Neeval, Walter G., Jr. 1977. *Yāmuna's Vedānta and Pāñcarātra: Integrating the Classical and the Popular*. Missoula, Mont.: Scholars Press.
Nigam, Sanjay. 1990. "Disciplining and Policing the 'Criminals by Birth,' Part 1: The Making of a Colonial Stereotype—The Criminal Tribes and Castes of North India." *Indian Economic and Social History Review* 27:131–64.
Nilakanta Sastri, K. A. 1955. *The Cōḷas*, 2nd ed. Madras: University of Madras.
———. 1974. *Aspects of India's History and Culture*. Delhi: Oriental Publishers.
Obeyesekere, Gananath. 1984. *The Cult of the Goddess Pattini*. Chicago: University of Chicago Press.
Oddie, G. A. 1979. *Social Protest in India: British Protestant Missionaries and Social Reforms 1850–1900*. New Delhi: Manohar.
Oden, Robert A., Jr. 1987. *The Bible without Theology: The Theological Tradition and Alternatives to It*. San Francisco: Harper & Row.
O'Flaherty, Wendy Doniger. 1980. *Women, Androgynes, and Other Mythical Beasts*. Chicago: University of Chicago Press.
O'Hanlon, Rosalind. 1991. "Issues of Widowhood: Gender and Resistance in Colonial Western India." In *Contesting Power: Resistance and Everyday Social Relations in South Asia*, ed. D. Haynes and G. Prakash. Delhi: Oxford University Press.

———. 1994. *A Comparison between Women and Men: Tarabai Shinde and the Critique of Gender Relations in Colonial India.* Madras: Oxford University Press.

O'Hanlon, Rosalind, and David Washbrook. 1992. "After Orientalism: Culture, Criticism, and Politics in the Third World." *Comparative Studies in Society and History* 34:141–167.

Olivelle, Patrick. 1995. *Rules and Regulations of Brahmanical Asceticism: Yatidharmasamuccaya of Yādava Prakāśa.* Albany: State University of New York Press.

Omvedt, Gail. 1983. "Devdasi Custom and the Fight Against It." *Manushi* 19:16–19.

Orr, Leslie C. 1992. "Women's Patronage and Power: Chola Royal Women and the Politics of Religious Endowments." Paper presented at the Annual Meeting of the Association for Asian Studies, Washington, DC.

———. 1994a. "The Concept of Time in Śaṅkara's *Brahma-sūtra bhāṣya.*" In *Strategies of Interpretation: The Indian Matrix of Religion, Philosophy and Text,* ed. Katherine K. Young. Atlanta: Scholars Press.

———. 1994b. "Food, Food Transactions and the Definition of Religious Community in Medieval Tamilnadu." Paper presented at the Conference on Religion in South India, Walker Valley, N.Y.

———. 1994c. "Women of Medieval South India in Hindu Temple Ritual: Text and Practice." *Annual Review of Women in World Religions* 3:107–41.

———. 1995a. "Devotion, Definition, and Difference: The Structuring of Sectarian Community in Medieval Chidambaram and Srirangam." Paper presented at the Annual Meeting of the American Academy of Religion, Philadelphia.

———. 1995b. "Retrospective Realities: Community and Leadership in a Medieval Hindu Temple." Paper presented at the Annual Meeting of the Canadian Society for the Study of Religion, Conference of Learned Societies, Montreal.

———. 1995c. "The Vaiṣṇava Community at Śrīraṅgam: The Testimony of the Early Medieval Inscriptions." *The Journal of Vaiṣṇava Studies* 3/3:109–136.

———. 1997. "The Lives of Women in Medieval Tamilnadu." Paper presented at the Second International South Asian Women's Conference, Los Angeles.

———. 1998. "Jain and Hindu 'Religious Women' in Early Medieval Tamilnadu." In *Open Boundaries: Jain Communities and Cultures in Indian History,* ed. John E. Cort. Albany: State University of New York Press.

———. 1999. "Women's Wealth and Worship: Female Patronage of Hinduism, Jainism, and Buddhism in Medieval Tamilnadu." In *Faces of the Feminine in Ancient, Medieval and Modern Indian,* ed. Mandakranta Bose. New York: Oxford University Press.

———. forthcoming a. "Jain Worship in Medieval Tamilnadu." In *Approaches to Jaina Studies: Philosophy, Logic, Rituals and Symbols,* ed. N. K. Wagle and Olle Qvarnström. Toronto: Centre for South Asian Studies, University of Toronto.

———. forthcoming b. "Women in the Temple, the Palace, and the Family: The Construction of Women's Identities in Pre-colonial Tamilnadu." In *New Horizons in South Indian Studies: Papers in Honor of Noboru Karashima,* ed. Kenneth R. Hall. New Delhi: Oxford University Press.

Orr, Leslie C., and Katherine K. Young. 1986. "Just Who Is Serving the God, and Singing and Dancing, in the Bhakti Hymns of the Āḻvārs and Nāyaṉmārs?"

Paper presented at the Conference on Religion in South India, Cape Cod, Mass.
Ortner, Sherry B. 1989. *High Religion: A Cultural and Political History of Sherpa Buddhism.* Princeton, N.J.: Princeton University Press.
Pandeya, B. K. 1984. *Temple Economy under the Cōḷas (c.* A.D. *850–1070).* New Delhi: Bahri Publications.
Parasher, Aloka, and Usha Naik. 1986. "Temple Girls of Medieval Karnataka." *Indian Economic and Social History Review* 23:63–91.
Parasher-Sen, Aloka. 1993. "Temple Girls and the Land Grant Economy, 8th-13th Century A.D." In *Social and Economic History of Early Deccan: Some Interpretations*, ed. Aloka Parasher-Sen. New Delhi: Manohar.
Pargiter, F. E. 1912. "Verses Relating to Gifts of Land Cited in Indian Land Grants." *Journal of the Royal Asiatic Society*, 248–54.
Pathak, V. S. 1960. *History of Śaiva Cults in Northern India from Inscriptions.* Varanasi: Dr Ram Naresh Varma.
———. 1987. *Smārta Religious Tradition.* Meerut: Kusumanjali Prakashan.
Penzer, N. M. 1924. "Sacred Prostitution." In *Ocean of Story*, Vol. 1, trans. C. H. Tawney. London: Charles J. Sawyer.
Perlin, Frank. 1981. "The Precolonial Indian State in History and Epistemology: A Reconstruction of Societal Formation in the Western Deccan from the Fifteenth to the Early Nineteenth Century." In *The Study of the State*, ed. Henri J. M. Claessen and Peter Skalnik. The Hague: Mouton.
Peterson, Indira Viswanathan. 1982. "Singing of a Place: Pilgrimage as Metaphor and Motif in the Tēvāram Songs of the Tamil Śaivite Saints." *Journal of the American Oriental Society* 102:69–90.
———. 1989. *Poems to Śiva: The Hymns of the Tamil Saints.* Princeton, N.J.: Princeton University Press.
———. 1998. "Śramaṇas against the Tamil Way: Jains as Others in Tamil Śaiva Literature." In *Open Boundaries: Jain Communities and Cultures in Indian History*, ed. John E. Cort. Albany: State University of New York Press.
Pillay, K. K. 1953. *The Śucīndram Temple.* Madras: Kalkshetra Publications.
Pollock, Sheldon. 1989. "Mīmāṃsā and the Problem of History in Traditional India." *Journal of the American Oriental Society* 109:603–10.
———. 1993. "Deep Orientalism? Notes on Sanskrit and Power beyond the Raj." In *Orientalism and the Postcolonial Predicament*, ed. C. Breckenridge and P. van der Veer. Philadelphia: University of Pennsylvania Press.
Ponchiroli, Daniele, ed. 1954. *Il Libro di Marco Polo detto Milione.* Torino: Giulio Einandi.
Ponnusamy, S. 1972. *Sri Thyagaraja Temple, Tiruvarur.* Madras: State Department of Archaeology, Government of Tamilnadu.
Pope, G. U., trans. [1900] 1970. *The Tiruvāçagam or "Sacred Utterances" of the Tamil Poet, Saint, and Sage Māṇikka-vāçagar.* Madras: University of Madras.
Prakash, Gyan. 1990. "Writing Post-orientalist Histories of the Third World: Perspectives from Indian Historiography." *Comparative Studies in Society and History* 32/3:383–408.
Prasad, Awadh Kishore. 1983. "Devadasis: A Study of the Temple Dancing Girls in South India (c. A.D. 800–1200)." Ph.D. dissertation, Patna University. Published in 1990 as *Devadasi System in Ancient India: A Study of Temple Dancing Girls of South India* by A.K. Singh. Delhi: H. K. Publishers.

Presler, Franklin A. 1987. *Religion under Bureaucracy: Policy and Administration for Hindu Temple in South India*. Cambridge: Cambridge University Press.

Price, Pamela G. 1990. "The State and Representations of Femaleness in Late Medieval South India." *Historisk Tidsskrift* 4:589–97.

———. 1994. "Honor, Disgrace, and the Formal Depoliticization of Women in South India: Changing Structures of the State under British Colonial Rule." *Gender and History* 6/2:246–64.

———. 1996. *Kingship and Political Practice in Colonial India*. Cambridge: Cambridge University Press.

Punekar, S. D., and Kamala Rao. 1962. *A Study of Prostitutes in Bombay*. Bombay: Allied Publishers.

Radhakrishnan, R., and N. Rajagopalan. 1984. "Modes of Bhakti in Tamil Devotional Literature." *Journal of South Asian Literature* 19:209–13.

Raheja, Gloria Goodwin, and Ann Grodzins Gold. 1994. *Listen to the Heron's Words: Reimagining Gender and Kinship in North India*. Berkeley: University of California Press.

Rajamanikkam, M. 1962. "The Tamil Saiva Mathas under the Colas (A.D. 900–1300)." In *Essays in Philosophy Presented to T. M. P. Mahadevan*. Madras: University of Madras.

Ramachandran, T. N. 1934. "Tiruparuttikuṉṟam and Its Temples." *Bulletin of the Madras Government Museum*. n.s.—General Sect., Vol. I, Part 3.

———. 1954. "The Nagapaṭṭiṇam and Other Buddhist Bronzes in the Madras Museum." *Bulletin of the Madras Government Museum* n.s.—General Sect., Vol. VII, No. 1.

Ramanujan, A. K., trans. 1981. *Hymns for the Drowning: Poems for Viṣṇu by Nammāḻvār*. Princeton, N.J.: Princeton University Press.

———. 1982. "On Women Saints." In *The Divine Consort: Rādhā and the Goddesses of India*, ed. J. S. Hawley and D. M. Wulff. Berkeley, Cal.: Berkeley Religious Studies Series.

Ramanujan, A. K., Velcheru Narayana Rao, and David Shulman. 1994. *When God Is a Customer: Telugu Courtesan Songs by Kṣetrayya and Others*. Berkeley: University of California Press.

Ramaswami Ayyangar, M. S. [1922] 1982. *Studies in South Indian Jainism*, Vol. 1. New Delhi: Sri Satguru Publications.

Ramaswamy, Vijaya. 1985. *Textiles and Weavers in Medieval South India*. Delhi: Oxford University Press.

———. 1989. "Aspects of Women and Work in Early South India." *Indian Economic and Social History Review* 26:81–99.

Ramesh, K. V. 1974. "Jaina Epigraphs in Tamil." In *Jaina Literature in Tamil*, A. Chakravarti. New Delhi: Bhāratīya Jñānapīṭha.

Rangachari, K. 1931. "The Sri Vaishnava Brahmans." *Bulletin of the Madras Government Museum* 2/2:1–158.

Reiniche, Marie-Louise. 1985. "Le temple dans la localité: Quatre examples au Tamilnad." In *L'espace du Temple I: Espaces, Itinéraires, Médiations*, ed. Jean-Claude Galey. Paris: Éditions de l'École des Hautes Études en Sciences Sociales. *Puruṣārtha* 8:75–119.

———. 1989. *Tiruvannamalai, un lieu saint śivaïte du sud de l'Inde 4: La Configuration sociologique du temple hindou*. Paris: L'École française d'extrême-orient.

Richman, Paula. 1988. *Women, Branch Stories and Religious Rhetoric in a Tamil Buddhist Text*. Syracuse, N.Y.: Maxwell School, Syracuse University.

Robinson, Sandra P. 1985. "Hindu Paradigms of Women: Images and Values." In *Women, Religion, and Social Change*, ed. Y. Y. Haddad and E. B. Findly. Albany: State University of New York Press.

Rocher, Ludo. 1986. *The Purāṇas*. Wiesbaden: Otto Harrassowitz.

Rukmini Devi. 1957. "The Spiritual Background of Bharata Natyam." *Marg* 10/4:5–6.

Rule, Pauline. 1987. "Prostitution in Calcutta, 1860–1940: The Pattern of Recruitment." In *Class, Ideology and Woman in Asian Societies*, ed. Gail Person and Lenore Manderson. Hong Kong: Asian Research Service.

Russell, R. V. [1916] 1975. *Tribes and Castes of the Central Provinces of India*. Delhi: Cosmo Publications.

Sachau, E. C., trans. [1888] 1971. *Alberuni's India*, abridged ed., ed. and intro. Ainslie T. Embree. New York: Norton.

Sadasivan, K. 1993. *Devadasi System in Medieval Tamil Nadu*. Trivandrum: CBH Publications.

Said, Edward W. 1979. *Orientalism*. New York: Vintage Books.

Sanday, Peggy Reeves. 1981. *Female Power and Male Dominance*. New York: Cambridge University Press.

Sarkar, Tanika. 1992. "The Hindu Wife and the Hindu Nation: Domesticity and Nationalism in Nineteenth Century Bengal." *Studies in History* 8/2:213–36.

Sathyanarayana, R. 1969. *Bharatanāṭya: A Critical Study*. Mysore: Sri Varalakshmi Academies of Fine Arts.

Schneider, David M., and Kathleen Gough. 1962. *Matrilineal Kinship*. Berkeley: University of California Press.

Schopen, Gregory. 1985. "Two Problems in the History of Indian Buddhism: The Layman/Monk Distinction and the Doctrines of the Transference of Merit." *Studien zur Indologie und Iranistik* 10:9–47.

———. 1988–89. "On Monks, Nun and 'Vulgar' Practices: The Introduction of the Image Cult into Indian Buddhism." *Artibus Asiae* 49/1–2:153–68.

———. 1990. "The Buddha as an Owner of Property and Permanent Resident in Medieval Indian Monasteries." *Journal of Indian Philosophy* 18/2:181–217.

———. 1991. "Archaeology and Protestant Presuppositions in the Study of Indian Buddhism." *History of Religions* 31:1–23.

Schrader, F. Otto. [1916] 1973. *Introduction to the Pāñcarātra and the Ahirbudhnya Saṃhitā*. Madras: Adyar Library and Research Centre.

Schulenberg, Jane Tibbetts. 1988. "Female Sanctity: Public and Private Roles, ca. 500–1100." In *Women and Power in the Middle Ages*, ed. Mary Erler and Maryanne Kowaleski. Athens: University of Georgia Press.

———. 1989. "Women's Monastic Communities, 500–1100: Patterns of Expansion and Decline." In *Sisters and Workers in the Middle Ages*, ed. J. M. Bennett et al. Chicago: University of Chicago Press.

Schussler Fiorenza, Elisabeth. 1983. *In Memory of Her: A Feminist Theological Reconstruction of Christian Origins*. New York: Crossroad.

Scott, Joan W. 1986. "Gender: A Useful Category of Historical Analysis." *American Historical Review* 91(5):1053–75.

———. 1987. "Women's History and the Rewriting of History." In *The Impact of Feminist Research in the Academy*. Bloomington: Indiana University Press.

Scott, W. Richard. 1987. *Organizations: Rational, Natural, and Open Systems*, 2nd ed. Englewood Cliffs: Prentice Hall.

Sethu Pillai, R. P. 1974. *Words and Their Significance* and *Tamil—Literary and Colloquial*. Madras: University of Madras.

Settar, S., and M. M. Kalaburgi. 1982. "The Hero Cult: A Study of Kannada Literature from 9th to 13th Century." In *Memorial Stones: A Study of Their Origin, Significance and Variety*, ed. S. Settar and Gunther D. Sontheimer. Dharwad: Karnatak University; Heidelberg: South Asia Institute.

Sewell, Robert. [1900] 1962. *A Forgotten Empire: Vijayanagar*. Delhi: Government of India Publications Division.

Shankar, Jogan. 1990. *Devadasi Cult: A Sociological Analysis*. New Delhi: Ashish Publishing House.

Sharma, Arvind. 1980. "The Notion of Cyclical Time in Hinduism." In *Textual Studies in Hinduism*. Delhi: Manohar.

Sharma, R. S. 1961. "Historiography of the Ancient Indian Social Order." In *Historians of India, Pakistan and Ceylon*, ed. C. H. Philips. London: Oxford University Press.

———. 1965. *Indian Feudalism: c. 300–1200*. Calcutta: University of Calcutta.

———. 1974. "Material Milieu of Tantricism." In *Indian Society: Historical Probings*. New Delhi: People's Publishing House.

———. 1980. *Śūdras in Ancient India: A Social History of the Lower Order Down to Circa* A.D. *600*, 2nd rev. ed. Delhi: Motilal Banarsidass.

Sharma, Tej Ram. 1978. *Personal and Geographical Names in the Gupta Inscriptions*. Delhi: Concept Publishing.

Shastri, Ajay Mitra. 1975. *India as Seen in the Kuṭṭanī-Mata of Dāmodaragupta*. Delhi: Motilal Banarsidass.

Shekhar, Indu. 1960. *Sanskrit Drama: Its Origin and Decline*. Leiden: E. J. Brill.

Shortt, John. 1870. "The Bayadère; or Dancing Girls of Southern India." *Memoirs Read before the Anthropological Society of London 1867–68–69*. London: Longmans, Green.

Shulman, David Dean. 1980. *Tamil Temple Myths: Sacrifice and Divine Marriage in the South Indian Śaiva Tradition*. Princeton, N.J.: Princeton University Press.

———. 1985. *The King and the Clown in South Indian Myth and Poetry*. Princeton, N.J.: Princeton University Press.

Silber, Ilana Friedrich. 1995. *Virtuosity, Charisma, and Social Order*. Cambridge: Cambridge University Press.

Singer, Milton. 1972. *When a Great Tradition Modernizes: An Anthropological Approach to Indian Civilization*. New York: Praeger.

Singh, A. K., 1990. *Devadasi System in Ancient India: A Study of Temple Dancing Girls of South India*. Delhi: H. K. Publishers.

Singh, R. L., ed. 1971. *India: A Regional Geography*. Varanasi: National Geographical Society of India.

Singh, Upinder. 1996. "Sanchi: The History of the Patronage of an Ancient Buddhist Establishment." *Indian Economic and Social History Review* 33/1:1–35.

Sinha, S. N., and N. K. Basu. 1933. *A History of Prostitution in India (Ancient)* Vol. I. Calcutta: S. N. Sinha and B. S. H. Association.

Sitaraman, B., N. Karashima, and Y. Subbarayalu. 1976. "A List of the Tamil Inscriptions of the Chola Dynasty." *Journal of Asian and African Studies* 11:87–181.

Sivaramamurti, C. 1983. *Panorama of Jain Art*. New Delhi: Times of India.

Sivaraman, K. 1973. *Śaivism in Philosophical Perspective: A Study of the Formative Concepts, Problems and Methods of Śaiva Siddhānta*. Delhi: Motilal Banarsidass.

Smith, H. Daniel. 1975. *A Descriptive Bibliography of the Printed Texts of the Pāñcarātrāgama*. Baroda: Gaekwad's Oriental Series.

Smith, Julian S. 1976. "Madurai, India: The Architecture of a City." M.Arch. thesis, Massachusetts Institute of Technology, Boston.
Sontheimer, Günther-Dietz. 1964. "Religious Endowments in India: The Juristic Personality of Hindu Deities." *Zeitschrift für vergleichende Rechtswissenschaft* 67/1:45–100.
Soundara Rajan, K. V. 1972. *Indian Temple Styles: The Personality of Hindu Architecture*. New Delhi: Munshiram Manoharlal.
———. 1975. "Jaina Art and Architecture in Tamilnadu." In *Aspects of Jaina Art and Architecture*, ed. U. P. Shah and M. A. Dhaky. Ahmedabad: L. D. Institute of Indology.
Spencer, George W. 1968. "Temple Money-lending and Livestock Redistribution in Early Tanjore." *Indian Economic and Social History Review* 5:277–93.
———. 1969. "Religious Networks and Royal Influence in Eleventh Century South India." *Journal of the Economic and Social History of the Orient* 12:42–56.
———. 1970. "The Sacred Geography of the Tamil Shaivite Hymns." *Numen* 17:232–44.
———. 1983. "When Queens Bore Gifts: Women as Temple Donors in the Chola Period." In *Śrīnidhiḥ: Perspectives in Indian Archaeology, Art and Culture* (Shri K. R. Srinivasan Festschrift), ed. K. V. Raman et al. Madras: New Era Publications.
———. 1984. "Heirs Apparent: Fiction and Function in Chola Mythical Genealogies." *Indian Economic and Social History Review* 21:415–32.
Sreedhara Menon, A. 1979. *Social and Cultural History of Kerala*. New Delhi: Sterling Publishers.
Srinivas, M. N. 1942. *Marriage and Family in Mysore*. Bombay: New Book Co.
Srinivasan, Amrit. 1983. "The Hindu Temple-Dancer: Prostitute or Nun?" *Cambridge Anthropology* 8(1):73–99.
———. 1984. "Temple 'Prostitution' and Community Reform: An Examination of the Ethnographic, Historical and Textual Context of the Devadasi of Tamil Nadu, South India." Ph.D. dissertation, Cambridge University.
———. 1985, November 2. "Reform and Revival: The Devadasi and Her Dance." *Economic and Political Weekly* 20/44 1869–76.
Srinivasan, K. R. 1960. *Some Aspects of Religion as Revealed by Early Monuments and Literature of the South*. Madras: University of Madras.
———. 1975. "South India." In *Jaina Art and Architecture*, Vol. II, Chap. 19, ed. A. Ghosh. New Delhi: Bhāratīya Jñānapīṭha.
Stafford, Pauline. 1983. *Queens, Concubines and Dowagers: The King's Wife in the Early Middle Ages*. Athens: University of Georgia Press.
Stein, Burton. 1960. "The Economic Function of a Medieval South Indian Temple." *Journal of Asian Studies* 19:163–76.
———. 1968. "Social Mobility and Medieval South Indian Hindu Sects." In *Social Mobility in the Caste System in India*, ed. James Silverberg. The Hague: Mouton.
———. 1969. "Early Indian Historiography: A Conspiracy Hypothesis." *Indian Economic and Social History Review* 6(1):41–59.
———. 1973. "Devi Shrines and Folk Hinduism in Medieval Tamilnad." In *Studies in the Language and Culture of South Asia*, ed. Edwin Gerow and Margery D. Lang. Seattle: University of Washington Press.
———. 1978a. "All the King's Mana: Perspectives on Kingship in Medieval South India." In *Kingship and Authority in South Asia*, ed. J. F. Richards. Madison: University of Wisconsin Press.

———. 1978b. "Temples in Tamil Country, 1300–1750 A.D." In *South Indian Temples: An Analytical Reconsideration*, ed. Burton Stein. New Delhi: Vikas Publishing House.

———. 1980. *Peasant State and Society in Medieval South India.* Delhi: Oxford University Press.

———. 1989. *The New Cambridge History of India, Vol. I.2: Vijayanagara.* Cambridge: Cambridge University Press.

Sternbach, Ludwik. 1942–50. "*Veśyā*—Synonyms and Aphorisms" and subsequent "First Supplement" and "Second Supplement." *Bhāratīya Vidyā* 4/1 (1942): 104–14; 4/2 (1943): 157–68; 5 (1945): *Miscellany*, 115–43, and *Supplement*, 1–19; 8 (1947): 256–67; 11 (1950).

———. 1965. *Juridical Studies in Ancient Indian Law*, Part 1. Delhi: Motilal Banarsidass.

Strenski, Ivan. 1983. "On Generalized Exchange and the Domestication of the *Sangha*." *Man* 18:463–77.

Stuard, Susan Mosher. 1987. "The Dominion of Gender: Women's Fortunes in the High Middle Ages." In *Becoming Visible: Women in European History*, 2nd ed., ed. R. Bridenthal, C. Koonz, and S. Stuard. Boston: Houghton Mifflin.

Subbarayalu, Y. 1973. *Political Geography of the Chola Country.* Madras: State Department of Archaeology, Government of Tamilnadu.

———. 1976. "The State in Medieval South India, 600–1350." Ph.D. dissertation, Madurai Kamaraj University, Madurai.

———. 1982. "The Cōḷa State." *Studies in History* 4:265–305

Subrahmanian, N. 1966. *Sangam Polity: The Administration and Social Life of the Sangam Tamils.* Bombay: Asia Publishing House.

Subramaniam, T. N. 1957. "Epigraphical Glossary." In *South Indian Temple Inscriptions*, Vol 3, Part 2, ed. T. N. Subramaniam. Madras: Government Oriental Manuscripts Library.

———. 1958–59. "Paḷḷaṉkōvil Jaina Copper-Plate Grant of Early Pallava Period." *Transactions of the Archaeological Society of South India*, 41–83.

Subramaniam, V. 1980. "The King-God Concept and the Arts." In *The Sacred and the Secular in India's Performing Arts*, ed. V. Subramaniam. New Delhi: Ashish Publishing House.

Suleri, Sara. 1992. *The Rhetoric of English India.* Chicago: University of Chicago.

Suresh Pillai, B. 1968. "The Raajaraajeesvaram at Tañcaavuur." In *Proceedings of the First International Conference Seminar of Tamil Studies*, Vol. 1. Kuala Lumpur: International Association of Tamil Research.

Suthanthiran, A. Veluswamy. 1986. "The Role of Hindu Mutts as Centres of Learning for the Tamils." In *Heritage of the Tamils: Education and Vocation*, ed. S. V. Subramanian and V. R. Madhavan. Madras: International Institute of Tamil Studies.

Swaminathan, A. 1978, January–June. "Aḍimaikaḷ (Slaves) in the Chōḻa Temples and Maṭhas." *Bulletin of the Institute of Tamil Culture*, 33–38.

Swaminathan, K. D. 1990. *Early South Indian Temple Architecture: Study of Tiruvāliśvaram Inscriptions.* Trivandrum: CBH Publications.

Talbot, Cynthia. 1988a. "Donative Inscriptions (Dāna-Śāsanas): Interpretations and Uses for Historical Research." In *Ajaya-Śrī* (Ajay Mitra Shastri Felicitation Volume), ed. Devendra Handa. Delhi: Sundeep Prakashan.

———. 1988b. "Gifts to Gods and Brahmins: A Study of Religious Endowments in Medieval Andhra." Ph.D. dissertation, University of Wisconsin, Madison.

———. 1991. "Temples, Donors, and Gifts: Patterns of Patronage in Thirteenth-century South India." *Journal of Asian Studies* 50/2:308–40.

———. 1992. "A Revised View of 'Traditional' India: Caste, Status, and Social Mobility in Medieval Andhra." *South Asia* 15:17–52.

———. 1994. "Female donors and their Families in Andhra, 1000–1649." Paper presented at the Twenty-third Annual Conference on South Asia, Madison, Wisc.

———. 1995a. "Inscribing the Other, Inscribing the Self: Hindu-Muslim Identities in Pre-colonial India." *Comparative Studies in Society and History* 37/4:692–722.

———. 1995b. "Rudrama-Devi, The Female King: Gender and Political Authority in Medieval India." In *Syllables of Sky: Studies in South Indian Civilization in Honor of Velcheru Narayana Rao*, ed. David Shulman. Delhi: Oxford University Press.

———. forthcoming. *Precolonial India in Practice: Society, Region, and Identity in Medieval Andhra.*

Tambiah, Stanley J. 1973. "Dowry and Bridewealth and the Property Rights of Women in South Asia." In *Bridewealth and Dowry*, Jack Goody and Stanley J. Tambiah. Cambridge: Cambridge University Press.

Tapper, Bruce Elliot. 1979. "Widows and Goddesses: Female Roles in Deity Symbolism in a South Indian Village." *Contributions to Indian Sociology* 13:1–31.

Tarachand, K. C. 1991. *Dēvadāsi Custom: Rural Social Structure and Flesh Markets.* New Delhi: Reliance Publishing House.

Tewari, S. P. 1987. *Royal Attendants in Ancient Indian Literature, Epigraphy and Art.* Delhi: Agam Kala Prakashan.

Thapar, Romila. 1976. "Dāna and Dakṣinā as Forms of Exchange." *Indica* 13:37–48.

———. 1987. "Traditions Versus Misconceptions." *Manushi* 42–43:2–14.

———. 1992. *Interpreting Early India.* Delhi: Oxford University Press.

Tharu, Susie, and K. Lalita, ed. 1991. *Women Writing in India: 600 B.C. to the Present, Vol 1: 600 B.C. to the Early Twentieth Century.* New York: Feminist Press at the City University of New York.

Thurston, Edgar, and K. Rangachari. 1909. *Castes and Tribes of Southern India*, 7 vols. Madras: Government Press.

Tirumalai, R. 1980. *Rajendra Vinnagar.* Madras: State Department of Archaeology, Government of Tamilnadu.

———. 1981. *Studies in the History of Ancient Townships of Pudukkottai.* Madras: State Department of Archaeology, Government of Tamilnadu.

———. 1982. "Glimpses of Chōḷa Townships in Śrīlaṅkā." *Journal of the Epigraphical Society of India* 9:14–19.

———. 1983. "The Brahmadeyas of Pudukkottai District." In *Śrīnidhiḥ: Perspectives in Indian Archaeology, Art and Culture* (Shri K. R. Srinivasan Festschrift), ed. K. V. Raman et al. Madras: New Era Publications.

Trautmann, Thomas R. 1971. *Kauṭilya and the Arthaśāstra.* Leiden: E. J. Brill.

———. 1981. *Dravidian Kinship.* Cambridge: Cambridge University Press.

Upadhyay, Bhagwat Sarau. 1974. *Women in Ṛg Veda*, 3rd ed. Benares: Nand Kishore & Bros.

Varadpande, M. L. 1983. *Religion and Theatre.* New Delhi: Abhinav Publications.

Vasudeva Rao, T. N. 1979. *Buddhism in the Tamil Country.* Annamalainagar: Annamalai University.

Vatsyayan, Kapila. 1968. *Classical Indian Dance in Literature and the Arts.* New Delhi: Sangeet Natak Akademi.

Velu Pillai, A. 1976. *Study of the Dialects in Inscriptional Tamil.* Trivandrum: University of Kerala.

———. 1980. *Epigraphical Evidences for Tamil Studies.* Madras: International Institute of Tamil Studies.

Veluthat, Kesavan. 1978. *Brahman Settlements in Kerala: Historical Studies.* Calicut: Sandhya Publications.

———. 1979. "The Temple-Base of the Bhakti Movement in South India." Paper presented at the Fortieth Indian History Congress.

———. 1993. *The Political Structure of Early Medieval South India.* New Delhi: Orient Longman.

Venkatachari, K. K. A.. 1978. *The Maṇipravāḷa Literature of the Śrīvaiṣṇava Ācāryas.* Bombay: Ananthacharya Research Institute.

Vergati, Anne. 1982. "Social Consequences of Marrying Viṣṇu Nārāyana: Primary Marriage among Newars of the Kathmandu Valley." *Contributions to Indian Sociology* 16:271–87.

Vijayavenugopal, G. 1979. "Some Buddhist Poems in Tamil." *Journal of the International Association of Buddhist Studies* 2:93–97.

Viswanathan, Lakshmi. n.d. "Devadasi Traditions of Dance in the Temples and Courts of Tamil Nadu." Report on research undertaken with the assistance of the Department of Culture, Government of India.

Vogel, J. P. 1911. *Antiquities of Chamba State*, part 1. Calcutta: Supt. Government Printing, India.

Wadley, Susan S. 1980. "The Paradoxical Powers of Tamil Women." In *The Powers of Tamil Women*, ed. Susan S. Wadley. Syracuse, N.Y.: Maxwell School, Syracuse University.

Waghorne, Joanne Punzo. 1981. "When the Mother Goddess Is Not a Mother." *Anima* 7(2):141–54.

———. 1984. "From Geertz's Ethnography to an Ethno-theology?" In *Anthropology and the Study of Religion*, ed. Robert L. Moore and Frank E. Reynolds. Chicago: Center for the Scientific Study of Religion.

———. 1994. *The Raja's Magic Clothes: Re-visioning Kingship and Divinity in England's India.* University Park: Pennsylvania State University Press.

Wagoner, Phillip B. 1993. *Tidings of the King: A Translation and Ethnohistorical Analysis of the Rāyavācakamu.* Honolulu: University of Hawaii Press.

———. forthcoming. "Understanding Islam at Vijayanagara." In *Shaping Indo-Muslim Identity in Pre-modern India*, ed. John Richards and Bruce Lawrence.

Walkowitz, Judith R. 1980. *Prostitution and Victorian Society: Women, Class and the State.* Cambridge: Cambridge University Press.

Watters, Thomas. [1904–5] 1973. *On Yuan Chwang's Travels in India, A.D. 629–645*, 2nd ed., ed. T. W. Rhys Davids and S. W. Bushell. New Delhi: Munshiram Manoharlal.

Weber, Max. [1922] 1964. *The Sociology of Religion*, trans. Ephraim Fischoff. Boston: Beacon Press.

Wemple, Suzanne F. 1987. "Sanctity and Power: The Dual Pursuit of Early Medieval Women." In *Becoming Visible: Women in European History*, 2nd ed., ed. R. Bridenthal, C. Koonz, and S. Stuard. Boston: Houghton Mifflin.

Whetten, David A. 1987. "Organizational Growth and Decline Processes." *Annual Review of Sociology* 13:335–58.

Whitehead, H. 1921. *The Village Gods of South India*, 2nd ed. Calcutta: Association Press.

Whitehead, Judy. 1995. "Modernising the Motherhood Archetype: Public Health Models and the Child Marriage Restraint Act of 1929." *Contributions to Indian Sociology* 29/1–2:187–210.

Willis, Janice D. 1985. "Nuns and Benefactresses: The Role of Women in the Development of Buddhism." In *Women, Religion, and Social Change*, ed. Y. Y. Haddad and E. B. Findly. Albany: State University of New York Press.

Yocum, Glenn E. 1982. *Hymns to the Dancing Śiva: A Study of Māṇikkavācakar's Tiruvācakam*. Columbia, Miss.: South Asia Books.

———. 1983. "Buddhism through Hindu Eyes: Śaivas and Buddhists in Medieval Tamilnad." In *Traditions in Contact and Change*, ed. Peter Slater and Donald Wiebe. Waterloo: Wilfrid Laurier University Press.

Young, Katherine K. 1978. "Beloved Places (*ukantaruḷiṉa-nilaṅkaḷ*): The Correlation of Topography and Theology in the Śrīvaiṣṇava Tradition of South India." Ph.D. dissertation, McGill University, Montreal.

———. 1987. "Hinduism." In *Women in World Religions*, ed. Arvind Sharma. Albany: State University of New York Press.

———. 1993. "The Pāvai Poems: A Study of Gender and Hinduism." Paper presented at the Annual Meeting of the American Academy of Religion, Washington, D.C.

———. 1995. "Theology Does Help Women's Liberation: Śrīvaiṣṇavism, A Hindu Case Study" *Journal of Vaiṣṇava Studies* 3/4:173–232.

———. forthcoming. "Āṇṭāḷ: God's Slave as She Who Rules." In *New Perspectives on Women in Hinduism*.

Young, Katherine K., and Leslie C. Orr. 1985. "Syncretism and Displacement: A Study of the Figure of the *Pāṇaṉ* in Tamil Poetry." Paper presented at the Conference on Hindu Syncretism, Carleton University, Ottawa.

———. 1988. "The Symbol of the Bard (*Pāṇaṉ*) in Tamil Hagiographies." Paper presented at the Conference on Religion in South India, National Humanities Center, Research Triangle Park, N.C.

Younger, Paul. 1995. *The Home of Dancing Śivaṉ: The Traditions of the Hindu Temple in Citamparam*. New York: Oxford University Press.

Zvelebil, Kamil V. 1977. "The Beginnings of *Bhakti* in South India." *Temenos* 13:223–59.

Zvelebil, Kamil, and Jaroslav Vacek. 1970. *Introduction to the Historical Grammar of the Tamil Language*. Prague: Oriental Institute in Academia.

Collections of Inscriptions and Reference Works Consulted but Not Cited

Alphabetical List of Villages in the Taluks and Districts of the Madras Presidency (Corrected up to September 1930). [1933] 1992. Madras: Government Press; New Delhi: Asian Educational Services.

Andhra Pradesh Government Epigraphy Series. 1968–70. Hyderabad: Andhra Pradesh State Government.

Andronov, M. 1969. *A Standard Grammar of Modern and Classical Tamil*. Madras: New Century Book House.

A Collection of the Inscriptions on Copper-plates and Stones in the Nellore District. 1905. Ed. Alan Butterworth and V. Venugopaul Chetty. Madras.

Corpus Inscriptionum Indicarum. 1955–77. New Delhi/Ootacamund: Archaeological Survey of India/ Government Epigraphist for India.
Indian Antiquary. 1872–1923. Bombay.
Indian Archaeology: A Review. 1960– . New Delhi.
Inscriptions of Bengal. 1929. Rajshahi: Varendra Research Society.
Inscriptions of Orissa. 1960–76. Bhubaneswar: Orissa Sahitya Akademi.
Jagadisa Ayyar, P. V. 1982 (reprint). *South Indian Shrines*. New Delhi: Asian Educational Services.
Karashima, Noboru. 1973. "A Bibliography of South Indian Epigraphy." *Journal of Asian and African Studies* 6:151–63.
Karnatak Inscriptions. 1941–69. Dharwar: Karnatak Research Institute.
Krishnamurthi, S. R. 1966. *A Study on the Cultural Developments of the Chola Period*. Annamalai: Annamalai University.
Kumaraswami Raja, N. n.d. List of the names and locations of and references to Śaiva sacred places in the hymns of *Tēvāram*. Provided by George Spencer.
Kuṭantai kalveṭṭukkaḷ. 1980. Ed. Nā. Mārkcīyakānti. Madras: Tamil Nadu State Department of Archaeology.
Mahalingam, T. V. 1985–. *A Topographical List of the Inscriptions in the Tamil Nadu and Kerala States*. 8 vols. New Delhi: Indian Council of Historical Research.
Nilakanta Sastri, K. A. 1963. *Development of Religion in South India*. Bombay: Orient Longman.
———. 1966. *A History of South India from Prehistoric Times to the Fall of Vijayanagar*, 4th ed. Madras: Oxford University Press.
Rangacharya, V. [1919] 1985. *A Topographical List of the Inscriptions of the Madras Presidency (Collected till 1915)*. 3 vols. New Delhi: Asian Educational Services.
Sethuraman, N. 1978. *The Imperial Pandyas: Mathematics Reconstructs the Chronology*. Kumbakonam: Author.
Sewell, Robert. 1882. *Topographical Lists of the Antiquarian Remains in the Presidency of Madras*. Madras: Government Press.
———. 1884. *Lists of the Inscriptions and Sketch of the Dynasties of Southern India*. Madras: Government Press.
Sircar, D. C. 1963. *Select Inscriptions Bearing on Indian History and Civilization*. Delhi: Motilal Banarsidass.
———. 1966. *Indian Epigraphical Glossary*. Delhi: Motilal Banarsidass.
Smith, H. Daniel. 1980. *An Annotated Index to Selected Topics Found in the Printed Texts of the Pāñcarātrāgama*. Baroda: Gaekwad's Oriental Series.
Ten Pandya Copper-plates (Pāṇṭiyar ceppēṭukaḷ pattu). 1967. Madras: Tamiḻ Varalāṟṟuk kaḻakam.
Yasoda Devi, V. "History of the Andhra Country (1000–1600)." *Journal of the Andhra Historical Research Society*, 25–27.
Zvelebil, Kamil V. 1974. *A History of Indian Literature: Tamil Literature*. Weisbaden: Otto Harrassowitz.
———. 1975. *Tamil Literature*. Leiden: E. J. Brill.

Index

Āŷvārs (*continued*)
on devotees and gift giving, 26
on feet of God, 52–53, 216n.17
on slaves of God, 53, 216n.18
temple women, no reference to, 6
See also bhakti literature; *titles of individual works*
Andhra Pradesh, 49–50, 181–82
androcentrism, 9, 195–96n.12
Āṇṭāḷ, 22, 240n.34, 259–60n.11
apsarās, 3, 6, 7, 108, 195n.7
ARE *(Annual Report on Indian Epigraphy),* 21, 35, 188–91
Arthaśāstra, 193–94n.3
ascetics, 32, 89, 109, 116, 216n.19, 258n.4
Āśvalāyana Gṛhya-sūtra, 202–3n.40
Atharva Veda, 217n.21
aṭiyār (slaves/devotees), 52–54
attendants, 112–15
flywhisk men, 112, 238n.27
flywhisk women, 89, 111, 112–13, 238n.28
functions of, 94, 112
lamp bearers, 112, 113–14, 239n.31
ornamental functions, 115, 239–40n.33
personal attendance on the deity, 111, 112, 114–15
presence at festivals, 112, 113, 238n.30
upasthāna, 193–94n.3
See also palace women
auspiciousness, 10, 17, 177, 200n.30

basavi (appointed daughter), 159, 256–57n.42
Bayly, S., 203–4n.43, 209–10n.59
bhakti, 11, 22, 23, 59, 208n.54
bhakti literature
as expression of love, 59, 220nn.33–34
See also Āŷvārs (poet-saints); Nāyaṉmārs (poet-saints); *titles of individual works*
Brāhmaṇas, 217n.21
Brahman assemblies, 30, 31, 70, 77, 115, 209n.58, 229–30n.29
Brahmans
gifts to, 25, 205n.47
inscriptional references, 30, 209n.58, 226n.14
and tending duties in temples, 233n.7
Brahman settlements, 22, 205n.47
Brahman women, 41
as donors, 68, 169
and family identifications, 155, 252n.31
overlap with temple women category (none), 43
and property transactions, 71–72, 226n.14
branding, slave, 120, 241n.39, 248–49n.21
British
and inheritance of status, responsibilities and privileges, 150, 249n.23
and notions of prostitutes, 14, 15, 198n.22, 199–200n.28
Buddhism, 23, 202n.38
and common religious culture with Hindus and Jains, 25, 204–5n.45
inscriptional references, 23, 201–2n.37
and women patrons, 205n.48
bureaucratization, 165–66, 258n.2, 259n.5

Cankam literature
on *kūtti,* 235n.13
on *pāṇar,* 109
on *paṟai,* 236–37n.19
puṟam literature, 55, 220n.34
on singers and dancers, 235n.14
See also titles of individual works
castes
inscriptional references, 30, 31
mēḷakkāraṉ caste, 237n.20
prostitutes as a caste, 15, 199n.26
and social organization, 209n.57
See also Brahmans; *veḷḷāḷas*
Champakalakshmi, R., 21, 203n.42
Chidambaram, 70, 122, 143–44, 145, 146, 246–47n.8, 247n.10
child of God, synonyms for, 59, 219nn.28, 30
children of temple women, 57, 150–51, 157–59, 227n.20
children of the temple *(koyiṟpiḷḷaikaḷ),* 42, 213n.6

Chingleput district, 211–12n.2
Chola period, 5, 20–21, 200n.31
chronological distribution of all temple women inscriptions, 181–82
chronological distribution of Chola period temple women inscriptions, 39–40, 43, 212n.3
chronological limits of study, 20–21, 200n.31
chronological pattern of women's donations, 69
Cilappatikāram, 7, 62, 221n.38, 235n.14, 256n.40
classification of women, 37–43
coming-of-age ceremonies, 253–54n.36
courtesans. *See* prostitutes

dance as symbol of sexual union, 17
dancers
  āṭiṉār, 237n.22
  cāntikkūttar, 104–5, 106–7, 110, 234n.12, 235n.14, 237n.20
  cānti kūttu, 126
  festival dancers, 105–6, 235–36n.15
  inheritance of festival dancer function, 236n.16
  kūtti kāl (dancer-tax), 104, 235n.13
  nartakīs, 6, 236n.7
  naṭṭiyāṭṭar, 236n.17
  naṭṭuvar (dance masters), 107, 236nn.17–18, 237n.20
  purchasing right to perform, 106
  shift from male to female dancers, 105–6, 106–7
  temple women as, 95, 102, 103–6, 105
dance traditions, 8, 126, 236n.17
dāsas, 55, 217nn.21–22, 221–22n.39
dāsīs, 55, 217nn.21–22
database and dataset inscriptions defined, 35, 183–84
  See also methodology
daughter of God. *See tevaṉār makaḷ*
Davis, R., 195n.8, 204–5n.45
deals
  to become attendants, 113, 114
  to become dancers, 106
  to become flywhisk bearers, 113
  and housing of temple women, 131
  and inheritance of status, responsibilities and privileges, 76, 152
  involving no support, 127
  by men, 75, 76
  motives in making, 77–78
  by nontemple women, 75, 76, 77, 228n.25
  to obtain service rights, 77–78, 228–29n.26
  to receive temple honors, 75–78, 228–29n.26
  to sing *Tiruvempāvai* hymn, 108
  by temple women, 57, 66, 75–78, 87, 108, 113, 228–29n.26
  See also donations; support, receiving
dedication ritual, 157, 253–54n.36
degeneration of *devadāsī* institution, 9, 10–12, 172, 173, 174, 197n.18
degeneration of Indian society, 10, 196–97n.15, 197n.16
degeneration of women's status, 11, 197n.17
descendents
  santāṉapraveśam, 75
  vaḻi, 117, 250n.25
  vaṟkattār, 19, 127, 151, 152, 236n.16, 250n.25
devadāsīs
  abolishment of, 4, 14, 16, 199n.27, 227n.21
  classes of, according to Thurston, 221–22n.39
  as compound word with *gaṇikā*, 194n.4
  defined, 3–6
  as defined by femininity and sexuality, 9, 14–17, 172, 174, 198n.24
  early use of term, 5–6, 193–94n.3, 194n.4
  hereditary eligibility of, 172

devadāsīs (*continued*)
as pan-Indian and transhistorical phenomenon, 9–10, 172, 174, 175–77
as passive victims of social forces, 9, 12–14, 172, 173–74, 177, 197nn.19–20
as *prasāda,* 16
relationship to kings and royal courts in Chola period, 43
relationship to kings and royal courts in seventeenth century, 42–43, 178, 214n.9
as singers and dancers, 102–3, 234n.10
and Tantric rituals, 16–17, 200n.29
and temple women as representatives of goddess-consort of male god, 146
term associated with temple women, 5–7
and *tevaraṭiyāḷ,* 5, 54–55
See also prostitutes; temple women
devadāsīs in recent history
ethnographic accounts of, 4, 193n.1
and initiation rituals, 253–54n.36
and prostitute label, 199–200n.28
status and associations with men, 252n.34
temple dedication of, 172
as wives of God, 157, 178, 253–54n.36
devagaṇikā, 7, 195n.7
devaraṭiyār, 18, 52
See also tevaraṭiyār
devotees. *See aṭiyār* (slaves/devotees); *tevaraṭiyār*
devotees, honored, 56, 57, 116
Dharmaśāstras
on forms of marriage, 224–25n.10
on gift giving, 25, 205n.47
Manusmṛti, 25, 205n.47, 221–22n.39, 224–25n.10
on women's property rights, 71, 224–25n.10, 226n.17, 227n.21
donations
chronological pattern of women's donations, 69
group donations, 83, 85, 232n.38
by Jain religious men, 222–23n.3
by kings, 28–29, 85, 222n.1, 232n.1
as a means to forge relationship with temple, 162, 168
motives for, 26–28, 80, 86–87, 206nn.49–50
by nonroyal women by temple type, 82–83, 85n.
number of gifts per temple, 224n.9
pūrta, 205n.47
reception of, by deities, 25–26, 205n.46
by royal women by temple type, 82–83, 85
temple authorities and village authorities, references to, 85–86, 232nn.40–41
by temple women by temple type, 82–83, 231n.35
by temple women outside hometowns, 79–83, 140
transfers of merit, 26, 83, 206–7n.50, 232n.37
value of, 67, 222n.1
See also deals; donors; set-up grants
donors
codonors with temple women, 85, 232n.39
expectations of, and involvement in temple affairs, 69
geographical distribution of donations by royal women, 69, 224nn.7, 9
geographical distribution of donations by temple women, 69–70, 224n.8
group donations, 83, 85, 232n.38
men as, 67
number of, who are named temple women *vs.* named temple men, 95–96
temple men as, 67, 96, 222n.3
temple women as, 65–70, 96
and type of temple, 81–83, 85
types of, and donative activities, 68–69
women as, 68, 223n.5
See also donations
drummers
as male-only function, 94
paṟaiyar, 31, 210n.61, 236–37n.19, 237–38n.24

as temple servants, 92–93, 94
uvaccar, 67, 89, 107, 109, 110, 120, 123, 236–37n.19, 237n.20

economic position, women's
in Chola period India, 170–71, 259n.7
in medieval Europe, 170, 259n.8
in post-Chola period, 259n.7
economic resources, access to, and religious activity, 71, 224–25n.10, 225n.11
elite and folk religion, 24, 25, 203n.41
emperumāṉaṭiyār (temple women), 218–19n.24, 229–30n.29, 238n.27, 239–40n.33

family identifications, 153–60
female-focused family patterns, 158–60
inscriptional references, 153–60, 252n.31–32
as relatives of men, 154–55, 252n.33, 253n.35
as relatives of temple women, 157, 158–59, 163
as relatives of women, 154
of slaves, 154
as wives, 155–56
family women, 41, 43
feeding houses
cālais, 117, 119
maṭhas, 32, 37, 119, 211n.63, 213n.7
paḷḷis, 32, 42, 213n.7
femininity and sexuality and *devadāsīs,* 9, 14–17, 172, 174, 198n.24
festivals, presence at, 105–6, 112, 113, 235–36n.15, 238n.30
feudalism, 10, 11, 29, 197n.16, 208n.54, 258n.3
folk and elite religion, 24, 25, 203n.41
food, 51, 70, 76, 228nn.24, 25, 228–29n.26, 242n.48
food preparers, 117, 119–21

gaṇikās, 6, 49, 194n.4, 199n.26, 215n.14
gardeners and garland makers, 92, 115–16, 232n.2, 240nn.35–36
geographical distribution of Chola period inscriptions referring to temple women, 43, 181–82, 211–12n.2
geographical distribution of donations by temple women, 69–70, 224n.8
geographical distribution of inscriptions in database and dataset, 183–84
geographical limits of study, 19–20
goddesses
Lakṣmī, 17
and marriage myths, 25, 204n.44
nācciyār (consort goddesses), 25, 247n.13
Śakti, 10, 17, 196n.14, 214n.10
yakṣīs, 202n.38
goddess-names and names of temple women, 146, 247nn.11–13
goddess worship, 24–25, 203–4n.43, 247n.13
gotras, 41, 224–25n.10
Grantha characters, 52

Hardy, F., 16, 24, 201n.35, 202n.39, 202–3n.40, 203n.41
Harijan women, 199–200n.28
head-cloth, 75, 121, 122, 228n.24
Heitzman, J., 22, 200n.31, 200–201n.33
on economy, 29, 208n.55
on influence of lords, 234n.9
on *kāṇi,* 241–42n.44, 242n.45, 243n.54
on local "lords," 249–50n.24
on method of study, 35
on *mirās,* 249n.23
on *paṟaiyar,* 210n.61
on place-names, 247n.9
on property relations, 249n.23
on role of witnesses, 207n.52
Hindu reform movement, 12, 13, 14–16, 197–98n.21
hometowns. *See* donations; places of importance for temple women
housing of temple women, 131, 243nn.52–53

hymns. *See* Āȳvārs (poet-saints); Nāyanmārs (poet-saints); singers; *titles of individual works*

inheritance, 73
- liability for fines or taxes incurred by sons or husbands, 227n.19
- from man to man, 73
- from mother to daughter, 73, 227n.20
- of property by temple women, 73, 227n.20
- of property by women, 226–27n.18, 227n.19
- of temple honors, 76
- women's, from natal family, 73, 224–25n.10

inheritance of status, responsibilities and privileges, 150–53, 249–50n.24, 252n.29
- in Āgamas, 250–51n.27
- and the British, 150, 249n.23
- and deals, 76, 152
- in definition of temple women, 8
- and fitness for functions, 152, 250n.26, 251n.28
- and rotation of duties, 251–52n.28
- and substitution, 251–52n.28
- *See also* descendents

initiation
- dedication ritual, 157, 253–54n.36
- *dīkṣā,* 219n.27
- and names, 148–49, 248–49n.21
- of women, 219n.27

inscriptions, Chola period, 183–84
- administrators, references to, 31–32, 99, 100
- Brahman references, 30, 209n.58, 226n.14
- Buddhist references, 23, 201–2n.37
- caste references, 30, 31
- distinctiveness of, 22
- earliest reference to worship, 23, 202n.38
- groups, references to, 31–32, 83, 85, 89, 101, 210nn.60–61, 232n.38
- information provided by, 26–33
- Jain references, 23, 201–2n.37, 214n.10
- number of, 21, 200n.32
- number of names in, 47–48, 95–96, 233n.5
- usefulness of, *vs.* texts, 26–27, 207n.52
- *See also* inscriptions referring to temple women

inscriptions, post-Chola, 175–76, 201n.34, 260n.14, 261nn.15–17

inscriptions referring to temple women, 19, 183–84, 185–91
- Chola *vs.* non-Chola inscriptions, 46–47
- chronological distribution of all, 181–82
- chronological distribution of Chola period, 39–40, 43, 212n.3
- as dancers, 95, 102, 103–6, 110–11
- geographical distribution of Chola period, 43, 181–82, 211–12n.2
- information provided by, 30, 208–9n.56
- methodology, 34–36, 38, 211nn.65–66
- with named temple women, 47–48, 95–96, 233n.5
- number of, 19, 35, 45–48, 181–82
- terms used for temple women, 48–63

inscriptions translated
- IPS 139, 126
- IPS 152, 79
- IPS 162, 111–12, 124
- KK 256 (TAS 6.15), 75
- NK 134, 18–19
- SII 2.66, 33–34
- SII 3.143, 111
- SII 4.134, 139
- SII 4.223, 121–22
- SII 4.558, 116–17
- SII 5.520, 98–99
- SII 5.701, 60
- SII 5.705, 102–3
- SII 5.1360, 65–66
- SII 7.526, 18
- SII 8.228, 135–36
- SII 8.333, 102
- SII 12.151, 70
- SII 13.88, 65
- SII 13.103, 144
- SII 13.170, 89–91

lamps, 111, 113, 115, 239n.31
gifts in support of, 66, 206n.49, 222n.1
in inscriptions, 18, 57, 60, 65–66, 78–79, 89–91, 117–18
legal debates about *devadāsīs,* 4, 193n.2
legislation to abolish *devadāsī* dedication, 4, 14, 16, 199n.27, 227n.21
literature
historical, 6–8, 215n.14
travel, 8, 195nn.9–10, 215n.14
See also Āy̆vārs (poet-saints); *bhakti* literature; Nāyaṉmārs (poet-saints); *titles of individual works*

Madurai district, 211–12n.2
Mahābhārata, 24, 202–3n.40, 217n.21
Mahānirvāṇatantra, 200n.29
māheśvaras, 32, 56, 57, 67, 75, 79, 210–11n.62
Māṇikkavācakar, 109
See also Tiruppoṟcuṇṇam; Tiruvācakam; Tiruvempāvai
Maṇimēkalai, 7, 235n.14, 256n.40
Manusmṛti
on classes of *dāsas,* 221–22n.39
on gift giving, 25, 205n.47
on women's property rights, 224–25n.10
See also Dharmaśāstras
maps, 20, 45, 140
Marglin, F., 7
on adoption into *devadāsī* families, 198n.23, 257–58n.45
on auspiciousness, 10, 17
on dance as symbol of sexual union, 17
on definition of temple women, 8
on *devadāsīs* as pan-Indian term, 5
on feminine symbolism, 196n.13
on payments to temple women, 74
on Puri *devadāsīs,* 257–58n.45
on relationship of *devadāsīs* to royal courts in seventeenth century, 178, 214n.9
on sacred prostitution, 16
on sexual activity as ritual, 17
on surviving *devadāsīs,* 199–200n.28
on Tantric rituals, 200n.29
on temple women as attendants, 239–40n.33
marriage
marital status of temple women, 4
matrilateral cross-cousin marriages, 226–27n.18
and property rights of women, 73, 74
and temple women status, 156
"marriage" to temple deity, 8, 74
goddesses and marriage myths, 25, 204n.44
and *devadāsīs* as wives of God, 157, 178, 253–54n.36
and transformation of woman, 259–60n.11
maṭhas. See feeding houses
matrilineal and matrilocal systems, 159–60, 163, 256–57n.42, 257n.43
Maturaikkāñci, 202n.39, 240n.34
merchants *(viyāpāri),* 31, 210n.60
methodology, 34–36, 38, 211nn.65–66
database and dataset, 35, 183–84
meykkīrttis, 28, 85, 99, 103, 122, 136, 139
muṟai, 18, 34, 111, 113
musicians, 108, 229n.28, 237n.20
Muslims, 204–5n.45

Nācciyār Tirumoḻi, 240n.34
Nakkaṉ, 146–48, 149, 248n.14–15
names for temple men, 147
names for temple women, 48–63, 144–49
and Chidambaram, 145, 146, 246–47n.8, 247n.10
and goddess-names, 146, 247nn.11–13
and initiation, 148–49, 248–49n.21
and Kanchipuram, 145
and male-deity names, 146–47
māṇikkam (ruby), 148, 149, 248n.20
Nakkaṉ, 146–48, 149, 248nn.14–15
and names of parents, 147, 248n.16
taḷicceri peṇṭukaḷ, naming of, 148, 248n.18

and Tiruvaiyaru, 246–47n.8
uṭaiyār as part of temple women's names, 52, 145, 247n.9
names of men with *dāsa* suffix, 55, 217n.22
names of temple women with *talaikkoli* title, 61–62, 148, 149, 220–21n.37, 248n.19
names of women with *dāsi* suffix, 55, 217n.22
Nāyaṉmārs (poet-saints), 6, 23, 202n.39
on celestial women, 195n.7
on devotees and gift giving, 26
feet of God references, 52–53, 216n.17
Kāraikkāl Ammaiyār, 22, 259–60n.11
on slaves of God, 53, 216n.18
temple women, no reference to, 6
See also bhakti literature; Māṇikkavācakar; *titles of individual works*
Neṭunalvāṭai, 202n.39, 240n.34
North Arcot district, 211–12n.2
North India, terms used for temple women in, 49–50

Ōcchar, 107, 237n.20
Orientalism, 9, 195–96n.12

palace men, 232n.39
palaces, 40, 212–13n.5, 228n.22
palace women, 228n.22
aṇukki (intimate), 41, 212–13n.5
declining visibility in inscriptions, 169
defined, 40–41, 212–13n.5
as donors, 68
and family identifications, 159, 252n.31, 256n.40
geographical distribution of donations, 69, 224n.7
named in inscriptions, 47
number of gifts per temple, 224n.9
overlap with temple women category, 42
peṇṭāṭṭi, 212–13n.5
poki, 41, 212–13n.5
See also royal women
paṉmāheśvarar, 18, 51, 60, 65, 100, 210–11n.62
See also māheśvaras
Paripāṭal, 202n.39, 216n.17
paternal lineage of temple women, 59, 220n.32
meaning of *il* infix, 60, 220n.35
in *Periya Purāṇam,* 6–7
term used for temple women in inscriptions, 37, 49, 60–63, 162
patrilineal family structure, 71, 159, 224–25n.10, 257n.44
Periya Purāṇam, 6–7, 259–60n.11
Periyatirumoḻi, 216n.18
place, temple men's association with, 138–39, 245n.3
place, temple women's association with
god identifiers, 136, 245n.1
hometown identifiers, 79–80, 136, 140, 230nn.30–31
linkage to deity, 136
linkage to place, 136
linkage to temple, 136
relationship between temple women and locality, temple, deity, 79, 161, 230nn.30–31
as seen in inscriptions, 136
temple-area identifiers, 138, 245n.2
temple identifiers, 136–37
places of importance for temple women
Kanchipuram, 140–41, 246n.4
Melapaluvur, 142
Takkolam, 143
Tanjavur, 141, 142
Tiruchatturai, 142
Tiruvaiyaru, 141
Tiruvalisvaram, 143
Tiruvannamalai, 143
Tiruvarar, 141
Tiruvidaimarudur, 141–42
Vedaranyam, 142, 231n.35
See also names of individual places
post-Chola period, 260nn.12–13
and agency of temple women, 177–78
changes occurring in, 174–75
decline in number of inscriptions, 201n.34

post-Chola period (*continued*)
and *devadāsīs* as pan-Indian and transhistorical phenomenon, 9–10, 172, 174, 175–77
effect of new rulers in, 176–77
inscriptions from, 175–76, 260n.14, 261nn.15–17
political arrangements in, 174–75
subcategories of temple women in, 221–22n.39
and women as symbols, 175, 177–79, 261n.21
and women's economic autonomy, 259n.7
prasāda
consecrated food, 228n.25, 242n.48
devadāsīs as, 16
distribution of sacred ash as, 228n.24
priests, 32, 123
and inheritance of status, responsibilities and privileges, 250–51n.27
as male-only function, 94
as temple servants, 92, 94
property. *See kāṇi*
property, women's *(strīdhana). See strīdhana*
property rights of temple women
acquiring of property, 73, 227n.21
inheritance of, 73, 227n.20
sources of income in recent times, 73–74, 227n.21
property rights of women, 70–74, 224–25n.10, 225nn.11–13, 226nn.14–17
inheritance of, 226–27n.18, 229n.19
and marriage, 73, 74
proportion of women owning land, 225nn.13
property transactions
by Brahman women, 71–72, 226n.14
complexity of, 225nn.12
and *mutukaṇs* (guardians), 72, 169, 226n.15
by women, 225nn.12–13
by women *vs.* by men, 71
prostitutes
attitudes towards, 14–15, 198–99n.25
as a caste, 15, 199n.26
dāsīs as, 55, 217nn.21–22
gaṇikās, 6, 49, 194n.4, 199n.26, 215n.14
Harijan women dedicated as, 199–200n.28
hereditary prostitutes, 15
and Hindu reform movement, 12, 13, 14–16, 197–98n.21
labeling *devadāsīs* as, 3, 4, 199–200n.28, 227n.21
as a medical issue, 14, 198n.22
receiving no temple support, 6, 194–95n.6
recruitment of girls, 13, 198n.23
sacred prostitution, 16
sūḷeyar, 49, 239–40n.33
temple women never labeled as, in Chola period, 50
term used for temple women, 49
term used in Āgamas, 50, 215n.14
veśyās, 6, 199n.26, 200n.29, 217–18n.23
vilāsinīs, 6, 49, 194–95n.6
in writings, 6, 194–95n.6
prostitutes of the gods, 7, 195n.7, 200n.29
Purāṇas, 6–7, 194n.5, 217n.21
Agni Purāṇa, 194n.5
Bhāgavata Purāṇa, 240n.37
Bhaviṣya Purāṇa, 194n.5
Brahmāṇḍa Purāṇa, 193–94n.3
Padma Purāṇa, 194n.5
Śiva Purāṇa, 194n.5

queens
decline of donations from, 169
defined, 40
as donors, 28, 68, 89–91, 223n.4
and family identifications, 155, 252n.31, 256n.40
geographical distribution of donations, 69, 224n.7
inscriptions referring to, 89–91, 212n.4, 232n.1
named in inscriptions, 47
number of gifts per temple, 224n.9
overlap with temple women category, 42, 213n.8
See also royal women

Rajaraja I, 21, 33, 207–8n.53
  and establishment of 400 temple women at Tanjavur temple, 33–34, 151, 161, 164, 245n.2, 250n.26
Rājataraṅginī, 6, 217–18n.23
Ramnad district, 211–12n.2
reform movement, Hindu, 12, 13, 14–16, 197–98n.21
Reiniche, M-L., 210n.60, 256n.39
religious concepts, abstract, 9–10, 195n.11, 196n.14
responsibility functions, 98–102
  accountants, 32, 67, 90, 94
  assigned to groups, 101
  increasing exclusion of women in, 98, 163
  of Jain men *vs.* Jain women, 233n.8
  managers, 31, 89, 90, 93–94
  performed by men, 101, 168, 234n.9
  performed by temple women, 95–96, 99–101
roles, attributes of, 132–33
royal power and influence, 164, 258n.1
royal women, 41
  and family identifications, 155, 252n.31
  geographical distribution of donations, 69, 224nn.7, 9
  named in inscriptions, 47
  number of gifts per temple, 224n.9
  temple type patronized, 82–83, 85
  See also palace women; queens

Śaivāgamaparibhāṣamañjarī, 202–3n.40
Śaiva Siddhānta, 22, 228n.24
Śaiva temples, 45, 60, 214n.10, 228n.24
Śākta temples, 214n.10
Śakti (goddess), 10, 17, 196n.14, 214n.10
śakti (powers), 9, 10, 25, 200n.29
Schopen, G., 203n.41, 206–7n.50, 207n.52
service rights, 77–78, 228–29n.26, 229n.28
set-up grants
  personnel referred to in, 91–95, 232n.2
  royal sponsorship of, 91, 232n.1
sexuality and femininity and *devadāsīs,* 9, 14–17, 172, 174, 198n.24
Shulman, D., 201n.35, 204n.44, 217–18n.23
SII *(South Indian Inscriptions),* 185–87
singers, 93, 232–33n.3
  deals made to sing *Tiruvempāvai* hymn, 108
  female *vs.* male terms, 108, 237nn.21–22
  number of female *vs.* number of male, 108
  pāṇar, 102, 109–10, 237–38n.24
  purchasing right to perform, 106
  status of singers, 109–11
  as temple servants, 93
  temple women as, 110–11
  temple women's exclusion from role of hymn singer, 107–8
  viṇṇappañ ceyvār, 110
śivabrāhmaṇas, 32, 56, 57, 67, 209n.58
slaves, 116–21, 163, 216n.18, 241n.40
  aṭimai, 43, 216n.20
  aṭiyāḷ, 43, 52, 54, 55
  branding, 120, 241n.39
  See also aṭiyār (slaves/devotees)
South Arcot district, 211–12n.2, 231n.35
Spencer, G., 21, 223n.4, 233n.7, 247n.5
Sri Lanka, 181
Srinivasan, A., 7, 195n.11
  on abstract concepts and temple women, 196n.14
  on adoption by *devadāsīs,* 198n.23, 229n.28, 257–58n.45
  on definition of temple women, 8, 193n.1
  on organization of temple area, 243n.53
  on paternal lineage of temple women, 220n.32
  on payments to temple women, 74
  on prostitution as medical issue, 198n.22
  on sexual activity as ritual, 17
  on social organization of temple women families, 257–58n.45

Srinivasan, A. (*continued*)
on surviving *devadāsīs,* 199–200n.28
on temple women as dancers, 234n.10
on temple women as focus of reform movements, 15, 197–98n.21
Srirangam, 82, 85n., 143–44, 231n.34, 246n.4
śrivaiṣṇavas, 32, 56, 57, 100, 116, 210–11n.62, 240n.36
Śrīvaiṣṇavism, 22
Stein, B., 21
on *brahmadeyas,* 205n.47
on Chola polity, 29
on economy, 208n.55
on inscriptions *vs.* texts, 207n.52
on kings in inscriptions, 29
on merchants, 210n.60
on *meykkīrttis,* 85
on post-Chola sectarian affiliations, 203–4n.43
on shrines for goddesses, 204n.44
on style of inscriptions, 28
on symbolism, 195–96n.12
on temples in Tamilnadu, 24, 203n.42
on *veḷḷāḷas,* 209–10n.59
strīdhana
and deals by men to acquire service rights, 77–78
in present-day Tamilnadu, 229n.28
women's property, 72–73, 77, 224–25n.10, 226nn.16–17, 229n.28
study areas, 35–36, 47–48, 67–68, 71–72, 79–81, 95–97, 138, 211n.65, 222nn.1–2, 223n.5
Kanchipuram taluk, 36, 252n.31
Kulattur taluk, 36, 231n.35, 252n.31
Kumbakonam taluk, 36, 71, 222n.2, 231n.35, 252n.31
Tirukkoyilur taluk, 36, 231n.35, 252n.31
śūdras, 205n.47, 219n.27
support, receiving, 243n.51
and attributes of roles, 132–33
housing of temple women, 131, 243nn.52–53
kāṇi (property), 42, 72, 126
kāṇi (support), 34, 126, 127–28, 241–42n.44, 242n.45
kāṇi-like arrangements, 128
and kings as source of support, 131–32, 173, 243–44n.54, 244nn.55–56
number of named temple women *vs.* named temple men, 97
proportion of female temple servants receiving support, 126–27
in return for donation (deal), 75–78, 228–29n.26
shares, 58, 128, 242nn.46–47
sources of support, 131–32, 243–44n.54, 244nn.55–56
temple men with no temple duties, 233n.6
temple women as individuals or as part of group, 128–29
temple women with no temple duties, 95, 233nn.4, 6
value of support, 129–30, 242n.49
See also deals
symbolism, feminine
and androcentrism, 9, 195–96n.12
femininity and sexuality and *devadāsīs,* 9, 14–17, 172, 174, 175, 177, 198n.24
in post-Chola period, 175, 177–79, 261n.21
and women's experience, 10, 196n.13

talaikkoli, 61–62, 148, 149, 220–21n.37, 248n.19
Talbot, C., 201n.34, 206n.49, 206–7n.50, 225n.11, 231–32n.36
taḷicceri peṇṭukaḷ (women of the temple district), 34, 47, 141, 142, 237–38n.24, 242n.46, 245n.2
naming of, 148, 248n.18
taḷiy(il)ār (temple women), 37, 162, 163
meaning of *il* infix, 60, 220n.35
term used for temple women, 49, 60–63

Tamilnadu, 199–200n.28
and Chola inscriptions, 21–24
economy, 29, 208n.55
inscriptions from, referring to temple women, 181
political system, 29
religious life in, 24–26, 203–4n.43
terms used for temple women, 48–63
Tanjavur, 33–34, 131, 141, 142
Tanjavur district, 43, 82, 211–12n.2, 231n.35
Tantra, 10, 16–17, 200n.29
TAS *(Travancore Archaeological Series)*, 188
teachers, 22–23, 40, 104, 201n.35, 213n.6, 238n.30
temple men, 35, 36, 211n.65
and association with place, 138–39, 245n.3
defined, 67
as donors, 67, 68, 222–23n.3
named in inscriptions, 233n.5
number of references to, 67, 222n.2
roles of, 95–98, 123, 124
śrīmāheśvaras, 67, 75, 79
terms referring to, 67
tevarkaṉmikaḷ, 18, 67, 75, 77
vaikhānasas, 67
temples
architecture of, 23, 201n.36
bureaucratization of, 165–66, 258n.2, 259n.5
koyil, 137, 164, 213n.6
organization of life in, 167–68, 259n.5
temple servants
accountants, 32, 67, 90, 94
aṭiyār, 43, 52, 53, 54, 55
cleaners, 93
cooks, 120–21
dārikās, 49
food preparers, 117, 119–21
gardeners, 92, 115–16, 232n.2, 240n.36
garland makers, 115–16, 240n.35–36
male-only functions, 94
managers, 31, 89, 90, 93–94
menial laborers, 116–20, 240n.36
nivantakkāṟar, 33
number of temple women involved in temple activities, 95
paṇicey, 216n.19, 241n.41
paṇiceyya peṇṭukaḷ, 122, 123
potters, 93, 115, 118, 122
pounders, 120, 240–41n.38
priests, 92, 94
roles of, referred to in set-up grants, 91–95
roles of temple men as, 95–98
roles of temple women as, 91–92, 94–98
sevakas, 238n.30
tevarkaṉmikaḷ, 18, 19, 67, 75, 77, 89
See also attendants; dancers; drummers; responsibility functions; set-up grants; singers; slaves
temple service
character and value of work performed by men *vs.* by women, 125–26
combinations of tasks, 124, 241n.42
and competition for positions, 125
descriptions of men's roles *vs.* women's roles, 123, 124
exclusivity of men's roles, 125
functions of temple women, 162
nonexclusivity of female roles, 125
number of men's roles *vs.* women's roles, 125
paṇi, 34
privilege *vs.* duty, 106
upacāras (ways of service), 202–3n.40
vague descriptions of women's duties, 121–26
temple types, 81–83, 85n., 230–31n.33, 231nn.34–35
temple women
branding of, 241n.39, 248–49n.21
as coherent social category, 38–40, 41, 43, 211n.1
defined by author, 5, 37–38, 161
defined by Marglin, Kersenboom, Srinivasan, 8
definitional features, overlapping of, 38–40, 63, 212n.3

family women classified as temple women, 43
first appearance of, 52
and inheritance of status, 150–51
most used Chola period term, 55, 218–19n.24
as a nonsectarian name, 52, 216n.16
to refer to males, 219n.25
shift in use of term, 98
synonyms for, 218–19n.24
term used for temple women, 49, 50, 52–57, 63, 162
timelessness and Indian history, 9, 195–96n.12
Tiruchirappalli district, 43, 82, 85n., 211–12n.2, 231n.35
Tirukkoyilur taluk. *See* study areas
Tirumantiram, 240n.37
Tirumoli, 241n.41
Tirumuraikanta Purāṇam, 238n.25
Tirumurukārruppaṭai, 216n.17
Tirunelveli district, 43, 211–12n.2
Tirupati, 101, 218n.24, 246n.4
Tiruppāvai, 216n.18
Tirupporcuṇṇam, 238n.26
Tiruttoṇṭattokai, 122
Tiruvācakam, 53, 240nn.35, 37, 240–41n.38, 241n.41
Tiruvaiyaru, 99, 141, 246–47n.8
Tiruvannamalai, 131, 143, 158, 256n.39
Tiruvarur, 81, 141, 246–47n.8
Tiruvāymoli, 109, 237n.23, 241n.41
Tiruvempāvai, 106, 108, 109, 213n.6
Tiruvidaimarudur, 60, 82, 85n., 103, 109, 141–42, 231n.35, 258n.1
transfers of merit, 26, 83, 206–7n.50, 232n.37

uṭaiyār
as lord, 58
as part of temple women's names, 52, 145, 247n.9
as "possessor," 31, 52
uvaccar. See drummers

Vaiṣṇava temples, 45, 214n.10, 228n.24
veḷḷāḷas, 31, 209–10n.59
victims, *devadāsīs* as, 9, 12–14, 172, 173–74, 177, 197nn.19–20, 23
Viṣṇudharmottara Purāṇa, 194n.5

worship
earliest references to, 23–24, 202n.38
elements involved in, 24, 202–3n.40
elite and folk religion, 24, 25, 203n.41
goddess worship, 24–25, 203–4n.43, 247n.13
poet-saints and worship of deity, 202n.39
pūjā, 202n.38, 219n.27
selling of worship privileges, 229–30n.29
upāsakar, 65

Yājñavalkya Smṛti, 205n.47
Yellammā, 199–200n.28, 214n.10
Young, K., 22, 195n.7, 196n.13, 201n.35, 209n.57, 232–33n.3